DATE DUE

			PRINTED IN U.S.A.

Strindberg's
Dramaturgy

Strindberg's Dramaturgy

Göran Stockenström, editor

UNIVERSITY OF MINNESOTA PRESS
MINNEAPOLIS

The University of Minnesota gratefully
acknowledges publication assistance
from the Swedish Council for Research
in the Humanities and Social Sciences and
from the Swedish Academy.

Published by the University of Minnesota Press,
2037 University Avenue Southeast, Minneapolis, MN 55414.
Published simultaneously in Canada
by Fitzhenry & Whiteside Limited, Markham.
Printed in the United States of America.
Design by Gwen M. Willems.

Eugene O'Neill's essay "Strindberg and Our Theatre"
appears by permission of Yale University.

LIBRARY OF CONGRESS
Library of Congress Cataloging-in-Publication Data

Strindberg's dramaturgy / edited by Göran Stockenström.
    p. cm — (Nordic series ; v. 16)
    Bibliography : p.
    Includes index.
    ISBN 0-8166-1612-4
    1. Strindberg, August, 1849-1912 — Criticism and interpretation.
2. Strindberg, August, 1849-1912 — Dramatic production.
I. Stockenström, Göran. II. Series.
PT9816.S698   1988
839.7'26—dc19   87-38090
                                                      CIP

Dedicated
to
the Memory of

Alrik Gustafson

(1903-70)
Scholar, Teacher, Humanist

Contents

Preface

In creating a modern theatre which we hope will liberate for significant expression a fresh elation and joy in experimental production, it is the most apt symbol of our good intentions that we start with a play by August Strindberg; for Strindberg was the precursor of all modernity in our present theatre, just as Ibsen, a lesser man as himself surmised, was the father of the modernity of twenty years or so ago when it was believed that *A Doll's House* wasn't — just that.

Strindberg still remains among the most modern of moderns, the greatest interpreter in the theatre of the characteristic spiritual conflicts which constitute the drama — the blood — of our lives today. He carried Naturalism to a logical attainment of such poignant intensity that, if the work of any other playwright is to be called "naturalism," we must classify a play like *The Dance of Death* as "super-naturalism," and place it in a class by itself, exclusively Strindberg's since no one before or after him has had the genius to qualify.

Yet it is only by means of some form of "super-naturalism" that we may express in the theatre what we comprehend intuitively of that self-defeating, self-obsession which is the discount we moderns have to pay for the loan of life. The old "naturalism" — or "realism" if you prefer (would to God some genius were gigantic enough to define clearly the separateness of these terms once and for all!) no longer applies. It represents our Father's daring aspirations toward self-recognition by holding the family kodak up to ill-nature. But to us their old audacity is blague; we have taken too many snap-shots of each other in every graceless position; we have endured too much from the banality of surfaces. We are ashamed of having peeked through so many keyholes, squinting always at heavy, uninspired bodies — the fat facts — with not a nude spirit among them; we have been sick with appearances and are convalescing; we "wipe out and pass on" to some as yet unrealized region where our souls, maddened by loneliness and the ignoble inarticulateness of flesh, are slowly evolving their new language of kinship.

Strindberg knew and suffered with our struggle years before many of us were born. He expressed it by intensifying the method of his time and by foreshadowing both in content and form the methods to come. All that is enduring in what we loosely call "Expressionism" — all that is artistically valid and sound theatre — can be clearly traced back through Wedekind to Strindberg's *A Dream Play, There Are Crimes and Crimes, The Spook [Ghost] Sonata,* etc.

Hence, *The Spook [Ghost] Sonata* at our Playhouse. One of the most difficult of Strindberg's "behind-life" (if I may coin the term) plays to interpret with insight and distinction — but the difficult is properly our special task, or we have no good reason for existing. Truth, in the theatre as in life, is eternally difficult, just as the easy is the everlasting lie.

So pray with us — and (although we don't need it, of course, but it may do some good) for us.[1]

Eugene O'Neill

O'Neill's recognition of Strindberg's importance to twentieth-century theater can be found in the inaugural program for the new Provincetown Playhouse, which opened in New York with a production of *The Spook (Ghost) Sonata* on January 4, 1924. The avant-garde arts theater, directed by the famous triumvirate Kenneth Macgowan, Eugene O'Neill, and Robert Edmond Jones, rediscovered in Strindberg's "behind-life" plays submerged parts of an aesthetic theater tradition that they themselves advocated as the dominating form of modernism.

Strindberg's view of humankind and his revolutionary stagecraft presented the needed challenge to the studio theater in MacDougal Street. In regard to their attempt to transcend realism, O'Neill reassures Macgowan about Strindberg's central place in their new repertoire: "That's experiment in this country. No one else dares to do him — yet we all laud him justly as one of the two or three 'great modern ones.' "[2] As late as 1951, O'Neill keeps reminding his friend, "I wish I could see some Strindberg. I think back to *The Spook (Ghost) Sonata.*"[3] The new Provincetown Players' production of *The Ghost Sonata* was followed in 1926 by *A Dream Play.* Hailed by followers of the experimental theater movement as a "milestone" in the

Figures 1-3. *Scenes from* The Spook [Ghost] Sonata *at the Provincetown Playhouse, New York, 1924, as pictured in* Theatre Arts Monthly *(April 8, 1924), pp. 217-19. Photographs by Francis Bruguière. Upper left, the masked ghost of the Milk Girl (Mary Blair); upper right, the Dark Lady (Mary Morris) and the masked Dandy (James Light); and below, from left to right, the Colonel (Romeyn Benjamin), the Fiancée (Marion Berry), Old Hummel (Stanley Howlett), the Dandy (James Light), and the Mummy (Clare Eames).*

New York theater season,[4] the performance of *The Ghost Sonata* was characterized by Agnes Boulton in *Theatre Arts Monthly:* "Feeling that Strindberg was the precursor of modernity in our present theatre; aware that there was no chance of this play of his being done elsewhere in this country, because of its difficulties of form as well as content; and seeing its possibilities for experimental production — indeed, its need for that — they made a fine and bold stand with this play as their first production and achieved an effect that was amazing, and which has been given intense interest and respect."[5] The critical establishment was far from receptive. Alexander Woolcott of the *New York Times* refused to take "these sickly phantasies in their strange garb" seriously.[6] The bitter review in the *New York Telegraph* was headed "An Odd Squawk."[7] In the years to come, Strindberg's reputation on American stages would confirm these diverging perspectives.

In the *Playwright as Thinker* (1946), Eric Bentley concludes that Strindberg is alien and still largely unknown to American audiences: "If it be asked how a major modern writer can be so little known, I can only reply that I do not know, but that is certainly the case."[8] In the mid-1950s, the critic and scholar John Gassner, concurs: "Strindberg himself, moreover, has not had a single conclusive triumph on the American stage. Nor is he likely to have one in the foreseeable future."[9]

Strindberg's profound influence on modern theater in general and American dramatists in particular — Eugene O'Neill, Maxwell Anderson, Tennessee Williams, and Thornton Wilder — was recognized, but it was not until the early 1960s that Strindberg gained the attention that O'Neill, in such prophetic terms, had proclaimed he would. It came as a result of the interest in the Theater of the Absurd. In his influential study of this movement, published in 1961, Martin Esslin delineates the tradition from writers like Dostoevsky, Joyce, and Kafka,

> "but the first to put on the stage a dream world in the spirit of
> modern psychological thinking was August Strindberg. The three
> parts of *To Damascus* (1898-1904), *A Dream Play* (1902), and *The Ghost
> Sonata* (1907) are masterly transcriptions of dreams and obsessions,
> and direct sources of the Theatre of the Absurd. In these plays the
> shift from the objective reality of the world of outside, surface
> appearance to the subjective reality of inner states of consciousness
> — a shift that marks the watershed between the traditional and the
> modern, the representational and the Expressionist projection of
> mental realities — is finally and triumphantly accomplished. . . . It is
> a significant and somewhat paradoxical fact that the development
> of the psychological subjectivism that manifested itself in Strind-
> berg's Expressionist dream plays was the direct and logical develop-
> ment of the movement that had led to naturalism. It is the desire to

represent reality, all of reality, that at first leads to the ruthlessly truthful description of surfaces, and then on to the realization that objective reality, surfaces, are only part, and a relatively unimportant part, of the real world.[10]

The Strindberg repertoire was finally expanded in the 1960s beyond the plays on the duels between the sexes (*The Father, Miss Julie, The Creditors*), for so long reduced to a reasonableness acceptable to its audiences.[11] A new breed of theater practitioners was now able to free itself from the naturalistic impulses of Strindberg's theater and to perceive that the apparent dislocation of form served to represent an inner universe on stage. A universe that was about alienation, ontological insecurity, the clichéd nature of language, the absence of logical cause and effect, but ultimately, about themselves. Directors began to search out the dream plays that had for so long been considered too "difficult." It was in the small, off Broadway theaters in the 1950s and in the off-off Broadway theaters in the 1960s that Strindberg was again presented, by a new avant-garde of theater artists.[12] In 1962 *Modern Drama* had devoted a full issue to Strindberg in the modern theater. His plays were now being discussed in the light of Beckett, Pinter, Albee, and Shepard. In more recent years Strindberg has been examined as postmodern, pointing to the obvious parallels between Richard Wilson's theater of images and Strindberg's *A Dream Play.*

Within the counterculture, represented by the flowering experimental theaters, Strindberg's influence is again felt. There have been more productions of his plays during the last ten to fifteen years than during the sixty years beginning with 1905 when Strindberg was first presented in New York by a Russian touring company with the famous Alla Nazimova as Miss Julie at the Bowery Theater.[13] What were critical invectives in 1924 when O'Neill used Strindberg as a model for his new aesthetic theater had by now become terms of acclaim. Strindberg had come full circle.

This perspective on the introduction of Strindberg's plays to the American stage reminds us that production and reception are mediating processes between the theater collective and its audience. It is a dynamic event, always in a state of becoming, which unfolds in its own time and space. The play takes on its meaning by the experience of its audience. This book examines how the design of signification is interwoven both in Strindberg's dramatic discourse and in the practice of staging his plays. It originates from the need to throw light on the formal characteristics of Strindberg's theater; to explore questions such as those raised by O'Neill, Esslin, and others; to concretize, describe, and interpret both the dramatic discourse and the staging of individual plays in their historical contexts. Its aim is to create a better understanding of Strindberg's impact on twentieth-century theater.

Preface

Strindberg's plays are stories first, remembered because what happened *mattered* to him. Below the clouded and tangled patterns of events, and behind them, are experiences, psychological realities of passionate importance. These accumulations of passion, sins, and sufferings were recorded by the dramatist and told through different tales on the stage. His plays represent incomplete and imperfect actions calling for a before and an after, as the events unfold in their own time and space on the stage. Through the theatrical process of signification they take on meaning and simultaneously point inward to central meaning structures. By the choices of the *mise en scène* and stage figuration, theater codifies history in terms of space and time. The visualization clarifies a large number of zones of uncertainty of the dramatic text and at the same time masks others. No production can ever really exhaust the text, which is always in a state of becoming. A tension between text and performance underlies the phoenixlike recreation through transformation, which ultimately takes place in the hearts and imaginations of the audience. This complex signification process, with its genesis in the collective consciousness, its origins in the dramatic text, its recreation through the theatrical process, and ultimate reception through the audience, has been studied by numerous critics and scholars. In this volume a select group of critics, scholars, directors, and theater practicioners have contributed their special insights into Strindberg's theatrical art.

Strindberg's renewal of theater did not take place uniquely as a result of stylistic and textual innovation within the dramatic canon, however revolutionary; but, equally important, through new ways of using the stage and the relationship to an audience, resulting in profound changes in the situation of reception and in the very nature of the theater event. The focal point of the collective exploration in this book is dramaturgy because it is integral to both of these perspectives. Dramaturgy examines how and according to which temporality the materials of the plot are disposed in both the textual and the stage space. It sets out from stage signs to reconstruct by comparison and analysis different signifying structures. In its endeavor to examine both the textual and the scenic macrostructures, dramaturgy deals with the double system of form and content. The basic principles of dramaturgy serve to illuminate the location of signs, to define what constitutes them as signs, and to understand the relationship between them and the laws governing their interaction. The ensemble of knowledge and skills gathered in this volume represents a number of different wedges with which to reach into the heart of Strindberg's theater. Different writers study both the ideological and the formal structures of Strindberg's plays, the dialectical tension between their stage form and their ideological content, and the specific mode of reception of various productions. Some of the writers consider primarily the textual and scenic macrostructures of the written text, whereas others focus on the performance as a unique system of signification. The dialectical tension between text and stage characterizes every chapter, whether the port of entry lies in the origins and development of Strindberg's theatrical forms or in their internal and synchronic functioning as a system of performance. Whereas the former approach is rooted in history, the latter deals with historically established forms as consequences of aesthetic choices. Both attempt to formulate the laws determining the composition and functioning of text and stage in Strindberg's theater. The composition of this book is in itself an attempt to develop a metalanguage that will enable readers to view both text and performance as a single field of study.

Part I, "Strindberg's Dramas: Historical Dimensions," establishes a historical context that reaches beyond theater. Delblanc places Strindberg in the tradition of Western humanism and explores the conflict between humanistic ideology and scientific determinism in the nineteenth century. Strindberg's solutions to this dilemma are penetrated by Sprinchorn, who uses Nietzsche and Strindberg as representative figures for this same conflict and impending crisis in the transition from the nineteenth to the twentieth century. Carlson probes Strindberg's relationship to history in the form of myth and the poetic strategies to make it credible in his analysis of Strindberg as a historian. Historical drama as a process of thought that can connect and make ultimate sense of the diverse persons and events represented on the stage is examined in my discussion of the dramaturgy of *Charles XII*. Myth and history, past and present, form the historical context of this study of Strindberg's dramaturgy.

Part II, "Strindberg in the Modern Theater: Dramatic Form and Discourse," examines Strindberg's impact on twentieth-century theater from the tradition of literary modernism. The growing experience of the fundamental uncertainty of the individual at the end of the nineteenth century is elaborated by Karnick in his discussion of Strindberg's modern understanding of dramatic roles. He analyzes his revolutionary use of the metaphor of role in the tradition and structure of postclassical literature from the eighteenth to the twentieth century. The dilemma of characterless characters in modern drama is pursued by Fuchs in the context of postmodernism in her deconstructive analysis of *To Damascus (I)*. Brandell surveys the changing images of Strindberg in different cultural contexts in an attempt to delineate textual and scenic macrostructures in Strindberg's dramas. For Brandell and Bark, the question of constant change versus fundamental unity is central. Bark defines the dream plays as a genre characterized by specific techniques for the representation of historical events in space and time and finds its roots far back in the literary tradition. Rokem has instead chosen Ibsen and Chekov as starting points for his study of the aesthetics of space and scenography in a narratological model analysis of *Miss Julie, A Dream Play,* and *The Ghost Sonata.* The nature of Strindberg's modernism, the inherent problem of stylistic designation, and unity versus infinite variety are issues central to determining Strindberg's position in the modern theater.

Part III, "The Naturalistic or Supernaturalistic Plays: Dramatic Discourse and Stagings," contrasts the naturalistic plays of the 1880s — *Marauders-Comrades, The Father, Miss Julie,* and *The Creditors* — with *The Dance of Death* (I) from 1900. The latter was selected because it is similar to the earlier plays in theme and form, but, composed after the Inferno crisis, the use of the same dramatic techniques are distinctly different. This creates the necessary focal point for a discussion of continuity or discontinuity and unity of style and technique in Strindberg's dramaturgy. McFarlane opens this discussion with his reflections on the small and the large in the philosophical framework of the nineteenth century as key dramatic techniques that simultaneously represent the verisimilitude of reality and the overriding structures of world history. Strindberg's intimate relationship to French drama and theater is documented by Gravier with illuminating examples from the repertoire of the theater of ideas and the well-made play. He raises important questions about the nature of Strindberg's naturalistic theater and concludes his chapter with a perspective on Maeterlink's theater of silence and the dream plays. Frederick J. Marker and Lise-Lone Marker examine Ingmar Bergman's expressionistic production of *Miss Julie* in Munich, 1981. By restoring some of the lost passages of the original, Bergman's adaptation opens an interesting perspective on Strindberg's aesthetic intentions. The question of naturalism versus expressionism is penetrated by Brantly in her close reading of *The Dance of Death* (I). Her examination of dramatic form and discourse delves into Strindberg's ideology as a counterpoint to the previous analyses in this section. Throughout, fundamental unity or revolutionary change, continuity or discontinuity, style and technique are used to investigate the nature of Strindberg's theatrical art, whether it be characterized as naturalistic or supernaturalistic.

Part IV, "The Dream Plays: Dramatic Discourse and Stagings," is an examination of the dramaturgy of the dream plays, juxtaposing analyses of dramatic discourse and stagings of representative plays arranged in chronological order — *To Damascus (I), Charles XII, A Dream Play, The Ghost Sonata,* and *The Pelican.* Tiusanen problematizes the earlier discussion of the style designated expressionism by comparing the dramatic techniques of *To Damascus* (I) with the stylistic features found in the plays of the Expressionist movement in the twentieth century. However, in Jacobs's study of the motifs of titanism and satanism and their shaping effect on the central conversion experience in *To Damascus* (I), he traces the lines back to the nineteenth-century romantic tradition. Söderström attempts a different approach in his discussion of Grandinson's first production of *To Damascus (I)* at the Royal Dramatic Theater in Stockholm in 1900. Strindberg's collaboration with Grandinson and his later plans for another Swedish production in 1909 are examined. Söderström's analysis and documentation throws new light on Strindberg's stagecraft in the first of his dream plays. I concentrate again on *Charles XII*, this time as a dream play. I explore the genesis of the play, its leitmotif technique, and its dream structure within the framework of historical drama as a genre requiring its own system of character relationships, poetic language, and dramatic progression in time. The dramaturgy of *Charles XII*, with its reduction of the public world of politics to the private realm of the king's consciousness, is made possible by a dramaturgy with close affinity to both *To Damascus (I)* and *A Dream Play*. In Holm's analysis of representative productions of *A Dream Play*, he demonstrates how the staging techniques of naturalism and expressionism failed to do justice to Strindberg's new theater art, until Reinhardt staged the play in Berlin in 1925. The theoretical ramifications of Holm's analysis of the dilemma posed by Strindberg's dramaturgy in *A Dream Play* is further probed by Törnqvist. Focusing on the transformation process from text to stage, Törnqvist examines major European productions. The theatrical solutions to the staging of *A Dream Play* are studied in their relationship both to theatrical praxis and to society. Susan Einhorn, in an account of her own successful staging in 1981 of *A Dream Play* in New York, bears witness to this dilemma. She describes the process she used, as a director, to find a central concept in the play around which to structure her production. In her frank and direct manner, she invites many observations on the problem of staging Strindberg in America in the 1980s. The last three chapters deal with the Chamber Plays. Bryant-Bertail presents a semiotic analysis of space and movement in *The Ghost Sonata*. She discusses the written text and the performance as a unique system of signification in operation. In her interpretation the motif of the tower of Babel becomes the dynamic metasign that unifies the diverse signsystems in the play. In his treatment of *The Ghost Sonata*, Berry begins by paralleling the breakdown of the separation between matter, mind, and spirit in the 1890s to Strindberg's own development during his Inferno crisis. This leads to an enlargement of the concept of reality as an all-inclusive formula for the dramatist. From this perspective Berry explores the intricate relationship between dramatist and audience in Strindberg's dramaturgy. Time, space, action, and character are analyzed from Strindberg's vision of the world, with an emphasis on its Buddhistic elements. From Walsh's 1982 production of *The Pelican* in Toronto, he presents a close reading of Strindberg's text to reveal the poetic tragedy as the underlying structure of the domestic melodrama. He defines different performance strategies as consequences of Strindberg's new dramaturgy, which allowed the intentional mixing of naturalism and expressionism as representational styles.

The questions of scholarly definition and description that have emerged from the historical context of the first two chapters, questions of unity or change, continuity or discontinuity, style and technique, and so on, are all crucial issues for our understanding of Strindberg's new dramaturgy. The major portion of this book is devoted to testing these issues by juxtaposing analyses of the dramatic discourse and stagings of representative plays. The methods used by the individual contributors are manifold and their answers at times contradictory. Like Strindberg, they have all been participants in the search for a finite order in the infinite variety of Strindberg's universe.

With the warp set up and the interweaving of the different threads, we can finally examine the texture and pattern of the dramatic web. From the vantage point of text or stage, critics and scholars may disagree on the interpretation of the little curlicues, their place in the design, and what part they occupy in the grand pattern. This diversity of approaches and interpretations offers an abundance of critical tools with which to penetrate the rich texture of Strindberg's dramaturgy and, thus, to understand its vitality and impact on twentieth-century theater.

Acknowledgments

This book was made possible by the sixth International Strindberg Symposium held May 3-5, 1983, at the University of Minnesota, Minneapolis. There were seventy-five participants representing thirteen countries. The twenty-three chapters in this book were symposium contributions from a number of recognized critics and scholars in the field of modern drama and theater, as well as from a new generation of American scholars and practitioners of theater. Their essays have been rewritten for publication with scholarly annotations. Photographs and illustrations have been added. All quotations from Strindberg's texts are in English. The Swedish original accompanies the English translation, however, where it appears necessary to a proper rendering. The index is particularly important, because most of the chapters span more plays and issues than their respective titles indicate.

The Strindberg symposium was part of the centennial celebration of the Department of Scandinavian at the University of Minnesota. Professor Alrik Gustafson (1903-70), to whom this book is dedicated, served as chair of the department from 1944 to 1970. His research and teaching on Strindberg and modern theater created a legacy shared by the Scandinavian and theater departments. His extensive collections on Strindberg and modern drama were donated to the University of Minnesota libraries after his death. An exhibit from this rich collection was shown during the symposium, thanks to the dedicated efforts of Austin McLean and John Jenson, curators of Special Collections and Rare Books.

The VI International Strindberg Symposium was cosponsored by the Department of Theater and I am grateful for the generous support of theater professor Wendell Josal, who co-chaired the symposium with me. Strindberg has a long history on the stages of the University theater. Perhaps best remembered is the magnificent staging of *A Dream Play* in 1945 under the direction of the legendary Frank Whiting. It was the first artistically success-ful production of this play in the annals of the American theater. Under the guidance of its present artistic director, Robert Moulton, who has many Strindberg productions behind him, all four Chamber Plays were staged during the 1982-83 season. The directors Jean Congdon, Warren Green, Dan Huizenga, Helene Mann, actors, actresses, and production staff deserve special credit. Important contributions were made by theater faculty Arthur Ballet, Eric Hagen, Dennis Hurrell, and Charles Nolte.

Without the inspiration and active support of many people, this book would never have come into being. The following most readily come to mind: the students who inspired me during the 1982-83 seminars on Strindberg on the Stage, five of whom contributed to this volume; my colleagues in the Department of Scandinavian for their helping hands whenever needed; and my teacher and friend Sven Delblanc, author, dram-atist, and scholar, who gave the Alrik Gustafson Memorial Lecture, "Strind-berg and Humanism," which appears as the first chapter of this book.

A special thanks to the three keynote speakers, Evert Sprinchorn, Manfred Karnick, and Gunnar Brandell, who graciously consented to undertake the difficult task of surveying Strindberg in the modern theater from their different cultural perspectives.

The publication of this volume is made possible by the University of Minnesota Press. I owe special thanks to my press editor, Marlene Tungseth, for her insightful, professional scrutiny and friendly advice, and to my production coordinator, Gwen Willems, for her inspired design and layout. To the director of the press, John Ervin, Jr., a special thanks for his tireless efforts on behalf of Scandinavian culture through the Nordic Series.

I am deeply indebted to my associate Sarah Bryant-Bertail, who was responsible for the initial language editing and gave freely of her time and translation and editing skills to make this book possible. A special thanks to Leslie Denny, our program coordinator, who mastered all the organizational details of this project with tact and efficiency; Joyce Momont, senior secre-tary of the Department of Scandinavian, who typed several versions of this manuscript with mindful attention to detail; and Kathleen Porter, principal secretary of the Department of Scandinavian, who gave me her support and assistance; to Deborah Regula and Paul Walsh for their careful proofreading and indexing skills.

I am greatly indebted to the individuals, publishers, and organizations who have graciously granted permission for use of their materials in this volme. Warm thanks to Evert Sprinchorn for the use of selected passages from his translation of *To Damascus* (I) in *The Genius of the Scandinavian Theater* (New York: New American Library, 1964), reprinted in *August Strindberg:*

Acknowledgments

Selected Plays, (Minneapolis: University of Minnesota Press, 1986). Special thanks to Dutton Publishing Co. for allowing us to quote selected passages from Evert Sprinchorn's translations of *The Ghost Sonata* and *The Pelican* in *The Chamber Plays* (1962) (rev. ed., Minneapolis: University of Minnesota Press, 1981). Doubleday Publishers Co. has graciously permitted us to quote selected passages from Elizabeth Sprigge's translation of *Dance of Death (I)* in *Five Plays of Strindberg* (New York: Anchor Books, 1960). We are greatly indebted to Walter Johnson for his work on behalf of the symposium and to the University of Washington Press for letting us use selected passages from the following volumes of Walter Johnson's standard American translation: *Charles XII* in *Queen Christina. Charles XII. Gustav III* (Seattle, 1955); *A Dream Play and The Ghost Sonata* in *A Dream Play and Four Chamber Plays* (Seattle, 1973); Strindberg's prefaces to the historical dramas in *Open Letters to the Intimate Theater* (Seattle, 1966).

Frederick J. Marker and Lise-Lone Marker have been especially kind in granting us access to illustrations from Ingmar Bergman's production of *Miss Julie* at the Residenz Theater in Munich, 1981, through the courtesy of Bergman and their own press office. Drottningholms Teatermuseum has graciously allowed us to reproduce an illustration from the original production of *Charles XII* at the Royal Dramatic Theater in Stockholm, 1902. Dr. Tom Olsson and Beata Bergström of the Royal Dramatic Theater deserve very special thanks for allowing us to reproduce a sequence of illustrations from stagings of *A Dream Play.* Susan Einhorn has been very helpful and kind in granting us access to illustrations from her own successful staging of *A Dream Play* at the Open Space Theater in New York, 1981.

Norsk Folkemuseum in Oslo has kindly allowed us to reproduce Christian Krogh's oil painting of August Strindberg from 1893, owned by Henrik Ibsen. The Director of the Strindberg Museum, Göran Söderström, has been equally helpful and kind, through the courtesy of the Strindberg Foundation, in supplying us with various illustrations, not least Strindberg's oil painting, *Scenery within a Scene (Dubbelbild),* Dalarö (1890).

I would also like to express my heartfelt gratitude to those organizations and individuals that have provided economic support, without which all our efforts would have been in vain—College of Liberal Arts (Fred Lukermann), American Scandinavian Foundation (Patricia McFate), Center for Northwest European Area Studies (James Munholland), Scandinavia Today (Marilyn Nelson), Northwest Airlines, Sunds Defibrator Inc. (Jan-Erik Bergstedt), Consulate General of Sweden (Karl-Erik Anderson), Svenska Institutet (Ove Svensson). I feel grateful to my friends, Matthew and Ann Walton, for their support.

A very special thanks to Cleyonne Gustafson whose enthusiasm and generous donations to the Alrik and Cleyonne Gustafson Strindberg Collection will ensure the future of Strindberg research at the University of Minnesota.

To all the aforementioned, as well as to my children, Truda, Trond, and Tone, I am deeply grateful.

In closing, I must mention two very special individuals, Walter Johnson (1905-83) and Timo Tiusanen (1936-85), who both contributed to this effort. Walter Johnson, outstanding American Strindberg scholar, had promised to chair the section on Strindberg and the historical drama, a topic he knew better than any one of us, but, unfortunately, he died a short time before our symposium. Timo Tiusanen, internationally recognized director and theater scholar, was a dynamic presence at our gathering. He staged a humorous scene to remind us not to take ourselves too seriously, an affliction most scholars suffer from. We are children of Mother Earth; we enter and we leave as part of the Great Spirit. What is asked of us is to live with courage and awareness moment by moment. Walter and Timo did just that. We carry their images in our hearts. May the warm hands of Grief caress us all.

PART I

Strindberg's Dramas:
Historical Dimensions

1

Strindberg and Humanism

Sven Delblanc

When I received the flattering invitation to lecture on Strindberg in memory of Alrik Gustafson, a great scholar and humanist whose name will be forever connected with the University of Minnesota, my reaction was one of humble soul-searching. And, soon after, I began to be tormented by the awkward and inevitable question: which Strindberg do they expect me to speak on? In his infinite variety he is as elusive as the Cheshire Cat, as versatile as Cleopatra.

Chauvinism, politics, religious zeal, and ideological hang-ups tend to distort the image of great writers, always in demand as figureheads, symbols, or scapegoats. Thus the image of Strindberg in West Germany is vastly different from that of Strindberg in East Germany or, for that matter, of Strindberg in America — in the few instances he is known here at all. Let us be frank: in Sweden we tend to overestimate his renown; lacking a Shakespeare we had to invent one.

Which Strindberg do we worship in Sweden today? In my opinion we may be inclined to minimize or neglect the mystic and metaphysical aspects of his work so as to emphasize his contributions in the fields of politics, satire, and social criticism. To educated Swedes — should such people exist — Strindberg appears as a pioneer of our blessed socialist state, worthy of our gratitude for his fearless criticism of the capitalist society of infamous memory. Being an ousider in our one-party state, I am inclined to regard this as a simplification — if not a distortion — and you may rest assured: I intend to bury that Strindberg, not to praise him.

Politics in a narrow sense was never that important to Strindberg, and we do him a disservice, since he was such an individualist, to connect him with political ideas he regarded from a distance, and with suspicion or scorn. Experimenting with ideas, inclining to the left or to the right, a liberal or a reactionary as it suited his mood, he was never the mouthpiece of a political party. Such an activity would not have seemed natural for his time, still influenced as it was by the romantic concept of the majesty of creative genius. It may be less anachronistic to connect this playwright with a concept more important to his generation — in short, to make some observations on the problem of Strindberg and humanism, however vast the subject, however impossible the task seems.

I consider Strindberg "the beleaguered humanist" who, with varying degrees of success, sought to plead humanity's cause in the turbulent nineteenth century, when new ideas arose to attack and undermine humanity's self-esteem. That he was often driven to the defensive, often defeated, must not overshadow the fundamental fact that he never submitted unconditionally to a church, an ideology, or a mechanistic view of human behavior. His heroic struggle is worth following through victory and defeat.

Venerable academic convention requires, however, that I first define terms such as humanism and humanist. In English, apparently, the word humanist can be used in a negative sense, denoting a person who lacks religious conviction yet, one might add, is not altogether evil. Oddly enough, humanist in the Swedish language may have a similar negative connotation, although it refers more to a person who lacks a political ideology, a definition obviously borrowed from Marxism.

In contemporary French both these negative connotations are probably implicit, but they are not necessarily the first meanings that occur to a native speaker upon hearing the word. To some extent it may be the influence of existentialism that brings a highly regarded French lexicon to define the term in this way: "L'humanisme est une philosophie centré non sur les idées abstraites mais sur l'homme concret." It was this that the young Sartre had in mind when he advanced his slogan: "L'existentialisme est un humanisme."

With some justification, Kierkegaard might have claimed that his religious thought was a form of humanism that concentrated on the concrete and rejected the Hegelian brand of academic philosophy — *idées abstraites* — as well as the contempt of ecclesiastical institutions for all things tangible, for the individual and his spiritual needs — *l'homme concret.*

But, for the sake of clarity, I will name some of the positive values I associate with the term humanism.

The idea that humankind is the measure of all things — *homo mensura* — is clearly central. Humanity is the point of reference and departure for all values, and human worth cannot be determined on the basis of religious or other ideological systems. As Immanuel Kant pointed out, humanity is an end in itself rather than a means to some end beyond the human: in this precept Kant was a true advocate of humanism. Humanism implies a high estimation of humanity as perfectible, rational, equipped with free will, a view of the human being incompatible with Christian pessimism and scientific determinism alike. Humanism also implies a skeptical or at least a pragmatic view of religious and other ideological systems — ideology must not be allowed to conflict with the best interests of humanity.

Humanism in the modern sense developed during the Renaissance. The philosophical systems of antiquity had again become accessible, and these were found to contain admirable moral doctrines that in no way rested on dogmatic or ecclesiastical foundations. In Livy and Plutarch one could read about great men, admirable *exempla* who had shaped their lives in accordance with the dictates of conscience and without the help of the Bible or an ecclesiastical moral code. The church's belief in the curse of original sin laid upon all creation was replaced by a bright and optimistic view of humanity, expressed most eloquently in Pico della Mirandola's great oration, *De dignitate hominis*. In poetic form, this same view would echo through the works of the greatest poet of the late Renaissance: "What a piece of work is man! How noble in reason! how infinite in faculties! in form and moving how express and admirable! in action how like an angel! in apprehension how like a god! the beauty of the world! the paragon of animals!" (Shakespeare, *Hamlet*, Act II, scene 2).

Yet Hamlet could find no delight in this quintessential clay, man delighted him not, nor woman either. He suffered that melancholy from which the equals of the gods were never freed, as Dürer was able to show with matchless art.

Shakespeare was well aware of humanism, its enthusiasm for human dignity and the wonders of a brave, new world. But in his conception of humanity, he is at once both older, more Christian and medieval, as it were, and more modern than sixteenth-century humanism. He has a sharp eye for human folly, human enslavement to the passions, human susceptibility to mass psychosis. He is at once close to the *dances macabres* painted in medieval cathedrals and to the absurdism of our modern stage.

De dignitate hominis — on the dignity of the human being. The title of this speech alone may convey something of the feelings of the Renaissance humanists, their pride in perfectible humankind, their joy at liberation from religious and scholastic bonds. Strindberg was well aware of this feeling, which he rendered in his plays set in the late Renaissance, *Master Olof* and *The Nightingale of Wittenberg.* Luther and Master Olof are both cognizant that they live in a time of transition, when the spirits awaken and it is a joy to be alive. They are, however, treated from the standpoint of modern, beleaguered humanism. A righteous revolt, undertaken against established authority but threatened by compromise and exploitation, is a strikingly "modern" theme in both plays.

It was Sigmund Freud who spoke of the insults humanity has had to suffer during our modern age, and among them he counted psychoanalysis itself, which emphasized the irrational element in our psyche and insisted on the power of the subconscious, thus eroding our belief in free will. Freud was no pioneer, however, because the first insults appeared as early as the eighteenth century; suffice it to name La Mettrie and d'Holbach, who endeavored to reduce the human being to a beast or a machine. And let us not forget Rousseau's "Contrat Social," whereby the human being was reduced to slave status under the will of the majority. Rousseau thus laid the foundation for those totalitarian political doctrines that have been the scourge of our century, this nightmare of history that seems to offer us no choice but that between the slavery of a Hitler or Stalin and the dubious freedom of the Marquis de Sade.

Another insult to humanity, another problem for humanism, was Darwin and the view of the human his work engendered. After him, it was no longer easy to regard human beings as angels or demigods: his interpretation of nature made us mammals once and for all. The influence of Darwin is directly or indirectly obvious in Strindberg's work, where we so often meet men and women locked in a battle for survival.

Reason had been the lodestar of the eighteenth century. During the early nineteenth century, romanticism had acclaimed feeling and imagination. After Darwin and the vast conflicts of the Napoleonic wars, moral philosophers turned their attention to human will as the most important of our faculties.

In Schopenhauer's pessimistic philosophy, it is the will to life, negating all reason, that rules and dominates humankind. In Dostoyevsky's work it is the will to freedom that makes us reject a rationalistic and scientific psychology, an idea best expressed in *Notes from the Underground.* In Nietzsche's later work, it is the will to power that overshadows all else. Strindberg follows in this tradition; the battle of wills is one of his great themes. Again and again he will show us individuals fighting to defend their integrity and to overcome the forces that seek to crush and enslave them. In this relentless struggle there is little room for mercy. And how much is left of humanism's respect for the individual on Strindberg's dramatic battlefields, littered as they are with the remnants of people defeated and crushed so that the hero may preserve his reason and his self-respect? The outlook for humanism is sinister indeed in this modern world of eternal struggle and a merciless battle of the wills.

It was accepted as a matter of course in an earlier and more sheltered humanism — Goethe's, that is — that we might achieve victory over crude force and over the demands of society by means of reason, self-control, and lofty argument, as well as triumph over our baser selves by means of resignation and self-denial; *Entsagung* was a key concept in Goethe's humanism.

Strindberg is more modern, more realistic if you like, when displaying people who are victims of their passions and at the same time vulnerable and helpless, sometimes shattered by the collective forces they have to contend with. Master Olof follows the inner voice of conscience and emerges in conflict with the Catholic church. A single individual in conflict with a mighty social institution — that is a classic theme of humanism, and we might expect a victorious ending or, at least, a tragic victory in defeat. But Strindberg is sufficiently modern to realize the moral problems of revolt, a revolt doomed to go wrong or to be exploited, in this case by another social institution. No appeals or lofty argument can soften the harsh *Realpolitik* personified in King Gustaf. He is not like King Thoas of Goethe's play, nor is Master Olof like Iphigenia of Tauris, serene and inflexible in her belief in human goodwill.

It remains for Master Olof either to continue the rebellion against this new opponent, at the risk of being crushed like Gert the Printer, or — as happens — to compromise, in hope of snatching something of value from the struggle and preserving it beyond the reach of cynical powers. Here we are far from Weimar, far from Goethe's harmonious world, and close to our own time, which so often presents the intellectual humanist with a similar choice always leading to partial defeat or dubious victory, to compromise or defeat.

But if human beings are animals, locked in a battle of life and death in the jungle of modern society, what then remains of humanism? Why, nothing at all, replied the writer Zola who, without scruple, showed us *la bête humaine* as the helpless victim of heredity, society, and animal instinct. This is as far from humanism as can be imagined, yet Strindberg hailed Zola as a master all his life. To some extent, he did this to "keep up with the times" —there was a streak of opportunism in Strindberg — but he also did it out of conviction. There was something in Zola that struck him as true, maybe the social Darwinism of the French master, something that agreed with his own vision of humankind and society.

What then is left of Strindberg the humanist, we may ask? The remarkable fact is that Strindberg remains a humanist, almost in spite of himself. This is exemplified in works such as *Miss Julie* and *By the Open Sea*. Here we find Strindberg the humanist struggling with Strindberg the modern scientist, just as later we shall find this same beleaguered humanist struggling with himself as religious believer.

Humanism uses tragedy as one means of expression; it is no coincidence that classical tragedy is obsolete and hardly ever attempted today. For an antique tragedian such as Sophocles, as well as his many followers, tragedy could be an expression of a humanistic belief in human dignity and worth. The hero may make moral errors and may fall victim to his passions, but the playwright gives him a chance to make a moral choice and thus gain redemption. The hero has free will even if it reveals itself only in the act of suicide. Taking one's own life was incompatible with the teachings of Christianity, but it was fully acceptable, not to say respectable, in the eyes of antique humanism. The last days of the Roman Empire saw an epidemic of the kind of heroic suicides glorified by stoic philosophy — Brutus, the virtuous tyrannicide, is one example among many. And, we may add, Strindberg could find the same high value placed on suicide in the Scandinavian tradition, in Old Norse literature and history. In terms of the primitive humanism of the Scandinavian heritage, it was a great and venerable act to take one's life rather than live in circumstances of disgrace, "like an old cow on straw."

The foregoing discussion brings me to *Miss Julie*. This famous play is a battlefield on which Strindberg the humanist meets Strindberg the naturalist, who is trying to present a biological picture of the human animal in imitation of Zola. He took great pains to invoke the French master, and he wrote a foreword that bears many characteristics of a rationalization. It seems obvious to me, however, that Strindberg the humanist emerged victorious when he had Miss Julie commit suicide and thus preserve her human dignity. In the course of his work, he had come to identify much too strongly with his heroine: he wanted to give her an end that somehow provided redemption. This end is in conflict with naturalism and the biological view of nature. Is not the instinct of self-preservation stronger than all else? Among the various models for the character of Miss Julie was a Swedish noblewoman who, after an affair with a servant, had no qualms about continuing her life, working in a restaurant in Stockholm. Such was reality and so, perhaps, would Strindberg the naturalist have wanted to end his play. But the humanist Strindberg had other ideas: he sought tragic atonement by virtue of suicide. There are contradictory impulses contending for power at the end of this drama, not to the benefit of the play's aesthetic effect. Strindberg the naturalist enlists the aid of all types of contemporary psychological explanations, including hazy ideas about hypnotism and suggestion, to make the suicide scientifically plausible, but the play does not gain by the attempt. The conclusion of *Miss Julie* remains confused and artistically unsatisfying. The playwright has not been able to choose sides; the humanist and the naturalist fight an indecisive battle right to the final curtain.

We find this same conflict in other texts from Strindberg's naturalistic period. *The People of Hemsö* is a study in social Darwinism, a fight for survival, a battle for territory. It is an animal struggle for life and death, at once farcical and cruel, but this was not enough for Strindberg the humanist. In the final scene he erects a mighty vault of tragedy over Carlsson's death. A human being facing death remains an exalted mystery for the humanist that Strindberg could not deny in himself. Consequently he was ready to sacrifice the stylistic unity of his work.

In few places does this conflict stand out more clearly than in the novel *By the Open Sea*, a study of the destruction of the superior personality. Borg, an independent thinker with a brilliant mind, is an outcast from the parochial scientific community of Sweden. He takes refuge on an island in the archipelago, where he tries in vain to create civilized surroundings that will calm his delicate nerves and satisfy his intellect. But the local people prove to be coarse and superstitious, and they instinctively hate this *Übermensch* whose personality reveals so clearly their own backwardness and raw vulgarity. Contact with a woman becomes an additional source of humiliation for Borg, who must demean himself to play the role of attentive admirer. The hero is gradually broken, physically and mentally, and ends as a drooling, helpless lunatic. Up to this point, Strindberg's approach to human behavior was naturalistic, but he was not content with a naturalistic ending for this novel. He has the deranged hero lift himself out of his degradation and regain his human worth through a heroic suicide. Thus the humanist wins yet another victory, although it may seem to be at the expense of plausibility. Consider how Beckett would have dealt with this material! We must admit that there are limits to Strindberg's modernism.

True humanism seems to presuppose a belief in human free will, a belief that nineteenth-century science and biology did their utmost to deny and replace with a deterministic view of human behavior. Again and again in Strindberg's naturalistic works, we seem to see determinism in operation, until once again the tragic conclusion brings free will into action and lends human dignity and grandeur to the destruction of the central character. In this way Strindberg as humanist seeks an emergency exit from the scientific labyrinth where human beings wander as predictably as programmed mice. But as we have seen, the humanist Strindberg always encounters difficulties in bringing his heroes to a tragic end with dignity and redemption; he often achieved his goal at the expense of plausibility and artistic effect.

In addition to having to wrestle with the ideas of his time, Strindberg also had to struggle with the neurotic elements in his own character, which drove him to deny free will and to embrace one or another deterministic explanation of human behavior or to accept the controlling power of fate or God. One lifelong problem was his inability to accept guilt, that all too familiar problem. We are reluctant to admit that we have injured a fellow being; we would rather blame the victim than ourselves. The simple rules we teach small children — to admit our faults, to ask for forgiveness, to repair the damage we have done — these rules apply to adults as well, whether they live within or outside a religious system. But although the rules apply, they are hard to uphold. For Strindberg, they were almost impossible to accept.

His customary way of dealing with guilt was to transfer it onto his victim, as he does in *A Madman's Defense,* in which he accuses his own wife of the offences he himself committed. This psychological mechanism can assume paranoid dimensions. One often gets the impression that a hostile world has conspired to drive August Strindberg to insanity and death and, consequently, that he is always to be excused — whatever he has done was done in self-defense.

But in his battle against guilt, Strindberg could seek other solutions as well. As he grew older he liked to think that God or providence had orchestrated his life, that he had been manipulated like a marionette to be given the greatest possible experience of life for the benefit of his writing. He applied the same line of reasoning to Shakespeare and expressed his wonder at a providence so cruel as to make that writer suffer Othello's jealousy, Macbeth's ambition, Lear's anguish over his ungrateful daughters, and so on. He took it for granted that Shakespeare had functioned as he himself did, and that he too had always written directly about his own feelings and experiences. Confronted with the immense variety of emotions in Shakespeare's plays, Strindberg recoiled in respect, amazement, and pity — what a life he must have led, that fellow Shakespeare!

All the same, the notion of God as a playwright and director who stages our lives for us can hardly be reconciled with the humanistic view: what free will is left to a human puppet appearing in a Punch-and-Judy show staged by the Almighty? Which leads us to this problem: how can his humanism be reconciled with the religious conviction he embraced toward the end of his life?

It is obvious that Strindberg's religious demand for submission always contested his urge for freedom. Insofar as it was possible, he took pains to attribute to ecclesiastical institutions the imposition of all kinds of servitude;

in this he remained a follower of Kierkegaard. He explained the fact that he was a member of the Swedish state church by viewing it as purely a matter of convention; there were other faiths he could consider accepting as well. His religious outlook remained ecumenical and syncretistic to the end.

Strindberg was hardly a Christian; if anything he felt closer to Judaism and very much at home in the Old Testament. In these archaic texts God may appear as almost human, as almost an equal in his intercourse with the mighty prophets, an equal with whom it is possible to fight and to come to grips. The prophets, serving as models and mouthpieces, could help Strindberg retain humanism and reduce the power of God:

> And Jacob was left alone; and there wrestled a man with him until the breaking of the day. / And when the man saw that he prevailed not against him, he touched the hollow of his thigh; and the hollow of Jacob's thigh was out of joint, as he wrestled with him. / And he said, Let me go, for the day breaketh. And he said, I will not let thee go, except thou bless me. / And he said unto him, What is thy name? And he said, Jacob. And he said, Thy name shall be called no more Jacob, but Israel: for as a prince hast thou power with God and with men, and hast prevailed.
>
> (Genesis 32: 24 - 28)

Just as Strindberg reduced God almost to an equal, he reduced Jesus to the level of a human being. The role of redeemer — or scapegoat, as Strindberg preferred to call it — was not unique to Jesus. It was a role that anyone at all might be called upon to play. Strindberg's later works are filled with people representing this moral function — to be subjected to suffering in order to help other human beings and redeem their sins — for instance, the Lawyer in *A Dream Play* or Eleonora in *Easter.* In this attempt to deprive Jesus of his divine role as Savior and apportion it out, as it were, among ordinary mortals, we find Strindberg the humanist trying to modify religious dogma to the advantage of humankind.

To sum up: humanity's moral guilt cannot be redeemed by Christ's sacrificial death; humanity must bear its own responsibility and atone for its own guilt. If and when a case of human suffering strikes our moral consciousness as unreasonable and indecent, we are dealing with a scapegoat, a human being chosen by God to atone for the sins of his or her fellow human beings. In this way Strindberg the humanist seeks to repudiate Christ's divinity, to take from Him what is unique in the miracle of redemption and to transfer this atonement to humanity. This is a humanistic reduction of religious dogma.

The struggle between humanism and religious belief is given dramatic expression in *A Dream Play.* Strindberg had arrived at the conviction that suffering in this world is a necessary punishment imposed on humankind by God, in order that we might overcome our will to life. But this concept collided with another idea, a stubborn conviction that suffering can be alleviated and social injustice ameliorated by human intervention. We are not simply passive victims after all.

Strindberg saw himself as an advocate of humanity, "pleading humanity's cause," in *A Dream Play* — an act of daring, maybe even of blasphemy. With the religious part of his personality, he feared God's wrath and punishment. We can see in his diary how his resignation to God's will came into conflict with his indignation over human suffering and with his belief in humanity's capacity to improve its own earthly circumstances. Here as always we find Strindberg the humanist doing battle with the great temporal or metaphysical forces that threaten to overpower humankind.

In his later years Strindberg took part in a great literary debate — with political overtones — called the Strindberg controversy. Socialists in Sweden have been pleased to make much of this final phase in Strindberg's development; it enables them to enroll a great writer in their ranks. But it poses the question of whether Strindberg ever took the course by which great writers submit to political ideologies and become their servants, contrary to the central ideals of humanism.

During the last years of his life, Strindberg at least once called himself a "Christian and a Socialist," but, as I have shown, he cannot really be called a Christian in any reasonable sense of the word. I do not believe he can be called a socialist either. The great controversy did, undeniably, have political consequences, but Strindberg was primarily interested in literary and religious questions. Whenever he made political statements, they were in line with nineteenth-century liberal tradition — against the monarchy, for increased suffrage, and against ossified, reactionary scientific and educational institutions. He always remained an adherent of the political ideas of 1848 and espoused a liberalism that was generally compatible with humanism. Nowhere did he endorse socialism's basic tenet — state ownership of the means of production. He criticized the socialism of Fourier and was to remain an opponent of collectivism. In my opinion he was a liberal and an individualist all his life.

I shall conclude with a personal statement. Now and again I look back with envy at the great eighteenth-century revolutionaries and individualists who sowed the seeds that were to blossom in 1776 and 1789. They all had one thing in common: optimism and faith in the future. They thought it sufficient to *écraser l'infame,* to crush the infamous church with all its superstition, and they never envisioned what new, cannibalistic churches and ideologies would arise in the coming centuries. They believed that the human being was perfectible, capable of developing into a good social animal, if enlightenment could be allowed to disperse the darkness of ignorance. They had no suspicion of the subterranean chasms of cruelty, hunger for power, and will to submission contained in the human soul; theirs was a humanism based on happy ignorance. Strindberg's humanism, on the other hand, had to struggle with a new, scientific view of humankind, with the precursors of psychoanalysis, with powerful and ambitious political ideologies. His humanism often succumbed to the pressure of contemporary ideas and to his own psychological need for submission and security. In that he was human, if not a humanist.

What is more remarkable is his persistent, stubborn return to a humanistic belief in human freedom and worth — despite the dictates of social and political authority and despite religious beliefs required by his own desire for atonement and peace. Many writers — altogether too many writers in this century — have betrayed humankind and submitted to cruel, totalitarian ideologies. Of Strindberg the humanist, despite all his vacillations and all his defeats, we can say with conviction that he fought a good fight. In his immense panorama of human suffering and human degradation, there is still a fundamental faith in human dignity and freedom. It is this faith that makes it possible for us to look back with respect on this beleaguered humanist, August Strindberg, our contemporary, our brother.

2

Strindberg and the Superman

Evert Sprinchorn

Although much has been written about the dramatic techniques that Strindberg invented or rediscovered, comparatively little consideration has been given to his thought and philosophy. In contrast to such dramatists as Goethe, Schiller, Ibsen, and Shaw, the Swedish writer appears, at least to many critics, to have no consistent point of view, no broad outlook. Rather, his plays and novels seem to emanate from a mind in which ideas are tossed about helter-skelter. Positions are taken but not adequately defended, and ideas are fired off as if the explosive effect were more important than the target.

Of course there have always been artists and philosphers who have proceeded toward their goals indirectly and whose methods of thought and investigation have been deliberately improvisatory and seemingly illogical. For them, systematic thinking has been a form of dogmatism to be avoided at all costs.

Nietzsche, for instance, must strike many of his readers as a chaotic thinker whose argumentative skill consists mainly in a brash assertiveness. Yet the careful student knows that chaos was the breeding ground of Nietzsche's philosophy and that his hammering style was meant to be destructive. He had to reduce the old cosmos to ruins in order to envision a new one. His emotionally charged, disruptive style is an essential part of what he had to say. What we know as Nietzscheanism is a special combination of art and philosophy. The same is true of Strindberg. In both cases it is impossible to appreciate the skills employed by the artist without comprehending the thoughts of the philosopher and vice versa.

With Strindberg, however, there has been a pronounced tendency, when judgement is passed on the value of his works, to separate method from meaning and form from content, and the result has been that his standing as a truly great writer has seemed rather shaky. The technician, the artist in the narrow sense of the word, has almost always been deemed far superior to the moral philosopher. When I was a university student I heard a professor of literature opine that *The Father* and *Miss Julie* were infernally clever plays but that their author could not by even those most kindly disposed toward him be considered a great writer, one worthy to rank with Tolstoy or Chekhov or Ibsen, because there was too much hatred in him. I still recall how this eminent man of letters shriveled up in my eyes when he had to admit that those two plays were all that he had ever read by Strindberg. Even in his own lifetime, or especially then, Strindberg suffered from similar treatment. In his native land the conventional gambit of critics was to praise him for his mastery of language and revile him as a detestable human being. In Germany, for a decade or so after his death, Strindberg was almost revered as a religious prophet, a Jeremiah denouncing a materialistic and godless age. At the end of that brief period, however, a leading German critic closed the books on Strindberg by proclaiming that the Swedish dramatist was indeed a theatrical wizard, but a wizard who had to resort to dramaturgical and stage tricks to conceal an emptiness of thought.[1]

In England and America the approach was not radically different. Since Strindberg's misogyny and mysticism were distasteful subjects, the commentators once again separated the artist from the ideologist. In their opinion, what Strindberg had to say was not worth saying but the way in which he said it was fascinating; and no one could deny that he had exerted a strong and pervasive influence on the course of developments in twentieth-century dramaturgy. Two pronouncements that appeared in the 1950s and 1960s may be taken as representative. The first comes from a standard handbook on the drama. Strindberg "has been both over- and underestimated, now being regarded as the equal of Ibsen (which, if only for lack of artistic wholeness, he could not be) and now merely as a brilliant theatreman, remarkable only for novelty of theme and form."[2] The second statement is more precise and revealing. An English critic wrote that "apart from . . . intensity, the other main secret of Strindberg's success may be . . . his style. . . . Since . . . he has pleased and excited, for the best part of a century, readers and audiences far beyond the limits of his own land, it would be futile to deny his powers. His pleasure-value is incontestable." However,

Strindberg, like Dostoyevsky, embodies "the assault of chaos and madness on all that is most valuable in Western civilization."[3] This same writer also strains to equate Strindberg's mentality with that of the Nazis, utterly ignoring the fact that Strindberg's reputation in Germany sank to its nadir during the Third Reich. And this same writer reveals his own kind of thinking, which one assumes must form a part of what is "most valuable in Western civilization," when he states that the characters in Tennessee Williams's *Cat on a Hot Tin Roof* "make me feel only that the best thing for the lot of them would be a humane and efficient gas-chamber."[4]

A large part of Strindberg criticism makes the same point in one way or another: Strindberg cannot be ranked among the indubitably great writers of the modern age merely on the basis of his dramaturgical skills or his eccentric personality. It does not follow, however, that he should for this reason be demoted to the rank of a second-rate thinker. I would turn the argument around and suggest that Strindberg's enduring influence has its roots in matters that are of concern to the thinking person of our times. By now we should be so familiar with the techniques that they should not blind us to the purpose they are meant to serve. Hitherto, his ideas have been detrimental to his reputation, and he has been esteemed for his proficiency as a teller of tales and maker of plays. Eventually his reputation will rest on his ethical and political philosophy, which will be seen as inseparable from the techniques he employed.

The novel *By the Open Sea (I havsbandet)*, for example, has more than its share of Strindbergian eccentricities, yet it deals with momentous philosophical issues (although this was hardly apparent when the novel was first published). It marks an epoch in Strindberg's career, yet it can be seen now as signally or foretelling a decisive rupture in Western consciousness.

The major transitional period in Strindberg's life was formed by the years leading into and out of his Inferno experience. These were the years when our century was in gestation, stirring rather violently in the womb of the nineteenth century. It was the time when the theories of Marx and Darwin had established themselves and their practical consequences were being felt; these were the years when Freud began drawing a new map of the human psyche; and when scientists were discovering that what they had thought were the elementary building blocks of matter were not elementary at all. Darwin had radically changed man's position in the great chain of being; Marx had completely inverted the old relationship between man's ways of producing and man's ways of thinking; Freud was about to undermine the bastion of reason itself, the human mind, thus finishing off what Rousseau had started; and the scientists were astonished to find that some of the basic and indivisible particles of matter were disintegrating and scattering waves of energy. Untune the string of order and hark what discord follows, warned Shakespeare. Well, here was a world filled with discord. Humanity was closer to the ape than to the angels; what we made with our hands determined what we thought and believed; and everything that had appeared fundamental and solid was turning out to be insubstantial and deliquescent. God, the social community, the ego, the atom — everything was breaking up. In a word, it was the time of the most stupendous revolution of humankind's perception of the universe since the Renaissance.

The issues were so complex, the crisis was developing along such a broad front, that only the most prescient and far-reaching minds could perceive at that time, even dimly, that the advance of Western man had brought it to the edge of an abyss. To many cultural historians the one mind that more than any other can serve as a microcosm of Europe in the latter quarter of the nineteenth century is that of Friedrich Nietzsche. His fevered brain seemed to glow with the reflections of a European *Götterdämmerung*. His writings — unsystematic, rhapsodic, aphoristic — image the flames he saw consuming Western civilization. And when the fire was most intense and brightest, when he was about to see in those flames a vision of the world as it might become, his mind suddenly collapsed. It is difficult to conceive of a life more dramatically right, more symbolic of the times, or more premonitory of things to come.

In his pursuit of truth — pure, Kantian, undogmatic truth — he claimed to see more penetratingly into his own times and more distantly into the future than his contemporaries. He saw that the vast upheaval that was about to take place was at bottom a moral and ethical revolution. "As the will to truth . . . gains self-consciousness," he wrote, "morality will gradually *perish* now: this is the great spectacle in a hundred arts reserved for the next two centuries in Europe — the most terrible, most questionable and perhaps also the most hopeful of all spectacles."[5]

With our perspective, nearly a hundred years later, we can see that Western civilization was in a state of chaos, however placidly and serenely life appeared on the surface, in that relatively long period of peace after the Franco-Prussian War. We can see now that the forces that were gathering then would explode on the fields of Europe in 1914. The great wars of our century should probably be regarded as the violent political catastrophes resulting from the collision of intellectual and cultural energies at the end of the nineteenth century. This was at first a subterranean collision because there were only a few thinkers and artists who sensed then that Europe was slipping into chaos.

One of these preternaturally sensitive souls was Strindberg, whose mental crisis in the 1890s reflects the great crisis of the modern age. To read Strindberg's works of this period as the revelatory products of a deeply disturbed man, as pages in a long case history, is to misread them. Their true significance lies in the fact that they record the tremors of a whole civilization about to collapse. It is as naive and unphilosophical to suppose that Strindberg's Inferno, which consisted of a series of psychological and scientific experiments, occurred simply by chance at the time of the great European crisis as it is to think that the formation of the Triple Entente merely coincided with the expansion of German commercial interests. Just as T. S. Eliot, during and after World War I, could not have pictured with such intensity the end of a world in *The Waste Land* without undergoing a very personal emotional crisis, so Strindberg could not have recorded the upheavals deep within Western civilization without experiencing those shocks deeply within himself. In the case of Strindberg, the crisis was deliberately self-induced so that he might gain the depth of insight that cultural historians achieved only after a generation or two.

It is possible that Strindberg realized what he had to do because of what happened to Nietzsche. The extraordinary aspect of the careers of these two men is that they intersect, and at just that moment when the majestic drama that comprises the history of the modern era requires it.

The year of the event is 1888. Georg Brandes came upon Nietzsche's writings and was so exhilarated by them that he gave a series of lectures in Copenhagen on Nietzsche's philosophy, labeling it aristocratic radicalism and introducing the German thinker to a wider European audience for the first time. Immediately recognizing that Nietzsche and Strindberg were kindred spirits in many ways, Brandes put the two in touch with each other. Strindberg read Nietzsche's *Beyond Good and Evil* in spring 1888, and later that same year he read *The Case of Wagner*, *The Twilight of the Idols*, and *On the Genealogy of Morals*. The following spring he read *Human, All Too Human*, and at some point he either read or read about *Thus Spake Zarathustra*.[6]

Strindberg himself confirms what scholars have noted: that the impact of the German philosopher is first noticeable in the preface to *Miss Julie*, composed in the summer of 1888.[7] In autumn he wrote the novelette *Chandala (Tschandala)*, his most Nietzschean work, although it is as misleading to say that as it is to say that Hitler was Nietzsche's truest disciple. Half a year later Strindberg again drew on Nietzsche for inspiration when he began to write *By the Open Sea*, which he completed in the spring of 1890.

At about that time Henrik Ibsen was making notes for one of his richest dramas, *Hedda Gabler*. With a sure sense of what was significant in the world around him, Ibsen elicited from a story by Strindberg an idea for a treatment of the new type of woman, from Brandes the plot device of a competition between a harmless liberal and an intransigent radical for an academic position, and from Nietzsche a far-reaching concept of cultural history in which the whole drama could be cradled.[8]

Nietzsche, Brandes, Strindberg, Ibsen — an extraordinary conjunction of intellects occurring in the two-year period from May 1888 to May 1890, with Brandes serving as a kind of message center or synapse. More than other thinkers of the time, these men perceived that Europe might well be about to undergo what Nietzsche called the transvaluation of all values. Christianity had ushered in the era of love, which was actually the era of remorse and resentment, of humility and meanness of spirit. Now, two thousand years later, the Christians, the meek who had inherited the earth, would yield to a new species of human being, the overcomer of repentance, revenge, and guilt: the superman. Thus spake Nietzsche.

The plot of *Chandala* is based on that historical development. The central figure is a research scholar who has been taught by school and society to treat his fellow human beings with kindness and to indulge their weaknesses. All he gets in return for his compassion and consideration is scurvy treatment from a lowborn gypsy, a rascal who takes advantage of the scholar's gentleness and gradually imposes his will upon him. Halfway through the novelette Strindberg begins a reverse movement. He introduces a teacher who speaks to the confused and degraded scholar as Nietzsche himself might have done.[9] The scholar pulls himself up and, using his superior intelligence, destroys the gypsy. Setting up a magic lantern that projects pictures on the clouds, he creates specters that reduce the gullible gypsy to a state of utter hysteria. His actual death is accomplished by hungry dogs who tear him to pieces. "The pariah was dead," Strindberg writes in the conclusion of the story, "and the Aryan had conquered, conquered thanks to his storehouse of knowledge and his being spiritually superior to the lower races."[10]

The reader is supposed to take this gruesome death as justified because of the ineradicable difference between master and slave. Strindberg clinches his argument by quoting from the Hindu code of Manu, the law of the caste system. He had come across the passage in Nietzsche's *The Twilight of the Idols,* which its author had mailed to him just in time to furnish Strindberg with a finale to his story. Accordingly, Strindberg changed the title from "Pariah" to "Chandala," the Chandala being the lowest social caste in India, "the fruit of adultery, incest, and crime," in the words of the Manu code. Nietzsche saw a similarity between the Chandala and the Christians, to his mind both were wretched failures whose professed religion of loving one's neighbor was really nothing more than the expression of the undying hatred they felt for those intellectually and spiritually above them. Nietzsche saw the code of Manu, its makers, and its victims as part of a single hideous system or morality. It was a point that was lost on Strindberg, and on most other readers, for that matter, just as it was lost on the Nazis.

Chandala is certainly one of the most distasteful stories that Strindberg ever wrote. To his credit, he was quick to repudiate it. In April 1889, he called it a poor book, a tedious work, and wished that he had never written it.[11] Shortly afterward, he set about writing *By the Open Sea*, a novel that reads like a parable about Nietzscheanism. It was obviously intended to be the reverse of Chandala. The career of the hero, Inspector Borg, runs parallel to that of the scholar in *Chandala* but in the opposite direction. Borg is introduced as an intellectual aristocrat, immensely superior in brains and education to the inhabitants of the remote and sparsely populated island where he has been assigned as government inspector of fishing. When we last see him, he is a defeated man who in a delirium sails out to the open sea to die alone and unlamented.

Although his end is precisely the opposite of the scholar's in *Chandala*, the two stories have the same two-part structure, which suggests that Strindberg was reworking material he had handled poorly the first time. At the beginning of the second half in each story, a new force enters the picture. In *Chandala*, the teacher arrives providentially to encourage the scholar to overcome those moral scruples that would allow him to be vanquished by the cunning of inferior, insignificant people. In the sea novel, a preacher arrives on the island to counteract the godless teachings of Inspector Borg, the scientist. In *Chandala*, Nietzschean notions of intellectual and spiritual superiority, of aristocratic radicalism, must be taught to the hero. He must root out of himself old ideas of right and wrong and of consideration for the less fortunate before he can avenge himself against his gypsy tormentor. In *By the Open Sea*, Inspector Borg is in total command of the situation on the island at the end of the first half of the novel. He has thoroughly cowed the ignorant inhabitants through his scientist's knowledge of the laws of nature. To underscore the fact that he is in a sense rewriting *Chandala*, Strindberg has the heroes of both stories employ their knowledge of optics as a means of subduing the little people. Inspector Borg intends to amuse himself, dazzle his fiancée, and overwhelm the villagers by putting on a magic show that will create the illusion of an Italian landscape on one of the barren islands of the Stockholm archipelago. In *Chandala*, the hero uses a magic lantern to defeat his presumptuous inferior.

Something significantly different happens in *By the Open Sea*. At the beginning of the second half of the novel, the mirage that Borg has planned takes place. But its effect is totally unexpected. By chance, the refracted light creates the image of a second moon. Instead of wiping out the superstitious awe of the fishing folk, as Borg had hoped, the mirage instills in them a religious awe, and the scientist, who had intended to enlighten the people, is looked upon as a miracle worker. He becomes the center of a force that he cannot control. And just at that moment a Christian preacher arrives at the island, witnesses the mirage, and calms the frightened people by reading to them from the Bible, from the Book of Revelation, no less. The ironic result of Inspector Borg's attempt to show the simple folk what science can accomplish is to drive them into the arms of the preacher and to reinforce their superstitions. Borg had "toyed with the powers of nature," Strindberg writes, "conjured up a devil to help him, or so he thought, only to find that everyone had been won over by the devil, so that Borg stood alone."[12]

Increasingly isolated from the common people, like Nietzsche's Zarathustra, and unable to make contact with them because he is afraid of losing his highly prized individuality and of becoming one of them ("When I lived with them," says Zarathustra, "I lived above them."), Borg is persecuted and ridiculed by them, is reduced to a physical wreck, begins to fear for his sanity, and eventually succumbs to the attractive power of the measureless sea. Like Zarathustra, he can find no true companion among the people of his time. "Thus I now love only my *children's land*, yet undiscovered, in the farthest sea: for this I bid my sails search and search."[13]

The sublime final pages of *By the Open Sea* contain other unmistakable allusions to Nietzsche's writings. Nietzsche had described how the free spirits of his time sensed that a new era was in the offing. "At last the horizon appears free again to us, even granted that it is not bright; at last our ships may venture out again, venture out to face any danger; all the daring of the love of knowledge is permitted again; the sea, *our* sea, lies open again; perhaps there has never yet been such an 'open sea.' "[14] In another passage Nietzsche had linked his vision of the progress of the human race with the movement of the solar system. "I hear with pleasure that our sun is swiftly moving toward the constellation of *Hercules* — and I hope that man on this earth will in this respect follow the sun's example?"[15] Inspector Borg, when he sails out into the open sea, sets a course for a star of the second magnitude, believing momentarily that it might be the star of Bethlehem, and then is relieved to discover that his star is the star Beta in the constellation Hercules — Hercules, "the moral ideal of the Greeks." So the superintellect Borg finds himself sailing out toward the Christmas star that signals the birth of a new era, "out across the open sea, the mother of all, in whose womb was kindled the first spark of life, the inexhaustible well of fertility and of love, the source of life and the enemy of life."[16]

Strindberg unquestionably wrote *By the Open Sea* as a response to Nietzscheanism and to what Brandes called "aristocratic radicalism." But the nature of that response seems ambiguous. The plot of the novel, which carries the hero into insanity, reads like a condemnation of the philosopher, whereas the description of Borg's last journey reads like a paean to Nietzsche and his vision of the future. Moreover, Borg bears a close resemblance both to Strindberg and to the highly developed individual whom Nietzsche saw as the goal of human striving. Nietzsche explained that the "higher types ... perish most easily as fortunes change. They are exposed to every kind of decadence: they are extreme, and that almost means decadents."[17] This fits Strindberg's description of the finicky and effeminate Borg perfectly.

Borg is also in many ways Strindberg's double. The writer and dramatist wanted first of all to be a scientist, and Borg's search for the underlying order of the universe duplicates Strindberg's investigations in natural science. As a matter of fact, the whole of chapter 3, with its detailed summary of Borg's intellectual development forming a parallel to an account of the evolution of the natural world, could with only minor changes serve as Strindberg's apologia. Even the ultimate collapse of the fishing inspector reflects Strindberg's own fears and imaginings, for Strindberg had an intimate acquaintance with the psychology of madness and the dangers of isolation. Some months before he began the sea novel and shortly after having received Nietzsche's last letters, he wrote, "I'm afraid Nietzsche has blinded me, and my brain is ulcerous from over-exertion. And he is driving me out of my mind! Because the incredible self-esteem shown in his books has made me feel the same way about myself. Which is no guarantee that my gray matter won't burst and split, and it probably will."[18]

Because Strindberg put so much of himself into Inspector Borg, it is tempting to read the novel as the sympathetic account of a Nietzschean hero, of a highly developed type of human being who is crushed by the stupid, unfeeling mob. The inferior type wins out through sheer force of numbers and because of the overrefinement of the intellectually superior human being. The structure of the novel, however, tells a different story and reveals Strindberg's intentions. Here we have an example of how meaning is revealed through form. What seems ambiguous on the narrative level becomes clear on the structural level. Stripped to its essentials, the novel can be seen to have a two-part structure. The last seven chapters correspond to the first seven in such a way that all that is done in the first half of the book is undone in the second half. In chapter 1, Borg arrives at the fishing village and is pictured as the all-knowing man of science, who because of his schooling is more adept at handling the forces of nature than the fishermen themselves. In chapter 8, the corresponding chapter from the second half, a lay preacher arrives at the village, and Borg is regarded by the people not as a scientist but as a miracle worker. In the second chapter, Borg is portrayed as a giant intellect. In the corresponding ninth chapter, the preacher, representing superstitious belief, gains ascendancy over the fishing folk. In the third chapter, which contains the section on evolution, Borg is placed at the end of a long line of development; he is a new variety of the human species. In the corresponding tenth chapter, Borg's assistant arrives, a man of brawn rather than brains. At the end of chapter 4, Borg falls in love with a girl. In chapter 11 he becomes jealous — in a very un-Nietzschean response — when she falls in love with the newly arrived muscular man. In chapter 5, Borg finds himself in a sexual dilemma: in making himself attractive to the girl, he feels he is lowering himself to the level of an inferior being. In the corresponding chapter 12, he finally and impulsively has sexual intercourse with the girl. In chapter 6, he realizes that the girl can be only a mother-woman to him, not the companion his finely tuned brain requires. In the corresponding chapter 13, he loses the girl. In chapter 7, the end of the first half of the novel, Borg plays God and creates the magnificent mirage that frightens the villagers. In the last chapter, Borg goes insane and sails out into the open sea, "the mother of us all."

I hope this outline shows how calculatingly Strindberg set the hero of the second half of the novel against the hero of the first half. If *By the Open Sea* is read primarily as a symbolic work, there can be little doubt that Strindberg's purpose in it was to settle accounts with Nietzscheanism and to abandon it. Although Inspector Borg may at first appear to be a kind of superman, certainly a superintellect, he becomes in the course of the novel a megalomaniac who thinks he is God the Father and who declines into madness, embracing God the Mother.

This interpretation will immediately prompt the objection that Borg no more resembles Nietzsche's ideal than does the scholar in *Chandala*. There is in him none of the exultant freedom, the dancing joy, the overflowing spirit of the philosopher's new man. Borg is a prudish, delicate, and sober intellectual, a caricature of the joyful scientist, the Dionysian dancer of indestructible spirit whom Nietzsche envisioned. To point up the parody, Strindberg even writes a scene in which the Inspector, infatuated with his girl, dances like a Hottentot for her enjoyment.

It would seem, then, that Strindberg meant Borg to be a stalking horse. But for what purpose? On the basis of what happens in the novel, only one answer makes sense. It is not Nietzsche's superman who is defeated by the little people; it is Nietzsche himself. The superman is not defeated, not even pictured in the novel, because he does not exist. To use Strindberg's own words: the superman "lacks any foundation in reality."[19]

Like Nietzsche, Strindberg saw the superman as arriving at the end of a long line of development, and both the philosopher and the artist-scientist wanted to see man surpass himself and overcome his past. But Strindberg disagreed with Nietzsche about how the new man would emerge from the old. The philosopher is not very helpful on this point. He grandly spurns science, abolishes Christianity, and imagines that along with it he has got rid of remorse and guilt, saying in effect that when enough good Europeans have done the same, they will have prepared the way for the emergence of the superman. No doubt Strindberg felt as giddy with the thought of what might be as many other readers have since that fateful year of 1888 when Strindberg first encountered Nietzsche. Then, immediately after Strindberg had fallen under the spell of the philosopher's incantations — it is difficult to imagine more dramatic timing — there arrived those mad letters from Nietzsche. The sudden collapse of Nietzsche's mind must have struck the Swedish writer as both a warning and a challenge.[20] Nietzsche had striven for the Dionysian, the passionate life, and had sought through supreme self-mastery, through self-overcoming, to create out of the chaos within himself a new order. But the struggle had torn him apart. He saw himself as Dionysus fighting against the Crucified One. When his mind gave way, he signed himself "The Crucified One."

To Strindberg, Nietzsche's insanity revealed the fatuity of dreams about the superman. "Zarathustra cures nothing," he said. "Couldn't even cure his own creator, who was at the end transformed into a loon (he shrieked like one in bad weather)." In kinder words he said that the human being is bound to the earth, and "the Earth Spirit takes its vengeance upon us when we try to exist as pure spirit."[21] The second half of *By the Open Sea* shows the would-be superman struggling against the earth spirit, against his lower instincts, and all in vain. At the end he must submit to forces much more powerful than his brain and much vaster than his individual being, forces so intangible and so amorphous that Strindberg could only convey their presence symbolically.

Still, there was a challenge in Nietzsche's exhortations, the great dream of human potentialities and of the enhancement of life, a dream Strindberg shared. Although Borg dies a failure, he did aim for greatness. He set his sails for Hercules. The ambiguity of the novel's close comes from the juxtaposition of two symbols: the constellation Hercules and the open sea, the one standing for the new human being, a new moral ideal, all that Nietzsche affirmed; the other, the sea, representing the instinctual life, the life of the unconscious, and humanity's evolutionary past.[22] Nietzsche had attempted to overcome the past, which was to him the source of a pernicious morality, an ethos fit for little people, not for giants. As long as human beings were bound to the moral code of the past, they would be unable to go beyond good and evil and attain true self-perfection. As long as they conceived of justice as based on revenge and punishment, their bad consciences would lead them to self-condemnation. The overcomer of the past would burst these bonds and give birth to the superman. Nietzsche wanted to replace Darwin with Zarathustra, the scientist with the artist-philosopher.

When Strindberg began to write his sea novel, he understood that Nietzsche, who claimed to see the truth naked, who despised the metaphysicians for creating systems of abstract thought that had no foundation in reality, who was so hard on those who separated experience from thought and morality from genealogy, had conjured up the dancing superman entirely out of his fantasies. Ruthless and penetrating when he studied the past and surveyed the present, Nietzsche turned out to be merely a wishful thinker who rubbed the lamp of history to bring forth a genie that would solve all his problems. Momentarily entranced by Nietzsche and then quickly disillusioned, Strindberg saw that the road to a higher level of existence went round about and that the Dionysian shortcut was a mirage. At the time he set to work on the sea novel he wrote to Brandes, "One must pass through (be fructified by) Nietzsche and then rid oneself of him."[23]

Like Nietzsche, Inspector Borg nobly puts himself above ordinary people by not feeling resentment against those who treat him with scorn and contempt; yet at the end he finds himself snarled in the coils of sexual jealousy and is drawn back to the primitive level of life that he thought he had overcome. Strindberg saw that the old codes of moral behavior were too deeply rooted to be extirpated with a stroke of the philosopher's pen, and that revenge, resentment, and remorse were more than notions taught in church and school; they were passions deeply seated in the human soul. Consequently, the path to the future wound its way through the realm of the emotions, through the unconscious, through the storehouse of the past. The way to Hercules lay across the open sea.[24]

By the Open Sea has usually and properly been viewed as a transitional work in Strindberg's career. Interpreted along the lines I have adumbrated, it can be seen as charting the course of his explorations during the next ten or twelve years. I would go further, however, and assert that as a symbolic novel it forms the best prologue to the twentieth century that art has given us. It encapsulates the moral history of the nineteenth century and points the way far into the twentieth.

Perhaps I am reading too much into this novel and into the confrontation of Nietzsche and Strindberg that formed its germinal idea. But if I am in error in ascribing so much significance to the story of a misguided intellectual who loses his mind among some primitive people on a barren island in the Stockholm skerries, I think it is the kind of error that should be made more often. I believe that Strindberg is not taken seriously enough as a man of ideas and profound insight, not simply into the workings of neurotic or psychotic minds but into the workings of historical and cultural forces. Critics who deal with these large themes do not hesitate to find in the novels of Mann and Joyce and in many a lesser writer the layers of meaning on which our culture is built. Yet Strindberg's plays and novels are almost always treated as forming the narrow realm of an eccentric artist standing on the periphery of our age and culture. I confess that I have always felt as I turned from Strindberg to Mann or Joyce or Eliot that I was entering a smaller and more constricted realm, not because Strindberg's characters are bigger or healthier than theirs but because his universe is so much larger, his intuitions so much more profound, and his horizons so much broader.

When literary talk turns to magic moments, and others tell of Hans Castorp's vision in the snowstorm, of the meeting of Irish Jew and substitute son in Dublin's Nighttown, of the echoes in the caves of Marabar, and of the memories aroused by madeleines soaked in tea, I think of a moment in chapter 9 of Strindberg's novel when Inspector Borg seeks solitude to reexamine himself. He sails out into a thick, almost impenetrable morning mist on a calm sea. Out of that mist there looms another boat, carrying the preacher. The preacher is seeking temporary isolation, too; only he needs it to commune with God. The preacher turns out to be a childhood acquaintance of Borg's, a poor farm boy who was humiliated by Borg and who ever since has felt himself to be one of life's failures.

I can see the ripples of history spreading from this chance encounter and flowing out into our time. Conjoined in the morning fog are the superman scientist and the superstitious believer, the overcomer and the undergoer, the aspiring Faust and the suffering Christ, the force that negates the past in favor of the future and the force that says the future is the past. Strindberg sensed the hollowness of Nietzsche's dream. He knew it was impossible to shrug off the past and the burden of guilt, not only impossible but unwise. Nietzsche declared that the priest had ruled human lives through the invention of sin and that the invention of sin was "the greatest crime against humanity [that] has been commited."[25] In our time we are more likely to believe that the scientist rules our lives and that some of science's inventions constitute the greatest crimes against humanity.

Strindberg knew that the irrational or mystical side of existence must intrude into the rational world of science as inevitably as the preacher intrudes into Borg's solitude out of the mist. He also understood that the moral ideal of the future, the Hercules ideal, must be formed out of both spheres of existence, the mystical or religious and the scientific or rational. Acting on that knowledge, Strindberg handled superstitions and intuitions as a geologist handles stones. There were secrets in them. Yet it is precisely here, in his investigations into the illogical and irrational, that he appalls most readers and critics. Embarrassed or contemptuous, they refuse to follow him out into the open sea.[26]

Strindberg and the Dream of the Golden Age: The Poetics of History

Harry G. Carlson

Strindberg drew on material from a variety of sources for his historical fiction and drama: autobiographical, historical, and philosophical — his own hopes and fears, details from his turbulent marriages, the facts and events of world history, and ideas borrowed from historians and philosophers such as Buckle, de Tocqueville, Swedenborg, Rousseau, and Schopenhauer. I will discuss the question of source from another point of departure: the poetic — the influence of particular metaphors on Strindberg's conception of history. Hayden White asserts that historians must first "*pre*figure as a possible object of knowledge the whole set of events" they find reported in documents. And "the prefigurative act is *poetic* inasmuch as it is precognitive and precritical in the economy of the historian's own consciousness. In the poetic act which precedes the formal analysis of the field, the historian both creates his object of analysis and predetermines the ... conceptual strategies he will use to explain it."[1]

In Strindberg's handling of historical fiction and drama — and the examples here will be drawn from both genres — the dynamic tension and interplay between metaphors from two sources play a significant role: the myth of the Golden Age, especially as it is depicted in Ovid's *Metamorphoses*, and the biblical images of the Fall and the Redemption of humanity.

As Ovid relates it, the Golden Age was a time when men and women trusted each other. They felt safe in their homes and had no need for laws or cities or warfare. Eternal spring was the only season: "Season of milk and wine in amber streams / And honey pouring from the green-lipped oak." The deity associated with the age was Saturn, god of agriculture. After his death, came the Age of Silver, when "Jove split up the year / In shifting Autumn, wild winter, . . . short Spring, [and] / Summer that glared with heat." Natural shelters no longer sufficed and people were forced to build houses. "Now Grain was planted and the plough pierced the earth."

In the third age, Bronze, human beings became more aggressive, without being warlike. The Age of Iron came last,

And from it poured the very blood of evil:
Piety, Faith, Love, and Truth changed to Deceit,
Violence, the Tricks of Trade, Usury, Profit;
* * *
Land, once like the gift of unlit air,
Was cut in properties, estates, and holdings:
* * *
War . . . lifted blood-clotted hands and marched the earth.
Men fed on loot and lust. . . .
Piety was overthrown, and Astraea [goddess of justice],
Last-born sister of the skies, left the blood-
Sweating earth . . . and turning
Lightly swiftly found her place in heaven.[2]

This abridged version of Ovid's description preserves the balance and structure of the original: only brief attention is given to the second and third ages; the basic tension is between the ages of Gold and Iron. If the Golden Age epitomizes an ideal of earthly life, the Iron Age reveals the meanness of the reality humanity inherits. Even the absences in the Golden Age are eloquent: with no laws or cities or wars, humankind and nature are one and at peace. The Iron Age brings a distinction between *meum* and *tuum*, mine and thine, and disharmony replaces harmony. From Ovid's day to the present, the expressive tension between these images has influenced us spritually as well as politically. Early Christians and contemporary Marxists alike concluded that the concept of property, mine and thine, divides human beings into classes and that the law often perpetuates the division. The virgin goddess of justice had no choice but to abandon earth for heaven.

One implication of this assessment of earthly life is that if justice and harmony are to prevail, a new cycle of ages would have to begin and the conditions of the Golden Age become reality, either once again or for the first time. We know, of course, that the Golden Age is ahistorical; it was only a dream, but a dream with great power. It helped to generate revolution in the past and may do so again in the future.

Strindberg turned again and again to Ovid's work, especially while he was in school (54, 468)[3] and Ovidian themes abound in *Lucky Per's Travels*, as Carl Reinhold Smedmark has pointed out.[4] During the Inferno years in the mid-1890s, Strindberg's letters speak of reading all the secrets of the world in the *Metamorphoses*.[5] But he also absorbed the imagery of the Golden Age indirectly, from reading works by Rousseau and disciples of Rousseau, such as the Unitarian Theodore Parker. Sven-Gustaf Edqvist has analyzed the significance of these sources[6] but in a narrower context and with a narrower purpose than I am suggesting. He makes a strong case for the thesis that Strindberg's flirtation with anarchism in the 1880s was stamped profoundly by Rousseau's ideas. It is also possible to say that both men, under the influence of the dream of the Golden Age, contributed importantly to a literary tradition with deep roots in antiquity. It is the implications of that tradition that I am interested in here.

All Rousseau's criticism of society — urging his contemporaries to abandon city life and to end their alienation from nature — echoes the discrepancies implied between the Golden and Iron Ages. "Man is born free," proclaims the opening line of Rousseau's *Social Contract,* "and everywhere he is in chains." In a passage from his *Discourse on the Origin of Inequality among Men* — a Strindberg favorite — we find the root of the problem:

> The first person who, having fenced off a plot of ground, took it into his head to say *this is mine* and found people simple enough to believe him, was the true founder of civil society. What crimes, wars, murders, what miseries and horrors would the human race have been spared by someone who, uprooting the stakes or filling in the ditch, had shouted to his fellow-men: Beware of listening to this imposter; you are lost if you forget that the fruits belong to all and the earth to no one![7]

Before Rousseau's time, poets who dealt either implicitly or explicitly with the shortcomings of the Iron Age tended toward nostalgia, to sketch, in contrast to present misery, a pleasant, primitive Golden Age landscape: Arcadia, a timeless, pastoral vision of the harmony of nature. Rousseau changed the focus, and another landscape took on new popularity: Utopia. If Arcadia is oriented toward the past, Utopia is oriented toward the future. Fichte summed up Rousseau's contribution succinctly: "*Before* us lies what Rousseau, in the name of the state of nature, and every poet, under the appellation of the golden age, have located *behind* us."[8]

In political terms, over the past three or four centuries Arcadianism has motivated the anarchist, who is "inclined to idealize a *remote past* of natural-human innocence from which men have fallen into the corrupt 'social' state in which they currently find themselves." Utopianism, on the other hand, has motivated the radical, who is "inclined to view the utopian condition as *imminent*, which inspires [his] concern with the provision of the revolutionary means to bring this utopia to pass *now*."[9]

Both landscapes — the Arcadian and the Utopian — figure prominently in Strindberg's works, as do the political extremes each inspires. During the early 1800s, he was especially interested in Russian anarchists and nihilists, but his awareness of the political implications of anarchy can be discerned at least a decade earlier. The most conspicuous anarchists of the sixteenth century were the Anabaptists, and their threatening presence plays an important if minor role in the history play *Master Olof*.

Utopianism, especially in its Rousseauistic sense as a practical program for transforming society, was a Strindberg enthusiasm in the mid-1880s, when he wrote a volume of short stories under the revealing title *Utopias in Reality*. One of the stories deals with an actual French experiment in collective living, the *Familistère*, founded on the ideas of the Comte de Saint-Simon. The latter, one of the promoters of socialism, affirmed in 1814 the significance of Rousseau's political contribution to the tradition of the Golden Age:

> The imagination of the poets has placed the golden age in the cradle of the human race, amid the ignorance and crudity of primitive times. It was rather the iron age that should have been abandoned there. The golden age of mankind is not behind us; it is ahead; it is in the perfection of the social order. Our fathers have not seen it; our children will get there one day; and it is for us to open the way for them.[10]

Strindberg's faith, however, in the possibility of perfecting the social order by means of a utopia was shallow and short-lived, and the loss of this faith is reflected in the different attitudes he held toward Golden Age ideals. In the early 1880s, in his two-volume study called *The Swedish People*, he wrote approvingly of the eighteenth-century Swedish Rousseau disciple, writer Thomas Thorild, who conceived an ambitious plan for a world republic: "New laws — the rights of nature! New customs, new ways of living — in freedom and joy. . . . In a word: the golden age realized — in a pure humanity" (*8*, 371). A decade later an important character in the play *The Keys of Heaven* is that tireless champion of chivalry, Don Quixote. In Cervantes's novel (which Strindberg first became acquainted with in his father's library), the Don says to Sancho Panza: "My friend, you must know that by the will of Heaven, I was born in this iron age of ours to revive the age of gold, or, as it is generally called, the golden age."[11] In Strindberg's play the Don says wearily: "I abandoned all illusions about a heaven on earth, since I realized that life is hell" (25, 158). One can sense both here and elsewhere in Strindberg's writings that over the years images of the grimness of the Age of Iron became less motivations to political action than existential observations.

The actual stages in the transformation from age to age are described in his witty 1884 novella, *The Isle of Bliss*. Secluded islands, separated from the ordinary world, where peace and eternal spring reign have been traditional features of the Golden Age landscape, at least as far back as Hesiod (eighth century B.C.), and the image held an almost magical fascination for Strindberg. In Hesiod's *Works and Days*, there is a description of Zeus's decision to establish such places. Rather than four ages, Hesiod has five, and the fourth of these he calls "the wonderful generation of hero-men, who are also / called half-gods, the generation before our own / on this vast earth." Some of these hero-men fought and died "for the sake of lovely-haired Helen," while on still others Zeus "settled a living and a country / of their own, apart from human kind, / at the end of the world. / And there they have their dwelling place, / and hearts free of sorrow / in the islands of the blessed."[12]

As with so many elements in Strindberg's life and works, islands of bliss or of the blessed had both real and poetic identities. The most frequent poetic name is the vernal Greening Island *(Grönskande ön)*, usually, but not always, associated with Kymmendö, in the Stockholm archipelago. He also called Kymmendö the Isle of Bliss.[13] European folktales contain many references to a Green Island, and the place was so popular that it was actually marked as a rock in the Atlantic on English maps until 1853.[14] On the Green Isle of Celtic myth, "the golden age is unending," and spirits of the departed dwell in radiant halls.[15] The Welsh name is Avalon, which Strindberg at one time intended as the setting for a play about the Viking hero Starkad.[16] Land of eternal spring and isle of departed souls also brings to mind the Arnold Böcklin painting *Toteninsel (Isle of the dead)*, which Strindberg indicated in stage directions was to appear at the end of *The Ghost Sonata* (45, 211).

In Strindberg's novella about the Isle of Bliss, Swedish colonists, headed for America in the 1600s, are shipwrecked on an Arcadian island where life is easy. In a discussion about how to maintain law and order, the colonists conclude that since no crime is likely to be committed in such a perfect place, there is no need for laws. The climate is mild and people need only the casual shelter nature provides. The seasons differ from one another only to the extent that different fruits and vegetables are available at different times. Envy and hate disappear. After some years, however, a volcano threatens to erupt and the colonists flee by boat. When they find land again, they must struggle to survive. The seasons are more regular, necessitating the building of more permanent shelters than were needed on the Isle of Bliss. Food must now be hunted or harvested. It is the Age of Silver.

Soon there are quarrels and class differences emerge. On the Isle of Bliss everyone was equal; now there are masters and servants. Step by step all the defects of the Iron Age are introduced in the new colony. Trade is established and along with it slavery. Taxes are levied and greed increases. Property becomes important and laws are passed regarding its ownership, disposition, and inheritance. Mine and thine become the foremost considerations. The death penalty is instituted for those found guilty of serious breaches of the law. An urban system appears, and people are once more alienated from nature. And of course everything is done in the name of progress. "Fear of hell vanished," the author tells us, "for people realized that hell already existed on Earth and things couldn't get any worse'" (12, 96).

Fifteen years after he wrote *The Isle of Bliss*, Strindberg made notes for a play containing a powerful indictment of earthly pain and injustice. Under the heading The Iron Age, he wrote: "Indra's daughter finds the Earth to be a madhouse, a prison, and human beings a collection of treacherous scoundrels or hypocrites, treacherous, thievish, cruel, stupid." Rousseau's warning to humankind from the *Second Discourse* — "you are lost if you forget that the fruits belong to all and the earth to no one!" — is echoed in the Riviera scene when Agnes asks the Lawyer why everyone cannot swim there. He answers that the beaches are private.

> DAUGHTER: But I mean outside of town, in the country,
> where the land doesn't belong to anyone.
>
> LAWYER: It all belongs to someone, . . .
>
> DAUGHTER: Even the sea? The great, open . . .
>
> LAWYER: Everything! If you're out on the sea in a boat,
> you can't even come ashore without getting permission
> and paying a fee.
>
> DAUGHTER: This is no paradise! (36, 293-94)

Nearly all Strindberg's treatments of the theme of the Golden Age are marked by ambivalence: on the one hand, there seems to be a denial of its viability, as in the Isle of Bliss novella, and, on the other hand, there is an affirmation of its justness and humaneness, its power to restore hope. Like the biblical image of Eden, the Golden Age is a lost ideal that galvanizes humankind into efforts to redeem it.

Both the Golden Age and Eden offer Arcadian landscapes of primitive oneness, goodness, and harmony. A parallel to the Iron Age is the hard life

Adam and Eve find when they are expelled from paradise after the Fall. The chief difference between the two systems is that the ancient world believed that the changing ages were aspects of a periodic cycle that endlessly recurred. Christians took another view: instead of history consisting of endless repetition, it had a happy ending. The loss of Eden would be redeemed and the Age of Iron disappear permanently with the Second Coming, after which Christ would reign for a millennium.

When August became the first emperor of Rome after the death of Julius Caesar, his reign was seen as the dawn of a new age. Virgil composed a tribute to it, at the birth of a son to a noble family: "The great line of the ages is born anew. Now [Justice] the Virgin returns, the kingdom of Saturn returns. Now a new race is sent down from heaven above. . . . Look benignly on the newborn boy, at whose coming the iron race shall first cease and a golden race will spring up in the whole world."[17] Such a prophecy of a new era, coming only decades before the birth of Christ, would later make Virgil seem a pagan prophet to Christians in the Middle Ages. The merging of these two themes, Christian and pagan — the fulfillment of the Promise in the millennium and the return of the Golden Age — provides the basic armature for a collection of short sketches Strindberg wrote in 1905, *Historical Miniatures*, an uneven and much neglected work. As evidence of Strindberg's conception of history, it is far more interesting and entertaining, and in some ways more revealing, than the long, rather pedantic essay he wrote two years earlier, "The Mysticism of World History."

In letters about the miniatures, Strindberg revealed his concern that they were too slight to stand as independent stories, which is true, but he also knew that whatever impact they might have was a cumulative one.[18] The themes of the Promise and the Golden Age ripple through them as through a musical composition.

One of Strindberg's reasons for adopting the Christian reinterpretation of the Golden Age theme was probably spiritual, a desire to make them conform with the confessionless Christianity he professed after the turn of the century. But another reason was certainly artistic. It is no accident that over the centuries, the image of the Ages of the World has proved more useful to painters than to playwrights. The Age of Iron is a fixed condition. Whatever potential for drama it possesses comes not from within but from without, in the possibility of change and reform. This may explain why *A Dream Play* has so often presented problems in production. So much of the play is devoted to a descriptive analysis of the Iron Age, with Agnes's repeated conclusion that human beings are to be pitied, that there is a risk of the action grinding to a halt in a series of static tableaux. For models of action in his plays, Strindberg often turned to the Bible, where the yearnings of the people of Israel to restore justice, to redeem Eden, are dramatized vividly and dynamically in the struggles between God and humankind, king and prophet, Messiah and Pharisee. If the theme of the Iron Age is descriptive, the biblical search for salvation is prescriptive. In *A Dream Play,* Agnes is a messiah figure come to an Iron Age world unaware of and unwilling to accept the challenge of salvation.

Historical Miniatures opens in an Iron Age setting in Egypt at the time of the birth of Moses. Rumors are that the gods who abandoned the earth are about to return. Although the people of Israel are in bondage, the promise God made to Abraham, to make of him a great people, is still alive. The next three stories are set in Athens, centuries later, and people are still wondering whether the gods will return. They discuss hopefully the prophecy in Aeschylus's play *Prometheus Bound* that Zeus will one day be overthrown by one of his own sons, a child born of a virgin. The fifth miniature is set in Rome, where Virgil dreams of the return of the Golden Age while Horace reminds him how closely the conditions of their own day resemble Hesiod's description of the Iron Age in *Works and Days.*

I must add at this point that these brief summaries do not do justice to Strindberg's narrative skills in the stories. In most of them he sets the plot in motion without identifying the characters, so the reader is left in some suspense: Who are these people? Why is the author asking me to listen to them? In this way the focus is on theme and variation, and exposition is at a minimum. To be sure, the approach has its dangers: the historical veneer is so thin in places as to be invisible, and development of character is sacrificed. But the narrative technique adopted is considerably more effective in the miniatures than in the dramatization Strindberg attempted earlier with virtually the same historical panorama for his cycle of plays on world history. Whatever is lost in the miniatures in the way of richness of historical detail is made up for in the brisk tempo and the cumulative power of the thematic repetition.

From Virgil's Rome the action moves to the Nile delta in Egypt. A man traveling with his wife and son learns from a local resident that God's Promise has been passed on from Palestine to Rome. The man is skeptical despite having been forced to leave his native land by a king who enjoyed power thanks to the Romans: Herod. Joseph takes his wife Mary and infant Jesus and moves on.

Several stories later a figure appears who interested both Strindberg and Ibsen: the fourth-century Roman emperor Julian the Apostate. In fact, as it is applied to Ibsen, "interested" is too mild a word. Julian was the central character in what was perhaps his most ambitious drama: the great sprawling *Emperor and Galilean.* Julian, originally a Christian, left the church and tried to reintroduce paganism. For Ibsen, he became a symbol of the need to establish a "third kingdom," something between or beyond the austere, often coldly inhumane asceticism of Christianity and the selfish, self-indulgent sensuality of paganism. For Strindberg, however, especially during his religious period after the turn of the century, Julian was the quintessential apostate. In the *Blue Book* essays, he grouped the emperor with Barrabas, Judas, and Nero and described him as a worshiper of Baal and Astarte. Nevertheless, as was true of his attitudes toward a number of historical figures of whom he disapproved — Charles XII and Gustav Vasa, for example — Strindberg was also clearly fascinated with Julian.

The setting in the miniature "Apostata," is Paris, or Lutetia Parisorium, as the Romans called the city. It is Christmastime, shortly before Julian will be declared emperor, and he has been sent with several legions to battle Germanic tribes. Still a practicing Christian, he hates Jesus, asserting that "three hundred and sixty years had passed since Christ was born and the world was more wretched than ever" (42, 121). Maximus, his adviser, confesses that although not a Galilean himself, he loves justice, to which Julian responds: "Justice and its goddess Astraea fled from the earth when the Iron Age began, and now she sits as a star in heaven" (123).

When soldiers under Julian's command begin preparations for celebrating Christmas, he determines to teach them a lesson, to demonstrate that the coincidence of three celebrations — Christmas, the return of the sun marked by the winter solstice, and the Roman festival of Saturnalia — proves that Christianity owes more to pagan forms of worship than it cares to admit. This kind of emphasis on the interdependence of religious ideas was attributed by earlier Strindberg scholars to his interest in the syncretistic atmosphere prevalent at the turn of the century. Martin Lamm, for example, pointed to the scene in act 3 of *Gustav Adolf* "where Mohammedans, Jews, Catholics, and Protestants hold separate divine services, but each read prayers that contain the same words, directed to the same God."[19] Strindberg was certainly interested in syncretism, but this interest was not limited to the period after 1900. Throughout his career he liked to juxtapose different mythic images in the same context, a technique I have described elsewhere as polyphonic:[20] emphasizing parallels for the sake of assonance and contrasts for the sake of dissonance. His blending of imagery relating to the return of the Golden Age with that of the Second Coming is a good example of such assonance.

In the miniature about Julian, we learn that the Romans celebrated their Saturnalia "in commemoration of the golden age of legend, which supposedly prevailed during the reign of the good king Saturn. The Earth was at peace then: the lion played with the lamb; the fruits of the land could be harvested without the need of farming; and no weapons were forged, for men were good and just" (42, 137).

Frazer tells us in *The Golden Bough* that during the Saturnalia "the customary restraints of law and morality [were] thrown aside" in favor of an orgiastic, carnival atmosphere. Mardi Gras is one of the descendants of the festival. One remarkable feature of the Saturnalia was a reversal of social roles. Slaves were permitted to drink as much as their masters and even rail at them, while "masters actually changed places with their slaves and waited on them at table."[21] The Iron Age, it would seem, was temporarily repealed, as the laws separating men were suspended in an atmosphere of ritualized equality. Historical time stood still as the ordinary order of life was reversed.

The high point in the Saturnalia celebrated in Strindberg's story is interpreted syncretistically by Julian's advisor, Maximus:

> "Have we not honored today the memory of the better times that once were and will come again, just as the light now returns with the returning sun? Times of reconciliation and peace on earth, when no one shall be master and no one slave . . . ."

> The congregation was exalted, and with tears in their eyes they fell into each other's arms, joined hands, and kissed each other's cheeks. A row of candles around the altar was immediately lit, a customary part of the Saturnalia to signify the return of the sun and adopted by Christians to honor the birth of Christ. . . . Then beggars were led forward and noblemen washed their feet, after which twelve slaves were seated at a table set with food, and their masters waited upon them. (42, 139)

Strindberg skillfully modulates the Saturnalian theme of the reversal of roles between master and servant into the theme of the Last Supper and Christ washing the feet of the disciples, recalling his admonition that "If any one would be first, he must be the last of all and servant of all" (Mark 10:44). Saturnalia becomes a reminder that a common goal of the Golden Age and the Second Coming is perhaps the highest goal, spiritually as well as politically, to which people can aspire: the brotherhood of mankind.

One terrible aspect of the Saturnalia was ritualistic sacrifice, mostly animal, but on occasion also human. Julian shocks the congregation at the Saturnalia-Christmas celebration by taking part in the bloody killing of animals.

The themes and trappings of the Saturnalia are all present in a play Strindberg wrote fifteen years before *Historical Miniatures:* a festival honoring the sun, a temporary abolition of social rank in an orgiastic atmosphere, and bloody, almost ritualistic sacrifice, animal as well as human.

The play, of course, is *Miss Julie.* Instead of a winter solstice, we have a summer solstice — midsummer eve, in Scandinavia an orgiastic, carnival time. The mistress of the manor condescends to join her servants in their festivities. Her father's valet, Jean, flirting with her, says: "We'll have to sleep on nine midsummer flowers, Miss Julie, to make our dreams come true" (23, 133). According to Mircea Eliade, magic herbs are picked at midnight on midsummer eve because it is one of "those critical moments which mark a breaking-through from profane to magico-religious time," and "popular belief has it that the heavens open and magic herbs receive extraordinary powers."[22] Profane time in the Age of Iron is suspended, and master and servant become equal. "On a night like this," says Miss Julie, "we're all just ordinary people having fun, so we'll forget about rank" (23, 123).

For the first time in her life, Julie realizes what a difficult world it is if you belong to the lower classes. In the real world, mistress and servant hardly speak to each other. Tonight they go to bed together. Just as there is a causal relationship implied between the Second Coming and the restoration of the Golden Age, so there is one implied between the Fall and the Iron Age, and this defines the structure of the play after Julie and Jean make love. After the Fall, after the orgy, the magic atmosphere of gaiety and equality vanishes. Julie wants Jean to address her in more intimate terms: "Call me Julie! There are no barriers between us any more" (146). He refuses. The barriers will be there as long as they remain in her father's house and, by implication, as the plot subsequently suggests, in this world. When Julie wants Jean to leave with her, he insists: "Think of Kristine in there. Don't you think she has feelings too?" "I thought so awhile ago," Julie says, "but not any more. No, a servant is a servant . . .," to which Jean responds cruelly: "And a whore is a whore!" (151). No girl of his class, he says, would have acted as crudely as she did.

Reversing roles has taught servant and master different things. Jean is disappointed; his conquest was too easy, and he discovers that Julie is not different from other girls. Meanwhile, she has learned humility. Kristine mocks her mistress and says that God favors the poor and the needy over the rich and powerful. "And the last shall be first" (182), she cites from the Gospel of Matthew (20:16).

By the end of the play, Julie's descent into humiliation and degradation is so complete that Jean can give her a reassurance of sorts: "You're no longer among the first — you're now among — the last." "That's true," she says, "I'm among the very last. I'm the last of all" (186-87). Once again in a Strindberg work, as in the miniature about Julian, a Saturnalian ceremony modulates into a ritual of purification. "If any one would be first, he must be last of all and the servant of all."

The forward movement in the miniatures emphasizes rising hopes, and the reader is left to conclude that the periods between the episodes involved the dashing or attenuating of these hopes. A story set in Rome on the eve of the year 1000 depicts people preparing anxiously for the end of the world and the coming of the millennium. On New Year's Eve masters and servants embrace one another tearfully. Old enemies shake hands and bury grudges. Meanwhile, in the ruins of Nero's house, the city's libertines have arranged a bacchanal. They don't fear the approaching end. "I've always thought," says one, "that we were already in hell" (42, 190).

A later story, set in the eighteenth century, depicts a discussion between Voltaire and Frederick the Great at Sans Souci. Looking back over the many inventions produced in their time, Voltaire declares that the Golden Age has surely returned. Some years later, in a letter, the king rebukes Voltaire for thinking badly of Rousseau. "I share his love of nature," says the king, "and his hatred of people. The other night, as the sun was setting, I thought 'Lord, how beautiful Your Nature is, and how awful Your people are' . . . This cursed race belongs to the Iron Age that Hesiod depicted. And it's supposed to be made in God's image — the devil's image, I say!" (307).

In the last and most interesting of the miniatures, "Judgment Day," Strindberg the dramatist begins to overshadow the writer of narrative, as the story evolves almost completely into drama. With his sure instinct for setting the right action in the right place and time, he places the scene in a watchman's tiny apartment in the north tower of Nôtre Dame Cathedral in Paris. The time is the seventh of November (or the eighteenth Brumaire, according to the new calendar) in 1799 — the eve of the end of the French Revolution. The watchman has little to do because the church lies in disuse. He is a bookbinder by night and has assembled an impressive library. One wall is covered with prints that depict the entire ten-year history of the Revolution, from the Tennis Court Oath in June 1789 to the emergence of Napoleon and the executive council, the directorate, which, through a coup, has fallen into Napoleon's hands on this very day. A proclamation of his appointment to the consulate is expected momentarily.

The old man has a biblical appearance: he is a centenarian and wears a beard like that of one of the apostles. "The Revolution is over!" he shouts, "What are you saying?" queries a voice from behind a bookcase. "The Revolution is over. — You can come out now, sir!" Grasping the bookcase and turning it like a door on its hinges, he exposes a beautiful little room in the style of Louis XV. A pale young nobleman of thirty steps out of his hiding place. Because he had once saved the old man from the guillotine, the old man has smuggled him into the tower and saved his life. "Sir," says the old man, "your time has come and mine is going out. The Revolution is over. . . . Tonight we are still brothers, but tomorrow you're the master and I'm the servant" (314-15).

From Saturnalia to Revolution — from the temporary, ritualized effort to restore the justice and equality of the Golden Age to the apocalyptic action that attempts to end the injustice of the Iron Age once and for all. Like the Flood or Ragnarök, the Revolution wipes the slate clean. As the old man says: "The Revolution was a Last Judgment" (317). The two men start quarreling over who was right and who was wrong, but quickly resolve to end their relationship peacefully. "Tomorrow, Jacques," says the young man, "watch out for your head" (316).

Jacques is disappointed but not bitter, not even over the loss of his family at the hands of the Revolution he still believes in. What sustains him is the memory of one glorious event: the Fête de la Fédération, on July 14, 1790, the first anniversary of the fall of the Bastille. The setting was the huge parade ground, the Champs-de-Mars, where the Eiffel Tower now stands.

"Twenty thousand men were supposed to clear the Champs-de-Mars," the old man says,

> but when they couldn't finish the job by the appointed day, the whole of Paris turned out. I saw bishops, chamberlains, generals, monks, nuns, ladies of society, workers, sailors, sewermen, and whores, side by side, with pick and shovel, trying to level the ground. Finally, the king himself put in an appearance and took part in the work! It was the greatest leveling work human beings ever accomplished; the heights were evened out and the hollows filled. And at last the great theatre of freedom was ready. On the altars of the fatherland wood cut from aromatic trees was set ablaze. Talleyrand, the bishop of Autun, attended by four hundred priests clad in white, consecrated the flags. The king, dressed in civilian dress, and the queen sat on the dais, and "the first citizen of the state" took an oath to uphold the constitution. Everything was forgotten, everything was forgiven. Animated by one spirit, a half million people assembled on the spot felt that day like brothers and sisters. We wept, we fell in each other's arms, we kissed. But we wept at the thought of how base we had been and how kind and good we were at that moment. Perhaps we also wept because we sensed how fragile it all was — Later, in the evening, all of Paris moved out into the streets and squares! Families had dinner on the sidewalks, the old and the sick were carried out under the open sky, food and wine were distributed at the state's expense. It was a Feast of Tabernacles, in commemoration of the Exodus from the Egyptian slavery; it was a Saturnalia, the return of the Golden Age! . . . And then . . . .

"Then," says the young man, "came Marat, Danton, and Robespierre . . . and the Golden Age went as it came." "But it'll come again," the old man responds. "Do you really believe in the return of the Golden Age?," the young man asks. "Yes," says the old man, "Like Thomas I believe when I have seen. And I did see on the Champs-de-Mars" (318-19).

Their conversation is interrupted by the clanging of bells in the churches of Paris, announcing Bonaparte's ascension to power. When they die out, the young man sighs in gratitude, "The Revolution is over!" to which the old man replies: "*That* Revolution!" (321).

In the marvelous coda Strindberg evokes in the last of his *Historical Miniatures*, the dominant themes merge and part and merge again. Despite the collection's shortcomings, in the ambivalent tangle of feelings, now hope, now despair, is revealed the scope and brilliance of Strindberg's understanding of history's drama: its epic structure and its human detail. The description of the Fête de la Fédération suggests a frenzy of liberty, equality, and fraternity that almost makes both the Promised Land and the Golden Age seem within reach. Then the Revolution, like the Saturnalia, runs its course, and the Iron Age returns. "Tomorrow," says the old man, "you're the master and I'm the servant." "Tomorrow," says the young man, "watch out for your head." But the hope never dies and the golden dream endures.

4

Charles XII as Historical Drama

Göran Stockenström

An examination of Strindberg's dramaturgy in rela-
tion to the twentieth-century theater seldom takes his historical dramas
into account, for obvious reasons. His cycle of history plays, spanning more
than five hundred years and representing ten Swedish monarchs from
Birger Jarl to Gustavus III, belongs to national history. The powerful effect
many of these plays have exerted in the Swedish theater has to a great
extent been lost when presented abroad. Their success is in a sense predi-
cated on the audience's awareness that it is witnessing a re-enactment of its
own past. Strindberg concludes in *Open Letters to the Intimate Theater* (1908-9):
"When one is going to write a historical drama, it is a little like writing an
assigned composition in school about a definite topic, to write a variation of
a theme on an already composed piece."[1] From the dramatist's point of
view, the attempt to imitate and make credible to an audience an external
historical reality restricts imaginative freedom.

The existing research on the historical dramas has stressed Strindberg's use of historical sources, the genesis of individual plays, the influence
of Shakespeare, Schiller, their place within the nineteenth-century historical
genres, and so on. As a body the historical dramas have been treated in a
number of surveys, of which the major work is Walter Johnson's *Strindberg
and the Historical Drama* (Seattle: University of Washington Press, 1962),

which presents not only the national cycle but also the earlier dramas and the incomplete world history cycle. Apart from possibly *Master Olof* (1872-77), none of these dramas has been exposed to the close scholarly scrutiny that we find in the extensive research on Strindberg's *major* works, and there have been few, if any, studies that deal exclusively with the dramaturgical aspects. Critics have in passing often elaborated on the interweaving of themes and the use of parallelisms, what Strindberg calls "polyphonic composition":[2]

> When I returned after twenty-five years to the historical drama, I did not have to bother with my scruples of 1872 when I wanted to depict historical men and women, so I went back to my dramatic technique from the first *Master Olof*. My purpose was, as it was my teacher Shakespeare's, to depict human beings both in their greatness and their triviality; not to avoid the right word; to let history be the background and to compress historical periods to fit the demands of the theater of our time by avoiding the undramatic form of the chronicle or the narrative.[3]

Acknowledging his debt to Shakespeare, Strindberg sums up a few of the dramaturgical principles that are to some degree applicable to all his historical dramas.

Charles XII partakes of some Shakespearean techniques but is not as representative as some of the earlier historical dramas in this respect. *Charles XII* deviates from the general norm in important ways. This is partly reflected in the genesis of the play, which stretches over a period of two years. He began the first draft in August 1899 and completed it in June 1901, and he had worked on it on at least four separate occasions. The following annotation from his diary reads: "*Charles XII*, which was written in 1901 although I never believed that I could write it."[4] The first revision resulted in a Shakespearean-influenced dramaturgy with its interweaving of public and private, and conspiracies as the central fable shaping the fall of the king. The suspense-filled action shifts from mass scenes to intimate scenes with the use of simultaneous staging areas. The ample use of local color balances protagonist and historical context, and the similarities to the *Saga of the Folkungs* (1899) are obvious.[5] Strindberg's *Charles XII*, such as it emerges in 1901, is stylistically and dramaturgically a very different historical drama, in many ways closer to Maeterlinck's *drame statique* than Shakespeare's histories. With its epic tableaux technique and distancing between protagonist and historical world, the action takes place mainly in the realm of the private, which in turn asserts a larger metaphysical pattern. The symbolization of the scenic space and the stylized poetic language demonstrate a close kinship to *A Dream Play* from the same year.

Charles XII *as Historical Drama*

As historical drama *Charles XII* was perceived to be a failure by most critics of Strindberg's time: "Drama implies action, and a character whose behaviour is only characterized by his refusal to act, is doomed aesthetically to fail as a protagonist of a drama . . . From its first inception *Charles XII* is presented as an epic and not a dramatic character."[6] Critics today, however, describe *Charles XII* as "extremely original," a "superb creation of the imagination," and they incorporate the text into the expressionistic tradition emphasizing its dreamplay technique or the existentialist tradition focusing on the shifting images of the self in the play.[7] What seemed to be obvious flaws to his contemporaries are reinterpreted in the context of modern theater as innovations. The sense of historical drama as a genre that implies a particular structure and type of language defined by literary tradition has been replaced by the general notion of *modernism,* which has as its focal point the idea of revolutionary change. The choice of perspective will of necessity yield totally divergent depictions of the same aesthetic *reality.* If the contemporary critics or audiences evaluated Strindberg's historical dramas first in their claim to represent an external historical reality, their modern counterparts view them primarily in terms of their fictive structures. To examine the dramaturgy of any historical drama requires an understanding of both processes. Even if all drama attempts to turn the past into present, the continuity between them is the central assertion in all historical drama. On the one hand, we retain a considerable awareness of the relationship of *Charles XII* to its historical sources and the changing frameworks through which this king has been viewed by historians. On the other hand, *Charles XII* is at least (if not more) a comment on Strindberg's own time.

Available research has demonstrated that Strindberg accepted the demand for historical truth as it was defined in the German aesthetics of the mid-nineteenth century.[8] In general Strindberg seems to follow the existing praxis from the nineteenth century in his use of historical sources. According to accepted theatrical conventions, playwrights could borrow from popular histories to create historical illusion. Strindberg declares: "History and the folk ballads have always and rightly been considered common property, which the writer has had the right to use and exploit. Fryxell, Afzelius, and Starbäck have been used for the purpose most advantageously since they have included more little human details than the dry chronicles and official histories."[9] Strindberg was also well read in the academic historical writings. His knowledge of the literature on Charles XII was substantial, and an existing bibliography indicates his familiarity with more than a hundred primary and secondary sources on the Caroline period.[10] At times it is possible to identify material borrowed from a farfetched and unlikely source. This body of texts belonged in one way or

43

another to the poetic consciousness, but for the play *Charles XII* it had little or no direct bearing. Strindberg followed the popular histories since they consorted well with the dramatic forms he was developing. The primary source for *Charles XII* was Anders Fryxell, who in his critical demythologizing of the king paralleled the story of the suffering people with that of their despotic ruler. Fryxell's dramatic style is noted by Strindberg: ". . . characters portrayed as if by an experienced dramaturge with scenography, setting and properties."[11] Fryxell's dramatic juxtaposition is developed and intensified by Strindberg in *The Swedish People* (1882) which is representative of his many depictions of the king and his people. Fryxell's critical perspective had its foundation in a providential view of history that conformed to Strindberg's newfound religious beliefs. It was also in line with his reinterpretation of history and served him well in his many attacks on the conservative establishment. Undoubtedly, he had Fryxell in mind when the Stranger reminisces in *The Burned House* (1907):

> I had reached the age of twelve and was tired of life. It was like going into a great darkness. . . . I didn't know what I was put on earth to do . . . I thought the world was a madhouse. I discovered that one day, when we marched to school with torches and banners to celebrate "the destroyer of our country." I'd just read a book that proved the worst ruler we ever had was the destroyer of our country, and there we were celebrating him with hymns and prayers."[12]

The annual festivity to celebrate the memory of Charles XII was an occasion to manifest a conservative ideology that Strindberg opposed. The characterization of the king as "the man who ruined Sweden, the great criminal, the hooligan, the idol of the ruffians, and the counterfeiter" in his preface to *Charles XII* in *Open Letters to the Intimate Theatre* evidences a critical stance that was to remain constant from Olle Montanus's portrait of the king in *The Red Room* (1879) to Strindberg's articles on Charles XII in *Speeches to the Swedish Nation* (1910).[13]

The contemporary meaning of *Charles XII* is clearly associated with the political implications that this historical figure carried for Strindberg. Erik Lönnroth, a historian, has analyzed the renaissance and political revaluation of Charles XII during the last two decades of the nineteenth century in the context of the Swedish government's conservative policies at home and abroad.[14] The astounding success of Heidenstam's *King Charles' Men*, published in two parts in 1897 and 1898, gave evidence to the same nationalistic sentiments. Heidenstam's interpretation of Charles XII as an incarnation of the Swedish spirit and his period as the only time when the same spirit showed itself in absolute national autonomy generated a widespread discussion of Sweden's national ideals in the newspapers. During the 1890s the historian Harald Hjärne emphasized the importance of the national heritage and exhorted Swedes to political self-assertion. Hjärne also outlined a comprehensive research program on Charles XII and the Caroline period. As a spokesman for these nationalistic tendencies, Hjärne launched his thesis concerning the historical role of Sweden as the outpost of Western culture in Eastern Europe.[15] In this light Charles XII's wars are reinterpreted, and he is seen as the true expression of Sweden's world historical mission. In a number of articles from the early 1890s, Strindberg countered Hjärne's view of Russia and contended that Sweden's mission as frontier guard against Asia was not motivated, since Russia had already been civilized by Czar Peter.[16] This viewpoint is echoed by Görtz and Ulrika Eleonora and expounded at length by Arvid Horn in his final monologue on the fate of Charles II in the play:

> That man, who is lying there waiting for his journey to the grave — for he is dead — was once the man of destiny . . . and success upon success attended him as long as he walked the paths of justice. But after that, when he wanted to walk his own paths eighteen years ago and to control the destinies of people and nations . . . then destiny took him by the ear and played blindman's buff with him! And this paradox that looks like a colossal hoax. He wanted to raise a strong Poland against Russia, but then he broke up Poland and did the work of Russia! Wanted one thing and did another! That is how destiny plays with those who want to play the part of destiny."[17]

The conservative ideology associated with the cult of Charles XII was also reflected in various ways in the social and political system in Sweden. The devastation this "tyrant" caused the Swedish people raised questions about suffering and justice. How could one explain the meaningless sufferings of the Swedish people during Charles XII's reign given a god that is omnipotent and good? As a result of the Inferno crisis, Strindberg the dramatist had gained insight into the moral functionings of his own scapegoat suffering, but the question of innocent suffering remained unresolved. It threatened his hard-gained belief in a meaningful and coherent universe as soon as his focus shifted from the suffering of the individual to that of the world.[18]

Strindberg perceived the king in the same scapegoat role he envisioned for himself. The play begins with the monarch's return to Sweden; eighteen years earlier he had lost sight of his divine mission and thus his public image is in total contrast with the lonely and guilt-ridden human being Strindberg presents. This account has obvious parallels to Strindberg's own life. Only through silence or pretense can Charles XII mediate between a private inner world, where his responsibility and guilt are constantly questioned and a public world, which no longer interests him and must be grasped with uncertainty. His role had shifted from the familiar despot to that of passive victim, who no longer controls events.

To portray the innocent suffering of the Swedish people and the destruction wrought upon the country, Strindberg uses an expressive scenography punctuated and paraphrased by choruslike arrangements representing different strata of society. The juxtaposition of king and country allows the dramatist to pursue a critical perspective at the same time as the private trauma of Charles posits an alternative to a world which rejects him. This contrast between the private world of the protagonist and the political world can be resolved only in tragic terms given the divine mission of the anointed ruler: "Surely suffering is redemption and death deliverance."[19] This pessimistic truth may be true for Charles XII but does not address the innocent suffering of the Swedish people. The problem that Charles XII poses to his own society is reduced to the private realm. Understanding is tantamount to forgiving and even *vox populi* offers the dead monarch their blessing. The balancing of books between God/Man/World is achieved from a purely metaphysical perspective. The contemporary meaning of Strindberg's portrayal of king and country is complex in its intermixture of social and religious vision, and it intimately relates to his position in the 1890s.

Strindberg's Inferno experiences are projected onto the process of history, and the poet envisages a religious evolution that will lead to the establishment of a new moral world-order: "Here you have the socialists' dream of a United States of the West, interpreted in a spiritual sense."[20] In the same way, the death of Charles XII represents the end of an absolute self and the emergence of a transcendent self on the private level and the end of political absolutism for a democratic system on the public level. Strindberg used his religious evolution as the model for social development and in history he found an abundance of literary analogies. Emerging as a result of the Inferno crisis, these ideas were developed into historical theory and first presented in 1903 . . . in a series of articles titled "The Mysticism of World History."

Every historical drama necessitates some particular historical pattern against which the action can be interpreted. In Strindberg's case the central meaning is articulated through a larger framework, which assumes a teleological direction. This is what makes sense out of the facts of history, and isolated episodes assume the most intimate connection as chains of events in a divinely guided historical process. In *Charles XII* the end of an era provides the ideal temporal location in which to situate this kind of perspective. The moment of transition creates a sense of continuity in which the era of absolutism is perceived in retrospect by the play's characters as a repressive system whose end is long past due when contrasted with the democratic freedom propagated by "the men of the future," Horn and Gyllenborg. The darkness might be placed in the past and the light in the future, but Strindberg is also playing on the audience's knowledge of historical events since the time of the play by alluding to the continued dissensions and party struggles that occurred during the Age of Liberty. By transferring the historical perspective from the original and legitimate pretenders to the throne — Fredrik of Hessen and Karl-Fredrik of Holstein — Strindberg strengthens the idea of continuity and universality so central to his historical philosophy. The unity which was represented by the era of absolutism, plunges into chaos when the king dies, but it contributes to the new order that is instituted through renewed divisions during the succeeding age. It is through this teleology that history achieves its forward impetus in Strindberg's historical dramas. He stresses this aspect in his analysis of Shakespeare's *Julius Caesar:* "But the audience ought to know that this is Augustus and that he is to defeat and succeed Brutus, because thereby the drama would give one endless perspective, without beginning, without end, something of world history's eternity."[21]

There are many similarities between Strindberg's and Hegel's philosophy of history, in which the idea of a will that guides the seemingly chaotic transformations and actions of individuals, peoples, and states holds together the panorama of history in its infinitely varied configurations.[22] The closest parallel from a dramatic point of view is, of course, Shakespeare's histories, in which the providential temporal framework of the medieval cycle and its restoration of the kingdom of God corresponds to the restoration of good rule through the establishment of the Tudor monarchy. Given their teleological direction, the various plays of a cycle achieved their unity through the anticipation of a common ending. The medieval audiences were well aware from the start of the universal Christian pattern, but recent scholars question how seriously audiences in the Elizabethan period entertained the system of order and degree that Shakespeare propagates in his dramas.[23] Strindberg's use of the cyclical development within a providential, temporal framework has undoubtedly been influenced by Shakespeare: "History in the large is Providence's own composition, and Shakespeare is a providentialist just as the ancient writers of tragedies were."[24]

After attending the opening of *Charles XII* in 1902, the drama critic Alfred Lindkvist in *Stockholms Tidningen* objected to the strange providential design, which dooms the king long before the action starts; his negative reaction was shared by most critics.[25] By portraying the king as "a ghost," "a living corpse," "a hated misty figure who walks in his sleep three quarters dead" — an essentially passive victim — and by superimposing a controlling myth, Strindberg had eliminated any possibility for dramatic action in the traditional sense. These aesthetic objections attacked the heart of Strindberg's philosophy. In a copy of Lindkvist's review, Strindberg made the following annotations: "In this [his philosophy] the author is certainly right, dear muckracker! But *that, you* are probably unable to grasp — *yet*!!!²⁶ All around him Strindberg perceived signs of the return of the powers inaugurating a new spiritual age where all religions would be unified and work for the same goal. The emphasis on the word yet and the triple exclamation marks attest to this connection concerning the inevitability of change from the materialism of the 1880s to a new religious transcendence in the 1890s. This process of change is projected onto Charles XII, whose inner development exemplifies the same religious awakening. Strindberg could easily conceive of himself and the king as scapegoats with exemplary roles to fulfill within the providential order. Strindberg's portrayal of Charles XII is, thus, very much part of his consciousness in the 1890s and offers his contemporaries the suffering and transcendence of the king at the expense of a suffering Swedish people.

The use of a religious, philosophical idea as controlling myth is applicable to Strindberg's whole cycle of plays on Swedish history (1899-1908). He prefers to use the names of the reigning monarchs to indicate the segments of history that he is dramatizing. Historical drama tends to deal with persons who wield power, and most plots treat the transference of that power, as different groups seek to replace the divinely anointed ruler. Strindberg always exploits the fact that the coexistence of person and office is never permanent within the social order. History invests *Charles XII* with a public, almost mythological, stature regardless of his role in the play. Our sympathies or those of Strindberg's contemporaries may be sharply qualified. He perceived his Swedish kings as world-historical individuals with a universal purpose that they must realize, much as he viewed his own mission as a poet. In Strindberg's dramas history is conceived of as essentially the story of rulers, whose rise or fall manifest the workings of the unconscious will. When Lindenberger characterizes Strindberg's cycle as "a series of significant psychological moments in history," it should be added that the dramatic focus is on those very moments that illuminate the higher universal order.²⁷

A dramaturgy that makes the historical process rather than the individual the chief carrier of action would necessarily receive the objections voiced by his critics. In his response to them, Strindberg stresses his philosophical perspective and points to the peripety at the end of the third act: "Horn and Gyllenborg, the men of the future, the men of the Age of Liberty have — after passive presentation in Act II — entered into active service and begin to sketch the perspective. Then something of world significance — historically — happens, symbolized by lowering the flag to half-mast: Louis XIV is dead. This signified the fall of Absolutism — and Charles XII's impending end."[28] The third act consists of processions of the king's victims: the widows of the captured lords, the widows of the executed traitors to the state, former royalists turned rebels, the President of the State Council, and the speakers of the four estates. These groups are defined by the epic narrator Malcontent, who comments to the Dwarf and the Man while mediating to the audience. One by one the different groups are turned away at the closed, silent house of Görtz. These processions manifest Charles XII's guilt on the political level, and the individuals of each group are all cornerstones in the critical historical tradition.[29] The peripety of the play is set at the end of this ceremonial act in a highly theatrical scene. The audience could hardly perceive the ideological implications of Louis XIV's anachronistic death as the peripety of the play. Neither could the audience be expected to see it in the apocalyptic, world historical perspective that Strindberg described: "Horn and Gyllenborg open completely a perspective of a new and better future even if that, too, was to be accompanied by new conflicts."[30] Originally Strindberg had intended to explore this idea in a trilogy in which *Charles XII* would be preceded by *Charles XI* and followed by *Fredrik I*. The trilogy would achieve a unity through its anticipation of a common ending and would be part of a series of trilogies, all centered at moments of transition, when the conscious will manifests itself. This ambitious idea was later reduced in scope, but Strindberg revived it when he was planning the cycle of world historical plays. The historical trilogy might serve as a better vehicle to project Strindberg's theory about history, but it is doubtful that any play by itself could exhibit a fully elaborated philosophy.

The dramaturgical consequences of this vision are obvious. The possibility of individual, heroic action is eliminated, and whatever political action Charles XII contemplates is meaningless from the beginning. Whatever plot the play offers is finally irrelevant. It is symptomatic that the conspiracies of the legitimate heirs to the succession do not appear in the play. Even those that have an actual motive for revenge admit that "the one who's to be hanged won't drown" or "neither point nor edge, neither fire nor water will have any effect until his time has come!"[31] The suspense of *what* is going to happen shifts to *how* the dramatist will approach the king's death. The ordinary suspense of plot is done away with, and the historical characters are made to re-enact Strindberg's cyclical model rather than to posit futures they might yet affect. A ruler at the brink of losing power still has a special fascination to an audience that knows the sad facts of Charles XII's death, but any heroic figure must be able to exercise some control over his own destiny to be a dramatically viable character. Although Shakespeare asserts a larger pattern in history, he manages to leave us in doubt about the inevitability of such a pattern through multiple points of view by which the audience comes to see the historical actions that are being enacted. However, in *Charles XII*, the inevitability of the king's death is repeated over and over again by the different historical figures. The impending death of the king or the fact that he is in a sense already dead is a symbolic theme devoid of historical and political meaning. The tightrope between the determinism that a dramatist needs to give a play its central momentum and the commitment to the individuality of particular moments and events is summed up by Herbert Lindenberger:

> Within the realm of historical writing, historical drama would stand somewhere between micro- and macro-history, between the concrete details of specific historical situations and the larger processes, forces and meanings to which they can be related —Its public locus is in itself a middle ground, for the public events it depicts are qualified by their reverberations within the private realm at one extreme and, at the other, within whatever metaphysical or religious realm it may choose to project around itself.[32]

The historical world of *Charles XII* can be conceived of as *history* only through the theatrical conventions that determine the relationship between the stage and the audience. Strindberg states in an article on historical drama that "the drama is an art form by means of which I must give illusion and an art form in which everything is illusory, language, dress, time above all. . . . Whoever believes anything else can try to write a historical drama in absolute keeping with the written records or the Swedish archives; then we shall go and take a look at him if he succeeds in interesting [anyone]."[33] What the dramatist acknowledges is that a historical drama creates its own world with a closed internal system of references. The historical materials must be translated into the dramatic conventions Strindberg saw fit to use in relation to his audience. It might be his Shakespearean "dramaturgy from the first *Master Olof*" that he advocated in his preface to the historical dramas or the epic tableaux technique of *Charles XII*. Whatever theatrical conventions it implies, it carries its own system of character relationships, poetic language, and dramatic progression in time. The relationship between the theatrical illusion and the audience is a special problem for the historical genre. Today we would, undoubtedly, feel the *The Father* (1887) is more *real* than *Charles XII*. The harsh contemporary criticism of Strindberg's version of Charles XII's history was not due to any expectancy of historical reality per se. It had to do with Strindberg's breaking of the rules that defined historical probability in nineteenth-century aesthetics.[34] In the case of *Charles XII*, it concerned the lack of heroic idealization that a monarch demanded.[35] The heroic stature awarded the Captain in *The Father* might, however, be more difficult for an audience to accept today. In classical drama this problem did not present itself because historical material had the same status as myth. When Sophocles presented the tragic myth in *Oedipus Rex*, his Athenian audience already knew it, and the only one that must experience it is Oedipus himself. Szondi states in *Theorie des modernen Dramas*: "Der sehende und dennoch blinde Ödipus bildet gleichsam die leere Mitte einer um sein Schicksal wissenden Welt, deren Boten stufenweise sein Inneres erobern, um es mit ihrer grauenhaften Wahrheit zu erfüllen. Diese Wahrheit aber gehört nicht der Vergangenheit an, nicht die Vergangenheit, sondern die Gegenwart wird enthüllt." (Oedipus, blind though seeing, creates, so to speak, the empty center of a world that already knows his fate. Step by step, messengers who come from this world invade his inner being and fill it with their horrible truth. It is not a truth that belongs to the past, however. The present, not the past, is revealed).[36]

In publicly known matters the historical reality exists within Strindberg's audience's knowledge of Charles XII's history. In *Open Letters to the Intimate Theatre,* Strindberg notes that Schiller, as history professor, could allow Joan of Arc to die actively in battle, instead of at the stake.[37] For a later dramatist this would be impossible, regardless of his dramatic intentions.

With *Charles XII* Strindberg gave himself a great deal of freedom by compressing the historical events into the period 1715-18 and locating it in Lund. In this way it was only the final act with the king's death at Fredriksten that had to operate in accordance with the audience's expectations. To make the necessary continuity between the past and the present, Strindberg, like most modern playwrights, made use of a number of traditional expository techniques to coax his audience into the historical world of *Charles XII.* He used the very common exposition "from below" with the help of the Coastguard and the Man, a returning prisoner of war, supposedly dead, who is developed into a parallel to the king during the course of the action. The Coastguard also serves as an epic narrator introducing the historical action with the presentation of the President of the State Council and the speakers of the four estates who had tried to depose Charles XII during the 1714 emergency session of parliament. It is through the piling up of concrete details, facts, and quotes from the sources that a sense of history is created for the audience. The set with its broken-down cottage, burned sites, and scrap piles and the leafless apple tree with one lone apple creates the symbolic space for the long-awaited return of Charles XII to his wasted and desolate kingdom on a windy December morning, 1715. The long, careful description of the king before his dramatic arrival and frozen, silent posture before the fire scenically reinforces the image of the absolute ruler. This image had been prepared and elaborated by characters representing all strata of Swedish society. The events surrounding Charles XII serve to establish a concrete reality within which the king's doom can be set. The king's entourage with the faithful servant Hultman and the dwarf Luxembourg create an intimate aura around the protagonist. The execution of the skipper of the brig Snapp-Opp dramatizes the theme of innocent suffering. Eventually Charles XII appears sick, silent, imponderable, and the action begins at long last. Strindberg uses one-fourth of the total action of the play for his careful exposition. The absent king is viewed from a distance through the eyes of his followers. All the historical personages reappear in different groupings during the succeeding acts until the grand summation of all the interwoven themes occurs in the grand finale of the play.

Strindberg utilizes a number of theatrical devices to implant the false image that has grown out of the discrepancy between the political role of the king and his authentic self. Strindberg's identification with Charles XII in this respect was obvious. The 1880s' image of Strindberg as a radical poet, that still persisted in many circles, no longer had any foundation. The frequent use of theatrical role-playing also mirrors Strindberg's essential belief that human beings are unfathomable in historical or other scientific terms unless a perspective from *Jenseits* is applied. Strindberg's use of theatrical ambiguity as well as the careful, step-by-step exposition are both familiar techniques of the historical drama. They serve to make his dramatic creation credible to his audience and to overcome his own hesitation concerning the historical reality he is trying to imitate.

By concentrating on the fate of Charles XII, the importance of the historical context is reduced. It begins to function primarily in terms of its effect on the protagonist. Except for his silent appearance, Charles XII is kept off the stage during the representation of his desolate country. The historical criticism of the political role of Charles XII is continued in the first scene of the second act and the largely ceremonial third act, and the king is absent on both occasions. It mirrors Strindberg's private dilemma in portraying the devastation of Sweden without making his protagonist responsible. This separation of public and private realms could be illustrated by one scenic object, the king's army bed with its blue silk cover. It is an important part of Strindberg's scenography in acts 2, 4, and 5, where it is given a central position with the silent king lying on it. The army cot occupies a permanent part of the stage space during three-fourths of the play, and the king spends one-fourth of his total time on stage upon it. Strindberg even made it part of the garden scenery to many critics' consternation. Yet this simple, blue bed, which in its absurd way may be as historical as anything else in the play, posits a private realm that is somehow altogether outside the public, political world. It serves to remind both critics and audience that the central action of *Charles XII* does not belong in the world of historical personages and events but in a private inner realm. The autonomy of the historical world is thus questioned. Strindberg's version of history starts to mirror his own existential search for meaning in a political world that he could reject but not escape.

Strindberg's inability to reconcile conflicting metaphysical and social perspectives made it natural for him to conceive of the individual historical segments that he chose to dramatize as essentially tragic. Within the larger framework of history, however, the sad story of Charles XII's death is only a single moment in a historical process guided by divine will. The tragic perspective on Charles XII and his period was already imminent in Strindberg's historical sources. It was easy for the dramatist to intensify themes and attitudes developed in his main source, Fryxell. The historical actions leading up to Charles XII's death offered a natural tragic unity. In his response to the critics at the opening of the play in 1902, he stated emphatically: "My *Charles XII* is a drama of catastrophe, consequently the last acts of a long epic, and thus imitates the classical tragedies . . ."[38] Strindberg's definition refers to tragedy as a genre with its own theatrical conventions independent of any notion about history as essentially tragic. Tragedy whether on classical lines or not is perceived as a separate form within historical drama, however hard it might be to distinguish the one from the other. If we compare the endings of *Gustav Vasa* as "historical drama" and *Charles XII* as "historical tragedy," we can see that the former stresses continuity and accommodation whereas the latter ends in a sense of total disruption. There is a corresponding shift of emphasis from the historical events to the universal perspectives of Charles XII. By transferring the historical vision to a wholly psychological realm, the king's fate is stressed at the expense of the fate of the community. By embodying the political workings of the community in the life of *Charles XII*, Strindberg emulates a conception of political power in line with the heroic conventions of tragedy but somehow alien to the socioeconomic perspective "from below" that characterized him as a historian in *The Swedish People.*

Even if Strindberg's point of comparison is the classical tragedies, it is obvious that Charles XII is not a tragedy within the Aristotelian tradition of drama, where plot is primary to character and catharsis the major means to persuade the audience. It would be much more fitting to describe Strindberg's "bourgeois tragedy," *The Father,* according to this formula, in which the tragic perspective emerges in the course of the action as a result of a conscious manipulation of the plot. Strindberg's tragic vision does not offer any real choices in *Charles XII,* and the conspiracies never materialize. The opposition against the king from the 1714 parliamentary sessions, the rivalry between the legitimate successors, Fredrik of Hessen and Karl-Fredrik of Holstein, the dissatisfaction of warring political groups represented by Horn and Gyllenborg and the personal motifs of all Charles's victims become only momentary diversions to create dramatic suspense. In his 1908 "Preface to the Historical Dramas," Strindberg qualifies his description from 1902: "My *Charles XII* is character drama and a drama of catastrophe, in other words the last acts of a long story, and it imitates in this respect somewhat the classical tragedies, in which everything has happened before, and it even resembles the much praised Dovre-dramas [Ibsen], which are only conclusions to dramas that have already been enacted."[39]

The term character drama refers to the central role of the protagonist but is also used to justify the love theme that dominates the fourth act: "Charles XII in the relationship to the female (the girl and his sister) had to be included at all costs."[40] The fourth act is the most theatrical act encompassing Emerentia Polhem's attempt to woo the king, his meeting with his sister, and the confrontation with Katarina Leczinska. Emerentia Polhem also figures in the parallel plot as fiancée to Emanuel Swedenborg. The interweaving of these themes establishes Swedenborg and Charles XII as scapegoats serving the divine will, with the "dreamer" and the philosopher functioning as a double who interprets the destiny of Charles XII. The magnificent scene with Ulrika Eleonora is the only scene that is integrated with the historical matters at hand through the struggle for succession.[41] The loosely connected scene with Katarina Leczinska and her economic demands is a conscious rearrangement of history to provide Strindberg the means to vent his aggression toward Siri von Essen.[42] In general these "love-scenes" tend to become altogether too biographical, to the point where Charles XII is made to exclaim: "Yes, you women! I have stood outside windows and looked into homes; that's why I saw more than others, because the ones who are inside see only their own. . . . The most delightful, the most bitter! . . . Love is almost identical with hate!"[43] The psychological parallels between the newly wed Strindberg and Harriet Bosse, and the aged monarch wary of his mission and the young, ignorant, and manipulating Emerentia are easy to detect.[44]

Even if the love-interest belongs to the most persistent and prevalent among the dramatic conventions in the historical drama, Strindberg's display of theatrical fireworks nonetheless implies a serious reduction of the historical world. Herbert Lindenberger points to the biographical emphasis of modern historical plays as an extension of the psychological inquisitiveness that has accompanied the domination of private experience within all forms of literature during the last two centuries. He identifies a modern genre — the biographical play — the genesis of which is traced to the martyr play with its specifically Christian models.[45] The exemplary king-martyr becomes an imitation of Christ as the protagonist, station by station, rids himself of the material world, turning suffering into transcendence.

The death of the king motif is the catastrophe that motivates the historical and political retrospection in the play. The crisis in the present serves to recreate the past, but the past is perceived only through the guilt-ridden conscience of the king. The characters and events of the play achieve what meaning they have only within that private perspective. In conventional dramaturgy cause-effect relationships create the necessary unity of action. In *Charles XII* this is replaced by the unity of a central protagonist juxtaposed to a historical world. It is symptomatic that Strindberg preferred the epic designation tableaux to act.[46] This dramaturgy served the dramatist's purpose of exposing the inner world of Charles XII in its relation to a metaphysical order. Strindberg's analytical technique is, indeed, more reminiscent of Ibsen than its classical predecessors. In both *Charles XII* and, for example, *John Gabriel Borkman,* the ill-fated events or tragic peripety happened some eighteen years earlier. It is only through a crisis in the present that both protagonists are forced to balance their books with a past that seems to elude them by the very lapse of time. The central action of Ibsen's play occurs within the inner recesses of his alienated and isolated protagonist. The same is true for *Charles XII,* but in Strindberg their primary realm is metaphysical, not psychological.

When Strindberg defends his dramaturgy to his critics, he uses the term dramatic repeatedly: "The inner conflicts of the tyrant when he seeks support from a well-known adventurer (Görtz), who during his absence had tried to dethrone him, are highly dramatic. . . . In the fourth act the suspense is sustained by waiting. . . . The kingdom is ruined, and only an honorable suicide remains. So — to Norway! This is dramatic, and it is the end of the act, too!"[47] "Dramatic" refers in these instances to an epic situation filled with suspense rather than the action of the play. The same holds true for his interpretation of waiting — not waiting for *what* is going to happen but for *how* it will happen. Suspense based on the action of the play is dispensed with, in its traditional sense. Strindberg's description of the dramatic peripety is in itself revealing: "So the drama has gone forward the whole time and thereby fulfills the requirements of drama, for only a drama that stands still is undramatic."[48] The problem confronting Strindberg was in many ways identical to that of Ibsen, how to represent the past within the consciousness of the king and still give the semblance of dramatic action.

PART II

Strindberg in the
Modern Theater:
Dramatic Form and
Discourse

5

Strindberg and the Tradition of Modernity: Structure of Drama and Experience

Manfred Karnick

Once Eugène Ionesco said: "On me prouva que j'étais très influencé par Strindberg. Cela m'obligea à lire le dramaturge scandinave: je me rendis compte, en effet, que cela était vrai." (They showed me that I was much influenced by Strindberg. This forced me to read the Scandinavian dramatist. I concluded that this was, in fact, true.)[1]

We know that Strindberg has broadly and variously influenced the literature of our century. There are excellent studies on this topic. Among these, *Strindberg et le théâtre moderne*, *Strindberg's Impact in France*, *Structures of Influence*, and *Strindberg und die Folgen* are characteristic titles.[2]

But Ionesco's remark points out that Strindberg's position in the history of modern literature can be defined in more than one way. The remark allows three conclusions that are not contradictory: (1) Strindberg influenced his contemporaries and successors directly. In his rather ironical comment, Ionesco affirms this and so admits that it is in general true, yet denies Strindberg's direct influence upon his own works; (2) Strindberg's work has sent out impulses that appear even in the works of those who know nothing of these impulses' origins. These authors find the possibilities of view and representation, modified by Strindberg, already present, "handed down," in a sense; and (3) Prevalent tendencies of postclassical literature are evident in Strindberg's work, tendencies that were introduced long ago and that have continued into our present time. They also existed outside his works, but it was he who paradigmatically condensed them in his texts.

The first conclusion sees Strindberg as a model, the second as a mover, the third as an indicator. I hold all three to be correct, but in my considerations will regard only the last, which seems to be the most far-reaching one. In so doing, the question of the influences — of earlier authors on Strindberg, of Strindberg on later authors — the question of Strindberg's still influential innovations are not yet answered — not at all. But these questions belong in a different methodological category. They provide stimulus, interesting comparisons and help in presenting the material, but they are not themselves the subject of this study. Rather, my question is: what is it, then, that makes Strindberg's work, singular as it is, altogether fundamentally representative and therefore important even today?

It is obvious that such a broad question can be only partially answered and that I can make but a few suggestions here. Beckett offers encouragement: "There are many ways in which the thing I am trying in vain to say may be tried in vain to be said."[3] To say it in vain in my own way here at the beginning, Strindberg's understanding of roles shall provide the direction. In his works, this understanding is expressed in many ways. The following passages from various works illustrate Strindberg's concept of role: "He was still searching for his role, and consequently he continued to lack in character."[4] "Woe to him . . . who does not know how to behave since he does not know how to play a role by memory."[5] So "he had to . . . take over, to learn and carry out a role. He wrote one."[6] The term role refers here to constraints on expectations in a social system and to the relation between self and society.

"Well, the Eternal seduced this deceptive prophet into rising and speaking, and the deceitful prophet feels irresponsible, since he played the role which had been imposed upon him."[7] Even the "hangman" who scourges me "only plays that role which was imposed upon him by Providence."[8] Here role refers to transcendental dependencies and to the relation between the self and the powers.

"Character" is "a role."[9] "So I have made my protagonists somewhat lacking in 'character'"[10] and have offered "no roles, no characters nor caricatures as it should be called."[11] In *Miss Julie*, "my souls are agglomerations";[12] in *A Dream Play*, "the persons split, double, multiply, evaporate, condense, disperse, assemble."[13] Here role is associated with Strindberg's poetics and the relation between the self and the drama.

Different as the spheres are to which Strindberg applies the term role, and no matter how long the intervals may be between these remarks, they concur on the assumption of an external determination and on the questioning of the self. This feature, which was spawned at the end of the eighteenth century, has, since the end of the nineteenth century, passed through literature as a specifically modern one. Strindberg writes: "The self is nothing on its own: it is a diversity of reflexes, a complex of impulses and desires, some of which are suppressed here and others unchained there."[14] Many others agree (Büchner, Tolstoy, Ionesco, and Brecht): "What is it in us that whores, lies, steals and murders? We are marionettes played by unknown powers, we are ourselves nothing, nothing at all."[15] "Man . . . is a fluctuating creature."[16] "We are not we ourselves. . . . Individuality does not exist. There are in us only contradictory or noncontradictory powers."[17] Individuality is an "accumulation of all social circumstances."[18] It would be easy to continue.

The growing fundamental uncertainty of the individual was bound to change the concept of drama. And it is clear, but less known, that this also had consequences for the self-image of the poet.

Drama had to change because the norm of the classical drama, which was based upon the protagonist's autonomy — his or her culpability and ability to decide — disappeared. When this premise ceased to exist, new, postclassical patterns appeared, and old, preclassical patterns, which had seemed obsolete, could be regenerated in the course of new evaluation. Strindberg's application of the metaphor of the role to social and mythological spheres indicates prerequisites set by the historical development of the human consciousness. Its application to the spheres of poetics indicates some consequences for drama. Several dramatists have experimented with it, with similar if sometimes deviating results, some before him, such as Lenz, Büchner, and Maeterlinck, and some after him, such as Jarry, Artaud, Pirandello, Beckett, Dürrenmatt, Weiss, Saunders, Handke, and many others.

The position of the poet had to change because the question of the self also applies to him or her: the poet is threatened by the disintegration and external determination that he or she describes. This description is the poet's means of self-integration and self-rescue. For the poet, freedom is in his or her writing. Life has no autonomous right to exist. It is only used, and this usage may be regarded as guilt. This is nothing radically new; however, in modern literature it appears in a new and sharper light, given our insight into the disintegration of the self. It almost seems that there remains only in the poet's own sphere of imagination that very freedom and culpability formerly ascribed to the characters of the drama. Again and again Strindberg made this complex relationship the subject of his work.

I would like to make these first assumptions clear by using examples from Strindberg's writing. These examples may be regarded as referring back to the three uses of Strindberg's metaphor of the role that is to say, to the social, the mythological, and the aesthetic role. The examples are *The Father*, in which the treatment of social status focuses on the relations between the sexes; *To Damascus I*, in which humanity's relation to the superhuman powers and the problems of the poet's existence are important; the epilogue to *Master Olof*, including its variation, and the prologue to *Inferno*, in which superhuman powers have become human characters.

In the exposition to *The Father*, motifs and themes are preluded on the level of the servants. The orderly is suspected of having made a servant girl pregnant. He asserts that his fatherhood cannot be proven. Both of them are deplored in a phrase that makes us keen of hearing: "Det är synd om flickan, ja; det är synd om pojken, ja." (Indeed, the girl is to be pitied; but the boy is also to be pitied.)[19] We know the most famous version of this Strindbergian leitmotif: "Det är synd om människorna." In *A Dream Play* this means: mankind deserves compassion. Because they are human beings, they are to be pitied, and, therefore, in spite of their guilt, they cannot individually be considered guilty. The theme is already introduced here. The Captain, who is shortly thereafter horrendously struck by doubt of his own fatherhood, passes the following judgment: "I don't suppose the lad's completely innocent, one can't be sure, but one thing you can be sure of, the girl's guilty, if you can say anyone's guilty."[20]

I will try to interpret the play from this line. The statement is a balancing act: whenever it seems to lean toward one side, its indecision draws it back to the other, prevents it from falling down, and drives it forward. The alternating direction of its impulses indicates the general structure of values in this drama. The drama itself is a balancing act.

It is clear that the first impression is that of a stronger valuation of guilt on her part. "Mankind deserves compassion" means in *The Father*: men — as opposed to women — deserve compassion. A man occupies the center of the play. The elements of the action are arranged so that they confirm his views. The poet seems to take sides subjectively. Nevertheless: *"I don't suppose the lad's completely innocent"* [my emphasis]. This statement by the Captain acknowledges a degree of responsibility on the part of his orderly, but his attitude seems overly rigid. His stubborn inflexibility to deal with the matter at hand serves to protect his own vulnerability. His attempt later in the play to kill his own daughter is not only the result of madness caused by women but also the expression of an egomaniacal motive that has been present from the beginning and becomes extreme only under severe stress.

> CAPTAIN: . . . You have two souls and you love me with one and hate me with the other. . . . You must only have one soul. . . . You must only have one thought, the child of my thought and you shall have only one will, mine.

BERTA: I don't want that! I want to be myself!

CAPTAIN: I won't let you do that![21]

Already in the first act this motif appears: "You see, it isn't enough for me to have given the child life. I want to give it my soul too."[22] Fatherly love manifests itself as a will to rule that overbearingly tries to pattern the child after the father's own character. Indeed: "I don't suppose the lad's completely innocent *one can't be sure*" [my emphasis]. The man's guilt is not finally decided. There is much to exonerate him. His inflexibility appears easily understood because of his actual situation at home and his position in a world of women; his influence upon the child is also a response and the counterpart to a similar influence from the other side. For *"one thing you can be sure of; the girl's guilty"* [my emphasis]. There is no doubt about that. For the spectator, the woman's guilt is attested to by the course of action, by blatant lies, tricks, and plots. She appears as a satanic intriguer who uses whatever means available with the result that her intrigue is a "psychic murder." She is guilty, *"if you can say anyone's guilty"* [my emphasis]; that is, if there isn't a special constraint of behavior under which even her individual responsibility is called into question.

It may occur to us that, in a social order that links all legal rights to the biological fact of fatherhood, hardly any possibility remains for the woman as soon as all bridges of understanding are destroyed. As a result she is actually driven to intrigues and cunning. The play ignores these arguments and presents two others; the first is an immanent one and deals with the communication between the sexes and generations; the second is a transcendental and mythological one.

The immanent argument is the result of a pattern of interrelation to which all the concerned persons are instinctively subjected. It is the pattern between mother/woman/daughter and father/man/son, which is dominant in the inner circle between the Captain, Laura, and Berta. Its key is fear, its principle is authority:

As regards the woman, the man can act only as an autonomous patron in relation to a protected charge or as a protected charge to an autonomous matron. In short, relationships are possible between father and daughter or between son and mother. Similarly, the woman, faced with the man, can behave positively only as protected charge to autonomous patron or as autonomous matron to protected charge — these are the relations between daughter and father and between mother and son.

"Care" means the exercising of authority; "shelter" can be gained only by submission. A tender relationship presupposes regression to a childlike dependency. I regret having to learn that we cannot speak of "infantilizing." Every attempt to determine the relationship in another way leads to a fight to exterminate. A balanced relationship between partners of different sexes, who accept each other's weaknesses, is definitely excluded in this pattern: "Do you hate me?" " Sometimes. When you are a man." "The mother was your friend, you see, but the woman was your enemy. Love between man and woman is war." "Weep my child. Your mother is here to comfort you."[23] Thus, the woman is only able to be tender to the man who is legally declared minor, tied, and helpless. Therefore, the father's attempt to kill his daughter who cannot be "his child" alone, who wants to be a person in her own right, can be regarded as the reflected image of the killing of the man, who has taken on the role of "man" and no longer plays the submissive child, by the woman, who does not accept her role as child.

If the mental experiment of substituting a son for the daughter in the play, a "Bertil" for Berta, is carried out, one recognizes how the entire drama would thereby lose its precarious balance.

Certainly, a slight tilt disrupts this balance. The attempt to kill the daughter remains the attempt of a mentally deranged man who has lost his self-control — in the play this remains an episode. It is not carried out. The drama as a whole is determined by the destruction of a man who loses his life in every regard. The weight of guilt, "if you can say anyone's guilty," still rests on the woman.

Nevertheless, it is astonishing to see how consistently Strindberg is able to treat and transcend his subjective male standpoint in the dramatic planning and to integrate his own reflexes in a pattern of reflexes and thus be able to behave in relation to his own behavior.

The characters are prevented from behaving toward their own behavior — which might be a definition of freedom. They operate in patterns of interaction that could be described in terms of communication theory according to Watzlawick, Beavin, Jackson as a "system"[24] or — psychologically — with Jürg Willi as "collusions."[25] They are not free. "I don't know that I ever planned, or intended, what you think I have done. . . . I didn't plot any of this — it just glided forward on rails which you laid yourself."[26]

Even the acting characters in this play — and no one is acting as effectively as Laura — are not autonomous persons and cannot carry out anything other than what happens in and through them. There is no doer of deeds.

The second argument presented in the play refers to just this. It is a mythological one: "You didn't want it to be like this, I didn't want it, and yet it happened. Who rules our lives?" "God alone rules." "The God of battle, then!"[27]

The tension between subjective standpoint and objective conception of fate seems to dissolve in favor of the latter. A "wrong" behavior that can be explained in terms of social psychology is established as an eternal law. Accordingly, the acting man and the acting woman are only agents of an overwhelming force called God.

That is a curious fact: otherwise in the play, religious elements appear only as female bigotry and enlightened male freethinking, as a means of delineating characters and positions. The action has been conducted only in pure immanent reality: scientific investigation and its sabotage, correspondences and their interception, household budget and its refusal, medical diagnosis and its falsification, influences from relatives and the dispute of the couple over the education of their daughter and so on.

Strindberg tries to open this domestic drama with a transcendental key. This will have meaning only if natural and supernatural determinants lead to the same point. From the basic experience of determination: "You didn't want it to be like this, I didn't want it, and yet it happened." Even the God who, in Strindberg's words, has been "abolished," along with "guilt," by "Naturalism,"[28] can be resurrected in the naturalistic tragedy. However, it remains questionable whether it is a gracious God.

It is also the question of the Stranger or the Unknown in *To Damascus* (I) that places the basic constellation of the naturalist tragedy into another context and that evaluates these constellations in a much more intricate way.

Again, in *To Damascus* (I), the man seems to play simultaneously the roles of father and child. The woman is his own creation to which he gives name and life like a father. At the same time, she is his mother, to whose apron strings he is tied. Again, it is a mother who is finally mightier than he. And again, supernatural and super-real powers seem to be the cause of worldly complexities and the pain with which people torture themselves and others. This play is, however, different from the naturalistic drama, because, in the former, natural and supernatural explanations do not remain at separate levels. They become permeable to each other and are interrelated by a context of guilt and penance, of punishment and instruction. How does that happen?

In this play, the interpersonal and especially the heterosexual relationships, which *The Father* regarded almost exclusively from the male standpoint, appear to be dependent on the disposition of roles the male protagonist himself determines. By comparison with Lucifer, this position is clearly seen as *superbia*, the pride with which the mortal man puts himself on a par with the divine director and creator of the world. This is punished and expiated by repetition. The presumptuous person who casts the roles, who, like a rebellious child, does not accept his status as a creature and is sent to do a penance that will lead him to confidential affirmation, like a reprimanded child — this man is a poet.

In *The Father* this was a minor motif: "you ought to have been a poet,"[29] Laura tells the Captain. In *To Damascus* (I), it is a central motif and determines the structure. The author's tendency to identify with the man leads to the consequence of the *Ich-Dramatik* becoming a poet's drama. This consequence explains the half-reality of the play of which Strindberg spoke;[30] it explains the configuration and the course of events.

For the Stranger, the elves are "nothing but a fairy tale!" "Frankly, I do not believe in them. . . . Yet they keep coming back."[31] This is a typical formulation. It shows the logical structure of the "balancing-act line" in *The Father*. The elves seem to owe their own reality to imagination, but they gain an autonomous life that cannot be controlled by imagination any longer, a life that takes possession of the imaginer — but that he cannot accept as reliable reality. For the Stranger plays: "O my God, you're playing with death!" "Just as I have been playing with life — wasn't I a poet? Despite being born with a morbid and melancholy turn of mind, I have never been able to take anything quite seriously — not even my own deep sorrows. . . . And there are moments when I doubt that life is more real than my poetic fancies."[32] In this manner he manifests his daydreams and nightmares, the pain of remembering, the possibilities of the self, and the oppressing fear of guilt —they become characters who then appear to him as real/unreal persons. Their subject comes from reality; their figurations owe themselves to his projections and obsessions. So the poet, an unknown to himself, tries to interpret himself through self-dissection: "I don't know whether it is someone else or myself I sense."[33]

Martin Lamm calls *To Damascus* (I) a "monodrama."[34] He is correct. But it is a monodrama in a double sense: the Stranger is the character *in*, and the creator *of*, the play. And again, this play is not only a play of self-vindication but also one of self-criticism.

The Stranger is a poet who takes notice of all events, including his own wounds and pains, without taking them quite seriously, so he — in this respect a changeling — is unable to grow and mature. For him, time spatially stands still. Above all, he is always confronted by the repetition of the same things — even in his marriages. The indifference of things in the "somewhere or anywhere" of space is reflected as the repetition of the events in the "sometime or anytime" of time.

Because the reason for the ambiguity in his handling of reality and his acting as its imaginary director is the fear of living reality, and because this fear is based on his inimical relation with the world and on a fundamental antagonism, the basic motif of sexual behavior is repeated in the behavior of the poet. In the play, these two elements are expressly made into one: "Are you religious?" "I am nothing." "So much the better; so you shall become something." "Yes — your name shall be Eve. . . . And now we come to your character."[35] The poet/man transforms the woman into Eve, the eternal mother of man, and himself into a child; he *simultaneously* transforms her into his own and himself into the creator. Here, social arrogance and religious presumption have become one thing: "I feel an urge to take the whole giant mass in my hand and knead it over into something more perfect, more lasting, more beautiful."[36] He transforms the world too. In Kierkegaard's words, whose *Gjentagelsen* is part of the background of *To Damascus* (I), "he commits the sin of writing poetry instead of living."[37]

Only after the recognition of his own limitations and guilt, and after the rejection of his antagonistic concept of life, can he take a new direction. It is a turn from repetition as an infernal curse to repetition as blessing and penance, which is connected with the substitution of the role of Jacob for the role of Lucifer. This is a turn away from the law of the Old Testament "An eye for an eye, a tooth for a tooth," to the law of the New Testament "Thou shalt love thy neighbor as thyself." This means a turn from evil toward good powers. If the dominant authorities appeared in the beginning to be antagonistic to the Stranger, as to the father in *The Father*, "as if two separate beings conducting" his "destiny,"[38] at this moment he decides on the tentative acceptance of a beneficent God as the final authority. The player — who had wanted to anticipate all experience by playing with his poetic imagination and who had rejected the message — has now accepted this message and feels as if he were a chessman or the subject of a game in which he has been playing a role: "It may seem like a game of evil, but it probably isn't. . . . I hated to be the dupe of life — that is why I became its victim!"[39]

It fully accords with the inner logic of the play that the dissolution of the arrogant poet's existence is an element of the turn. "Well — then you are on the right road," says the mother. "But I am also bankrupt. . . . I have lost my poetic inspiration," confesses the Stranger.[40] Yet a warning is necessary. Even this confession is poetry. It is the poet who is played and who plays being played. The end is ambiguous. As in the beginning, "the Stranger is seated on the bench underneath the tree. He is drawing in the sand. . . . 'I am still writing in the sand.'"[41] It remains undecided whether he has walked through the stations of his play or whether these stations passed through his mind as mere mental images. But this is not a determining factor in the space/time of the play. The state of waiting, in which all apparitions return again and again, and the repetitive wandering, are the same in their basic structure. The development of the play does not describe a linear forward and backward movement with a lightninglike *metanoea* repentance, at the point of reversal, as the title *To Damascus* might suggest; rather, it describes a circle — "like a serpent," Strindberg tells us — "which bites its own tail": "Pilgrimage, punishment, devouring, *and everything begins again in the same place,* where the play ended and where it began,"[42] and where it can begin the next repetition.

The last word of the Stranger is a mixture of question, hope, and doubt: "Perhaps." This is not a word with finality.

It is therefore perhaps symbolically apt and, in a sense, "correct" that the Stranger should limp. He thus suffers the same injury as Jacob, and, at the same time, as a "limping devil," he carries the sign of his Luciferian disposition, of which he cannot be rid. Strindberg considered at one point entitling the piece *Robert le Diable.*[43]

And if the order of creation that we find existing was, indeed, according to Strindberg's old suspicion, a perverted and maybe even a maliciously administered one, then the verdict on the poet must not only be balanced by an acquittal, but his Luciferian claims must also be restored.

Consequently, the poet's acquittal is suggested when God himself is put on trial in *To Damascus* (III), and the poet is acquitted when the question of guilt falls back on God in *A Dream Play*: "Is the fault theirs or yours?"[44] This recasting of the world — its mirrored inversion by the poet — is justified if the world itself is inverted. The attorney for the gods enlightens the defense lawyer for humanity concerning this: "Do you know what I see in this mirror here? . . . The world, but as it really is! . . . Yes, for it itself is inverted!"[45] This distortion is explained by the lateral inversion that took place during the "stamping" of the archetype. The inverted world can in principle be countered, its inversion neutralized. This world is described as being a vision in a dream:

> DAUGHTER: . . . Thus it is that the world, life and mankind are but a phantom, an illusion, a dream vision —
>
> POET: My dream!
>
> DAUGHTER: A true dream.[46]

Only the dreamers within a dream, among whom is the poet, can grasp the inversion of the world and perhaps overcome this inversion by means of a counterdesign. They dream themselves *out* of the dream and *into* the reality of an undistorted world — and are thereby in advance of humanity.

The acquittal, however, does not cancel the verdict. Both judgments belong together. The poet, a mortal who entered into the game of life, in order to leave the game and thus free himself, must injure, become guilty, and suffer punishment. Only as one emancipated can he confront reality with its counterpossibility, can he change the world and perhaps dream it into its rightful shape. The position of the poet is ambivalent, for so, too, is the world.

Strindberg states his suspicion of the world's inversion and ambivalence most directly and, at the same time, most intricately in his short miracles plays.

In the epilogue to *Master Olof* and in the prologue of *Inferno*,[47] Strindberg's main characters are "God or the evil power"; "Lucifer . . . the good power"; the Eternal, invisibly above both of them and returning only after myriads of years; Adam and Eve on earth; and later, human beings. They do not appear on stage but are only mentioned. "The God of strife" is polarized into the battle of the gods, human antagonism is changed into antagonism among the gods. Events proceed in the course of action and reaction:

God creates the earth and man and wants to gloat over
the silly actions and the suffering of his creatures —
Lucifer's rebellion and fall; he liberates the human
beings to mortality;
God creates love as the possibility of sexual
reproduction —
Lucifer liberates the human beings from life by causing
the Flood;
God saves the most unknowing couple —

So it goes until the undecided ending. In the first version, the humans do not accept the liberator sent by Lucifer and take him to be evil. "They do not know anything yet, those fools!" And in the second version, the creator damns his creation and tries in vain to take back his curse. The earth, damned by God, races along in its orbit, and the creator cringes in humiliation before the invisible Eternal. The angels call this madness. This is simple in its basic concept but is realized only through a complicated system. The complication follows from the reversal of God's and Lucifer's values, from the assumption of a wicked *demiurge*, creator of the material world, and of a fraternal fight over the path of humankind, from the change of directions between "threat" and "help" and from the reversal of their associations with "life" and "death." These particularities could in part be elucidated by enumerating a lot of sources from the sixteenth century, by baroque and romantic traditions of fictionalizing Lucifer, by gnostic traditions, and by references to Goethe's *Faust* and to some of Schopenhauer's and Eduard von Hartmann's works.

Leaving this tradition aside, it is, nevertheless, important to mention one model and counterpart that should not be overlooked. What I have in mind is the baroque *teatrum mundi* of Calderón: "El gran teatro del mundo."

There are quite a number of common structural features in Calderón's and Strindberg's plays. In addition, both plays exhibit the same differences in relation to the modern classical drama and its Aristotelian principles. I will describe some of these common features because they may help the reader understand Strindberg's dramatic art.

Contrary to Aristotelian principles, the plot is not structured as an organized order of events. Aristotle recommends that the structural union of the parts be such that: "if any of them is displaced or removed, the whole will be disjointed and disturbed. If, however, the presence or absence of a part has no impact on the whole it is not at all part of the whole."[48] Held up to this principle, the different structure of the *teatrum mundi* does not build a "whole," as it is defined by Aristotle. The beginning is not developed as a traditional exposition of the initial situation; on the contrary, it is *stated* as the act of creation and the beginning of life. The characters are called forth by God's will. They do not influence each other. Their meeting serves the purpose of demonstrating various possibilities of behavior. Their fates do not follow from previous actions but are determined by external forces, and thus they transcend the action. Likewise, the sequence of characters and events does not take the form of a causal chain; it is rather a sequence of separate elements, and these could be augmented, reduced, or rearranged without doing much harm to the texts. For all the elements are variations of a pattern. The principle of their temporal arrangement is not development but repetition.

Therefore, the plot of the *teatrum mundi* does not reside in itself. The characters and events of the *teatrum mundi* continually refer to the world —and from the world back to the theater: the set of characters is chosen according to the *extra*dramatic logic of representativeness, not according to the necessities of an *intra*dramatic conflict. The characters entering the scene represent something else: social status, behavioral patterns, humanity as a whole. In accordance with the pervading transcendental point of view, the characters' actions are commented on epically.

These are the structural parallels between Calderón and Strindberg, baroque and modern *teatro del mundo*. Its revival is the revival of a preclassical pattern. There is, however, a fundamental difference, with which all their other variances are interwoven. It concerns the character and the quality of decision. And it is this difference that changes the preclassical pattern into a postclassical one.

To Aristotle, tragedy shows "men in action."[49] Action is more important than character: "Character is that which reveals moral purpose, showing what kind of things a man chooses or avoids. Speeches, therefore, which do not make this manifest, or in which the speaker does not choose or avoid anything whatever, are not expressive of character."[50] In the modern classical drama, the predominance of action is abolished in favor of an interplay between character and action, but the dramatic protagonist completely retains the quality of his decision and thereby the principal disposition for his tragic flaw. Hegel writes: "Ein wahrhaft tragisches Leiden wird über die handelnden Individuen nur als Folge ihrer eigenen — ebenso berechtigten als durch ihre Kollision schuldvollen — Tat verhängt, für die sie auch in ihrem ganzen Selbst einzustehen haben" (A true tragic suffering is burdened upon the active individuals only as a result of their own deed, a deed which is at the same time justifiable and yet, in its consequences, guilty and for which they are totally and personally responsible).[51] It is important to realize that this criterion, the possibility to decide and become guilty, also applies to Calderón's characters (along with some modifying criteria), and in part applies to Strindberg's gods. It does *not* apply, however, to Strindberg's humans after the Fall.

By using epic style, Calderón shows that the individual is again and again confronted with a fateful decision, an ordeal that is demanded of all human beings. The question is whether to accept one's role in life or to be at odds with it. The code is clear: "Obrar bien — que dios es dios" (Do well —for God is God).[52] As human beings are endowed with a strong will and can thereby rule their passions, they are free to choose their roles and attitudes toward the code, and therefore they can be called to account on the day of the final judgment. Because the characters on the stage of life are in each single action directly related to the supreme stage in heaven, there is no place for the causality of a worldly interplay that follows its own rules. Since human decisions are oriented toward God's decisions, the play is —despite its episodic structure — strongly directed toward the end.

With Strindberg this is not so. A human being is an object in the battle of the powerful, a struggle that takes place *within* the person. The inimical brothers God and Lucifer determine the action. The compulsion to decide between them is perhaps just as crucial as the decision between good and evil in Calderón, but human beings cannot make this decision according to established criteria. What does "doing well" mean if God is no longer God, if there are two gods fighting with each other and above them an eternal god? How can a character manifest himself if there is such a fundamental uncertainty as to what to choose or what to reject? The very order of life, on which any decision is based, is fragmented.

Therefore, the repetitive structure does not show a sequence of examples related to the eternal order; rather, it shows a permanent antinomy. Through its permanence, the field of the powers turns into the "normal" state of the world for human beings. Thus, to human beings, "judgment" cannot be the final instance of decision toward which the process of their lives is oriented. It is plainly the bitter path of life on earth, it is a "hell" in which they suffer through a meaningless time whenever the creator acts as an autocratic tyrant; it is a purgatory where they must undergo penance for sins they are not individually guilty of wherever the *demiurge* — not knowing it himself — acts as a tool of the Eternal. And the verdict that awaits even him after myriads of years must change when the definition of the role of the creator changes. Even the verdict on the Fall must change. Strindberg tried out all these possibilities in *Inferno* and *Legends* and in *A Dream Play*, expanding on the theme of the miracle plays. All elements may be turned in the opposite direction by one move: the evaluations change with the respective orientation toward the prince of the world — Satan, that is — or to eternal providence. Because of this ambiguity human beings cannot orient themselves anymore, nor can they make well-founded autonomous decisions. The ambiguity of values and the antinomy of powers cause the heteronomy of the individual.

In Calderón's play, the role player cannot choose his role, but he can decide how he wants to *play* his role. In Strindberg's play, however, the human beings are "played" from the very beginning.

What the naturalistic tragedy presents in the real world of everyday life and what the symbolist "station drama," morality journey play, develops in the dreamlike half-reality between imagination and reality is, in the miracle plays, a struggle conducted by personalized "powers," including all that involves human beings. In summarizing, I will stress the common features and leave the differences aside, point out Strindberg's innovations compared with this classical tradition and note the following connections.

The same unceasing movement between evaluation and counterevaluation is repeated everywhere. "I don't suppose the lad's completely innocent, one can't be sure, but one thing you can be sure of, the girl's guilty, if you can say anyone's guilty." The elves are "nothing but a fairy tale!" "Frankly, I do not believe in them. . . . Yet they keep coming back." The powers are either inimical ones who gloat while they make people suffer, friendly ones who educate people by making them suffer, or perhaps inimical ones who educate without knowing it. As concerns this dialectical evaluation, the differentiation between pre- and post-Inferno dramatic art has a modifying but not crucial effect.

The spheres of power in the world are polarized, and for human beings this is the state of the world. There is no way out. If one looks for it, one is only led back to the starting point. Whether one is fixed to a place or restlessly underway is of no importance. Repetitive structures and circular figures are characteristic of this. Time is transformed into space/time, and in these coordinates humans are driven by impulses that are not their own. "I don't know that I ever planned, or intended . . . any of this — it just glided forward on rails." "There is someone inside me who gloats over your suffering, but it is not me."[53] As the powers of the world fight over — and also within — a person, he or she may split up into several persons, even visibly on stage. The fragmented ego is transformed into an ensemble of characters that enacts the collective fate of all human beings.

Autonomy, formerly ascribed to the character, is now attributed to the *action*, and this already applies to naturalist drama. In Lamm's words: "Even when the heroes rebel and believe themselves free, a higher hand holds the strings."[54] Action is transformed into *happening*. Somebody acts. Something happens. "Everything goes its course," as Strindberg writes at the end of the prologue to *Inferno* or "something is taking its course," as Beckett states.[55]

You will have noticed that what I have said can also be applied to more general possibilities of modern drama. Among their preconditions are changes in how religious authorities are evaluated and changes in the use of metaphors of role and theater. These changes reach back into the last third of the eighteenth century, into the great process of upheaval before the Industrial Revolution.

Let me remind you of Blake's, Shelley's, Victor Hugo's, and Byron's defenses of Lucifer or Prometheus, their denunciations of a victorious Jehovah or Jupiter as a tyrant, and the new emphasis on the pitfalls of religious relationships. Their typical formulation is found in Lenz, Büchner, and Strindberg: "It must needs be that offenses come; but woe to that man by whom the offence cometh!"[56] In our century, we refer back to classical myths in describing the situation created by double-bind pitfalls as a *machine infernale*. The notion of a gracious God is done away with or is held up to bitter ridicule. Instead of a gracious God, there is the external agency of a sadistic chief experimenter who uses the characters as his objects for experimentation. "The sentence 'God is dead,' " writes Reinhard Baumgart, "forms the key line here. Yet still it seems as if the one declared dead was meant to hear the sentence, maybe even answer it, even if it was by saying 'Yes.' "[57] One still tries to understand the fragmented, enigmatic, frightening world with the help of elements of the decaying order of religious values and to make it understandable *as* a hostile or meaningless world.

What remains on the most reduced level is the consciousness of being forced to play; what remains is the experience of role determination and black comedy. The latter takes Lenz's concept of comedy very literally. Autonomy alone makes characters capable of tragedy; heteronomy is comical. But our laughter about it is not comfortable — for we ourselves are involved. The symbol of heteronomy is the marionette, which was introduced into aesthetic discourse at the end of the eighteenth century. Büchner's famous line could serve as a motto for wide spheres of modern literature: "We are marionettes, played by unknown powers; we are ourselves nothing, nothing at all!"[58]

But certainly not for all spheres. Their variety is not completely comprehended by this motto, nor can I present it here. I will, however, make two final distinctions that are interesting in this context: on the one hand, along with the model of the godless *teatrum mundi* and the situation of being forced to play, there is, carrying further one potential pointed out by Strindberg's ambiguous view of the world, the religious *teatrum mundi* of Claudel, Eliot, and Hofmannsthal. On the other hand, there is the conscious denial, by Brecht and others, of any model of *teatrum mundi*.

Most of the twentieth-century authors whom I have explicitly or implicitly mentioned drew directly from Strindberg. Keeping in mind Ionesco's remark cited at the beginning of this chapter, I was not concerned here with these relationships, not concerned with Strindberg as a model and mover, but with Strindberg as an indicator. I know that he left most of his followers behind, that many of them preferred significantly simpler and more ideological solutions. Strindberg himself was skeptical of ideologies. He used *and* he neutralized them. His form of protest against being played was the art of depicting being played.

6

Strindberg "Our Contemporary": Constructing and Deconstructing To Damascus (I)

Elinor Fuchs

As time separates Strindberg from his dramatic critics, two almost contradictory motions are occurring. On the one hand, Strindberg is being classicized, absorbed back into the long tradition of dramatic art; forerunners, models, and patterns are appearing that were at first obscured in the intense light of his originality. Strindberg was not so long ago too modern to be a romantic, too expressionistic to be a symbolist, and too scientific to be an occultist. But these latter categories and many others are now being brought to bear as critics undertake the project of linguistic, musical, mythic, ritual, and even alchemical analysis of Strindberg's work. Yet while Strindberg is being reconnected to his time and with past dramatic tradition, he paradoxically seems more original, for with each successive generation of theater artists one aspect or another of his strategies and preoccupations has proven his uncanny power to forecast the drift of theater and the larger culture it reflects.

Strindberg's progress has not yet been charted fully even up to Beckett, and not at all beyond Beckett. But as soon as one begins to examine the avant-garde theater of the late 1960s and 1970s, Strindberg's force can be felt in the background. Three-quarters of a century after *A Dream Play*, which in Evert Sprinchorn's characterization contains more memorable pictures and images than any other play in world literature,[1] an entire wing of the

American experimental theater came to be called the theater of images.[2] One cannot fail to see in Robert Wilson's surrealist panoramas and mythic themes the seed of Strindberg's chrysanthemum.

In this essay I shall attempt to extend Strindberg's presence, if not his direct influence, beyond modern drama into the postmodern world of the American experimental theater. To do so I must employ two critical vocabularies — the traditional vocabulary of dramatic interpretation, with its interest in the meanings that arise from the interaction between dramatic content and dramatic structure; and the subversive discourse of the post-structuralists, who throw doubt on such meanings by examining the lacunae and contradictions embodied in the clearest texts. It is perhaps fitting that the Strindberg text that occasions this divided exploration is his masterpiece of double structure, *To Damascus* (I).

Of the six theatrical elements identified in the *Poetics*, Aristotle asserts that plot is the most important and is the "soul" of tragedy. But at the beginning of the nineteenth century, romantic critics looked back at the dramatic model of Shakespeare and concluded that character is the cornerstone of dramatic art. Dramatic conflict, as Hegel said, lay not so much in a collision of actions but in the divided psychic and spiritual realm within the human being.[3] Although never articulated as such in post-Renaissance dramatic theory, a notion emerged of "complete character" analogous to Artistotle's view of "complete action." It is still taught today that dramaturgical excellence in characterization comprises the positing of a character who undergoes development, crisis, and a resolution that signals change or growth.

Yet even as the Romantic critics elevated character to the place in the Christian dramaturgical pantheon that plot had assumed in the Greek, there was evidence that the whole self was collapsing. The fragmented, mechanical self of Büchner's *Woyzeck* and the onion self of Ibsen's *Peer Gynt* are among the initial contributions to a new way of regarding human nature in the theater. Strindberg sketched a theoretical framework to this development in his concept of "characterless characters" in the preface to *Miss Julie.*

In the 1890s the project of the symbolist playwrights might be described as the search for something other than character in dramatic structure that could restore a sense of wholeness to what they saw as a diminished art. The Belgian poet and literary critic Albert Mockel, for instance, linked this impoverishment to the depiction of psychological character, as had Nietzsche before him. Mockel wrote that the protagonist of the *drame idéal* should have two selves, one accessible and one remote, so that the audience, instead of focusing on merely the "anecdotal and the individual," could also experience the "eternal history of man."[4] Strindberg's pilgrimage plays both expressed and emerged from this search for a new structural principle to replace exhausted notions of plot and character.

Many experiments were tried in the last years of the century. In his early plays Maeterlinck tried two at once: universalizing his characters through generalization (e.g., the Old Man, the Young Girl), a device Strindberg later borrowed, and writing for marionettes, sensing as Kleist had done earlier in the century that marionettes were capable of a metaphysical presence that the fragmented and contradictory human image could not evoke. Maurice Bouchor had a similar intuition, and his mystery plays for marionettes acquired a kind of cult following in Paris in the early 1890s.[5]

A number of writers in the Parisian occult, such as Jules Bois, experimented with ritual and mythic dramatic schemes. A young American symbolist named Sadakichi Hartmann, who went to Paris briefly in 1892 as a journalist, conceived a vast world history project for the stage, predating Strindberg's by more than a decade, that would include epic dramas on Christ, Buddha, and Confucius. He succeeded in bringing out the first of these, *Christ*, in a private printing in 1893. The volume announced the entire three-part scheme and was dedicated to none other than August Strindberg, in whose library in Stockholm an unmarked copy can be found.[6] Finally, the "magus" Péladan wrote mythic plays that were produced in his Rosicrucian salons during Strindberg's tenure in Paris. Péladan's rules — that the best art was ideal, redemptive, and Italianate — were better observed by Strindberg in *To Damascus* (I) than in any of Péladan's own "Wagneries."[7]

Many of these *fin-de-siècle* attempts to theatrically depict the "eternal history of man" were dramatically feeble, but they created an artistic-spiritual environment that was formative for Strindberg during his years in Paris. When Strindberg finally turned his own hand to the problem of making the "ideal invisible" visible on the stage, he hit upon a brilliant synthesis of two popular medieval forms, the passion and the morality play. In so doing he returned to the allegorical mode with its concomitant journey structure, a form that achieved enduring power in twentieth-century dramaturgy. It is as shortsighted to attribute Strindberg's arrival at this synthesis to personal psychological factors as it is to label it expressionism,[8] for its roots run deep in Western theater and its branches have grown into a mystery play genre that has become the primary vehicle for metaphysical inquiry in modern drama.

The revival of interest in allegory has been a major event in twentieth-century literature. In the past two decades, a number of sophisticated critical studies have attacked stereotyped ideas of the intellectual debasement and formal rigidity of allegory. At the same time, allegory has derived vitality from an entirely new quarter, criticism, where interpretation itself has been recognized as a species of allegorical thinking. Only in theater, which tends to lag behind other disciplines in critical adaptation, is allegory still an ugly word.

The allegorical mode in modern drama, or the modern mystery genre, has certain consistent characteristics that distinguish it from tragedy, comedy, melodrama, and even tragicomedy, to which it is philosophically most allied. These characteristics are all present in *To Damascus* (I), the first play of this type. The form, to sketch a brief poetics, has a two-level plot typically comprising a quotidian and a mythic dimension. It has patterned, schematic action that is based not on probability but on the formulation of its own rules. Conflict is rarely embodied in antagonistic characters; rather, it goes on between structural levels. There is frequently a symbolic, universalized treatment of stage space, and time is presented in a systematic, often cyclical pattern derived either from nature or from myth: for instance, the movement of a cycle of seasons, a human lifetime, or the entire cycle of sacramental history from Creation to the Last Judgment. The action usually assumes the form of a progress but may occasionally take on other forms favored by allegory, such as a battle or debate. Character is abstract, the substitution of dualistic devices such as fragmentation, projection, and *figura* for a solid, psychologically developed self. This splintering of character constitutes a crucial bridge between modern and postmodern dramatic methods.

What distinguishes this modern mystery from its medieval prototypes is irony — the manifest clash of levels or the ambivalent relationship of the central character to the mythic content and pattern of the play. German expressionist drama affords many examples of such dramatic structures, one of the most successful being Georg Kaiser's *From Morn to Midnight*, in which an insignificant bank clerk who revolts against bourgeois life simultaneously depicts an Everyman figure who ends his life in an ironic version of the Christian Passion. This pattern, however, is not limited to expressionism.

Artaud's surrealistic play, *The Spurt of Blood*, evinces a similar mystery pattern. Beneath the confusing and seemingly random appearances of a young man on a mysterious search, a fat medieval knight, his wetnurse, a priest with a Swiss accent, and an enormous whore, can be found the firm structure of Christian sacramental history. This entire experiment, incidentally — an irreverent miniature mystery play — had first been tried by Strindberg as an epilogue to *Master Olof* and published as *Coram Populo* in 1896. The Artaud play begins in Paradise with the innocent bloom of young love and proceeds to a Fall in which "bodies, hands, feet, scalps, colonnades, porches, temples, and alembics" fall to earth with sickening slowness. It now reverts to the young man's search for purity through varied terrestrial obscenities and culminates in an apocalypse filled with images from Revelation, including the Great Whore, fire, and blood. It ends with a new heaven and a new earth in the revival of the young girl, who exclaims, "The virgin! Ah, that's what he was looking for."⁹

The pattern emerges again in Brecht's *Badener Lehrstück*, in which a hybrid of the morality and the Christian cycle becomes a vehicle for a Marxist explication of the class struggle. The collective "protagonist" is a group of flyers whose airplane crash is a lightly disguised version of the Fall. Most of the play is a spiritual winnowing that rids the flyers of individualistic bourgeois ideas, and salvation is anticipated at the end through submersion in the historical lifestream of the masses.¹⁰

There is no better example of this allegorical mode in modern drama than *Waiting for Godot*. Although Beckett calls it a tragicomedy, it behaves more like a modern mystery play. Beneath the superficial debts to Strindberg — the two-part repeating structure, the tree that leaves miraculously, the rich blind man echoed from *A Dream Play* — there is a deeper debt to the mystery structure of *To Damascus* (I): at one level, or from one point of view, two ragged bums with sore feet and weak kidneys; and at the other, a morality journey play fused with the Passion. The metaphysical journey in the modern mystery would seem to have reached its end here, for Beckett has narrowed the quest to a fixed point. There is nowhere to go in this journey of stasis, and no satisfaction to be wrenched from the mythic world, for all that comes back from it are our own cultural conventions —figures in white beards and little boys asleep in the hay. One might think that with Beckett, *To Damascus* (I) had reached the end of its usefulness as a directional pointer for advanced theater.

Yet there is something about *To Damascus* (I) that evades the very genre designation that helps give it clarity and that illuminates the ensuing avant-garde tradition in modern drama. Its combination of colloquial and formal tones is so extreme, as Richard Gilman complained,¹¹ that it almost refuses to cohere; an uncertainty — or, to use a Derridaean term borrowed from symbolic logic, an undecidability — that undermines stable interpretation. In all its self-reflexive doubleness and conflation of texts, it could be seen to be a work not only about confession, therapy, guilt, and reconciliation but about itself, its own strategies, and the essential problem of conveying meaning.

Seen in this light, which perhaps is not the dominant one but is the one that persists, the play displays sudden kinship with the postmodern theater of fragments and collage, a theater in which meanings arise from a juxtaposition of theatrical elements in ironic relation, in which authors efface themselves in others' texts, and in which characters are dissolved into kaleidoscopic role shifting. Unlike the *To Damascus* (I) we know (or think we know), this postmodern *To Damascus* points to the unreliability of "truth" and the breakdown of metaphysics.

Deconstruction may be said to take as its starting point Derrida's overturning of the priority accorded speech over writing in a metaphysical tradition that he traces from Plato through the structuralists. Derrida asserts, on the contrary, that spoken language, along with the very thought that speech reflects, must be fished from an already existing sea of language, an *écriture* in which myriad cultural influences have left their untraceable traces.[12] This "deprivileging" of speech in relation to writing simultaneously deprivileges nature in relation to culture and substitutes a boundless subjectivity and relativism for the "idealist" structuralism that Derrida and other poststructuralist writers critique. In answer to philosophers who have studied speech as a validation of the workings of consciousness, Derrida enlists Freud, who says, as Derrida interprets him, that consciousness itself is conditioned by writing — as it were, previously inscribed.[13] This critical perspective represents a special problem for theater, or at least for theater critics, who have always prided themselves on recognizing the distinction between the munificent art of the stage and the straitened art of the text. Although Derrida does not by and large write about drama and theater, his thought makes us attend to the paradox that drama is writing that fosters an illusion of spontaneous speech. The question that poststructuralist thought in general poses for theater is whether dramatic reading by actors bringing to texts the interpretive sign-systems expressed by eyes, gestures, and vocal inflections does not once more reassert the hegemony of speech over writing, lowering the boom of an especially restrictive "closure" on the inherently undecidable text.

A poststructuralist poetics of performance would perhaps teach that rather than reaching for consistent meanings, performance attention should be devoted to the dissociations, contradictions, "absences," and grating juxtapositions discovered in the text. A deconstructive approach to the performance of text, then, would be subversive: not interpretive but deinterpretive; not providing answers and seeking closure but raising questions and opening closure. And finally, one can imagine that texts created for such a theater would embody strategies that resist footholds of consistent meaning. As Derrida puns, "Il n'y a aucun de hors-texte," meaning that nothing lies outside the text and that the text has no outside from which to make a safe and stable interpretation.[14]

The title of this chapter imitates Jan Kott not only because of Strindberg's protean ability to refresh his contemporaneity but because Kott's work was a protodeconstructive reading of Shakespeare, an effort to show that, in the very heart of a long-taken-for-granted-harmony and transcend-ence in a number of the major plays, lay contradictory elements of despair and dissolution. Kott in effect challenged closure of meaning in Shake-speare. In *To Damascus* (I), Strindberg seems to invite such a challenge as well.

My first question about *To Damascus* (I) is not whether it submits to deconstructive reading — presumably every text does — but whether it does not anticipate a theater that already reflects and implies deconstruc-tive ideas. Have we ever adequately addressed, for instance, the mystery in the fact that the entire play is a parenthesis inserted into writing — the sand writing at the beginning and end of the play? Arguably, this writing has not ceased during the play's action, for the Stranger notes in the last few lines that he is "still at it" — that is, writing.[15] Not only has the Stranger perhaps never ceased writing — lending a bit of practical support to the view that the play is a kind of dream play, a daydream, as Strindberg later asserted —but he has never ceased writing *in the sand*, writing in a substance subject to continuous change, so that no meaning can possibly endure in it.

If we regard the play as a latter-day Christian mystery, the writing in the sand may suggest Christ's writing on the ground in the story of the Woman Taken in Adultery (John 8:6-8). The Stranger is, after all, a figure of Christ among others, and forgiveness and charity are themes of both the Biblical parable and the Stranger's journey. But there is an additional, more playful, and perhaps more mysterious way to "read" this writing. The Stranger himself is a writer, and he is the Unknown One, a being subject to such change that — like writing in the sand — perhaps no fixed meaning can be attached to his experience. The books he writes are subject to the same potential for "misreading" for he represents them as the urgings of justice and liberation, but others account them the work of the devil. And nowhere in the play do we find out what the Unknown One is writing or what he has written — that too is unknown. We do learn that the Stranger doubts that "life is any more real than my novels," which lends an eerie unsubstantiality to both the charges against his work and his defense of it.

Yet, although these texts are present in the play only as absences, numerous other texts and their writers are present in their absence. The Bible, Virgil, Dante, Swedenborg, Kierkegaard, and a number of fairy tales permeate the text but are unrepresented as such. In this intense intertextu-ality, our unknown but present author-character almost disappears, as he becomes the hero of *The Divine Comedy*, Saul, Paul, Adam, Cain, Christ, Aeneas, a fairy-tale knight, Caesar. His soul, even more than Miss Julie's, is "patched together," an agglomeration of "past and present cultures."[16] I quote, of course, from Strindberg's preface to *Miss Julie*, which in light of deconstruction appears more radical than it did one hundred years ago.

Surely the inscrutability of the Stranger is no serious thing, just a veneer over the events in Strindberg's life. Indeed, to critics, the play's blatantly autobiographical nature has been one of its most disturbing factors. Yet it is precisely the "distancing" of the most intimate material that gives *To Damascus* (I) some of its strongest deconstructionist affinities. Granting the "death of the subject," Roland Barthes writes: "Today the subject . . . can return at another place on the spiral: deconstructed, taken apart, shifted, without anchorage: why should I not speak of 'myself' since this 'my' is no longer the 'self'?"[17] "It should all," he declares in the frontispiece of *Roland Barthes*, "be considered as if spoken by a character in a novel."

The disappearance of the sense of self into the maw of culture (or the sea of *écriture*) in postmodern society may be what has opened the door to an autobiographical intimacy in theater unprecedented except for Strindberg's example. The documentary account of the suicide of actor-writer Spalding Gray's mother in the abstractly patterned *Rumstick Road*[18] is perhaps the best-known example of a genre of performance in which artists paint their own bodies before audiences,[19] or actual photographs of performers' or writers' lives are incorporated into a production design.[20] This erasing of the distinction between self and other, between artist and art object, can no longer be understood in terms of psychopathology. Rather, it can be regarded in the predictive *To Damascus* (I) as the deconstruction of the primary binary opposition of subject and object.

Although it has sometimes been suggested that *To Damascus* (I) is a "message" play whose clarity amounts to ethical prescription, does not this same "undecidability" between conflicting terms overlie the play's entire structure? Let us look further at this message. If there is a point where the play's germ is delivered entire, it must be in the second Kitchen scene and in the Mother's speech after the Stranger's visitation of heart pain. But who is delivering the message? Does not the Mother partake of the unknown along with the Stranger? All the characters are contaminated with unknownness to the degree that they are aspects of the Stranger or that their actions are projections of his powerful emotions. Therefore, can we trust the Mother? She is full of vengeful fury at first but turns kind when he becomes kin; her turn itself may be a projection of the Stranger's changing mood instead of an autonomous action. Even if we grant the Mother independence, her new role as spiritual counselor to the Stranger is questionable, for she has admitted to using religion "in the same way I'd make use of a hair shirt and a stone floor."

The Stranger has just understood the Mother for the first time, and speaks "sincerely, without irony." While this direction can be taken as a further clue that we have arrived at a moment whose clarity we can trust, it also tells us that the foregoing speeches of the Stranger have been, or *perhaps* have been, tainted with insincerity and irony. Furthermore, as we are never again instructed that the ironic mode is absent, this very strange direction can serve to reinforce the mistrust it appears to relieve, a mistrust that must wash onto the other characters to the extent that they function as projections.

At this point the message is delivered. The Mother says: "My son: You have left Jerusalem and you are on the way to Damascus. Go there. The same way you came here. And plant a cross at each station, but stop at the seventh. You don't have fourteen as He had." If there are questions about the speaker, there are even more about her puzzling speech. This latter-day Saul is to complete a linear journey from Jerusalem to Damascus in Escher-like fashion by describing a circle, leading us either to question whether the true journey has been mysteriously deflected or to conclude that Jerusalem and Damascus are, on some level, the same place. The place of ugly persecution, in other words, merges with the place of absolution. Each partakes of the other, the two modes blur and blend, and — like the subject and object recently discussed — risk disappearing into each other.

There is another journey suggested, the journey of Christ making his sorrowful way to Golgotha. This journey too is ambiguously presented by the Mother. Does "stop at the seventh" mean that a journey previously completed in fourteen stages can now be dispatched in half the number, or that only half the journey will be taken? And if the latter, should we conclude that two incomplete or fragmentary journeys — one modeled on Paul and the other on Christ — have been prescribed? Is it then possible that the Stranger's vacillating behavior at the end of the play is not so much a failure of nerve, a falling away in the face of the firm logic of his journey, as it is a predictable end to a journey whose deferral of its objects and difference from its models (these two qualities being combined by Derrida in the neologism central to deconstruction, *différance*,[21] the damned worm in the apple of meaning) make its ambiguous outcome inevitable?

One may say on the one hand that I am speaking in riddles when the metaphysic here is perfectly clear. On the other hand, the Stranger tells the Mother that she is "speaking riddles." One thing is certainly clear — if we bring a Christian, metaphysical closure to the text, the outcome of the play will differ from our expectation of it, which must then be deferred. The allegorical journey described in *To Damascus* (I), the mystery play, the journey in which more can be found than meets the eye, is at the same time an ironic journey in which less can be seen than meets the mind. We, the readers or spectators, may have "privileged" one line of meaning over another, thus pushing the play too confidently toward a closure perhaps deliberately exploded in the very lines that suggest it. If we then do not accept a closure which asserts that this play is about the torments of guilt and the way out through a contritional Christian mysticism, what can we say it is about? The distinguishing trait of the postmodern text lies in its self-reflexive nature: it is about itself, about writing and reading and misreading. To the extent that Strindberg anticipates the postmodern, his text may be about these things as well.

Just as the play has characterless characters — that is, characters who are fragments and figments and mysteries — so it has in a sense actionless action. There is plot enough, but it plots itself: very little physical action or psychological volition is required to further it. The characters appear caught in the amber at each station. So suspended, one of their most persistent activities is interpretation, or, in an extended sense, reading. In a tireless search for meaning, they continuously peer into the curtain of inscrutability that shrouds the text. Before, "all I saw was objects and movements, forms and colors," says the Stranger at the outset, but "now I see meanings and connections." Characters read one another's minds, or strive to read. Stranger to Beggar: "I cannot make out whether you are satiric or incoherent." The Doctor reads lips. The Lady reads the wallpaper. The Stranger reads the tablecloth. The Lady's crocheting is an "endless scroll." The scenery in the Ravine is scanned for meaning. The Werewolf's face is sighted in the cliffs. The Old Man reads omens in magpies. The Lady and her husband used to read the Curse from Deuteronomy over the Stranger. The Confessor recites, that is, reads from memory, the *Dies Irae*, and the Beggar reads snatches from Latin authors. The Confessor reads the Curse from the breviary on the lectern. Everyone reads, and misreads, the Stranger's books. And on and on, until finally the reading of a letter brings respite.

"Misreading" is what some deconstructionists say is the closest we can ever come to unriddling literature. Literature itself, according to Harold Bloom, is produced in a dialectical process of strong misreadings.[22] If we permit ourselves to lift for a moment the metaphysical closure that has made a unit of *To Damascus* (I) and the unshakable belief systems that some of its dominant inner texts embody, we might venture to say that it is a play of, a play on, misreading.

In *Allegory, The Theory of a Symbolic Mode*, Angus Fletcher sees in obsession the psychoanalytic analogue of the allegorical mode and in compulsion the mechanism of its characters, a theory broadly applicable to the structure and characters of the mystery play genre previously outlined. For a postmodern theater — a theater of nonclosure and autorepresentation, in which there is nothing outside the text or outside the world of the stage to give ultimate validation to any reading over any other reading — one might guess that the correct psychoanalytic analogue would be not obsession but paranoia, an illness that manifests itself in the construction of false systems, or in misreading.[23]

It is paranoia that fuels the action of *To Damascus* (I), not only in its use of the mechanism of projection to deal with mental conflict, the persecutory fears of its protagonist, its febrile spinning out of reading after false reading, but in its entire literary structure, which can be seen compiled in two "readings" or two conflicting systems applied to the same characters and locales. In this (my own) reading, the mirror structure of the play can be understood as a reversal — a true order succeeding a false one — and, more importantly, as a self-reflecting system of readings more concerned with change than with truth. Reality, after all, is unaffected by this process. The letter was in the post office from the outset. The entire drama is spun out of the endless play of interpretation. Is it correct to think that the Stranger is paranoid in the first half of the play and gradually regains sanity in the second? No, for when he sees the masts of three ships in the fourteenth scene, it is he who reads in them a "new Golgotha," although none appears.

The parabola of thought traced in this essay begins with the fragmentation of dramatic character experienced in nineteenth-century theater, leads to a discussion of an allegorical dramatic strategy that subordinates character to a schematic dramatic structure, and suggests how that very structure then tends toward the same indeterminacy earlier found in character. This shift in perspective on *To Damascus* (I) may be seen as the shift from a modern to a postmodern point of view.

When one examines postmodern theater itself, it is surprising how many of its traits are foreshadowed by *To Damascus* (I). I previously discussed the incorporating of autobiographical material into a formal pattern that both drains it of personality and enlarges the "I" to enclose the entire process of art. The formal visual patterning, the jarring mixture of tones, the tendency toward allegory, and above all the fragmentation of character are all attributes of the experimental theater since the early 1970s. This theater has adopted the "dream play" principle to the extent that no sustained narrative can be followed through the traditional means of plot and character; rather, one follows levels or channels of information — visual, aural, characterological, and so on — constructing one's own dramatic "allegory."

If one examines the new theater for its "soul" — to return in true Damascus fashion to our Aristotelian starting point — one would have to say that it now resides not in plot or in character but in the intertextual, interstitial flux that arises from a play of all theatrical elements. Such a formal theatrical aesthetic is neither Greek nor Christian but is remarkably consistent with the teachings of Buddha, who discovered that there was no such thing as a continuous "self," and no external god in the universe, only the endless play of mental and physical functions in an impersonal process beyond closure. Is it possible that the insignia of an Eastern worldview is present in the deconstructive mind of the poststructuralists and in the new deconstructive theater? If so, it must be acknowledged that, not only in the predictive power of his new forms but in his attraction to Buddhist thought, Strindberg is once more our contemporary.

7

Macro-Form in Strindberg's Plays: Tight and Loose Structure

Gunnar Brandell

In an international perspective, Strindberg is above all a dramatist, the author of a handful of plays that are staged and filmed again and again in different countries. All the international Strindberg symposia have more or less exclusively dealt with Strindberg's plays. Egil Törnqvist and Evert Sprinchorn have recently published full-length Strindberg studies in English, on Strindbergian drama and on Strindberg as dramatist, respectively. Such studies have been a well-established trend since the 1890s when Strindberg acquired his earliest reputation as a dramatist at the theaters in Paris and Berlin.

I see things from a slightly different angle because I am Swedish and because I am working on a complete Strindberg biography. It is not a question of reducing Strindberg's importance as a portal figure to twentieth-century drama. This is well established and has been confirmed each time his plays have been brought to new life in connection with every modern trend, from expressionism to postmodernism. Nor can it be doubted that, for Strindberg himself, dramatic writing was a favorite endeavor. But I must insist on the fact that Strindberg had many other roles and dimensions, if only for the reason that his dramatic achievement cannot be fully understood unless one takes into account his experiences and ambitions in other fields.

Gunnar Brandell

I shall begin with the character of Strindberg's dramatic creativity. He wrote fifty or sixty plays — there is of course no exact number; one can arrive at the total in different ways — which is a considerable amount. But he did not devote much time to them, at least not to the actual writing. He wrote his plays extremely fast. As always with Strindberg there are exceptions to the general rule, and in this case at least one: *Master Olof*, on which he worked repeatedly for nearly a decade. But *Miss Julie*, another masterfully structured play, was finished in three weeks, and the first part of *Dance of Death*, as far as I can determine, was written in ten days. The natural point of comparison and contrast is, of course, the steady flow of plays from Ibsen's pen. Ibsen's plays seem to be the result of regular work and mature reflection; there are no failures or trifles. Compared with Ibsen's, Strindberg's plays sometimes stand out as improvisations, as in the three I mentioned — brilliant, yes, but some of them were less successful with audiences than others.

Strindberg's playwriting, unlike Ibsen's, is highly irregular. His dramas were conceived in periods of intensive dramatic production, separated by long intervals devoted to other activities. If I leave aside *Master Olof*, the first of these periods covers the years 1880 to 1882 with the more or less romantic dramas; then there was an interval of four years until 1886 to 1888 when he wrote the so-called naturalistic plays; these were followed by the one-act plays and the fairy-tale play, *The Keys of Heaven*, written in 1889 and 1892, respectively; then came the famous Inferno interval when for six years Strindberg did not think about writing plays; after that came the longest period of all, the four years between 1898 and 1902, which saw the sensational and well-known revival of Strindberg's dramatic productivity. *The Nightingale of Wittenberg* emerged in 1904; and last, in 1907-9 there was the final phase that included, among other things, the Chamber Plays. This is only a sketchy outline. Regarded at a closer range, these periods would fall into subperiods because Strindberg was usually also working on other projects. An exact timetable is difficult to establish, but I think it likely that Strindberg devoted at most ten years of his life to writing plays. That would approximately break down into five plays per year.

The current explanation of this irregular productivity is that Strindberg turned to drama whenever he saw a chance of being produced and took up other things in the meantime, *faute de mieux*. This is, I think, only part of the background, but as such it is obvious. In the first of the periods I have outlined, he had access to the ordinary Stockholm theater; in the second he had the newly established experimental theaters in Paris and Berlin in mind; in the third he had plans to start a theater of his own; in the fourth he wrote for the regular Stockholm theater again; and in the last phase, he wrote for the Intimate Theater.

Macro-Form in Strindberg's Plays

It is still difficult to imagine Strindberg as a steady purveyor of plays to some theatrical institution. His entire literary output, not least his playwriting, bears witness to his restlessness, his need to change direction, try new formulas and different projects. The fact that the theaters were sometimes open to him and sometimes closed probably suited his temperament and his kind of creativity fairly well. He was a man of many dimensions and, to use Thomas Mann's phrase, of many "ingenious detours."

It is true, however — and this is prerequisite to the following discussion — that Strindberg wrote his plays with the stage in mind. There may be one or two exceptions to this rule, too, but I doubt it. That playwriting is writing for the theater now seems self-evident, but it was not so obvious in the nineteenth century. Ibsen's *Peer Gynt* was not originally intended for the theater; Strindberg's corresponding play, *Lucky Per's Journey*, was written for the stage. Strindberg was not a regular theatergoer, but his "theater of the mind," the one he dwelt in when writing his plays, was fully equipped: it had a stage, actors, settings, costumes, props, lights, sometimes an orchestra, certainly an audience, and even a foyer — although on this last point Strindberg's main concern was to keep people away from it.

Such a theater was in Strindberg's mind even when he wrote his "heavy" plays, like the first part of *To Damascus*, which at the time was sometimes considered a closet drama. Strindberg himself was of another opinion. It should be staged, he wrote to a friend *"C'est du théâtre."* In his case we can make the notion dramatic technique easier to handle by reducing it to simple but, for the producer, fundamental things such as setting, cast, length, and overall composition. Strindberg was also aware, of course, of certain other features that may be thought of as part of dramatic technique, in a wider sense: plot, themes, motives, characterization, and dialogue. But such things are as a rule better analyzed in one's armchair than in the theater, and with this in mind I leave them aside.

Among Strindberg's plays there is a group of about twenty — the historical plays — that I shall also leave aside. They constitute an important part of Strindberg's dramatic production, and some of them have been successful, at least in Sweden. They too are written for the stage, most for theaters in Stockholm and other Swedish cities. Although it would be interesting to compare Strindberg's historical plays with the kind of conventions reigning in the theatrical establishment to see what he accepted or rejected, the inquiry would delve too deeply into Swedish history. Strindberg himself pointed to the reason for this when he stated in his *Open Letters to the Intimate Theater*, "Writing historical plays is a bit like a piece of composition or writing about a prescribed subject." The composition in a historical play cannot be separated from the handling of the raw material — that is, the historical facts and persons. The situation thus changes from play to play, and the critic must analyze them individually, one after the other, as Walter Johnson did. In this survey, which aims at categories rather than individual plays, I must disregard the subject.

I propose that the rest of Strindberg's plays can be divided into two categories — the tightly composed and the loosely composed. About twenty clear cases fall into the first category and ten into the second. I doubt I will encounter opposition if I point to *A Dream Play* as the most extreme case of loose composition. With regard to the tight plays, there are several possible choices, but a good case could be made for *The Creditors* being the most strictly composed. With these examples in mind, it is easy to see that the loose plays have been more in favor with literary opinion and the experimental theaters. It is the author of *A Dream Play* rather than *The Creditors* whom we think of as the forerunner of modern, "non-Aristotelian" drama, whereas the latter plays, along with some others of the tight variety, have met with more success in the conventional theater.

That we should find these two poles in Strindberg's dramatic writings is not surprising given his general outlook and temperament. Constant change and fundamental unity are, throughout his life, the two poles of Strindberg's experience. This double vision can be found in everything he wrote, but it is perhaps best illustrated by Superintendent Borg in *By the Open Sea*. This character, like Strindberg, has double vision. He seems to be two different people: one dominates everything by means of rational understanding and willpower; the other is a poet who lets himself be carried away in the constant flux of changing sensations. As a natural philosopher, Strindberg propagated the formula of an "infinite order in the great chaos," and believed in both Heraclitus and Pythagoras. As a creator of his own dramatic world, he had free choice and could write, on the one hand, plays in which everything on the surface is flux and reflux and the meaning seems to lie somewhere behind it all and, on the other hand, plays with a strict, almost mathematical composition — perhaps embodying a secret or two, but only in the playwright's mind, not in the play itself. These structures are created in a spirit of experimentation.

There are very few theoretical statements about drama in Strindberg's writings; he avoids generalizations and keeps very close to the particular drama he has in mind. For example, in the famous preface to *Miss Julie*, he certainly tries to convince his audience that he has written a "modern" play, but whatever implications or presuppositions you may find in or deduce from his text, he does not say that modern drama in general should be of this particular kind. The same is true of the equally famous preface to *A Dream Play* — of which, incidentally, there are two different and partially conflicting versions. Unlike Brecht or Artaud, Strindberg had no theory of drama in general, and he certainly did not want one. In the most theoretical of all his statements, "On Modern Drama and Modern Theater" (written in 1889), he distributes praise and blame unsystematically and with a certain amount of nonchalance, and concludes that we should strive for a "free theater, where one is free to do everything except to lack talent and to be a hypocrite or an imbecile! And if we do not get such a theater, we shall have to manage without it!" In *Letters to the Intimate Theater*, he says approximately the same thing, and Törnqvist rightly uses the sentence as an epilogue to his own book: "No predetermined form is to limit the author, because the theme determines the form."

Implied in this demand for freedom is a criticism of conventional drama and of the audience's preconceived expectations. (Someone had to pay for the freedom Strindberg wanted to grant to the theater and to himself as an author.) In Strindberg's mind, it was the audience who had to give up its conventions, expectations, and habits. One outstanding feature in his reflections about theater is his lifelong fight against intermissions between acts. In practice, because his control was not unlimited he had to make various concessions with regard to dividing acts and intermissions. But fundamentally, he thought it inappropriate that the audience should be permitted to eat, drink, and chat in the middle of a play. If such behavior were allowed, he thought, everything was in danger: the unity of the play, the illusion, the message, and the atmosphere. So, when writing for the theater, even though he felt free to do what he wished, he tried every possible way to avoid intermissions or at least to make them nonobligatory. This is a general tendency with both his tight and his loose plays.

One obvious way to avoid intermissions is to use the same scenery throughout the play. This is observed in all the plays I classify as tight, and it provides for unity of place. Within reasonable limits, unity of time is also observed. In several cases time is identical with the actual time of performance, whereas in other cases, such as in *The Father*, the time of action is extended but still held within the classical limit of twenty-four hours. At the other extreme is *Easter*, in which the action takes several days, but, since the days are related to Easter week, the time factor is controlled. Unity of action is strongly underlined in all these plays, even those that are quite unique in other respects, such as *The Bond* and *Swanwhite*.

Apart from this general adherence to principles in the Aristotelian tradition, there is also in Strindberg's tight plays a tendency toward the reduction of scenic elements. In these plays Strindberg makes little use of lighting devices or stage props or indeed anything that would change the scenery. In *Miss Julie* the daybreak at the end of the play signals an important scenic shift, the only one of its kind besides the entry of the farm people.

In *The Father* the scenery is changed from day to night when the curtain is raised for the second act. Between the second and the third act one lamp is exchanged for another, but that is all. In *The Creditors* this tendency reaches its aesthetic extreme. The play can be performed, Strindberg wrote proudly, "with one table, two chairs, and no sunrise" — the last remark is directed against Ibsen's *Ghosts* or his own *Miss Julie*.

Another way to tighten the play is to reduce the cast of characters. This too was one of Strindberg's experiments. He wrote three short plays with only two characters in each — *Pariah, Simoon,* and *The Stronger* — the last of which has only one speaking part. This kind of reduction also filled him with pride. In a letter to his third wife, at a moment when he was planning a theatrical tour around Sweden for the two of them, he wrote, "Give me two people and I shall create a world; give me three, and I shall move it."

The difference between a created world and one that moves is reflected in the contrast between a short play of Strindberg's and a full-length one. He wrote three plays with three characters, and interestingly enough they are generally considered to be among his best: *Miss Julie, The Creditors,* and *The Dance of Death* (I). These plays give testimony to Strindberg's talent as a playwright because the three-character form is no doubt difficult to master. In the theater it evidently has some advantages, and although it demands a great deal from the actors, it also gives them great opportunities. Many actors from all over the world are famous for their performances in these plays.

The preceding discussion gives some idea of the almost mathematical simplification that Strindberg aimed at in some of his tight plays. But the analysis does not stop there. Given three actors, designated A, B, and C, it is easy to discern the three possible confrontations in the play: A-B, B-C, and C-A. By making each of these confrontations interesting in its own way, the dramatist can lend variation to a play with reduced elements. I think Strindberg was quite successful in this respect, but his method cannot easily be reduced to a technical formula; it is a question of invention, psychology, dialogue, and other not so well defined factors. Nevertheless, when he wrote *The Creditors*, Strindberg was so sure of himself that he did nothing to conceal the mathematical construction of his play — which of course could easily have been done with a few extra entries and exits. *The Creditors* is structured exactly according to the mathematical formula. First Gustav and Adolf are alone on stage, which takes thirty-two pages in the text; then Tekla and Adolf appear for twenty-three pages; followed by Tekla and Gustav for nineteen pages. After this there is another half-page scene, with all three characters on stage in which Adolf falls sick. Those are the only confrontations that are mathematically possible, and Strindberg presented them on a descending scale to accelerate the play.

The situations are less schematic in the other two plays of this group, but the three-part division is clearly discernible and the proportions are similar. In *Miss Julie* the first part ends when the farm people arrive and Miss Julie and Jean retire to Jean's room. The second part consists of their long conversation in the middle of the night, and the third part begins with daybreak and Kristin's entrance into the kitchen. The proportions are twenty-six, twenty-three, and twenty-one pages, respectively. In the *The Dance of Death* (I), the first part, which ends with the Captain's stroke, is slightly shorter than the second. The last part of the play begins with the Captain's pantomime, which is scenically underlined with *entre-acte* music. The proportions in this case are forty-five, forty-nine, twenty-two. Strindberg needed less time to take this play back to where it started than he did to prepare for the tragic ending in *Miss Julie*.

It is perhaps a pity that most of the plays in which Strindberg experimented with a reduction of the scenic elements have been classified as realistic or naturalistic. This designation may be correct from the point of view of content, at least to a certain extent, but with regard to form, it would be more precise to call them classical. In a general way, reduction of the scenic elements is also a formula that applies to French classical drama, and at least one such play, *Bérénice* by Racine, has the same reduced cast as the Strindberg plays I mentioned; however, in *Bérénice* there are six roles because each of the three characters has a confidant serving as his or her double. This of course does not make Strindberg's plays less "modern." Reduction is also a strong tendency in twentieth-century theater, as, for example, in Beckett. To keep within the French tradition, Sartre in *Huis clos* applies a formula similar to Strindberg's in *The Creditors* or *The Dance of Death* (I).

Strindberg's experimentation in the opposite direction, with the loose dramatic form, also led to some remarkable results, among them *To Damascus* (I) and a *A Dream Play*. If tight is classical, then loose is, from the point of view of form, romantic. This is a kind of drama in which the unities — much hated by the romanticists — are abandoned for the scenic elements of surprise and entertainment. In its simpler forms it became a "magic circus" of the kind Schikaneder practiced in *Die Zauberflöte* — which, incidentally, Strindberg read just before writing *To Damascus* (I).

This type of theater practiced a trick called *changement à vue*, which is a scene change in full view of the audience. Strindberg used it in many of his early plays and, of course, in his fairy-tale play *Lucky Per's Journey*. In this he simply followed the general trend in romantic fairy-tale plays, but since the magic theater was less common in Sweden than in Vienna, producers and audience probably thought of those changes as difficult to arrange. It worked, under the guidance of theater director Ludvig Josephson — the man who turned Ibsen's *Peer Gynt* into a play for the stage — and it was considered a great success. The play became Strindberg's most appreciated production, and the stage manager was called on stage at the end of the first performance to share the triumph.

For Strindberg, it was the beginning of his lifelong preoccupation with open scenery change in the theater. But he was probably already aware of the problem when he wrote his play. This can be deduced from the way he arranged his scenery. There are seven settings in *Lucky Per's Journey*, and they correspond in pairs in a so-called circular composition. The first and the last setting are in the church; the next two, the second and the sixth, represent, respectively, the seashore and the forest — both nature settings; next are the calif's palace and the rich man's banquet hall, which are also similar to each other. The fourth setting, an isolated case, is the open square in front of the town hall, which makes this particular scene stand out as the central one and perhaps something of a play-within-the-play.

When Strindberg, in the first part of *To Damascus* (I), arranged the scenes in a similar way, *Lucky Per's Journey* was in his mind. *To Damascus (I)* had been well received before in Sweden, and it once again became a success. In a letter Strindberg called his new play "as fantastic and brilliant as *Lucky Per* but set in the present." And this time the use of the circular composition, with the scenes returning in reverse order, was motivated not only philosophically but also dramaturgically, from a practical point of view. He pointed out to a friend, who wished to persuade theater directors to stage the play, that there were, in fact, a number of different settings but that they were "used twice." As a result, the asylum scene stands out in this play the same way as the town hall scene does in *Lucky Per's Journey*. It also gives some coherence to a play that would otherwise easily fall apart in a series of tableaux vivants, although the coherence can be considered slightly artificial. This would not be the case if Martin Lamm had been right when he said that in *To Damascus* (I) we have the impression of sinking deeper and deeper into a dream and then, in *To Damascus* (II), of gradually emerging from it. But I am not convinced that Lamm is right on this particular point. The kind of steady progression, or regression, he speaks about simply cannot be found in the play.

Strindberg himself is partly responsible for this kind of commentary. He made two important public declarations on *To Damascus* (I). One of them is well known: in the preface to *A Dream Play* he talks about *To Damascus* as his "former dream play," but he does not say whether he means part I or II or both. In the second declaration, which has escaped much attention, he talks about *To Damascus* (I) and relates the circular composition to music, not to dreams; the composition, he says, reflects different stages in life, youth, and old age. In a commentary on the scenery in the director's log, Strindberg writes:

> Same scenery as in *The Last of the Knights* but in reverse order. This contrapunctual form, borrowed from music, which I have used in *To Damascus* (I), has the effect that the listener's memories are awakened by the various localities where the memories originated, and by this means the play seems to be enacted far ahead in life with much behind. Accumulated sensations arise, echoes from better times resound, the hard seriousness of age predominates, the fallen are counted, crushed expectations are brought into remembrance.

If we choose to rely on Strindberg's own interpretation here, it is obviously to be doubted that *To Damascus* (I) with its circular composition, apart from the asylum scene, should be regarded as a dream play at all. And what about *A Dream Play* itself, which at first glance is the most loosely composed of all Strindberg's plays, the best contrast to the tight plays? Here there are no unities at all, whether of time, place, or action. The colorful scene changes incessantly, usually without the curtain being drawn, and both with and without stage blackouts. In contrast to the term reduction, the best catchword here is redundancy, especially with regard to the roles that are, to use Strindberg's own term, reduplicated. Magic tricks are performed throughout the play, when, for instance, a tree loses its leaves and is finally transformed into a coat rack. Strindberg's favorite old device, the *changement à vue*, is pushed to its limits.

Up to a certain point, however, the chaos is only apparent. As Spinchorn has pointed out, Strindberg made intermissions possible at two different points, which would divide the play into three fairly equal parts — as are so many others — roughly corresponding on the thematic level to Agnes's descent from heaven, her stay in the lower spheres, and her return, respectively. In the Swedish script he did not number the parts, acts, or scenes because he wanted the intermission to be short and insignificant. Sprinchorn's observations are totally confirmed by a French version, probably translated by Strindberg himself (the original is in his handwriting). In it the scenes are numbered from one to seventeen, and after the first one the script contains the clearly written direction *Ridå* (curtain) — in Swedish! There is also a division sign after the second part in the French version, whereas in the Swedish text there are only blanks.

The French manuscript is interesting from other points of view as well. When *A Dream Play* was published in Sweden it was generally thought of as a closet drama, impossible to produce on the stage. Strindberg's opinion was different; he wanted it to be staged. Otherwise he would not have translated the play (or allowed it to be translated) into French and sent it to Lugné-Poe. He was well aware of its staging difficulties, however. To persuade Lugné-Poe to produce it, he wrote an introductory note saying — somewhat misleadingly — that the play needed backdrops only. "There are only ten such backdrops, and they are used more than once sometimes." Strindberg knew fairly well what was feasible for the stage and what was not, but when this conflicted with his dramatic vision he adhered to the latter, postponing decisions about the technical problems. After Strindberg's death the many remarkable productions of *A Dream Play* confirm that he had been right in his priorities — even if the dramaturgical solutions have differed from what Strindberg had in mind.

Strindberg himself saw only one performance of *A Dream Play*, the premiere at the Swedish Theater in 1907. Strindberg considered it a failure, despite the fact that he and the director Castegren had made great efforts, even transporting projection machinery from Germany to produce the "dissolving views" that Strindberg liked so much because they reflected his sense of life as constant change. The machinery did not work, however, so, as he stated, they "gave up." A few years later Strindberg made plans for a production of *A Dream Play* at the Intimate Theater and envisioned a radical simplification using a curtained stage and symbolic stage props, but the project was never realized.

With *A Dream Play* Strindberg carried his experimentation in dramatic form as far as possible in two opposite directions — the tight and the loose—each one corresponding to one side of his general outlook and temperament. In all his periods of intensive playwriting, Strindberg felt free to work in one direction or the other, and free also — especially in his historical plays — to use more conventional and intermediate forms. This is true also of the last period. Among his Chamber Plays some, such as *The Pelican*, are of the tight type, and others, like *The Black Glove*, are very much of the loose kind. The most interesting and puzzling one, *The Ghost Sonata*, is fascinating in what I would call its discontinuity — in the dialogue, the conception of characters, the action. All this is perhaps interconnected in its thematics, but it does not propose a new formula with regard to overall dramatic form.

In the very diversity of Strindberg's work, not only as a dramatist but in general, lies a temptation for us to make a choice. It is easy to acknowledge the fact that, internationally, Strindberg the dramatist has had more importance than Strindberg the novelist, but whom should we prefer? In this particular situation I would not want to choose between *The Dance of Death* (I) and *A Dream Play*, two of Strindberg's most outstanding plays written within only one year of each other, but one of them wonderfully tight in its composition and the other wonderfully loose. Arthur Rubinstein, of all people, came to my rescue when, in a television program, he compared himself to his great rival Horowitz. He said that Horowitz was the best pianist and he himself the best musician. Strindberg in his work is both: both a virtuoso of dramatic construction and a poet of the stage.

8

Strindberg's Dream-Play Technique

Richard Bark

When Strindberg wrote his preface to *A Dream Play*, he called *To Damascus* (I) "his former dream play." So in a sense the author has given his approval for us to call these two plays — and perhaps others, such as *The Ghost Sonata* — "dream plays," bearing in mind that although they are different in character and technique, there are more things that unite them than separate them — above all a basic view of reality.

When *To Damascus* (I), *A Dream Play*, and *The Ghost Sonata* were first published, the critics discovered their "dream atmosphere." Ever since then, scholars, professionals in the theater, readers, and spectators have tried to ascertain how Strindberg created this dream atmosphere in the text and how it could be portrayed on stage.

The term "dream play" already existed in Swedish (*drömspel*) as well as in German (*Traumspiel*) before Strindberg used it (although it did not exist in English and French), but in those days it meant only the presence of a dreamlike reality in a play. Strindberg seems to be the first one to have used it to designate a dramatic genre, and as such it is used in present-day English.

To experience reality as a dream is nothing unique for Strindberg. Human beings have done so throughout history. Even during his so-called naturalistic period, Strindberg could express such a concept. In a letter to the author Axel Lundegård, November 12, 1887, he wrote concerning *The Father:* "It seems to me as if I am walking in my sleep; as if fiction and life were blended. I do not know if *The Father* is fiction or if my life has been one; . . . Through much writing my life has become a life of shadows."[1] It is easy to find paraphrases of these statements in *A Dream Play.* But the point here is that, when he wrote *The Father,* he did not depict reality as dreamlike. The fact that directors have tried to stage *The Father* and *Miss Julie* as dream plays is a different issue. It is after the Inferno crisis that the depiction of reality as dreamlike will become the dominant aspect of Strindberg's work.

A study of Strindberg's dream-play technique must start from an understanding of the author's experience of reality at the time of the Inferno crisis. In the books *Inferno* and *Legends,* it is obvious that he conceives reality as being like a dream. There is, of course, a basic level of fictional reality; he is walking on the street or sitting in a café when, suddenly or gradually, this reality is transformed into a dreamlike one. And all this is depicted with the same naturalistic means as before. In this way Strindberg remains a naturalist; the same view of reality that is expressed in *Inferno* and *Legends* is in his dream plays. Strindberg has never depicted a "real" sleeping dream in his plays (perhaps with the exception of the Alchemists' Banquet and the Inn scenes in *To Damascus* [II]). It is always reality that he depicts as dreamlike. And it is in this way that I use "dream play" in connection with plays, a term depicting a reality that is partly dreamlike, a reality that temporarily has the atmosphere of a dream.

It is true, however, that sleeping dreams have been staged from the very beginning of theatrical history — ever since the ghost of Clytemnestra appeared in front of the sleeping Furies in Aeschylus's *The Eumenedies* — not to mention dreams in the medieval mystery and miracle plays, in Shakespeare's dramas, in the baroque, the romantic, and the symbolistic theater.

There was a time when Strindberg was regarded as having been totally ignorant of the technical aspects of the theater. Nothing could be more wrong, as later research has proved. His writings about theater, his letters, and his discussions with directors and actors give the picture of a professional man of the theater. His plays themselves are the best proof of his theatrical knowledge, proof that he wrote them with the stage before his eyes.

When Strindberg was twenty years old, he tried to become an actor and was accepted as a pupil at The Royal Dramatic Theater in Stockholm. Even though he did not have great success in this endeavor, he did have the opportunity to work as an extra in many Royal Opera productions, including Bjørnson's *Maria Stuart i Skottland,* Halm's *Fäktaren från Ravenna* (The Swordsman from Ravenna), Birch-Pfeiffer's *Ladyn av Worsley-Hall,* and such operas as Hérold's *Zampa,* Halévy's *Judinnan* (The Jewess), Rossini's *Wilhelm*

Richard Bark

Tell, Verdi's *Ernani*, and Meyerbeer's *Afrikanskan* (The African Woman). Meyerbeer's opera featured one of the most magnificent shipwrecks that had ever been put on a Swedish stage. Strindberg, with his sharp powers of observation, of course registered everything concerning the techniques of the stage. The fact that the changes of scenery in *A Dream Play* could be a problem, did not deter a theater professional who had actually seen the most advanced machinery.

Strindberg wrote his dream plays for a stage that perhaps did not exist at the time but that *had* existed when he was young. It was something he knew as well as his own writing desk — a stage that had been destroyed by realism and naturalism, by what he called "byggandet på scenen" ("building on stage" [i.e., realistic scene construction]), which created endless intermissions and made fast scenery changes impossible. Strindberg wrote for the elegant machinery of the baroque theater with its potential for "changements à vue," which he himself had used in *Lucky Per's Journey* (written at the beginning of the 1880s).

It is misleading to say that it is the technique of the modern theater that has done full justice to Strindberg's later plays. They could have been produced in his time on a baroque stage with entertaining and astonishing effects. Of course, today such effects would seem old-fashioned and unsatisfying. But a production of *A Dream Play* at The Drottningholm Court Theater could, in the right hands, be a sensation in our time as well.

Many scholars have tried to explain how a dream atmosphere is created in Strindberg's dream plays — as literature and as stage productions. Most of them say the effect is created when something "dreamlike" is put into the text or staging. This is self-evident — if not a case of circular reasoning. Attempts have been made to characterize this dreamlike quality as distortion, immobility, slow motion, chiaroscuro, and soundlessness, and in addition as exaggerated rapidity, visual sharpness, and loudness — opposite characteristics! The dream effect, then, can be created through any means at all; it is the *context* that matters, the circumstances in which these techniques appear. With this in mind, the dreamlike effect could better be defined as a violation of time and space. Of course there must be some technique for creating dream atmosphere, but manipulating iconic elements — that is, elements that imitate an actual sleeping dream — may not be sufficient.

In Strindberg's dream plays there is always a sort of reality (fictitious, of course) established, but this reality is either suddenly or gradually transformed into a dreamlike one and then, in a permanent motion, returned to its original state. Sometimes "objective" reality and dreamlike reality appear simultaneously. The boundaries are impossible to draw. It is through special relationships, changes, and contrasts between these two levels, that the dream atmosphere is created, above all as it is expressed in the relation between the protagonist and his or her reality. Dream atmosphere is always created in contrast with the "reality" of the fictitious world of the play. I shall delineate these structures beginning with the protagonist, who may be confronted with a dreamlike reality as the spectator of a play-within-a-play, or perhaps drawn into it, becoming a dream character.

Strindberg is often regarded as one of the forerunners of expressionism and this is of course correct. But we must stop examining Strindberg in the light of expressionism as if he had been an expressionist himself, and instead emphasize how he is different, in order to discover his uniqueness. We cannot be content with regarding *To Damascus* (I) as a "drama of the soul" (which is the most important aspect of expressionism), acting in a "landscape of the soul," a drama that takes place entirely inside the Stranger, who is the protagonist. In *To Damascus* (I) there is an objective reality and the presence of a higher power that intervenes and directs everything. (There is also a god in the background of *A Dream Play* and *The Ghost Sonata*; in *A Dream Play* it is the god Indra, but he has already created the world once and for all and no longer intervenes.)

To Damascus (I) starts entirely realistically, but after a while dreamlike things begin to happen that have the effect of abolishing time and space. The Stranger is a kind of representative of reality throughout the play, increasingly tortured by fear. He looks at all these things as would a spectator of a dreamlike play-within-a-play. He exists on two levels: the real and the dreamlike. What he sees has an objective existence within the fiction of the play, but since we see these things partly through the eyes of the Stranger, we have the impression that we are looking into his soul. He also has visions and hallucinations, but they are never made visual or audible in the scenic dimension. There is a great difference between what the Stranger *says* that he experiences and what he *is shown* to experience (consider, for example, the vision in the Lady's crochet work and the sound of the grinding mill).

Let me mention *some* of these dreamlike plays-within-a-play, to which the Stranger is a spectator and which thereby take on a dream atmosphere. When he wants to give the Lady a new name, he shouts, "Fanfares!" and makes a gesture toward offstage; but instead of fanfares a funeral march is played. The Beggar has a scar similar to that of the Stranger, and when he learns that the Beggar, like himself, has received it from a close relative, he says: "No, now I am becoming afraid. May I feel if you are real?" and he touches the Beggar's arm and confirms, "Yes, he is real!" But the Beggar is still a sort of double — an evident violation of time and space. Then the six brown-clad pallbearers enter and, when the Stranger asks why they are mourning in brown and not in black, they answer that it *is* black, "but if

Your Grace so commands, it will be brown to you." At the Doctor's Home he is confronted with the so-called Werewolf (the Doctor, husband of the Lady); an arm and a leg of a corpse, which the Doctor pulls out of an icebox; and the Madman Caesar, who bears the name the Stranger had in school.

At the Hotel Room everything is quite different. Here the Stranger is no longer a spectator of a play-within-a-play. Both he and the Lady are trapped in a dreamlike situation — becoming, in a way, dream characters themselves.

In the Asylum scene the Stranger makes his most obvious appearance as a spectator of a dreamlike play-within-a-play . He is sitting at a table to the left, and at a table to the right there is a strange party:

> *The brown-clad pallbearers from the first act; the Beggar; a Woman in mourning with two children; a Woman, resembling the Lady but who is not the Lady, and who is crocheting instead of eating; a Man who resembles the Doctor but is not he; the Madman's double; the doubles of the Father and the Mother; the Brother's double; the Parents of the "Prodigal Son" and others. All are dressed in white but over their clothing is gauze in various colors. Their faces are waxen, deathly white; and their whole appearance and gestures are ghostlike.*

These people also have an objective existence (within the fictitious world of the play) although here they abolish time and space. The Stranger has only to ask the inevitable question: "Are they actually like that?" and the Abbess answers: "If you mean are they real, yes, they're terrifyingly real." In his next question he directly refers to the play-within-a-play: "Is it a play being performed?" Then the Confessor confuses everything even more — by introducing the doubles as actually *being* the characters they resemble.

After the Asylum, the scenes reappear in reversed order, and the dream atmosphere gradually disappears — as in an awakening.

In *To Damascus* (II) the structure is quite different — more similar to the one at the Hotel Room in part I. In part II the Stranger is outside the dream atmosphere only when he listens to the Doctor's speech while sitting on the bench of the accused; and when he sees his children, their new parents, the Doctor, and the Madman on the bridge. In all other cases he is drawn into a dreamlike situation and becomes a part of it, transformed into a dream character himself — for instance, at the Alchemist's Banquet and the Inn scenes, which he afterward refers to as a dream, an actual sleeping dream. It is obvious that here Strindberg is very close to expressionism, but it would be wrong to interpret all his dream plays on the basis of these scenes.

A Dream Play begins as pure baroque theater, when Indra's Daughter descends to earth in a cloud chariot. Although she comes from heaven, from a world of gods and myths, she functions as a representative of reality throughout the play — sometimes in company with the Officer, the Lawyer, or the Poet. She walks through the play as the spectator of many dreamlike plays-within-the-play, wherein time and space are abolished. The growing castle, for example, is situated on another level of reality, a violation of time and space. The Daughter and the Officer "then stop, frozen in their gestures and mime" and watch a scene in the parents' home. She takes the Door-keeper's place in the theater corridor to "sit here and look at the children of man," and she sees how the Officer is waiting for his beloved Victoria who never comes, and how he grows older and older — a dream character. She sees the world transform before her eyes: for example, a tree becomes a coat rack, which becomes a candelabra, while people on stage are frozen in their positions. In the Promotion scene in the church, the Lawyer enters a dreamlike situation and becomes a dream character when the Daughter, who actually remains outside, places the crown of thorns on his head. Although she is performing the crowning, she does not become a dream character. The levels are thus mixed.

In the room where a hellish marriage is enacted, the Daughter becomes a part of the dream level when she is nearly choked by Kristin's papering of the windows. We can also observe the people standing in the doorway as silent spectators of the scene.

At Foul Strand the Daughter again sees several strange people: a quarantine master, two patients exercising on some gym machinery, an old dandy in a wheelchair, an old coquette, her lover, a poet with a pail of mud, and a loving couple who have to go into quarantine. At Fair Haven she sees Ugly Edith, whom nobody wants to dance with but who achieves a moment of triumph by playing Bach on the piano. During the School scene, the Officer becomes a dream character when he cannot give the answer to two times two.

And after all this comes the Coal Heavers' scene — a totally realistic scene without any dream atmosphere, although the Daughter and the Lawyer are spectators during it. Here there is no violation of time and space (the shift to the Mediterranean is only mentioned in the stage directions) and the Coal Heavers are really not dream characters.

The drama concludes with a magnificent dreamlike play-within-a-play: the "defile," where all the people in the drama enter offering their attributes to the fire, with the Daughter and the Poet as spectators. Finally, at the end of the play, the Poet alone remains a spectator while the Daughter enters the burning castle, returning to her father in heaven.

In *The Ghost Sonata*, the Student's role as a spectator is not as clear as those of the Stranger and the Daughter. In the first act, Hummel is a kind of lecturer and the Student a spectator, when, for example, the former describes the strange people in the house just as they become visible in the windows (as on an inner stage) and in the street: the Colonel, the statue of the Mummy, the Fiancée, the Caretaker's Wife, the Woman in Black, the Aristocrat, the Young Lady, the Dead Man, the Beggars, the Milkmaid.

In the second act in the round drawing room, the Mummy is introduced by the two servants as a character in a play-within-a-play while she sits in her wardrobe as on an inner stage, chattering like a parrot. The "ghosts" in the ghost supper constitute by their immobility and silence the dreamlike violation of time and space. But from the moment the Mummy stops time by stopping the clock, several levels of a dreamlike reality are introduced: the Milkmaid enters — seen only by Hummel — and at last he goes into the closet to hang himself, with all the other characters functioning as spectators.

In the third act in the hyacinth room, the Cook belongs to a dreamlike level: she stands in the doorway like a character in a play-within-a-play, with the Student and the Young Lady as spectators. The Student loses his temper and reveals all the rottenness in the house. His speech kills the Young Lady, who escapes into another world. She is joining the other ghosts, becoming a dreamlike character, while the Student is a spectator of her death and of the transformation of the hyacinth room into the Isle of the Dead — the final abolition of time and space.

I have exposed the structure of some of the dream play scenes in these three plays. In the history of their productions, one can see how directors have attempted to realize their two-layered structures. In the first productions — during the period of symbolist theater — directors tried to make everything on stage as dreamlike as possible while the spectators themselves were designated as dreamers of the plays. For the 1900 production of *To Damascus* (I), Grandinson and Grabow erected an extra stage (three steps high) on the main stage and framed it with an additional proscenium in the shape of an arch. In only one scene — the Asylum — was the Stranger (played by August Palme) represented as the spectator of a play-within-a-play, watching the doubles who were placed on an inner stage within an additional arch. For their production of *A Dream Play* (1907), Castegren and Grabow also used an extra proscenium in the shape of a poppy-arch, but this time it was not possible to remind the spectators of their role as dreamers. In *The Ghost Sonata* at Strindberg's Intimate Theater (1908), everything on stage was made to look like a dream, and the Student (played by Helge Wahlgren) was represented in a totally realistic way — a failed concept in most respects. In the Bernauer-Gade production of *A Dream Play* (1916), the stage was given an extra proscenium as well: a huge oval with a transparent veil, behind which everything was enacted within a fairy-tale framework, giving the audience the function of dreamers. Moreover, Indra's Daughter (played by Irene Triesch) was made a spectator of several plays-within-a-play, in which the Officer (played by Ludwig Hartau) was part of the most dreamlike of these. In Reinhardt's production of *The Ghost Sonata* (1916), the Student (played by Paul Hartmann) was a spectator of many plays-within-a-play, in which Hummel (played by Paul Wegener) appeared in the most dreamlike sequences.

Molander and Skawonius succeeded in making the settings for *A Dream Play* (1935) transformations of each other . The Daughter (played by Tora Teje) was often a dream-play spectator to scenes in which the Officer (played by Lars Hanson) portrayed a memorable dream character. In Molander's *To Damascus* (I) (1937), Lars Hanson created a protagonist who was fearful, wondering always whether or not he was dreaming. In Molander's *The Ghost Sonata* (1942), both the Student (played by Frank Sundström) and Hummel (played by Lars Hanson) were represented as "real" people — that is, spectators of plays-within-a-play — one of which, the ghost supper, at last engulfed Hummel.

In Ingmar Bergman's production of *A Dream Play* (1970), the drama was shown as a theatrical event that the Poet was creating while it took place on stage. The Poet, his creation, and the audience were all on the same level — as in Brecht's theatrical Verfremdung. Bergman was at that time not interested in creating the illusion of a dream, nor in creating any illusion at all. For his 1973 production of *The Ghost Sonata*, he perceived the play as Strindberg's dream and wanted gradually to penetrate deeper and deeper into the consciousness of the author. However, there was no clear expression of this intention in the production, other than an increasingly intense acting style. In Bergman's *To Damascus* (I) and (II) (1974) the Stranger (played by Jan-Olof Strandberg) was a part of the dream level, a character in sleeping dreams — "a mental landscape" created through an intensified expressionism in stage design and acting.[2]

Why so much fuss about dream atmosphere? Is it that important? I think so. If we exclude this effect from Strindberg's plays, we exclude a view of life: life as a dream — which I think is the basic aspect of the dream plays. If we can create a dream atmosphere on the stage of our minds, and in our theaters, we will gain the impression of a much truer reality, as if we were seeing behind the surface of illusion and reality into inner reality.

I have tired to demystify Strindberg and to show that dream atmosphere has nothing to do with imitation of sleeping dreams but that it relies on a particular scenic structure that is simple and practicable. Dream atmosphere is not achieved through exterior means or theatrical tricks (although they can help). It can be created in daylight in any space if the audience is made aware of this structure through visual means.

It is very difficult — if not impossible — to create a dream atmosphere in the theater if the director wants to depict actual sleeping dreams, but it is quite possible if reality is to be depicted as a dream, which is Strindberg's method. His dream atmosphere seems to build on the contrast between two levels: the transformation of reality into dreamlike reality and the relation between the protagonist and his or her world, in which he or she sometimes becomes a dream character in his or her own dream but ultimately is a spectator of a dreamlike play-within-a-play.

It is impossible to create an absolute illusion of reality on stage, but through the dream-play technique it is possible to create an absolute illusion of a dreamlike reality. Nobody in theater can deny that what is shown on stage really *is* a dreamlike reality — and this is perhaps Strindberg's greatest contribution to the history of drama and theater.

9

The Camera and the Aesthetics of Repetition: Strindberg's Use of Space and Scenography in Miss Julie, A Dream Play, and The Ghost Sonata

Freddie Rokem

The question of how that which the writer-dramatist wants to communicate is passed on to the reader-spectator as experience or knowledge was one of Strindberg's primary concerns. In several of his plays, the actual process of passing on information and the issue of its authenticity are placed in the foreground, thus confronting us as spectators with problems that careful narratological and rhetorical analysis of fiction has taught us as readers to carefully sift and weigh for possible counterversions that are in some way embedded in the text itself.[1]

In this paper I investigate how the visual information, based primarily on our perception of the scenographic elements in some of Strindberg's major plays, is "narrated" by the dramatist through the manner and order of its presentation to us. The playwright's selection of *locus* and events are the key to the narratological scheme of the play. An examination of how the dramatist-narrator has visually "cut into" the fictional world of his characters with his selection of stage events will clarify how the rhetorical devices affect us. Watching a theatrical performance (and reading a script) implies that we are constantly adjusting visual and verbal information to make it coherent. By concentrating here on the visual aspects, I hope to fill a gap in the appreciation of Strindberg's genius.

Freddie Rokem

In an interview about his art as a stage director, Ingmar Bergman made the following comparison between Ibsen and Strindberg:

To me, the most fascinating thing about Strindberg is that enormous awareness that everything in life, at every moment, is completely amoral — completely open and simply rooted. . . . With Ibsen, you always have the feeling of limits — because Ibsen placed them there himself. He was an architect, and he built. He always built his plays, and he knew exactly: I want this and I want that. He points the audience in the direction he wants it to go, closing doors, leaving no other alternatives. With Strindberg — as with Shakespeare — you always have the feeling that there are no such limits.[2]

This statement is true in several respects, finally, because Strindberg has presented us with a very subjective view of the world, a view that not only changed several times during his own career as a writer but also took sudden and unexpected turns within the individual works themselves. I will show how this subjectivity operates in the theater.

In Strindberg's dramatic production, the stylistic developments that had been started by Ibsen's decision — after writing *Peer Gynt* — to place the dramatic action in the bourgeois drawing room, now came full circle: in Strindberg's expressionistic plays we again find ourselves in the vast landscapes that have to be understood and interpreted as metaphorical explorations of the vast inner landscapes of the subjective mind. In *Peer Gynt* there is an excursion into these inner landscapes when Peer visits the world of the trolls. It can take place, however, only after Peer hits his head on the rock and faints (act 2). It is thus motivated on the "realistic" level of plot in the progression of the play. In Strindberg's post-Inferno plays, the so-called expressionistic ones, the motivation for this exposure of the inner regions of the mind is, however, only "aesthetic." This means that it is based solely on an acceptance by the spectator of the literary and theatrical conventions through which the protagonist's mental life is presented.

These aesthetic intentions were given a rather negative interpretation during Strindberg's own lifetime when the post-Inferno plays were originally published and performed in Stockholm (the first decade of this century). Even in the recent study *Tragic Drama and Modern Society* by John Orr, these conventions are seen as a limitation that finally hinges on Strindberg's own madness. Orr claims:

The limitation of Strindberg is seen more easily by comparison with the painting of Munch or Kokoschka. Here the expressionist method was used to enlarge the figurative dimensions of art and represented a step forward in the history of painting. But theatre invariably imposes a distance between the spectator and the hero which has to be overcome both technically and thematically by the actor's performance. It has no equivalent of the novelist's "point of view" which can lead us, through indirect speech, into the mind and sensibility of the character. Strindberg's attempt at such direct exposure through dramatic speech can be compelling and equally disturbing, but the sense of distance is always there. The attachment of an expressionist method to the exploration of the human unconscious ultimately led him to a pathological vision of the world.[3]

If, on the other hand, we accept the aesthetic "limitations" or "givens" of the theater as an artistic medium, limits that involve the fundamental issue of how and to what extent the inner privacy of the mind can be presented to an audience during a live performance, then the methods of perception developed by Strindberg do not seem as disturbing as Orr implies. Strindberg is, rather, bringing the narrative techniques of the theater into areas of perception that had not been explored before. As Orr rightly observes, the questions of point of view and narrative technique lie at the center of Strindberg's communication with his audience. This shift of emphasis in the modes of theatrical communication and perception has determined the nature of Strindberg's plays on almost all levels, although I will concentrate primarily on the visual implications of the shift. The major change Strindberg effects is the gradual abandonment of the realistic stage convention wherein the proscenium arch is the aesthetic frame through which the dramatic action and the fictional world are statically presented and perceived.

In the dramas of Ibsen and Chekhov, for instance, the proscenium arch is basically equivalent to the imaginary fourth wall that separates the stage action from the audience. It is a dividing line that places the dramatic action and the audience in a *static* relationship to each other. In Strindberg's plays, however, there is a constant manipulation of our vision and point of view, which in many respects resembles the function of the narrator in a novel or even the camera in a movie. Strindberg has elaborated a *dynamic* dramatic/ theatrical method of presentation through which he shows us his heroes and their fictional world from several changing points of view during the progress of the action. This also leads to a different, and sometimes much closer, involvement of the reader-spectator in the fictional world Strindberg presents than in those of Ibsen and Chekhov.

Susan Sontag, in an article analyzing the differences between theater and film, quotes Panofsky's formal distinctions between seeing a play and seeing a movie:

Freddie Rokem

In the theatre (Panofsky argues) "space is static; that is, the space represented on the stage, as well as the spatial relation of the beholder to the spectacle is unalterably fixed," while in the cinema, "the spectator occupies a fixed seat, but only physically, not as the subject of an aesthetic experience. In the theatre, the spectator cannot change his angle of vision." In the cinema the spectator is "aesthetically in permanent motion as his eye identifies with the lens of the camera, which permanently shifts in distance and direction."[4]

Sontag subsequently argues against Panofsky's attempt to keep the two art forms separate. Sontag quotes from several movies and theater styles to show that only in the use of "a realistic living room as a blank stage"[5] — that is, in the plays of Ibsen — does the theater become as static as Panofsky claims. Here I will argue, in concurrence with Sontag's views, that Strindberg developed theatrical techniques in which the eye of the spectator actually "identifies with the lens of the camera, which permanently shifts in distance and direction," and that he has actually turned this lens into an invisible narrator in some of his plays. I will primarily focus on *Miss Julie, A Dream Play,* and *The Ghost Sonata*. These plays illustrate Strindberg's fundamental dramatic-theatrical devices that bridge the distinctions often made between the pre- and post-Inferno plays. These similarities do not of course completely erase the important differences between these two periods in Strindberg's creative life.

No matter what final meaning we ascribe to Ibsen's plays, his principal characters are usually involved in quests toward understanding and overcoming specific past events that have become overshadowed by guilt. When these past experiences resurface, there is usually some kind of catastrophe. By "closing doors," as Ingmar Bergman expresses it, Ibsen really leaves "no other alternatives" for his heroes. In Chekhov's plays, all the doors have been opened, but his main characters have no deep urges or possibilities to use them to change their lives or move on to new situations or places. His protagonists are caught somewhere between paralysis and despair, which, precisely because the doors have been opened, involves them in very painful struggles. In the context of Chekhov's major plays, these struggles are understood neither as failures nor as successes, just as phases of suffering and despair, mixed with varying degrees of irony.

These fundamental differences of presentation of the fictional world are also expressed on the level of scenographic presentation. In Ibsen's realistic plays, the setting very often focuses on a single physical point, which, in terms of the play's action and the main character's past, is a visual representation of the past catastrophe. Examples of this principle are the attic in *The Wild Duck* or the mill stream in *Rosmersholm*. Chekhov, on the other hand, presents a scene that leads in several different directions. His protagonist stumbles because he or she is not sure which choice to make, whereas Ibsen's fails because his or her choice is undermined by a sense of guilt from the past.

In Strindberg's plays, it is never clear what his main character's world looks like and whether it has one or many focal points. This obviously makes it much harder to interpret his plays and is probably one of the reasons why so much of the criticism and interpretation of his work had drawn correlations between Strindberg's own life as son, husband, father, and writer and his literary output.[6] There was for a long time no other direction to take. His poetry, novels, and dramas have in several cases even been treated as private documents or "diaries" of a struggling individual, who in his writing sought a final and public outlet for his personal suffering. Strindberg himself is largely responsible for directing his critics toward this kind of criticism by writing the confessional autobiographical novels *The Defense of a Madman* and *The Son of a Servant.'*

Several of his plays, such as *Miss Julie, The Father, To Damascus* (I), and many more, have also been given biographical interpretations. In them he exposes not only the private lives of his characters but also his own private life in the public sphere of the theater. This of course is a further development of the dialectic between the private and the public, a very important aspect of theatrical communication, which in this case is realized in the form of open confession.

In analyzing the works of Ibsen and Chekhov it is possible to use the visual focal points in their fictional worlds as "keys" to interpreting the strivings and dreams of the characters. One of the salient features of these focal points, whether they are singular or multiple, seen or unseen, reachable or unattainable, is that apart from being physically present in the fictional world and in the consciousness of the characters, they are *static*. Once such a focal point has been established, in Ibsen's plays for example, there is a relatively high degree of certainty that it will remain in place until the characters have concluded their struggle at the end of the play. One of the primary guarantees and safeguards for this static quality is the steady frame of the proscenium arch through which the fictional world is perceived. And in Chekhov's plays, where there are several focal points or where the physical point of view changes in different acts, for example, in *The Cherry Orchard*, they still remain rather constant.

However, the assumptions that are part of the realistic tradition are drastically altered in Strindberg's plays. It is possible to identify two important features in several of his plays which, by being present in varying degrees, change the whole relationship between the presentation of the stage action and the perception of the audience. The first feature is a visual focal point that constantly changes or occasionally disappears or is very difficult to find; this feature is present in the proposed set for the play as well as in the consciousness of the characters in relation to the world they inhabit. The second important feature, which relates to the first, is the superimposition of some kind of "filter" or "camera" on the fictional world presented on stage. With the help of this "camera," Strindberg directs the audience's perception and vision of the stage world in a manner similar to the manipulations of the narrator in the novel and the camera in the movies. The camera has of course frequently been compared to the narrator.[7]

I am using the concept camera very deliberately here because Strindberg succeeded in arriving at theatrical effects that resemble the way a photograph "cuts out" a piece of reality: not a symmetrical joining of one wall to the other walls in the house — the basic fourth-wall technique of the realistic theater — but rather an asymmetrical cutting-out. Furthermore, Strindberg used cinematographic techniques resembling zoom, montage, and cut, which are highly significant from the strictly technical point of view and for the meaning of the plays. Historically, photography and movies were making great strides at the time and were art forms to which he himself — as photographer and as movie writer — gave considerable attention and interest. During Strindberg's lifetime, both *The Father* and *Miss Julie* were filmed as silent movies by the director Anna Hofman-Uddgren and her husband, Gustaf Uddgren, writer and friend of Strindberg, but only *The Father* has been preserved.[8]

Strindberg thus developed dramatic theatrical techniques that, like the movie camera, can bring the viewer very close to the depicted action and, at the same time, can quite easily change the point of view or direction of observing an event or succession of events. The disappearance or near disappearance of the static focal point is largely the result of the introduction of these different photographic and cinematographic techniques. When the characters, the action, and the fictional world are continuously presented, either from partial angles or from constantly changing ones, it is often impossible for the spectator to determine where the focal point is or what the central experiences are in the characters' world. This in turn is a reflection of the constant and usually fruitless search of the characters for such focal points in their own lives.

Whereas Hedda Gabler's lack of will to continue living was based on her refusal to bear offspring within the confines of married life, Miss Julie's despair primarily reflects her unwillingness merely to exist. Of course, there are external reasons for her suicide, and Strindberg has taken great care both in the play and in the preface almost to overdetermine her final act of despair. Nevertheless, as several critics have pointed out, there are no clear and obvious causal connections between her suicide and the motives presented. Instead, this final act of despair is triggered by an irrational leap into the complete unknown, as she herself says "ecstatically" (according to Strindberg's stage direction) in the final scene when she commands Jean, the servant, to command her, the mistress, to commit suicide: "I am already aleep — the whole room stands as if in smoke for me . . . and you look like an iron stove . . . that resembles a man dressed in black with a top hat — and your eyes glow like coal when the fire is extinguished — and your face is a white patch like the ashes."[9] These complex images within images resemble links in a chain, and they illustrate the constant movement or flux of the despairing speaker's mind. For Miss Julie there is no fixed point in reality, no focal point, except her will to die, to reach out for a nothingness.

In Strindberg's description of the set in the beginning of *Miss Julie*, he carefully specifies how the diagonal back wall cuts across the stage from left to right, opening up in the vaulted entry toward the garden. This vault however, is only partially visible. The oven and the table are also only partially visible because they are situated exactly on the borderline between the stage and the offstage areas. The side walls and the ceiling of the kitchen are marked by draperies and tormentors. Except for the garden entry, there are no doors or windows. As the play reveals, the kitchen is connected only to the private bedrooms of the servants Jean and Kristin; there is no direct access to the upper floor where the count and his daughter, Julie, live except through the pipe-telephone.

In his preface to the play, Strindberg explained: "I have borrowed from the impressionistic paintings the idea of the asymmetrical, the truncated, and I believe that thereby, the bringing forth of the illusion has been gained; since by not seeing the whole room and all the furnishings, there is room for imagination, i.e., fantasy is put in motion and it completes what is seen."[10] Here Strindberg describes the imaginative force of this basically metonymic set. But rather than following the custom in realistic theater of showing the *whole* room as part of a house that in turn is part of the fictional world of the play, Strindberg very consciously exposes only *part* of the room. He claims it should be completed in the imagination of the audience. As Evert Sprinchorn comments: "The incompleteness of the impressionist composition drew the artist and the viewer into closer personal contact, placing the viewer in the scene and compelling him to identify with the artist at a particular moment."[11]

The audience comes closer not only to the artist through this view of the kitchen from its interior but also, by force of the diagonal arrangements of the set, to the characters inside the kitchen. This is because the fourth wall, on which the realistic theater was originally based, has been moved to an undefined spot somewhere in the auditorium, the spectators are in the same room as the dramatic characters. It is also important to note that, to achieve this effect, Strindberg also removed the side walls from the stage, thus preventing the creation of any kind of symmetrical room that the spectator could comfortably watch from the outside. Furthermore, the audience is not guided regarding the symmetries, directions, or focal points in the set itself, which the traditional theater strongly emphasized. The only area that is separated from the kitchen is the garden, visible through the vaulted entry, with its fountain and, significantly enough, its statue of Eros. Thus, the physical point of view of the audience in relationship to the stage is ambiguous.

What is presented is a "photograph" of the kitchen taken from its interior, drawing the audience's attention to different points inside or outside as the play's action develops. The set of Miss Julie can, furthermore, be seen as a photograph because while the spectators get a close view from the inside of the kitchen, they also experience an objective perception of it and the events taking place there through the frame of the proscenium arch. The comparison between Strindberg's scenic technique in Miss Julie and the photograph is compelling because of the very strong tension between intimacy and closeness on the one hand and objectivity and distance on the other; this sort of tension has often been observed to be one of the major characteristics not only of the play but also of photography, as the practice of documenting and preserving large numbers of slices of reality. The photograph also "cuts" into a certain space from its inside, never showing walls as parallel (unless it is a very big space photographed from the outside), at the same time it freezes the attention of the viewer upon the specific moment. In photography the focus is on the present (tense), which is "perfected" into a "has been" through the small fraction of a second when the shutter is opened. Barthes even goes so far as to call this moment in photography an epiphany.[12]

This is also what happens in Miss Julie when the attention of the audience is continuously taken from one temporary focal point to the next by force of the gradual development of the action. Our eyes and attention move from the food Jean is smelling to the wine he is tasting, to Miss Julie's handkerchief, to Kristin's fond folding and smelling of the handkerchief when Jean and Miss Julie are at the dance and so on. In Miss Julie these material objects force the characters to confront one another and to interact. They are not objects primarily belonging to or binding the characters to the distant past toward which they try to reach out in their present sufferings — as are the visual focal points in Ibsen's plays or even the samovars and pieces of old furniture in Chekhov's plays. The objects in Miss Julie are first and foremost immersed in the present, forcing the characters to take a stance and their present struggles to be closely observed by the audience.

In Miss Julie the past and the future have been transformed into fantasy, so the only reality for the characters is the present. Because Jean and Miss Julie are forced to act solely on the basis of the immediate stimuli causing their interaction, and because the kitchen has been cut off diagonally leaving no visually defined borders on- or offstage, it is impossible to locate any constant focal points, either outside or inside the fictional world of the play and the subjective consciousness of the characters. This "narrative" technique achieves both a very close and subjective view of the characters and a seemingly objective and exact picture of them. The temporal retrospection has also been diminished because Jean and Miss Julie are not as disturbed by irrational factors belonging to a guilt-ridden past as, for example, the Ibsen heroes are. Strindberg's characters are motivated primarily by their present desires.

This of course does not mean that there are no expository references to the past in *Miss Julie*; on the contrary, there are a large number of references to specific events in the lives of the characters preceding the opening of the scenic action. The play, in fact, begins with a series of such references, all told by Jean to Kristin. Thus, we learn that Miss Julie is "mad again tonight" (inferring that it is not the first time this has happened), as represented by the way she is dancing with Jean. And to give her behavior some perspective (just before her entrance), Jean relates to Kristin how Miss Julie's fiancé broke their engagement because of the degradations he had to suffer, jumping over her whip as well as being beaten by it. These events are, however, never corroborated by other characters in the play. Miss Julie's subsequent behavior does to some extent affirm Jean's story, but we can never be completely sure.

What is specific to Strindberg's plays is not the omission of the past — which absurdist drama emphasizes — but rather a lack of certainty regarding the reliability of what the characters say about that past. And since in many of Strindberg's plays there is no source of verification other than the private memory of the character speaking, the past takes on a quite subjective quality. Miss Julie gives *her* version of *her* past and Jean relates *his*, and the possible unreliability of these memories is confirmed when Jean changes his story of how he as a child watched her in the garden. Unlike the past in most of Ibsen's plays, which is objectively verified through the independent affirmations of other characters. There are certain important events that cannot always be completely verified, such as the real identity of Hedvig's father in *The Wild Duck*, but the characters act on the assumption that they know. And there is enough evidence, given by several characters independently of one another, to grant that they are right.

The major outcome of past actions, guilt, is objectified in Ibsen's plays. That is the reason why it can be given a specific geographical location in the outside world, which becomes the "focus" (in all respects) for it. In Strindberg's fictional worlds there is definitely an awareness of past actions, that is of guilt, but it exists as a private limbo in the subjective consciousness of the individual characters and thus cannot be projected onto the objective outside world. That is why in Strindberg's plays there is either no visual focus or a constantly moving one.

In *Miss Julie* the two principal characters continuously try to turn their respective opponents into the focal point onto which their own guilt and related feelings of inadequacy and general frustration can be projected. That is one of the major reasons for their sexual union and the distrust and even hatred to which it leads. Just how fickle those focal points are, however, can also be seen as in Miss Julie's last desperate attempt to find some kind of support in Jean for her step into the unknown realm of death. Jean's face has become a white spot, resembling to Miss Julie the ashes of a fire because the light of the sun — which is rising at this point in the play — is illuminating him. Again the present situation becomes the point of departure for her wishes. And when Miss Julie wants to die, her wish is thus focused on Jean's illuminated face. In *Ghosts* Ibsen used the same images (the fire and the sun) at the end of the last two acts as objective focal points. Strindberg has compressed these images into one speech in which they are projected onto Jean by the fantasy of Miss Julie's subjective consciousness. Ibsen gives a "scientific" explanation of Oswald's madness for which the sunset is a circumstantial parallel, whereas Strindberg lets the sunset motivate the outburst of Julie's death wish, as expressed from within. Thus the preparations for the introduction of expressionism, wherein everything is projection, had already been made in Strindberg's pre-Inferno plays.[13]

In *A Dream Play*, in which the subjective is much more emphatically central than it is in *Miss Julie*, Strindberg wished to integrate and develop the complex procedures of perception related to photography with an explicit moral vision of humanity. In *A Dream Play* there is not only a single lens photographing the stage of tragic events at one relatively fixed point in time and space as in *Miss Julie* but a complicated camera that zooms in and out on the events and juxtaposes different images in space and time through a dream filter, using a montage technique.

In his first expressionistic play, *To Damascus* (I), in which the protagonist quickly moves from one place to another, Strindberg used a variation of the "station drama,"[14] employing a mirror construction. This means that the scenes of part II, after the climax in the Asylum, are arranged in reverse order from part I and lead the hero gradually back to the place where he began. In a letter to a friend, the Swedish author Geijerstam, Strindberg described his use of this structure:

The Camera and the Aesthetics of Repetition

The act lies in the composition, which symbolizes the repetition (Gentagelsen) Kierkegaard is talking about; the events roll up towards the asylum; there they reach the edge and are thrown back again; the pilgrimage, the homework to be done over again, the swallowings; and then things start anew, where the game ends it also started. You may not have noticed that the scenes roll up backwards from the Asylum, which is the backbone of the book which closes and encloses the plot. Or like a snake that bites its own tail.[15]

When Strindberg in his short preface to *A Dream Play* also refers to the "nonconnected but seemingly logical form"[16] of the dream used in this play (as well as in the earlier *To Damascus*), the assumption that the mirror construction has also been applied would not be far-fetched. In *In A Dream Play*, however, the realization of the mirror construction is only partial and very fragmentary. In its present form, the play contains the following scenes:

1. prologue in heaven
2. garden with growing castle
3. a room in the castle
4. another room in the castle with the dead parents
5. opera corridor
6. Lawyer's office
7. church
8. Fingal's Cave
9. living room behind Lawyer's office
10. Foul Strand (Fair Haven behind)
11. Fair Haven (Foul Strand behind)
12. classroom in yellow house in Fair Haven
13. by the Mediterranean
14. Fingal's Cave
15. opera corridor
16. outside the castle

Lamm claims that Strindberg had actually intended at some point to repeat the scheme of mirror construction from *To Damascus* (I) but that he later abandoned it. Ollén has called the structure of the play "Contrapuntal" in an attempt to reflect Strindberg's own use of musical terminology to describe his dramatic structure, as in the Chamber Plays. Sprinchorn has likewise argued that the repetition of certain scenes reinforces the cyclical structure for the purpose of what he sees as a Freudian "secondary elaboration."[17]

However, as can be easily seen in the preceding enumeration of scenes, Strindberg has actually repeated only three scenes in part II. Going backward, scene 16 repeats the location of scene 2, scene 15 returns to that of scene 5, and scene 14 to that of scene 8. It is worth noting that in the last three scenes of part II the locations of three different scenes from part I (2,5,8) are repeated, and that each time two scenes from part I (3-4 and 6-7) are skipped in the return. Scene 13, the scene with social pathos, which takes place by the Mediterranean, does not appear in part I and, as a matter of fact, Strindberg added it, along with the opening scene — the prologue in heaven — to the already finished play at a later time. In one sense the scenes of Foul Strand and Fair Haven are also repetitions because each time the other is shown in the background. The aesthetic technique Strindberg employed in the scenic depiction of the two beaches, which is where the so-called edge mentioned in his letter about *To Damascus* (I) is located, will be carefully analyzed below.

In the kind of artistic economy that Strindberg practiced in *A Dream Play*, the scenes missing in the mirror construction are not completely absent, however. Instead of visually repeating the scenic images from part I in reverse order in part II, Strindberg often repeats on the level of dialogue and appearance of representative characters. These repetitions become in effect reminders of the scenes that are missing. They also, interestingly enough, usually appear in the text in the exact reverse order from part I, so that we are at least reminded of the mirror construction. In part II the Lawyer's dwellings, the church, and the Lawyer's office are not presented as full scenes but are referred to textually; the journey of Indra is proceeding in reverse order. The Lawyer appears at the end of the schoolhouse scene (scene 12) asking his wife to return to their home (scene 9 in part I). At the end of his second appearance in Fingal's Cave (scene 14) the Poet has a vision of the church tower, which returns us to the church (scene 7 in part I), which then came before the cave (scene 8). At the end of the second opera corridor scene (scene 15) the Lawyer again appears, reminding his rebellious wife of her duties and thus repeating the scene in the Lawyer's office (scene 6 in part I). In this last example the strict order of the mirror construction is, however, somewhat upset.

One interesting instance of this verbal repetition of scenes is the description of the soldiers marching on the tower of the church (end of scene 14), an image Lamm refers to as "one of those places in *A Dream Play* where the reader is called upon to make fruitless interpretations."[18] In the framework of the scenic structure of the play, however, Strindberg actually makes us return to the church (scene 7 in part I) through the powerful image of death. This poetic description recalls the complex arrangement of image within image seen in *Miss Julie* when the fire in the oven is extinguished, when one image becomes involved in the next through a constant metamorphosis between light and shadow. The Poet in *A Dream Play* is describing soldiers marching on a field while the sun is shining on a church so that its shadow can be seen on the field. Through the juxtaposition of images on the field, they appear to be actually walking on the church tower:

> Now they are on the cross, but I perceive it as if the first one who is walking on the rooster must die . . . now they approach . . . the corporal is the first one . . . haha! A cloud is approaching, covering the sun of course . . . now they are all gone. . . . The water of the cloud extinguished the fire of the sun! The light of the sun created the dark image of the tower, but the dark image of a cloud muffled the dark image of the tower.[19]

What we see on the field is actually some kind of photographic image, a "dark image" (*mökerbild* in Swedish), a negative through which the movement of the cloud is transformed into another image. It is worth emphasizing that in both plays Strindberg superimposed images of light and shadow — a technique closely related to photography — to create the different images of death.

In addition to the complex metamorphosis on the level of imagery, the scenery onstage changes from Fingal's Cave to the corridor outside the opera while the poet is speaking (from scene 14 to 15), thus superimposing additional images upon the already rather complex visual images presented. This combination of verbal and visual images could without a doubt be termed theatrical montage, in analogy to Eisenstein's "film montage."

Before I analyze how and when the "edge" of *A Dream Play* is reached, I must make some general remarks about the technique of "zooming" in *A Dream Play*. What the audience actually *sees*, at least in the first part of *A Dream Play*, is a fictional dream world, a world with a "dream atmosphere" (*drömstämning*), to use Bark's terminology,[20] in which the walls of the castle and of other dwellings are peeled off, crumble, or simply go through various metamorphoses, gradually drawing the audience closer and closer toward the fictional offstage world, in the direction of some kind of center that remains elusive. This is, as a matter of fact, a visual version of Peer Gynt's famous onion, which leaves him with empty hands after it is completely peeled. Strindberg very carefully specifies in his stage directions that the transitions from scene 2 to 8, 9 to 13, and 14 to 16, respectively, stress the continuity of movement from scene to scene. Backdrops and screens are removed, replaced, or turned when the curtain is open, and objects that had a certain function in one scene are transformed through the dream to reappear with a different function in the next.

One of many such changes is the transformation of the organ in the church in scene 7 into Fingal's Cave near the ocean in scene 8, a shift effected primarily by lighting, as the stage directions indicate. The continuity between the different locations presented on stage is strongly stressed and represents Strindberg's theatrical expression of the connectedness of images in the dreamer's mind. Strindberg has introduced a theatrical, aesthetic continuity as a reflection of the dream, thereby underscoring its isolation from all kinds of everyday reality. As Harry Carlson has explained, the aesthetic principle behind these transformations is the revelation of "a critical continuity of identity between the two scenes. Objects have changed, but somehow remain the same. One implication is that no matter how the two locations may seem to differ from each other, underneath they are fundamentally alike: we are still in a world of illusion and pain."[21] I must stress, however, that this identity is not static because there is flux and movement from place to place effected by the zoom action of the "camera" through which we perceive Strindberg's fictional world.

The two outdoor scenes at Foul Strand and Fair Haven (10 and 11) are extremely important with regard to the visual aesthetics of *A Dream Play*. When we see the ugly landscape of Foul Strand in the foreground in the first of these two scenes, beautiful Fair Haven can be made out in the background on the other side of the bay that separates them. In the following scene, after the short blackout prescribed in the stage directions, the relative positions of Foul Strand and Fair Haven have changed so that Fair Haven is now visible in the foreground, the bay again in the middle ground, and Foul Strand submerged in shadow in the background. This kind of visual technique, which can be termed a "turn-around," has been used by Strindberg several times. The "turn-around," or "edge," as Strindberg calls it in his letter to Geijerstam, is the place from which the scenes are rolled up backward again. The very important innovation in *A Dream Play*, however, is the interesting manipulation of the spectator's point of view. It can be described as a change of position on the part of the audience so that after the "turn-around," the fictional world is perceived from exactly the opposite standpoint: in each of these two scenes the other place is seen in the background. Through the change of angle or "camera" position, the audience is allowed to see the action from a vantage point behind the scene, thereby viewing from behind what was formerly seen from the front.

With the help of Strindberg's "camera lens" on the action, the audience can not only follow the heroine from one point in space to another as in picaresque "station drama" but also examine the fictional world by perceiving it through specific angles, perspectives, and sudden jumps from one point in space to another diametrically opposite point in space. In cinematographic terms, the camera has moved, and, from the audience's perspective, Indra's slow and gradual return to heaven is now seen from the completely opposite angle.

It is thus as a result of the "turn-around," or reversal of directions, that the backward movement in the scenic succession is actually precipitated. Now the camera that had been zooming in toward the open seaside lands-cape of the archipelago has been turned the opposite way. But instead of returning directly to the home of the Lawyer and his rebellious wife, we are given a look into the schoolhouse where the grown-up Officer is sent back to the schoolbench and where normal everyday logic breaks down. At this point the Lawyer appears again to remind his wife of the duties that still remain: "Now, you have seen almost everything, but you have not seen the worst. . . . /Repetition. . . . Returns. . . . Going back! . . . Redoing the homework. . . . Come!"[22] Both Agnes and the Officer thus have to return in humiliation to a former traumatic situation of confinement. This is, however, not simply a return to a trite childhood or marital reality; in the larger structure of the play, the heroine is taking the route back to heaven, the place from where she originally came.

Strindberg has, as he explains in the letter to Geijerstam, employed the Kierkegaardian moral-psychological concept of *gentagelsen*, or repetition, in *A Dream Play*. In 1843 Søren Kierkegaard had published an introspective work called *Repetition: An Essay in Experimental Psychology*, which Strindberg clearly knew about or had read. Kierkegaard's work is a philosophical and autobiographical explication of the moral-psychological concept of repetition. He writes:

> When one does not possess the categories of recollection or of repetition the whole of life is resolved into a void and empty noise. Recollection is the pagan view of life, repetition is the modern view of life, repetition is the *interest* of metaphysics, and at the same time the interest upon which metaphysics founders; repetition is the solution contained in every ethical view, repetition is a *conditio sine qua non* of every dogmatic problem.[23]

In *A Dream Play* Kierkegaard's moral concept is also used as an aes-thetic structuring principle in that the idea of return is the basis for devel-opment of the plot and for the succession of the dramatic locations. Strind-berg also applied it on the moral level of the play in that the central lesson Indra learns about humankind is that everything in life is repetitious. This is true of the small and the large duties of everyday life, the fixed return to childhood and, of course, the constant suffering of all humankind, which is the central theme repeated over and over again in the play. One could even claim that Strindberg attempts to unify the ethical and aesthetic spheres, presented as irreconcilable opposites in Kierekegaard's *Either/Or*, by showing in *A Dream Play* that repetition is an aesthetic concept as well as a moral one. For Indra and the Poet, beauty is contained within the ethical law based on her return to heaven, which, in terms of the play's aesthetics, is structurally worked out as a formal repetition. The theme and concept of repetition is thus embedded in the play in multilevel fashion to interweave its aesthetic and moral dimensions.

It is also possible to compare Strindberg's methods of theatrical composition and perception with the perceptual modes developed at about the same time by Picasso in his cubist paintings.[24] In his attempt to depict a three-dimensional reality in a two-dimensional medium, Picasso gave a pictorial account of how he moved around the depicted objects in space by showing through paint on canvas what these men and women looked like from different angles simultaneously. Strindberg, working in the three-dimensional, temporal medium of theater, also depicted characters and objects from several angles and points of view. By repeating the events and locations from the first part of *A Dream Play* from *behind* the scene in the second part, the audience is visually drawn into the fictional world from two completely opposite points of view.

This multiple perspective technique is also comparable to the complex structure developed by Stoppard in *Rosencrantz and Guildenstern are Dead*, in which a certain number of episodes in the backstage world of *Hamlet* are independently dramatized. We can even imagine two audiences — one watching Shakespeare's play and the other watching Stoppard's — sometimes seeing the same play from diametrically opposed angles but usually watching different parts of one fictional world. The actor in Stoppard's play tells Rosencrantz and Guildenstern what they, as actors, are really doing in the theater: "We keep to our usual, more or less, only inside out. We do on stage the things that are supposed to happen off. Which is a kind of integrity, if you look on every exit being an entrance somewhere else."[25]

The aesthetics of repetition Strindberg in various ways developed has been extremely important for writers like Beckett, Pinter, Ionesco, and Genet and for modern theater and art in general.[26] Suffice it to mention here that when we are watching *Waiting for Godot* we have no idea how many times the ritual of waiting has been repeated before the play starts and between the two acts. This kind of repetition is very different from the probing of their own past in which Ibsen's protagonists are involved or the nostalgia in which Chekhov's are caught. Strindberg's protagonists are trapped in a condition that, once we accept the premises and the presentation, is a universal Sisyphean limbo, not just a psychological probing into the tragic past of an individual. One of the primary features of this Strindbergian *condition humaine* is the fact that the protagonists are caught and imprisoned in behavioral patterns and in a fictional world they are never sure they can leave or transcend, not even at the moment of death, unless of course the protagonist is a divinity, as is Indra's daughter in *A Dream Play*.

In *The Dance of Death* (I), for example, the central theme is that there is definitely no transcendence from the repetitive patterns Edgar and Alice have created in their marriage. The five opening lines of the play are extremely indicative of the kind of repetitive life the couple has led for almost twenty-five years:

THE CAPTAIN: Would you like to play something for me?

ALICE: What shall I play?

THE CAPTAIN: What you want!

ALICE: You don't like my repertoire!

THE CAPTAIN: And you don't like mine![27]

The Captain's request to hear his wife play something is not granted at all at this point; much later she plays the "Dance of the Bojar," during which he has his famous fainting spell, a symbolic death within a life that is very much like death. Alice does not answer but retorts with another question, which leaves it up to the Captain to decide what music he wants to hear. But he also refuses to make a decision and returns the initiative to Alice, who refrains once more by claiming that he does not like her repertoire, to which he in turn retorts that she does not like his.

This kind of procedure in which both partners refuse to gratify the other one is repeated over and over in *The Dance of Death* (I) until, ironically enough, they agree at the end of the play to seek reconciliation in the celebration of their twenty-fifth wedding anniversary. The repetitive patterns of behavior from which their marriage suffers are expressed implicitly on the level of the dialogue itself. The use of the word repertoire, ambiguously referring to Alice's playing the piano as well as to all the petty tricks of their married life, is the key to the motif of repetition in the play; this repertoire is constantly repeated.

The principle of repetition, as Strindberg developed it in his plays, was an attempt to artistically concretize something beyond the particular fate of the individual and to reach a dramatic formulation of a universal human condition. Strindberg's characters are not primarily motivated as individuals trying to find a solution to a personal problem, as are Ibsen's, but are representative types of human beings, caught in an existential dilemma in which there apparently is very little or no chance for redemption.

The spatial-scenographic metaphor most frequently used by Strindberg to express this universal condition is the presentation of different kinds of closed spaces from which the main characters cannot escape. The kitchen in *Miss Julie*, the Captain's hiding room in *The Father*, and the straitjacket into which he is tricked are motivated primarily on the realistic level, even though they achieve a more general social or spiritual significance. In *The Dance of Death* (I), however, the tower in which Edgar and Alice "live" is a metaphysical and spiritual prison that makes it impossible for them to escape from their "death in life." In *A Dream Play* this imprisonment is dramatized on a grand scale through the separation and opposition between the worlds of matter and spirit. There remains only one channel of communication between them through which the daughter of Indra but not the mortals can escape. The sufferings of this world are a universal condition for which there is no solution — except for death itself.

In my opinion the play by Strindberg that most forcefully presents death, not only as the accidental outcome of a situation where all other solutions have failed but as the one necessary escape from the confinement of the base repetitiveness of the material world, is *The Ghost Sonata*. Here the Young Lady gradually withers away into a death that is the logical result of the degraded and depraved spiritual condition of humanity. Not even the love of the Student can redeem her from this universal depravation.

I am particularly concerned with how the scenography expresses this separation from life and the growing awareness that ultimate truth lies beyond life in *The Ghost Sonata*.[28] The visual representation is in this case too, of course, parallel to the textual elaboration of the same theme: behind the façade of appearances and that which *seems* to be true about the lives of the characters in the play, a very different truth has been hidden. What we initially perceive is false. Hypocrisy and deception reside behind the walls of the modern well-to-do bourgeois house presented in the first act. As they are gradually exposed, they threaten to shatter the very foundations not only of the house but of society and the whole social order as well. The play's revolutionary message has, however, been immersed in an atmosphere of resignation and religious sentiments so that when *The Ghost Sonata* ends, the only future that seems to remain is one of eternal death. The three short acts of the play present a gradually intensified revelation of the rotten foundations of the house as well as of society itself. Visually this is presented by a gradual zooming in toward the center of the house.

The first act presents the exterior facade of the house, the street corner with a fountain, and a telephone booth; and through the windows on the facade, the so-called oval room is visible. In the second act, the Strindbergian camera has zoomed in on the oval room, which now opens up into two different directions in the background: to the right is the green room where the Colonel can be seen, and to the left is the hyacinth room where the Young Lady is visible from the beginning of this act and where the Student later joins her. The third act takes place in the orientally furnished hyacinth room, which was visible in the background during the second act. This succession accentuates the continuity of the fictional space throughout the three acts. But instead of zooming in on the scene in the hyacinth room from the oval room and thereby gradually drawing the audience into the fictional world in straight one-directional fashion, Strindberg has effected a "turn-around" with his camera, displaying (in act 3) the oval room — which was the setting for act 2 — in the background with the Colonel and the Mummy visible through a door on the right. The kitchen, from which the destructive forces of this act appear in the form of the vampiric Cook, appears in the background on the left.

The effects this "turn-around" can have on an audience are quite stunning. At the end of the ghost supper in the second act, the mad Mummy who has been imprisoned in the closet for twenty years is finally released. The Mummy is actually the Young Lady's mother, who conceived her with Hummel, her former lover, outside of her marriage. It is mainly the guilt resulting from this union that has led the Mummy to a state of death and madness, and only through the mock reunion with Hummel (who, because he killed the Milkmaid, is even more guilt-ridden than she) can she be released. When Hummel takes over her place in the closet, it is a ceremonially structured revenge, which in a way is also a minor "turn-around," wherein the characters exchange points of view. Hummel, his sinful past now completely revealed, is, by taking the Mummy's place, thus "liberating" her, while one of the servants, Bengtsson, places a death screen in front of the door of the closet. After all the characters present have pronounced a ceremonial "amen" over the death of Hummel, Strindberg directs the audience's attention toward the hyacinth room — in the background behind the oval room — where the Student is singing a song of reconciliation and hope with the Young Lady accompanying him on the harp. The older generation has found no resolution to their conflicts and guilt except in hatred and revenge, so the audience is naturally guided to the only existing hope: the younger generation.

The setting of the third act confirms this hope because, as mentioned above, it takes place in the hyacinth room where the young couple has been seated throughout the second act. Thus our attention has gradually become focused on the young couple and the possibility of a happy future for them. Because of the "turn-around," the older generation — having definitely outplayed its role — has been placed in the background. The "turn-around" changes the audience's point of view in relation to action in space, since it is now viewing from "behind" what was formerly seen from the "front," as in *A Dream Play*. Moreover, the "turn-around" changes the audience's temporal points of reference: in act 2 the young couple in the background represent the future and its possibilities, in act 3 the characters in the background represent the lost past and its guilt and limitations.

Strindberg has also achieved another interesting effect in the passage from the second to the third act, an effect involving our perceptions and interpretation of time as well as space. The first words uttered in the third act are the Young Lady's exclamation "Sing now for my flowers!" They seem to refer directly to the song about the sun that the Student has just sung at the end of act 2, while he and the Young Lady were still in the background. Thus there seems to be a temporal continuity in the plot, as in Ibsen's *John Gabriel Borkmann* in which all the acts are consecutive. What at first seems to be temporal continuity is in fact underlined by the spatial continuity of the same two rooms in both acts. This sense of continuity is further reinforced by the continuing presence in act 3 of almost all the characters from act 2. The Student and the Young Lady are now in the foreground instead of the background, and the Colonel and the Mummy — "the parents" — remain in the oval room following the fatal ghost supper that has just ended.

After approximately five minutes of performance, however, the audience learns through the young couple's conversation that Hummel's funeral has already taken place; thus it is *not* seeing a scene directly subsequent in time to the death scene of Hummel that took place at the end of act 2. This detail is one of the ever more numerous contradictions between what the audience *thinks* it sees and what is actually presented. Törnqvist affirms this interpretation of the play: "The fundamental theme or leitmotif of *The Ghost Sonata* is found in the conflict between illusion and reality, between *Sein* and *Schein*. In the antithesis between mask and face, façade and interior, word and deed, in the depiction of the dead — everywhere we are confronted with the fundamental idea that the world is not what it looks like and mankind not what it seems to be."[29] Strindberg has transformed not only the Student (who, as Törnqvist has pointed out, is the protagonist-observer in the play) but also every spectator into an active participant-observer in the revelation of deceptions and lies and the discovery of something that at least for the moment *seems* to be closer to the truth. The audience thus becomes involved in the actual process of discovery, Aristotelian *anagorisis*, not only through the mediation of the characters and their dialogue but through directly presented theatrical events. In this kind of direct presentation the spectators are no longer passive eavesdroppers who can sit back and pass moral judgments on what they see. Instead they have become active participants in the process of perception and interpretation itself, just as the protagonist perceives and interprets what to him *seems* to be the truth.

The "camera" Strindberg has introduced as a mediator between the fictional events and the audience does not necessarily bring the audience closer to the truth of the depicted reality in *The Ghost Sonata*. Rather, it brings it so close to the action, selecting the angles and points of view in such a narrow manner, that the moment new information is available, enabling the audience to make new connections and draw different conclusions — which the very limited "camera angle" has left unexplored or ambiguous — the fictional reality itself has to be reinterpreted and reevaluated. The problem is not that the "camera" lies; it just gives a very limited and selective slice of reality, one that can heavily distort the images projected, especially in their relationship to the fictional world as a whole. By presenting in *The Ghost Sonata* the possibility of distortions of fictional reality and by emphasizing the role of the spectators as participant-observers in such clear terms, Strindberg has in effect precisely identified the limitations in the methods of representation and perception that the realist theater thought it could solve unambiguously by tearing down the fourth wall of the drawing room, thereby opening it up for what was considered "objective" observation. Strindberg showed, however, that the closer the distance from which spectators observe an event, the more "subjective" their viewpoints.

The Ghost Sonata also contains an image of inversion that is related to the light-shadow images from *Miss Julie* and *A Dream Play*. In the latter plays, death is seen as a photographic image in which there is some kind of exchange between light and shadow. In *The Ghost Sonata*, this reversal is conceived in terms of language and silence. Hummel claims that languages are codes and that words actually hide the truth. It is only through silence that everything is revealed, he says. Furthermore, it is when the Student wants to tell the Young Lady "his" truth about her beauty that she gradually crumbles behind the death screen. When the screen makes its second appearance in the play, to separate the Young Lady from the world, the Student can only give her his blessings for having been able to escape from all the madness and suffering of this material world.

Just as what the audience sees is a clouded reality, what it hears is masked truth. Silence alone hovers over truth, as in Wittgenstein's enigmatic final statement in his *Tractatus Logico-Philosophicus*: "Wovon man nicht darüber, reden kann, muss man schweigen" (What we cannot speak about we must pass over in silence). In *The Ghost Sonata*, this silence is realized through that final exit behind the death screen where some kind of truth can supposedly be reached. But the living have no access to it. In its unattainability it resembles the frustrated attempts of Didi and Gogo to reach the world of Godot, who is situated beyond the place where they are now.

Strindberg leaves no road unexplored in his effort to materialize the grandeur of that beyond. The final gesture of the play, when *"the room disappears; Boecklin's* Toten-Insel *becomes the backdrop,"*[30] is Strindberg's desperate effort to make the immaterial perceivable. The movement of the "camera" in space thus becomes completely frozen, showing the barren landscape that cannot be further penetrated. If only because the audience's perceptions cannot stretch any farther.

PART III

The Naturalistic
or Supernaturalistic Plays:
Dramatic Discourse
and Stagings

10

Strindberg's Vision: Microscopic or Spectroscopic?

James McFarlane

In *The Father*, when Laura seeks to convince the Doctor that her husband is mentally ill, she offers as a self-evident absurdity the fact that he should claim to explain distant cosmic phenomena by peering into a microscope at little bits of rock.

LAURA: My husband's mind is unbalanced. . . . Is it sensible for a person to claim to see in a microscope what is happening on another planet?[1]

Whereupon the Doctor has to admit that it seems to be a *prima facie* case. But Strindberg immediately permits the Captain to put the record straight.

CAPTAIN: My duties don't give me time for extensive research, but I do think I'm on to a new discovery. . . . I've been submitting meteorites to spectral analysis, and I've found carbon! Evidence of organic life! . . .

DOCTOR: You can see that in a microscope?

CAPTAIN: Good God, no! A spectroscope!

DOCTOR: Spectroscope? Ah, forgive me, Well then, you'll soon be able to tell us what is happening on Jupiter.

CAPTAIN: Not what *is* happening, but what has happened.

James McFarlane

It is thus firmly established that the objects in question are not any old pieces of rock but meteoric stones, that the instrument being used is not a microscope but a spectroscope, and that the submission of meteoric stones to spectrum analysis in this way is an entirely reputable research undertaking. Strindberg thereupon creates an early opportunity for the Doctor to make the situation incontrovertibly clear to Laura (and of course to the audience):

> DOCTOR: You were mistaken . . . when you told me that he'd arrived at these astonishing results about other heavenly bodies using a microscope. I now learn that it was a spectroscope. So he is not only free of any suspicion of mental derangement, but indeed has made a positive contribution to science.

I have included these familiar scenes to demonstrate how very determinedly Strindberg drives his point home and how explicit is his use of what I suggest must be considered a key dramatic image in the understanding of Strindberg.

In its barest essentials, it is an image that juxtaposes the "small" (i.e., the closely focused scrutiny of a relatively tiny object) and the "big" (a problem of veritably cosmological proportions in respect of objects remote in time and space and otherwise beyond the reach of human comprehension); and it then further juxtaposes two different ways in which, in this particular set of circumstances, the small and the big are brought into mutual and meaningful relationship. One (the spectroscopic) is revealed as the appropriate, legitimate, and authentic and the other as the inappropriate, illegitimate, and inauthentic.

As I contemplate the problems of attempting to define the characteristic genius of Strindberg, of attempting to place him in the historical context of nineteenth- and twentieth-century literature, and of assessing his contribution to the enormous cultural shifts and displacements of the modern world, I find both this particular image and the use to which it is put by Strindberg in this drama powerfully suggestive.

One possible and even rewarding way open to the cultural historian of charting the development of modern thought might indeed be to see it as a continuing preoccupation with the small and the big. In one sense of course this has been a matter that has occupied the human mind since the very dawn of consciousness. But the attention lavished by thinkers, writers, and artists since the early nineteenth century on natural phenomena of ever-diminishing smallness and ever-increasing bigness has taken on the characteristics of an obsession. In recent years our concern with these things has taken us to the very limits of human understanding; and the penetration into first the atomic and subsequently the subatomic world has, in its intensity of purpose, been matched only by our exploration on the very frontiers of time and space of phenomena of literally cosmic significance. Western science has obeyed a compulsion to explore places where, indeed, instruments like the microscope and the telescope — instruments essentially designed to enlarge or reduce the dimensions of the observed phenomena into the normal range of human vision and understanding —no longer suffice. More and more our understanding of the physical world depends on abstract and imaginative constructs based on phenomena that can be only indirectly and obliquely observed themselves — constructs that it becomes disturbingly apparent are usually incompatible with the simple, sturdy framework of common sense that adequately serves us in our ordinary quotidian affairs.

We should nevertheless be conscious of two related but fundamentally different ways of approaching these concepts of small and big. Strindberg, who in so strange and visionary a manner presages and anticipates many of the profounder shifts in our modern sensibilities, was responsive to this distinction, not only in his use of individual images but also in his protracted and anguished efforts to read sense into the nature of existence as he saw it and experienced it, and to communicate his "reading" in dramatic and narrative imagery. It is — as the reader will surely acknowledge — a dauntingly big subject, and this brief paper is (I readily confess) an absurdly small assault on it. As such, and within its severe limitations of time and scholarship, it takes on all the trappings of self-caricature.

I will briefly describe a few of the more familiar ways in which the nineteenth century conducted its debate into the nature of the big and the small and some of the characteristic ways in which it manifested itself in literary debate.

One of the classic nineteenth-century statements in defense of the small is found in that well-known passage in which Adalbert Stifter, in the preface to his collection of Novellen entitled *Bunte Steine* (*Stones of Many Colors*), defends his practice in these tales of peasant life: what he movingly refers to as "the gentle law" (*das sanfte Gesetz*).

Weil wir aber schon einmal von dem Grossen und Kleinen reden, so will ich meine Ansichten darlegen. . . . Das Wehen der Luft, das Rieseln des Wassers, das Wachsen der Getreide, das Wogen des Meeres, das Grünen der Erde, das Glänzen des Himmels, das Schimmern der Gestirne halte ich für gross: das prächtig einherziehende Gewitter, den Blitz, welcher Häuser spaltet, den Sturm, der die Brandung treibt, den feuerspeienden Berg, das Erdbeben, welches Länder verschüttet, halte ich nicht für grösser als obiger Erscheinungen, ja ich halte sie für kleiner.

As we once and for all speak about the Great and the Small, I want to present my views. . . . The gentle breeze, the murmur of water, the growth of corn, the waves of the sea, the earth turning green, the radiance of the sky, the gleam of the stars, are things which I consider great: the majestic approach of a thunderstorm, the flash of lightning that cleaves houses, the tempest that lashes the breakers, the fire-belching mountain, the earthquake that lays waste whole lands, are phenomena which I do not consider greater than those others, in fact I consider them smaller.[2]

And just as with outer nature, so also with the inner nature of humankind:

So wie es in der äusseren Natur ist, so ist es auch in der Inneren, in der des menschlichen Geschlechtes. Ein ganzes Leben voll Gerechtigkeit, Einfachheit, Bezwingung seiner Selbst, Verstandesgemäsheit, Wirksamkeit in seiner Kreise, Bewunderung des Schönen, verbunden mit einem heiteren, gelassenen Sterben, halte ich für gross: mächtige Bewegungen des Gemütes, furchtbar einherrollenden Zorn, die Begier nach Rache, den entzündeten Geist, der nach Tätigkeit strebt, umreisst, ändert, zerstört und in der Erregung oft das eigene Leben hinwirft, halte ich nicht für grösser, sondern für kleiner, da diese Dinge so gut nur Hervorbringungen einzelner und einseitiger Kräfte sind wie Stürme, feuerspeiende Berge, Erdbeben.

And as it is with external nature, so it is also with the internal nature of mankind. A whole lifetime of fairness, simplicity, self-mastery, understanding, effectiveness within an allotted sphere, reverence for beauty: such a life, with a calm and peaceful death to end it, is what I consider great. Mighty emotions of the soul, terrible outbursts of anger, the thirst for revenge, the fiery spirit that hurls itself into action, the man who demolishes, changes, destroys, and in his passion often throws away his own life; for these things too are the products of particular and unilateral forces, just as are storms, volcanoes, and earthquakes.[3]

This was a defensive posture imposed on many a writer and thinker in the Hegelian age — an age that tended to give its attention to the larger shifts in history, to the nature of the *Weltgeist,* and that strove to achieve those comprehensive all-embracing formulas that would illuminate the continuing progress and vast sweep of history. To these ambitious minds with their eye forever on some grand design, the notion of an authorship that addressed itself to the minutiae of existence was beneath contempt. As Hebbel, in an unbelievably heavy-handed epigram (printed in *Europa* in 1849) once put it:

Wisst ihr, warum euch die Käfer, die Butterblumen
so glücken?
Weil ihr die Menschen nicht kennt, weil ihr die
Sterne nict seht!
Schautet ihr tief in die Herzen, wie könntet ihr
schwärmen für Käfer?
Säht ihr des Sonnensystem, sagt doch, was wär
euch ein Strauss?
Aber das musste so sein; damit ihr das Kleine
vortrefflich
Liefertet, hat die Natur klug euch das Grosse
entrückt.

Did you know why the bees enjoy the buttercups
so much?
Because they do not know human beings, because they do
not see the stars!
Look deep in your hearts, how could bees
enrapture you?
If you could see the solar system, tell me then
what would a bunch of flowers be to you?
But it must be that way; having supplied you splendidly
with the Small,
Nature has wisely removed you from the Great.

The miniaturist's (or microscopic) view of life and of human endeavor was nevertheless quick to claim science as an ally. The claim that the patient observation and careful collation of small detail would eventually coalesce into that more genuinely larger truth that brings true insight into the nature of things was one that gained wide allegiance. The writer felt encouraged to compile a kind of inventory of the natural world, adding item to minute item in an accumulation of detail, all in the confident hope that the particularities would eventually compose themselves into a generality by which our understanding would ultimately be enriched.

Weil aber die Wissenschaft nur Körnchen nach Körnchen erringt,
nur Beobachtung nach Beobachtung macht, nur aus Einzelnem das
Allgemeine zusammenträgt, und weil endlich die Menge der
Erscheinungen und das Feld des Gegebenen unendlich gross ist,
Gott also die Freude und die Glückseligkeit des Forschens unver-
sieglich gemacht hat, wir auch in unseren Werkstätten immer
nur das Einzelne darstellen können, nie das Allgemeine, denn dies
wäre die Schöpfung: so ist auch die Geschichte des in der Natur

Grossen in einer immerwährenden Umwandlung der Ansichten über dieses Grosse bestanden.

As science achieves knowledge grain after grain, observation after observation, deriving the universal from the individual, and as the numerous phenomena and the given field is infinitely great, God has made the joy and bliss of research inexhaustible. For these very reasons we can only in each instance reproduce the individual, never the universal, for the latter would be Creation. This is why the history of the Great in nature consists of a continuous change of views about this Great.[4]

It was believed that each small detail of life repaid a loving scrutiny, often mirroring the otherwise incomprehensibly big, focusing it, making it assimilable, rendering it accessible to our necessarily limited vision and comprehension. It was a view of life and literature that built up over the century to a veritable cult of the small, the minute; the conviction grew that in these things a significant reverberation was present that would reveal to the devoted attention of those of practiced sensitivity truths that would otherwise escape registration. One recalls the tradition of this "gentle law" that runs from Novalis and Wordsworth, through the subdued discipline of the German poetic realists and on to Maeterlinck who (in *Le Trésor des Humbles*) turned resolutely away from high passion and outsize emotions:

Il m'est arrivé de croire qu'un vieillard assis dans son fauteuil, attendant simplement sous la lampe, écoutant sans le savoir toutes les lois éternelles qui régnent autour de sa maison, interprétant sans le comprendre ce qu'il y a dans le silence des portes et des fenêtres et dans la petite voix de la lumière . . . il m'est arrivé de croire que ce vieillard immobile vivait en realité d'une vie plus profonde, plus humaine et plus générale que l'amant qui étrangle sa maitresse, le capitaine qui remporte une victoire ou "l'époux qui venge son honneur."

I have grown to believe that an old man, seated in his armchair waiting patiently, with his lamp beside him; giving unconscious ear to all the eternal laws that reign about his house, interpreting, without comprehending, the silence of doors and windows and the quivering voice of the light . . . I have grown to believe that he, motionless as he is, does yet live in reality a deeper, more human and more universal life than the lover who strangles his mistress, the captain who conquers in battle, or "the husband who avenges his honour."[5]

When, in the 1890s, this was extended to the observation of the ways of the mind — especially the unconscious mind — the parallel with the microscope was often not merely implied but specifically invoked. As Hamsun, in a well-known passage, once put it: "We would learn something of the secret stirrings that go on unnoticed in the remote parts of the mind, the incalculable chaos of impressions, the delicate life of the imagination seen under the magnifying glass."[6]

It is a view of existence to which Strindberg too was at times and in appropriate circumstance quite ready to give his allegiance; a faith that patient observation of minuter events can reveal a kind of order in the apparent chaos, by virtue of which we would be assisted to comprehend the macrocosmic world. In this connection I think particularly of *I Havs-bandet* (*By the Open Sea*), and especially the fascinating chapter 3 in which Borg takes along "en stor sjökikare," a sort of marine observation glass, through which he views the silent drama of life under the sea and which he confesses he interprets, "not with the dreamy imagination of the poet . . . but with that of the scientist," and by virtue of which he feels he gains in insight into God's very purposes.

The reader is probably wondering why I have not so far mentioned the essay that meant so much to Strindberg in matters of this kind, the very title of which could so easily serve as a motto for this paper. The essay of course is that provocative study by Georg Brandes of Shakespeare's *Henry IV* that first appeared in 1869 as "Om 'Det uendeligt Sma' og 'Det uendeligt Store' i Poesien" (On the Infinite Small and the Infinite Great in Poetry) and that was reprinted a year later in his collection of critical essays *Kritiker og Portraiter* (Critics and Portraits).

Strindberg is known to have paid close attention to the piece and to have been much impressed by it. Even if (as Joan Bulman in her monograph *Strindberg and Shakespeare* would have us believe) the proposition "It had very much the effect of a blast of dynamite, removing the wall of rock that had hitherto stood between him and his genius" is something of an over-statement, one can at least readily accept that the essay and the comments made in it on the nature of Shakespeare's dramatic art had a deeply formative influence on Strindberg's own development as a dramatist.

Strindberg himself indicated that, at the time when he read Brandes's essay, he was at a stage in his own intellectual development where he found himself questioning some of the currently prevailing views about the con-cept of beauty and wondering how it was that certain Dutch paintings of inn scenes had an undeniable kind of beauty even though some of the details were in themselves unbeautiful, even sordid.

In the midst of these speculations a book came into his hands [he writes of himself in the third person] which broke like a lightning flash through his dark doubts and threw a new light on the whole world of the beautiful. It was Georg Brandes's *Kritiker og Portraiter* which came out in the summer (of 1870). . . . No new complete system was presented here, but it cast a new light over the whole thing. All those things borrowed from German philosophy — order, content and form, the beautiful, the sublime, the characteristic — were missing.[7]

In this essay, as is well known, Brandes examines the methods Shakespeare used to depict a heroic character like Hotspur. It is not my purpose here to summarize the essay in any detail; but one can say that it has to do with the creation of a toweringly heroic figure through the medium of small, indeed trivial, and yet, in some strange and oblique way, *telling* detail. Some of the particular phrases Brandes used do nevertheless merit scrutiny, because I suspect that the deeper significance of them has not always registered.

He indicates how the characters succeed in

describing themselves in every sentence they speak without every saying a word about themselves; or, if they are described by others, it is done not through any report of their qualities in straightforward general terms . . . but by means of small things, small characteristic anecdotes which imply a quality without naming it. They do not become any less heroic for that. But behind the outer, superficial qualities can be glimpsed these deeper and more significant qualities which are their cause.[8]

Of the characters in the opening inn scene of the second act of *Henry IV*, Brandes writes:

They do not say a word about Prince Henry and Falstaff; they talk about the price of grain and the fact that "this house is turned upside down since Robin Ostler died." Their talk does not directly relate to the action of the play, but it conveys the scene of the action. . . . Never, in poetry, was so much given by so little. . . . All the senses are involved: one sees, hears, smells. . . . One does not know what makes the situation overwhelm one with the full compelling power of reality; but the reason is that Shakespeare has again touched our nerves by the infinitely small which serves as the basis for every sensation.[9]

He concludes that, in our effort to grasp the meaning and purpose of an entire historical epoch, it is only by taking as one's starting point this matter of "the infinitely small" that we find it possible to move on to an understanding of "the infinitely great."[10]

But — and this is perhaps the real crux — this is a different method of deploying and interpreting small observed detail than that which compiles items into a generally accumulative assembly of significance. What we are dealing with here is a form of *encoded* information, of detail that, no matter how long one were to scrutinize each item as a discrete piece of information, would never of itself yield up anything of its true contributory significance. No direct *microscopic* examination — of the then prevailing price of grain, of who Robin Ostler might have been, of how the house might have been turned upside down — will vouchsafe anything other than merely contingent relevance; the details are only obliquely, indirectly meaningful, yet all the more powerful for being so. To achieve understanding in these circumstances, things need to be passed through a complex, intermediate, interpretive stage, subjected to a kind of transformational process before their essential significance begins to emerge.

Again, I turn to spectrosopy. Although this process, which Strindberg calls spectral analysis, dates back (in its simpler manifestations, at least) to Sir Isaac Newton and the seventeenth century, it was not until the second half of the nineteenth century and the beginning of the twentieth century that it was systematically developed. In its earliest form, it concerned essentially the study of the spectrum of natural light — that colored band into which a beam of light is decomposed by means of a prism. The real breakthrough in the use of the fundamental techniques involved did not really occur until the years 1859 and 1861 when Bunsen and Kirchhoff, through their work in spectrum analysis, created a new and powerful weapon for the chemist, the mineralogist, the astronomer, and the cosmologist.

At the time *The Father* was written, it took a very alert and well-informed mind to appreciate what was happening in the field of spectroscopy to the point where this particular branch of science would commend itself as a useful source of dramatic imagery. Much more than this, however: it took a mind in very special rapport with the direction and ultimate potential of scientific enquiry — especially those aspects of science that to the commonplace mind (such as Laura's) would have appeared merely absurd and irrelevant — to make such confident, intuitive use of a mode of scientific enquiry that was to figure so formidably in the creation of the new post-Newtonian physics and the new cosmology.

Over the last one hundred years, these new spectroscopic techniques have moved inexorably from a relatively simple analysis of the light from planets, stars, and other large and distant bodies — whereby an informed study of the spectral lines gives an insight (otherwise unattainable) into the composition of objects infinitely beyond our reach and comprehension — into areas where other radiations and emissions at frequencies beyond everyday perception (ultraviolet rays, infrared rays, and X-rays) came to play a crucial role. In lay language, the new techniques made possible the understanding of certain natural phenomena through the study of radiated emissions and the unique spectrum (i.e., the particular pattern of frequencies and intensities) they cast. And as one follows the modern developments of these techniques into the mid- and late twentieth century, one becomes aware of how (for example) nuclear magnetic resonance spectroscopy and the related disciples of X-ray crystallography have totally transformed our understanding of the natural world.

But how does this relate to Strindberg and to his astonishing capacity for prefiguring the fundamental patterns of modern scientific and philosophic enquiry? It is in his conviction — which grew progressively stronger in the last twenty years of his life — that many of the smaller and seemingly inconsequential things of modern living are unexpectedly found to be charged with high-intensity meaning. To the commonplace mind — to the Lauras of this world — these things may seem only like undifferentiated stones, bits of commonplace rock, not worth a second look and certainly bereft of anything of great significance. The Captain (and of course Strindberg) knows better. He recognizes many of these seemingly commonplace things as meteorites, as objects ordinary and innocuous in appearance but nevertheless possessed of a high charge of significance for anyone equipped with the right (spectroscopic) vision and with the skill and knowledge and sensitivity to deploy it.

If I were to continue this study, the next (and infinitely more fascinating) step would be to hold these hastily sketched ideas up to the concrete reality of Strindberg's texts: particularly those works with the highest levels of *encoded* meaning, such as *To Damascus* (I-III), *A Dream Play*, *The Ghost Sonata*, and (supremely) *Inferno*. In the latter work, where the narrative is conducted so persistently in terms of radiations, vibrations, frequencies, and magnetic and other forces and where the anguished examination of contingent objects is not for their surface or material or structural qualities but for their encoded significance, the image of the spectroscope is a pervasive presence.

Consult an English dictionary today and you will find that a spectroscope is defined as "an instrument specifically designed for the production and examination of spectra." If you then look up "spectra," you find not unexpectedly that its meanings and usages go much further back in time than its twentieth-century applications. The oldest recorded meaning of "spectrum" in the English language is "an apparition or phantom or ghost" (1611); and its next oldest is "an image or semblance" (1693). And that in itself prompts me to suggest — not entirely frivolously — that the English-speaking world rename *Ghost Sonata*, *The Spectral Sonata*.

11

Strindberg and the French Drama of His Time

Maurice Gravier
(Translated by
Sarah Bryant-Bertail)

August Strindberg wanted to be heard by his Swedish public, but at the same time he also sought to write "modern" plays. To be accepted by the audiences of his day, he had no choice but to create a place for himself within the repertory of his time; before he could introduce the innovations he desired, it was necessary to accept a certain theatrical tradition. In the nineteenth century, however, such a tradition, in the true sense of the word, did not yet exist in Sweden. After the great world classics, particularly the ancients and Shakespeare, it was French drama that was most strongly represented on the Swedish stages. Where contemporary theater was concerned, only the drama of Norway was becoming a serious competitor against that of France. As for the Swedish plays, even the most recent of them did not please Strindberg; he judged them all to be extraordinarily old-fashioned:

> In which of our plays do we see reflected the events of 1809, 1814, 1844, 1848, 1865? In *The Foundling, The Pamphleteer, Master Smith, The Sister of Eve, The Worker*? In none. Perhaps in some servile play written for a coronation or a national holiday. Would we have recoiled before the idea of drawing up our subjects fully into passionate life? But we have never had passionate life; the solutions to our prob-

lems have never been truly dramatic. We are by nature too ponderous — that is, resistant to the drama.[1]

And so Strindberg turned his eyes toward the French theater of entertainment and the Parisian-style "theater of ideas." "In France," he wrote, "the theater reflects the life of society like a faithful mirror, perhaps too faithful. It has become a place of public discussion where all questions are judged by either catcalls or applause."[2]

The French theater of that day was related, on the one hand, to journalism and, on the other, to the very old tradition of vaudeville. In the French "theater of ideas" the authors, to convey their messages, their "ideas," present an ingenious scenario, a plot that is solidly established and then cleverly unraveled, all in the style of the well-made play, or *pièce bien faite*. Since the early nineteenth century there had been a very lively exchange of ideas on theater in Western Europe, an exchange that had two focal points: Paris and Vienna. In these cities similar themes were treated, taken up by others, and later adapted to local requirements practically everywhere in Europe — "updated" and "localized" to the point where the original play was often scarcely recognizable. The main points of transit — and of transformation — were Berlin and Hamburg. Among the points of destination, Copenhagen was especially important (here the adaptors quickly became creators, in particular, J. L. Heiberg and Overskou), followed by Stockholm (where Blanche adapted less than he innovated and invented), and finally Christiana (now Oslo) and Bergen, where the directors, espeially the young Henrik Ibsen, were attempting themselves to initiate the techniques of a European vaudeville that was generally more Parisian than Viennese.

At the beginning of the nineteenth century, French vaudeville resembled a sketch or a series of sketches, scenes of the type that were to be found later in the end-of-the-year revues or cabarets. But one man profoundly modified the structure of vaudeville, introducing complex and refined action — a subtle mechanism that, through a series of accidental encounters and misunderstandings, provoked an unfailing and almost mechanical sort of laughter. In this type of vaudeville, we find the germ of the well-made play, which is the comic counterpart of what for tragedy was the venerable old melodrama with its well-calculated and always reliable effects. The man who sparked this transformation was Eugène Scribe. He made his debut on a modest stage at the fair and later became the chief playwright of the distinguished Théâtre de Madame (later known as Le Gymnase) on the Boulevard; and, finally, he gained access to the Comédie-Française. While he himself was ascending the social ladder, his productions — based on the principle of the well-made play — underwent a profound transformation.

Strindberg and the French Drama of His Time

From pure vaudeville Buffoonery in *Le Pacha* (The Pasha) in 1817, Scribe passed to the comedy of intrigue, often in historical costume, as in *Bertrand et Raton* in 1833 and *Le Verre d'eau* (The Glass of Water) in 1840, then to the comedy of manners in modern costume, *La Camaraderie* (The Comradeship) or *La Courte échelle* (The Short Ladder) in 1837, and finally to the problem play, in which he dealt with topical political themes. *Bataille de Dames* (The Battle of the Ladies) of 1851 was, for instance, a kind of feminist manifesto written in collaboration with Ernest Legouvé. The technique — one might even say technical virtuosity — of Scribe eventually imposed itself abroad, in particular, in Denmark with Heiberg and in Norway with the young Ibsen during his Bergen period. They myth of the well-made play continued to inspire and guide French dramatic criticism until quite late in the nineteenth century, with Francisque Sarcey as its chief propagator and defender.

At this point I had hoped to supply a correct and concise definition of the well-made play, and did in fact search for one in the critical works of Sarcey. Actors of course believe that they know what it is and will tell you without hesitation that it is a play that is "well-knit" or "well-crafted," responses which no doubt signify that the genre in question is solid and resistant to rationalistic or easy critical formulation. But the perfection implied doesn't seem completely spontaneous: one senses a bit too much the author's intention — the "fabrication." I leafed through an account of the famous series of columns entitled "Rez-de-chaussée," which appeared in the Paris daily *Le Temps*, columns written assiduously by the "bon Oncle Sarcey." In turning those pages, I was able to recapture a very clear impression of the powerful vitality of the theater in the latter half of the nineteenth century. The theater of that era was an industry that could make a profit and did not require, with rare exceptions, any sort of subsidy.

The French "theater of ideas," from Emile Augier to Alexandre Dumas the Younger, also produced many plays that were "well-made" in addition to being socially edifying. They were all equipped with their *scènes à faire*, "obligatory scenes"; that is, scenes that were no only dramatically interesting but also charged with the important task of conveying the message intended by the author. The didactic elements were often contained in lengthy tirades that began to appear more and more like exercises in the development of symbolism (one is reminded here, in microcosm, of the parable of the fruit bowl containing almost all good fruit; the few bad pieces, however, which are deceptive in appearance, will quickly contaminate all their neighbors).

Ibsen made his debut when Norwegian theater was dominated by well-organized historical drama that was decorative and evocative of the opera, and he himself even succumbed for a time to the temptation to work within this genre. But when he was able to escape the repertory imposed upon him by his Bergen employers, he abandoned the "national-historical" or "rustic-folkloric" theater and he too began writing well-made plays. The first of his great social dramas, *Pillars of Society*, was a kind of vaudeville wherein, however, the author only rarely aimed to make the audience laugh. But Ibsen's rather complicated plot with its extraordinary mishaps and misunderstandings (involving ships rather than just persons) recalls Scribe's techniques precisely. There already appears here a certain type of symbolism hardly removed from that found in the French "theater of ideas" of the same era.

The first great play by Strindberg set in modern times, *Marauders*, later revised and titled *Comrades* (1886-87), is a refinement of the same dramatic aesthetics. Yet as early as 1882 Strindberg had noted the importance of economizing the means of theatrical production and had sketched out plans for a theater through which he might escape from the constraints of a style that seemed to him to be outdated. Four years later he nevertheless wrote *Marauders-Comrades* which shows that he was trying out the recipes of traditional theatrical cuisine. He too wanted to write his well-made play. Why this concession — one might even say regression? Perhaps simply because *Marauder-Comrades* was not so much a direct creation as a reply: he wanted to oppose Ibsen's *A Doll's House* with a stinging and apt response of his own. In many respects, *A Doll's House* is related to the well-made play. As its parody, *Marauders-Comrades* consequently had to present itself as a play of this genre.

The dramaturgical construction of *Marauders-Comrades* is simple and relatively clear, especially in its first version (*Marauders*), indicating that Strindberg had wished to apply the rules of Parisian-style know-how. There is detailed and minute presentation of a dozen male and female characters belonging to the milieu of Bohemian artists and writers, the use of interesting secondary motifs, and the introduction of the main plot, which shows the development of the careers of two painters, a man and a woman bound by marriage yet rivals because both wish to be admitted to the French *Salon des Artistes*. It is a question of knowing whether both will be admitted or, in case one of them fails, who will be eliminated. Upon this thematic framework, Strindberg embroiders a misunderstanding involving the paintings rather than the people. The husband has entered his own painting under his wife's name and the wife, likewise, under the name of her husband. At the close of the action the rejected painting is carried into the studio of the two painters during the course of a celebration: the wife, who had believed herself to be the one admitted, is now humiliated, while the husband, whom we had pitied, suddenly appears in the triumphant role. The abrupt reversal of the situation permits us to judge the two protagonists and to see how they react individually and in relation to each other. This is an instance of the famous *scène à faire*: in accordance with the laws of the genre, Strindberg has placed this scene near the end and to make us wait for it he introduces many picturesque episodes that allow him to describe with a great deal of verve the artistic cabal of the two painters and the literati that surround them.

But, despite all the care Strindberg has taken, *Comrades* is not a well-made play — in the literary and everyday sense of the term it in fact comes close to being a poorly made play. One is overwhelmed by the superabundance of motifs and exasperated by the frequency of pedagogical speeches. Here and there we find tirades that recall Dumas the Younger: the speech of the "marauding women," for instance, shows us to what extent the teachings once propagated by Dumas had found their last refuge in a symbol, a cliché that had by now fixed itself painlessly in the memory of the spectator. Strindberg is thus a prisoner of his set purpose: he wishes to write a parody of *A Doll's House* and so recovers certain visual motifs from Ibsen's play to hold them up to ridicule — the motif of disguise, for example. In Strindberg's parody, the poor husband must disguise himself as a woman, agreeing to wear his wife's bracelet as the symbol of his enslaved condition in regard to his wife, who henceforth exercises authority in the household. Axel's acceptance of his wife's bracelet is a reversal of Nora's breaking off her alliance to Helmer by no longer wearing upon herself the sign of a marriage of which she wishes to erase all traces. As the parodist, Strindberg is concerned with precise details and transparent allusions to Ibsen's original, but this concern renders his task difficult and causes the clarity of the play to suffer. Above all, Strindberg did not write this "comedy" with the serenity he would have imposed upon himself if he had intended to judge the society of his time impartially. On the contrary, he dwells constantly upon his own personal troubles and is not always successful in maintaining distance from his characters. In examining the position of the masculine partner in the "modern" marriage, he sometimes seems so irritated, bitter, and pessimistic that we must ask ourselves whether he is writing a drama, comedy, or perhaps a tract. He has a great deal of trouble ending the play, and debates for a long time whether he will guide Axel and Bertha toward serenity and reconciliation or whether he will opt for a denouement that brings the play to a grating, clashing halt. It is the second option that finally triumphs. The comedy becomes less and less comic as we approach the harsh, explosive final scene. However, the essential fact to consider here is that Strindberg was a writer who was evolving very quickly. Even while he finished writing *Comrades*, he had already almost ceased to believe in the value of the well-made play, if indeed he had ever done so. His imagination and his philosophical and aesthetic aspirations had already moved much farther on.

Maurice Gravier

After *The Red Room* (1879) was published, Strindberg was classified by the Swedish critics as a naturalist, to the surprise of the author, who claimed not to have yet read Zola at that time. Later, however, Strindberg was to become a fervent admirer of the great French novelist, and even seemed to have the ambition to become a naturalist himself, particularly in the field of theater. He informed himself about the French theatrical productions of the naturalists and read with interest the theoretical works of Zola and Louis Desprez as far as they concerned the theater and the transformations that naturalism would effect in dramatic literature. Strindberg was not concerned with the fact that Zola, although an incontestable master of the novel, was only a mediocre playwright. He was aware, for instance, that Zola's play *Thérèse Raquin* was a rather flat adaptation of his unforgettable novel of the same name. In fact, the French naturalistic theater as a whole never rose above the mediocre or won much international acclaim, and in France itself only Becque has survived until today. Even though he knew Becque personally and was received graciously by him, Strindberg did not hold him in high esteem. In his eyes Becque represented what he termed "shabby realism" *(smårealism)*. Actually, there were hardly any literary works of the French naturalists—or at least theatrical texts of that time—that inspired Strindberg.

But there was to be a French institution that would, on the other hand, offer him a great deal of hope, about which he had read in the press: the creation of the Théâtre Libre in Paris. An employee of the gas company had created a "free theater," and now independent writers were given an opportunity to see their works produced. This event was especially important to Strindberg, who had suffered official ostracism and whose plays had too often been disdained by directors, particularly when he tried to have *Master Olof* staged. He dreamed of creating the Free Scandinavian Theater, and actually did organize one, though it was to be short-lived. For the Théâtre Libre of Paris, he took to writing plays that escaped all classification. The Théâtre Libre was neither an official institution nor a commercial enterprise but rather a place that was open to all innovations.

The question inevitably arises of whether it can be said that Strindberg was a naturalist. The plays that have been called naturalistic do not in fact conform to any one classification. *The Father* does not resemble *Miss Julie* or *The Creditors*. With each play Strindberg seemed to be creating a new genre and never really approached French-style naturalism at all, except perhaps in *Miss Julie*, the only one that he himself specifically characterized as naturalistic. In *Miss Julie*, the decor must in a sense approach reality. The playwright is preoccupied in this drama with recreating, through a multitude of small details, the festive atmosphere that reigns at the outset in the chateau on the evening of St. John's Day. But through this concise drama, Strindberg also shows that he is turning his back on "shabby realism."

146

Strindberg and the French Drama of His Time

Rather than an adherence to a style, what is found in all the plays written between 1887 and 1891 is a certain faith of the author, a confidence in science, an evident positivism, sincere if a bit too forced in manner. He proclaimed himself an atheist, although a religious note could also be heard in most of his major works, even at that period — at the end of *Miss Julie* and *The Father*, for example. In any case, Strindberg believed in science, or at least in certain areas of science. In the second half of the nineteenth century, the natural sciences were particularly highly esteemed, as exemplified by practitioners Charles Darwin and Claude Bernard. But what interested Strindberg above all was medical science — especially the study of the nerves. Charcot, for instance, impressed the Parisian elite — the upper classes and the artists. As for Strindberg, he could have lectured alongside Maupassant and Freud when they held their public demonstrations and discussions of the patients at Salpêtrière. He read with passion the studies of the neurophysiologists, psychiatrists, and psychologists of the new school. The French novelists began very quickly to put the new research to their own uses, especially the Goncourt brothers, Bourget and Maupassant, the latter of whom might have used himself for a clinical case study. The "literature of the nerves," as it was termed, had been born, but not the theater of the nerves, at least not in France. On the other hand, the Scandinavians soon showed an interest that led to fascinating and fruitful experiments: Ibsen had opened the way with *Rosmersholm* and Björnson triumphed in Paris itself with *Beyond Our Power*, but it was above all Strindberg who exploited with unflagging perserverance this rich vein. In France, on the official stages and those of the Boulevard and the salons, the playwrights were still light-years away from being able to profit from the new science of psychology, the phenomena of hypnosis and of suggestion via the unconscious: all this seemed nearly magical to the writers and their naive public alike. At the beginning of the century, Hoffman had already invoked mesmerism, which he took to be scientific, to help the public accept his *Tales*. Alexandre Dumas the Elder had covered the same terrain with *Joseph Balsamo*, and, nearer to Strindberg, there was Rydberg with his gripping novella *Singoalla*. The distance between this last work and *Miss Julie* is not so great.

With *Miss Julie* Strindberg was returning to the concept of theater that he had formulated in 1882, a theater that was more economical in its means. He wanted to concentrate the attention of the spectator upon what was essential — an intention that seems radically opposed to the aesthetics of naturalism, which calls for the cutting out from reality of "slices of life" that the author pretends not to have chosen, but to have left for the spectator to sort out! If one takes one by one the three main works of Strindberg's "naturalist" period, it is in *The Creditors* that he most definitively realizes the ideal sketched out in his 1882 essay. *The Creditors* is truly a masterpiece in its rigor, logic, and economy, but it is also the work of a virtuoso. This time, in addition, it is a well-made play in the French sense of the term. Not surprisingly, it more easily won a favorable judgment from the pitiless French critics of that time.

Three characters constitute the cast of *The Creditors*: a woman named Tekla and her two successive husbands, Gustav, from whom she is divorced, and Adolf, who is her present spouse. The first has an advantage over the second; Gustav has an opportunity to get to know Adolf in advance and to understand his predecessor's strengths and weaknesses. Adolf, however, has never actually met Gustav and would be unable to recognize him if they did encounter each other. Actually this is nothing more than a vaudeville situation, at least at the outset. Gustav's aim is to place himself in Adolf's good graces, to act upon him by suggestion, to have him "ripen" in a sense, thus to render him malleable and vulnerable to the impending revenge. The moment the curtain rises, there is an encounter in a hotel room between these two sharp adversaries so unequal in strength: Gustav who knows his adversary well and Adolf who has no idea of the identity of the man opposite him. We the audience also have an advantage over the naive Adolf: we operate from the same plane as Gustav, in that we soon learn who Adolf is, whereas the latter remains confined to ignorance of the situation as a whole and is left to debate with himself in uncertainty. This initial scene, the first *scène à faire*, to use Sarcey's terminology, is great in its own right, with its sensational effects and all the subtle psychological developments that Strindberg knew how to create. But, in contrast to the typical well-made play, this conversation between the two men not only serves as the play's exposition but also advances the action that is rapidly being delineated. The audience eagerly awaits more such sensational scenes, and Strindberg soon accommodates them with two. Adolf vanishes at an opportune moment and, although not at first obvious, he has gone to the adjoining room — his own — where he will soon become an auditory witness to the second *scène à faire* in which Tekla and Gustav draw closer together. Tekla first appears to believe that this encounter between herself and her former husband is one of pure chance. Yet she soon guesses that the whole scenario has been staged by Gustav, the cruel puppetmaster who pulls the strings.

This represents one of the oldest schemata of dramatic literature, that of the-play-within-the-play. As spectators, we first take the greatest delight in the scene of coquetry that Tekla is playing with Gustav. Then, when we become more aware of the situation and realize that it is being played more for Adolf's sake than for our own and that it is all meant to make him suffer, it takes on a very unique aspect and becomes completely tragic. Each line rings with added resonance and becomes ambiguous, exactly like in vaudeville where the lines do not mean the same thing to the unknowing character to whom they are addressed as they do to the spectator who is perfectly cognizant of the entire situation. Strindberg has taken care to inform us in advance of Adolf's very precarious state of health: he is an epileptic and the slightest annoyance could precipitate a serious or even fatal crisis. On the other side of the door, Adolf is reacting constantly to what he hears. The door is shaken by the blows he deals it to express his anxiety and anger. This prepares the audience for the denouement — for that epoch not merely surprising but quite shocking. At a time when the theater most often contained nothing more than simple salon conversation aimed at the bourgeoisie, the sight of Adolf leaving his room — unsteady, pale, and foaming at the mouth — was hard for the audience to accept. Such spectacles belonged more right among the exhibits of the *Musée Dupuytren,* a celebrated medical science museum in Paris. Adolf collapses on the stage in the arms of Tekla, who remains as frivolous, emotional, and loving as she has always been. A sarcastic and nontalkative Gustav observes all this. He has succeeded perfectly in his enterprise: his "psychic murder" has been flawlessly carried out according to plan.

Contrary to *Comrades, The Creditors* is a well-made play in every sense of the term. In the latter, certainly, there is no methodical, slow exposition distinct from the body of the action. The characters, few in number and lacking any precise sociological definition, are quickly set before us like factors in a simple equation. The exposition is cleverly incorporated into the unrolling of the action and does not retard it. Only much later, in the last moments of the play, does the author venture to slow down the development of the plot; and he doesn't seek to create suspense in us about what the denouement may be. In other words, even if he constantly keeps us breathless, he does not play on the pleasure or anxiety linked to our waiting. The directly juxtaposed *scènes à faire* have their own life and at the same time are incorporated into a well-oiled mechanism; without a single intermediary element being necessary, the action progresses naturally. Moreover, the author retains all his freedom to maneuver and is able to introduce, without any pedantry, the psychological and philosophical developments that to him seem new and important (for example, the impure exchange involving the successive husbands of the same wife). Thus Strindberg seems to have found a solution to the squaring of the circle. He has written a well-made play but has eliminated all the somewhat caricatural and archaic aspects of this genre and yet retained all the advantages offered by its being a well-defined discipline of dramatic art. He succeeds in his intent because his dramaturgical construction is simple — or seems to be simple. He plays with his material in the manner of a virtuoso who has imposed severe limitations upon himself, taking no recourse to any but paradoxically limited means. He clearly turns his back on the kind of naturalism that tries to grasp life in all its troubling multiplicity and that refuses to discard the useless if picturesque details — details that drown the phenomenon that the author intends to analyze and develop.

The Creditors particularly pleased a French public who found itself at ease when confronted with a pure and logical dramatic construction. For their part, French actors also felt at ease with dialogue that was written a bit *à la française* and that "rolled" easily. But Jean Bollery, an excellent Strindbergian actor in the French theater, offers a warning: "One has somewhat the impression of playing ping pong. However, one should not let oneself be tempted by this impression: *The Creditors* is not a French play. It is important to leave to this drama all of its mystery." Nevertheless, such warnings have not prevented the public and actors of France from thinking that this work is a well-made play.

After *The Creditors*, Strindberg's "naturalistic" theater followed more uncertain paths. The inspiration was never again to be as lively or original. Sometimes with his one-act plays, for example, *Debit and Credit*, he falls into a certain mean dryness that rather reminds one of the Fench *théâtre rosse*, a comedy of a cynical cast wherein virtue goes unrewarded and vice unpunished. This vein of naturalism finally dried up completely.

When Strindberg again began to write for the theater, it was in a wholly new atmosphere, the one that followed the *Inferno* crisis. He no longer held the same beliefs, and the aesthetic principles to which he had formerly adhered were likewise not spared in the upheaval. He lived in an atmosphere held together by his new religiosity. Moreover, there was a change taking place in the literary climate itself, both in Western Europe as a whole and particularly in France. For too long the French had merely bantered sarcastically about the mystery surrounding the Scandinavian writers; they had not wanted themselves to be invaded by the "mists of the north." Now, however, they began to speak with reverence of a new Flemish master, the French-speaking Maurice Maeterlinck. Strindberg had at first delayed his admiration of Maeterlinck, but he too eventually admitted the importance of the latter playwright and came to consider him capable of rejuvenating the dramatic style of that epoch. Strindberg in fact exhorted his actors — in particular, Harriet Bosse and Fanny Falkner — to read the dramas of Maeterlinck.

With Maeterlinck the French fled from the loquacious, rationalistic "theater of explication" and took refuge in the "theater of silence." The dialogue was interspersed with long pauses that were supposedly charged with heavy undertones. Theater was no longer a dramatic art that called for full lights on the set; rather, it preferred dim lighting or half-darkness and action as clumsy as the dialogue that served to support it. The texts of this new drama also escaped temporal determination. They demanded neither modern costumes nor precise archeological reconstitution; instead, they seemed to unfold in a timeless age in a kind of enchanted fairyland. Such a fairyland particularly agreed with Maeterlinck, as it had several times done with Strindberg. But Maeterlinck's fairylands were more mysterious and a bit more charged with melancholy than were Strindberg's.

How can we rediscover the mysterious affinities that connected Strindberg to the Flemish playwright who began his career in Paris? A few clues are obvious, in certain sequences of *A Dream Play*, in fairytales such as *Swanwhite*, and above all in the mysterious *Advent* and *Easter*. In Strindberg's eyes Maeterlinck never became a true master, but he perhaps awakened in him some harmonies that would not have been realized otherwise.

Strindberg followed very closely the development of the French theater. However, he imitated little of what he had read or seen in Paris (to tell the truth, he rarely attended the theater, and no more in Paris than in Stockholm). Above all, he studied through documents the French innovations and sought to determine French tendencies. He succeeded in placing himself at odds with the French theater and, at the same time, in going even farther than that theater in the direction that it seemed to him to be indicating. In summary, the French theater was able to aid him in a highly useful area: French writers and technicians of the theater and, especially, French psychologists and psychiatrists led him to define himself and to be aware of the scope and the power of his genius.

12

Love without Lovers:
Ingmar Bergman's Julie

Frederick J. Marker and Lise-Lone Marker

"Love Without Lovers" was the working title for a
film Ingmar Bergman never finished. We are borrowing this evocative
phrase, however, to describe all three dramas of corrosive sexual combat
that he brought together to form the Bergman Project — as his mammoth
triple production of *A Doll's House, Miss Julie,* and *Scenes from a Marriage,*
staged sequentially in Munich in 1981, has come to be called.[1] It would be no
exaggeration to say that, in each part of this triptych, the spirit of Strindberg
seemed the presiding influence and inspiration.

Nora, as Bergman called his boldly economical revision of Ibsen's play,
was very consciously steeped in the caustic reassessment of the play that
we find in Strindberg's foreword to *Giftas* (sometimes translated as *Married*).
As for the rewritten stage adaptation of Bergman's own film, both its tone
and its tautly concentrated structure now seemed far more Strindbergian
than had been the case in the earlier, more conciliatory screenplay. Yet it is to
Bergman's *Julie* that our adopted phrase applies most readily and aptly. His
most recent German production of Strindberg (which also played a three-
day engagement at the Royal Dramatic Theater in Stockholm) was remarkable, above all else, for a precisely defined, at times even dreamlike rhythm
that it imparted to an utterly loveless, destructive struggle raging back and
forth among the sexual combatants — all three of them — in this complex work.

"It's never difficult," Bergman remarks in an interview. "With Strind-berg you never run into difficulties because you can hear his way of breathing — you can feel his pulse rate — you know *exactly* how it's meant to work. Then all you have to do," he adds casually, "is recreate that rhythm."[2] Musical analogies and techniques are always congenial to this director, but in his intensive preparations for *Julie* they were uppermost in his mind. Strindberg himself, of course, refers directly in his famous preface to *Miss Julie* to the crucial strategy whereby his elliptical dialogue "gathers material in the first scenes that is later picked up, repeated, reworked, developed, and expanded like the theme in a musical composition."[3] As Bergman and his actors rendered this text, a distinctly musical rhythm governed its emotional design — a rhythm built on deliberately sustained phrasing, lighter and more acute stages of dissonance, beats of rest, changes of tempo, and what can be described only as monologue-arias. As a result, a form of progression emerged that was associational rather than merely sequential, expressive and suggestive rather than literal or declarative. Here, as it were, was a living illustration of that punctuation (as Strindberg likes to call it in his *Open Letters to the Intimate Theatre*) without which "acting becomes flat as a musical composition without nuances, without piano and forte, without crescendo and diminuendo, accelerando and ritardando."[4]

"In my case," Bergman reminds us, "it has always been a matter of reading closely. And interpreting in the same way a conductor interprets a score."[5] The process of orchestrating this particular composition for perfor-mance led him — almost as the conductor of a symphony might be led — to examine the emendations and dynamics recorded in the composer's origi-nal score, in this case, Strindberg's holograph manuscript of the play, which contains cuts and changes introduced both by the playwright and by the cautious Josef Seligmann, who undertook to publish the contentious new work after Bonnier had turned it down.[6] One of the most significant changes of emphasis that Bergman introduced sprang from his decision to restore the original manuscript version of the story, as told by Jean near the beginning of the play, about the desertion of Julie's rebellious suitor. Here, without the spurious deletions made in Strindberg's text by the presump-tuous Seligmann, is how the passage in question now sounds in Bergman's *Julie:*

CHRISTINE: So you saw it, did you?

JEAN: I certainly did. One evening they were down in the stable yard, and Miss Julie was putting him through his training, as she called it. And do you know what that meant? She made him jump over her riding whip, like a dog you'd teach to jump. He hopped twice, and each time he was given a rap. But the third time he grabbed the whip out of her hand *and struck her across the left cheek with it.* Then off he went.

CHRISTINE: You don't say. And you actually saw it happen? You don't say. So that's the reason she paints her face so white now!

Beneath her white, death-mask makeup, this Julie bore an ugly scar on her face — inflicted, as Jean informs Christine with satisfaction, when the angry and mutinous fiancé Julie has been trying to subjugate at last rebels and hits back. This humiliating injury became the outward sign of a deep, inner lesion in her spirit. "It is now a marked, stigmatized Julie who makes her first appearance," Bergman told a Swedish interviewer. "A mortally wounded woman — whose wounds gradually reveal themselves."[7] Beneath the commanding and haughty presence the actress Anne-Marie Kuster conveyed in the role, there festered a thinly concealed anguish and despair that foretold her ultimate destruction. It is precisely this acute sense of festering spiritual malaise — of "something *menacing* going on which we don't speak about because we have no words"[8] — that is the hallmark of Christine Buchegger. This actress, who played both Hedda Gabler in Bergman's Munich production and Katarina Egerman in *From the Life of the Marionettes*, was also to have portrayed Miss Julie — a character Bergman clearly regards as related in significant ways both to Ibsen's Hedda and to his own Katarina. Buchegger suffered a nervous breakdown that forced her director to reassign the role to Kuster, scarcely three weeks before the opening. It is characteristic that, as outspoken as he is in praise of Kuster's ability and courage, Bergman has remained fascinated by that even stronger quality of intense inner suffering and alienation that Buchegger's performances tend to convey — so fascinated, in fact, that he subsequently restaged *Julie* as a touring production, simply to see this actress play the part.

Hence, in a very physical sense, this Julie must bear the mark of her destiny from the outset — and, what is equally important, both Jean and Christine *know* the meaning of the scar and recognize, with sure predatory instinct, the vulnerability it signifies. In Bergman's version, Jean seizes upon this palpable sign of Julie's defeat, using it as a weapon in the struggle between them. When, for instance, Julie finishes recounting the story of her father's humiliation and the origins of her own hatred of men, a line previously deleted in Strindberg's manuscript gives Jean a new, crueler rejoinder:

JEAN: I saw it all — down by the stable.

JULIE: What did you see?

Love without Lovers

JEAN: What I saw. The way he broke off the engagement. *You can still see it there on your cheek.*

In general, the dominant image of Miss Julie this production projected is crystallized in an informal note made by the director in his copy of the play: "She is a big, helpless animal who is done to death by smoothly functioning beasts of prey. Who is still bound by conventions. Defeated by her own kind, destroyed by the others. The moral is simple: 'Miss Julie has no finesse.' This "simple moral" is, of course, Jean's, spoken by Michael Degen with infinite vulgarity while he chewed his kidney dinner and sipped contentedly on his master's burgundy.

An even more radical sequence of changes that Bergman introduced served to counterbalance the fact that, in his interpretation, Julie was so manifestly doomed from the beginning. In his version, she also became, decisively, the mistress of her own fate rather than simply the victim of Jean's hypnotic (perhaps even diabolical) influence. The entire final movement of this production was shaped by its director's observation that "she forces *him*. From the moment she decides, she becomes stronger than anyone else."[9] The two sharp rings of the bell, announcing the Count's return, instantly transformed Degen's impudent and cocksure kitchen Casanova into the cringing valet again, rendered impotent by the burden of "this damned servant boy sitting on my back." But it was emphatically *not* the unseen presence of the Count that, in this case, chiefly influenced Julie.

Even while she pleaded, with profound weariness, for Jean's help, she already held the razor firmly in her hand. As she stood motionless in the middle of the room, bathed in the sunlight that filled the kitchen with a white, brilliant radiance, she seemed to be intently engaged in her own inner struggle, rather than caught in some kind of hypnotic trance. Julie's familiar "trance" speech ("The whole room is like smoke around me") was the one major cut that Bergman made in the text. The fragment of a command she at last wrings from Jean in this version ("Go now — go out to the barn and — ") was hardly a command at all, spoken as it was, virtually in tears, from the chair beside the stove where he crouched. Only an instinct for self-preservation appeared to propel the panic-stricken valet into action. As Julie prepared to leave, he hastily scooped up handfuls of the money she had taken from her father's desk and — lest he should bear the blame for her theft — brutally crammed the bills into the pockets of her dress. Unheeding and completely absorbed in her own choice — her decision to die — Julie walked calmly and without hesitation into the bright sunlight outside. Jean, for whom the making of such a choice was incomprehensible, snatched up his master's boots and breakfast tray with an air of relief. During one or two of the rehearsals, Degen was even heard to whistle as he hurried away!

Frederick J. Marker and Lise-Lone Marker

Julie stands outside the world of "reality," which, in Bergman's interpretation, is a very tangible world represented by Jean and the wine he
steals from the cellar, by Christine and the noisome food she fries on her
cast-iron stove, and by the six other watching, leering servants who bear
witness to the humiliation and destruction of the Count's daughter. Julie's
rejection of this "real" world was a process of gradual disillusionment and
steadily growing revulsion. The progressive stages of this process were
orchestrated, almost in a musical fashion, to form an ironic and insistent
counterpoint to her erotic encounter with Jean.

Very early in that encounter, the prattle of her childishly explicit erotic
challenges was snapped, abruptly and unexpectedly, by the intrusion of a
completely different tone. Her utterly dreamlike meditation on the "strangeness" of everything in life — "all of it scum drifting on the water, drifting
along, until it sinks, sinks down!" — was conceived as a monologue that
gazed inward, at something that Jean would never be able to comprehend.
However, the Jean that Degen drew was, above all, an able and quick-witted
actor, and he was swift to pick up his cue, following Kuster's lead, with his
own animated, improvised "dream" of ambitiousness. When more tangible
physical advances failed, Degen resorted to his reliable histrionic skills. At
first, Julie's sense of revulsion and incipient self-disgust rose dangerously at
his colorfully embellished but loathsome tale of his coprolitic adventures in
the Count's outdoor "Turkish pavilion." But his subsequent sobbing recital
of the deprivations of "a poor farmer's child" gave him a fresh hold on his
naive and illusion-prone listener. The recital reached its peak of exaggeration when Degen casually mopped his tear-stained face with a handy
kitchen towel! With the approach of the servants singing their ribald song
(the text of which was made more explicitly malicious in Bergman's version
than in Strindberg's play), Degen had the pretext he needed to hurry Julie
into his own room. He took the opportunity with cynical composure,
without a trace of erotic passion.

The unseen seduction is the turning point in the play. Following it,
their masks now laid aside, Julie and Jean sit through the rest of the brief
Midsummer night discussing alternatives. With the rising of the sun that at
last dispels the darkness (and "the spooks"), Julie realizes that she has
neither illusions nor alternatives left.

Bergman replaced Strindberg's ballet of "peasants in their Sunday
best" with a different choreographic interlude, intended to provide a far
harsher and more explicitly ironic comment on the seduction than does the
Midsummer folk dancing described in the text. (Perhaps, as Smedmark
suggests in his detailed notes on the original manuscript, the playwright,
too, may have had second thoughts and other alternatives in mind.)[10] "I
think the people *are* a threat," says Bergman. "In my production there's no

ballet — just some peasants who come in and sing this . . . very obscene little song. People looking around for something to drink, looking around for Jean, sitting around there in the kitchen doing obscene things." [11] The grotesque antics of the drunken, copulating servants who invaded the kitchen underscored the true, sordid nature of Jean's easy conquest; it became the rough equivalent of the rutting of Diana, Julie's wayward lap dog, by the porter's mutt. Lars, the grossest of the six servant figures invented by Bergman, rapped out the tempo of the ribald song on Jean's bedroom door. Christine's arrival dispersed the rowdy, mocking servant chorus; left alone, she sat wrapped in a black shawl, facing away from Jean's door, perfectly aware of what was taking place in the next room. Then, as she glanced at the door, she heard a noise from inside and quickly disappeared. "But," Bergman continues, "when she returns in the second part of the play, she already *knows* what has happened." She and everyone else on the estate, one might add. In other words, the presence of these sneering intruders and of Christine transformed the sexual act into a ritual of humiliation for Julie.

In Strindberg's play, when the Count's daughter reappears from Jean's bedroom, she takes out a powder puff and nervously powders her face. By contrast, Anne-Marie Kuster's Julie emerged in extreme physical pain, retching and bleeding visibly from her scar and from her ruptured hymen. "When Jean gives her the second 'wound' — her second physical humiliation at the hands of a man — it destroys her," Bergman explains. "If you look closely at the play, you'll find that poor Miss Julie's physical suffering is terrible. She has convulsions as well. As you can see in the text, her mother suffered from convulsions and paralysis — some kind of epilepsy — and Julie has inherited that sickness from her mother. Suddenly she has the same sort of epileptic seizure."[12] The strong emphasis throughout Bergman's production on a more overt and intense ordeal of physical suffering on Julie's part was no shock tactic, however, but a concrete means of externalizing the self-destructive anguish and despair within her.

At first, the emotional nausea and revulsion that overwhelmed her following the seduction made no impression whatever on Jean, who devoted himself to his train schedule, his cigar, and his scheme for acquiring a hotel ("with first-class accommodations for first-class customers") and perhaps even a Rumanian count's title. However, once Julie's revelation that she had no money of her own had effectively closed off that alternative, his manner toward her shifted abruptly from callous indifference to open hostility. Not, as Jean insists, that he has no pity for her — following the first of her two panic-induced convulsions, he smugly consoled her with a glass of the wine he had pilfered from her father's cellar; then, as she lay huddled on the floor after her second seizure, he patted her sympathetically on the

Figure 4. *Jean (Michael Degen) and Julie (Anne-Marie Kuster) in a scene from Ingmar Bergman's 1981 production of* Julie. *Photo by Jean-Marie Bottequin, courtesy of Ingmar Bergman and the Residenztheater, Munich.*

back, his cigar still held in his hand, while he told her the truth about his concocted fable of the servant boy's tragic romance.

This Jean gradually became, in his own way, as visibly consumed by the bitterness of his disillusionment with false ideals as Julie herself was. "You almost always see Julie played as very beautiful, delicate, fragile — a creature of Meissen porcelain. And Jean as the big, brutal, insensitive one," Bergman argues. "And that's all wrong — because Julie is the one who is big and clumsy, you see, and it's Jean who is the aristocrat."[13] "What scullery-maid do you think would play up to a man the way you did? Have you ever seen any girl of my class cheapen herself like that? I've only seen it happen among animals and loose women," the class-conscious valet shouts with resentment — but the real source of Jean's bitterness was given full expression in the unused lines from Strindberg's original manuscript that Berg-

Love without Lovers

man's version restored: "But I know it's done among your class. That's what they call being liberated or emancipated or something educated like that." And so, seated in his and Christine's favorite corner chair beside the stove, Degen's lackey-aristocrat literally shook with a mixture of fury and chagrin as he pondered his "discovery" that he had been duped by the false glitter of cat's gold — "that the hawk's back was as gray as the rest of it" after all.

Julie, meanwhile, was already far away. She struggled for her life, as Bergman observes, "in a very, very hopeless kind of way — hopeless because she wants to die." She had barely enough resistance to fight off Jean's sudden and explosively violent attempt to force her to have sex with him again. The introspective, dreamlike tone in her voice became steadily more insistent, until it completely suffused her long, exhausted monologue about her ingrained family heritage of sexual strife and hatred of men. Jean, however, barely listened. The alternatives — to stay, to run away together and die or torment one another to death, to live by renting sleazy villas to the "loving couples" who visit the rainy shores of Lake Como — were not encouraging, and they dwindled rapidly in the rose-colored dawn that preceded the sunrise.

Julie's reminder of "the consequences" that might result from their affair was cleansed of its faintly melodramatic air in this production; it became instead an idea that Jean seized upon as an unlooked-for solution to his problem — the means of convincing Julie that she must run away alone. When she returns to the kitchen dressed for travel, however, she has stolen enough of her father's money to cause Jean to reconsider his plan. All through the elegiac dream-monologue in which she describes her "child-hood memories of midsummer days," this Jean sat at the kitchen table frantically counting the cash. The amount was sufficient to persuade him to go with her — but his brutally indifferent destruction of the irksome greenfinch released in Julie the final eruption of a self-abhorrence and a despair that she could no longer contain. *"Here Julie goes to pieces"* is the simple, emphatic notation found in the director's copy at this point.

The arrival of Christine, dressed for church in funereal black, put an end to Jean's plan of escape — but by that time Julie's own awareness of the utter futility of further struggle had already overtaken her. Kneeling before this implacable agent of self-righteous moral indignation, Julie pleaded with her for a compromise in which she herself no longer believed. The tempo of her appeal increased to lightning speed; then it faltered, came to a halt, and died away. When it was finished, she collapsed at the kitchen table and sank her head down between her arms.

Christine, the cook, developed in Bergman's *Julie* into something very different from the supporting servant character described in Strindberg's preface to the play. The playwright calls her "a female slave, spineless and

159

phlegmatic after years spent at the kitchen stove, bovinely unconscious of her own hypocrisy, and with a full quota of moral and religious notions that serve as scapegoats and cloaks for her sins — which a stronger soul does not require since he is either able to carry the burden of his own sins or to rationalize them out of existence."[14] It is essential to grasp the fundamentally changed attitude toward this crucial character that is inherent in Bergman's whole approach. The essence of the change is contained in the director's remark that "she rules not only her kitchen, but also Jean. *She* is the reason why Jean is a winner — because Christine is the strongest of them all. She knows that one day she will sit in this house with Jean — one day they will rule this house together."[15] This sense of her strength and of the control she is in fact exercises found expression in the Bergman version in a variety of ways.

The young, strongly sensual Christine created by Gundi Ellert was Julie's antithesis. She embraced and fondled Jean with a laughing, possessive animality that stood in marked contrast to the shy, awkward behavior of her mistress — who, moreover, inadvertently walked in on their passionate lovemaking on two occasions. Almost from the outset, in a mimed sequence that replaced the "pantomime" described in Strindberg's text, this Christine communicated both her acute awareness of her lover's propensity for philandering — as readily with household rivals like Clara or Sofie as with their mistress — and her determination to maintain a tight surveillance on his activities. During this new pantomime, she proceeded to strip off her cook's top, wash herself carefully, dry herself with a towel, and unpin her hair before a small mirror — and as she was doing this Sofie and Clara, the two servant girls, appeared outside the windows of the kitchen, peering in. The latter, clearly Christine's chief rival for Jean's affections, came inside and whispered something to the cook, giggling and sniggering as she did so. Angrily, Christine pushed her away and chased her out the door with the towel. As the two girls ran off, she impatiently opened the door and peered outside. Then, while she picked up a wreath of white flowers and tried it on, Jean returned alone, laughing and combing his brilliantine-slick hair. This sequence of actions established an atmosphere of spying and eavesdropping — an atmosphere that was to remain an intrinsic part of the ritual of psychosexual humiliation and counterhumiliation that was a cornerstone of Bergman's interpretation.

"Is it possible?" Christine asks Jean, with an angry clatter of dishes and pots, the next morning — but her vigil in the darkened kitchen during the seduction left no doubt that she knew the answer to her own question. Her knowledge — coupled with her own sense of humiliation — fueled the self-righteous wrath of the hieratic denunciation she pronounced, like a high priestess before the altar of her cast-iron stove, over Julie. (Christine is

unmindful, to be sure, that her text, from Matthew 19, is immediately preceded in the Bible by the parable of the unmerciful servant who is damned for his failure to show compassion for other human beings.) When she left for church, the glance of mutual understanding and conspiracy that she exchanged with Jean spoke eloquently enough of the attitude shared by these two "smoothly functioning beasts of prey" toward their exhausted quarry. "They are," as Bergman puts it, "absolutely certain, both of them — absolutely certain that the future belongs to them."

Christine is rooted, in a very tangible sense, in the midst of a "real" world that both repudiates and is repudiated by Julie. The six nonspeaking servant figures that Bergman's version introduced were a further means of strengthening the atmosphere of concrete reality to which the ferocious cook Christine belonged (although she would doubtless consider herself a notch above these lower types). In his notes (again based on hints scattered throughout Strindberg's text), the director assigns each number of this mocking chorus of prying onlookers to a particular position in the sociosexual hierarchy of the place. Thus Clara, the housemaid, "considers Jean her personal property"; Sofie, lowly scullery-maid, is pregnant from an affair with Johan, the stable foreman; Anna, a stable-girl, goes out with Lars, the gross and self-important coachman, but she is otherwise "everybody's property." This largely unseen but deftly suggested dimension of sexual entanglements existed on a plane somewhere between Christine's affair with Jean and Diana's brush with the porter's mutt. This added dimension deepened the sense of love without lovers — of what Bergman calls "the fantastically brutal, cruel eroticism that runs beneath the surface of the play." In addition, the presence of this servant chorus of malicious snoopers and eavesdroppers amplified the tangible hostility of a society that participates willingly in the exorcism of its enemy, the outsider. ("No, Miss Julie, they don't love you," Jean warns her as the singers of the ribald song approach. "They take your food — but they spit at you afterwards. Take my word for it!")

Christine's kitchen kingdom, around which the watchers prowled and down into which Julie quite literally descended in this production, likewise became a manifestation of the "real" world to which everyone in sight belongs, except the rootless and self-dispossessed Julie. As such, it was a place where realistic specificity (down to the smells of food cooking and coffee brewing on the stove) existed at maximum intensity, with a completeness of detail that it first took many by surprise. The realism of the kitchen setting was thus virtually magical — a picture of sharp focus and precise representation, outside of which, beyond the windows that looked out on the park, no other reality existed. (And those windows were made increasingly opaque by Bergman as rehearsals went on.) Magic realism is a

Figure 5. *Christine (Gundi Ellert) confronts the exhausted Julie (seated) while Jean looks on, in Bergman's 1981 production of* Julie. *Photo by Jean-Marie Bottequin, courtesy of Ingmar Bergman and the Residenztheater, Munich.*

term that is sometimes used to describe the work of certain modern painters who, by employing an exceedingly exact realistic technique, try to convince their viewers that extraordinary and dreamlike things are possible simply by painting them as if they existed. "Painting reality with an edge — with a meaning" is how the American painter Andrew Wyeth once described his own style in an interview. "It's what is behind it that's important. . . . It's fairly true, but it's certainly not accurate perspective," Wyeth goes on to say. "I change things terribly from what is really true." In very much this same manner, Bergman's production exploited a cool, camera-sharp surface fidelity to create what director and painter alike would call a "distillation" — a charged image of the prison world of the spirit where Julie acts out her dreamlike and hopeless struggle to exist.

Ibsen's Nora, for example — and, in particular, Bergman's Nora in his Munich Project — is the center and, therefore, as it were, the creator of her stage world; when she leaves, she takes that world away with her. The kitchen world of Christine and the others possessed an objective and remorseless permanence of its own, and Julie's departure from it was a thing that would make very little discernible difference. The only small, pathetic reminders of her passage through it were the empty birdcage and a light traveling shawl she left behind. The familiar significance often attached to another object in the play — the Count's boots — mattered far less in this interpretation. This Julie chose her own destiny; bravest at the last, she took her own way (to purloin a phrase from Shakespeare's Octavius Caesar). And so, it was that abandoned shawl, draped forlornly over the back of a kitchen chair on the empty stage, that caught one's eye and flooded one's imagination.

Naturalism or Expressionism: A Meaningful Mixture of Styles in The Dance of Death (I)

Susan Brantly

What could Strindberg have been thinking of when he wrote *The Dance of Death* (I)? Karl-Ivar Hildeman has indicated the influence that Strindberg's observations of his sister's marriage had on the characters and events in the play.[1] Furthermore, Hans Lindström has pointed out that a number of Strindberg's close acquaintances had died during the year he wrote *The Dance of Death* (I), causing his thoughts to revolve around questions of life and death.[2] As Evert Sprinchorn has shown, Strindberg's thoughts were also still occupied with hell and purgatory and the Swedenborgian shape of the universe.[3]

Strindberg was specifically influenced at the time by his reading of Paul's letter to the Romans. In his diary on September 9, 1900, Strindberg took down some key quotations from this book of the Bible which are worth looking at carefully. The first quotations are taken from Romans 1:25-26, 28: "Who changed the truth of God into a lie . . . For this cause God gave them up unto vile affections . . . And even as they did not like to retain God in *their* knowledge, God gave them over to a reprobate mind, to do those things which are not convenient." Strindberg's own commentary to these passages is, "Thus, the sin [is] itself a punishment."[4]

At the beginning of *The Dance of Death* (I), the Captain belongs to the ranks of those who are punished by sin. He is an atheist who worships his creature comforts and denies God's truth. In Paul's words, such men are "filled with all the unrighteousness, fornication, wickedness, covetousness, maliciousness; full of envy, murder, debate, deceit, malignity; whispers, / Backbiters, haters of God, despiteful, proud, boasters, inventors of evil things, disobedient to parents, / Without understanding, covenant-breakers, without natural affection, implacable, unmerciful" (Romans 1:29-31). The Captain, in complicity with his wife, is guilty of all these sins.

Strindberg goes on in his diary, however, to quote even more extensively from chapter 7 of Paul's letter. Strindberg sums up this chapter as dealing with the problems of the spirit and the question of free will. More specifically, Paul deals with the conflicts between the spirit and the flesh. In a journal entry on September 9, 1900, Strindberg not only writes down but also underlines verses 15, 19, and 24-25: "For what I want to do I do not do, but what I hate I do. . . . For what I would, that do I not; but what I hate, that do I. . . . For the good that I would I do not; but the evil which I would not, that I do. . . . O wretched man that I am! Who shall deliver me from unrighteousness, fornication, the body of this death (sin). . . . so then with the mind I myself serve the law of God; but with the flesh the law of sin." Thus, the will to do good is defeated by the flesh. Purity of the spirit is unattainable while the spirit is in the flesh. The body is death; ergo, the death of the body brings life. Or in the words of Edgar in *The Dance of Death* (I): When death comes, life begins."[5]

Strindberg also mentions in his diary that he finished *The Dance of Death* (I) on October 31, 1900. This entry appears on the page after Strindberg's notations on Paul's letter. More than a month after the completion of the play, Strindberg was still deliberating about the questions raised in Romans. On December 11, in a letter to Axel Herrlin, he paraphrases the notes he made on September 9: "Now I believe firmly that sin itself is the punishment. But that you despise it and yourself is certainly good for the moment of death, which shall always remain the moment of liberation. The seventh chapter of Romans seems to have solved the riddle. 'Who shall deliver me from this body of sin (sic)?' The longing for innocence and beauty makes itself felt the strongest after sinning! That is peculiar! Is that the mission of sin?"[6] Notice that in his citation of Romans, Strindberg substitutes the term the body of sin for that of the body of death. Sin is equivalent to death. Precisely these thoughts on the function of sin, the conflict of spirit and flesh, and death as the only release were the matters foremost in Strindberg's mind when he wrote *The Dance of Death* (I).

One of the major dramaturgical problems facing Strindberg was how to project on stage the very private struggles between the spirit and flesh so that an audience could follow them. Actually, a very well-developed apparatus for depicting the pull of the flesh lay near to hand: naturalism. Of course, when referring to naturalism in this context, I speak of a modified naturalism entailing only the techniques developed for describing the nature and nurture of characters. Strindberg's naturalism in *The Dance of Death* (I) is clearly separated from the main literary tradition by the author's belief in God. Zola's meticulous recording of details pertaining to nature, nurture, and immediate environmental influences becomes pointless if one adheres to the belief that an individual's fate is ultimately controlled by a transcendent deity. In Strindberg's view, however, this technique enabled him to describe the evils of the flesh in scientific detail.

Strindberg believed that reason and scientific observation could prove God's existence. The disciplines of natural science and theology were compatible. In *Inferno*, Strindberg writes, "I had been well acquainted with the natural sciences since my childhood and had tended toward Darwinism. But I had discovered how unsatisfying can be the scientific approach that recognizes the exquisite mechanism of the world but denies the existence of a mechanic."[7] Scientific observation helps to describe the genius of the mechanic. With Strindberg's new religious insight, the empirical facts of the universe did not change, but their significance did.

Thus, it is quite possible to submit *The Dance of Death* (I) to a naturalistic reading. Through dialogue, the audience gets the traditional information about the nature and nurture of the three main characters. For example, Alice tells the Captain: "Just as you cringe to all your inferiors. Although you're a despot, at bottom you're a slave." At another point, Kurt says to Alice, "I knew you had a cruel and domineering streak in your nature." Before Kurt arrives both Alice and Edgar express a desire to see him, "Because he always gave in." Alice is a tyrant who views herself as a captive slave, and Edgar is a born slave who behaves like a tyrant. Unsuspecting, tractable Kurt gets caught in the crossfire.

Among other things, the play is about a fight for dominance. Alice and Edgar, who have reached a stalemate in their own conflict, compete for dominance over the weak-willed new arrival. The Captain's strategy is to gain control over Kurt's children and seduce his wife. Alice counters this tactic by attempting to ensnare Kurt sexually. Alice and Edgar are evidently not new to this sort of game. Before Kurt arrives, they speak of a previous incident: "But what was interesting in the experiment was how happy we were as soon as we had stranger in the house — to begin with."

Alice and Edgar compete for dominance not only over friends and houseguests but also over their own children:

ALICE: They couldn't stay at home. He set them against me. . . .

KURT: And you against him.

ALICE: Yes, naturally. Then it came to taking sides, canvassing, bribery. . . . So, in order not to destroy the children, we parted from them.

This theme is a direct carry-over from Strindberg's naturalistic play *The Father*, in which parents also war over who will dominate the child. Dominance and survival of the fittest were favorite themes of Strindberg's pre-Inferno naturalistic plays.

Strindberg does not neglect to give an account of the nurturing of the main characters. We are told that the Captain as a young man was forced to give up the pleasures of youth to support his brothers and sisters. Because of these privations, he has developed an inflated opinion of himself and a horror of having to be grateful to anyone. When the Captain first saw Alice, he fell passionately in love with her and seduced her. After they were married, their love turned to love/hate. Alice tells Kurt, "It's a quite unreasoning hatred. It has no cause, no object, but also no end. And why do you think he fears death most? He's afraid I shall marry again." The Captain is drawn to Alice by a compelling sexual attraction and later falls prey to a Darwinian compulsion to ensure fidelity in his mate.

As Strindberg's dialogue also reveals, Alice is not a novice in tampering with affections, particularly Kurt's. Alice asks him, "Do you remember when we were children and got engaged? Ah! You were shy, of course." Even when she was a child, Alice's favorite sport was ensnaring men. Her ambitions to become an actress were thwarted by Edgar's seduction. Her audience was reduced to one, and after twenty-five years of marriage, Edgar is thoroughly familiar and bored with her repertoire. Thus, when a new spectator arrives, Alice leaps at the opportunity to play her favorite role, seductress.

Another source of Alice's animosity toward Edgar is her contention that he wooed her under false pretenses: "But, you see, he cheated me. He promised me a good life — a beautiful home — and there was nothing but debts. . . . The only gold was on his uniform, and that wasn't gold either. He cheated me." This dissatisfaction also harks back to a premise expressed in *The Father*: a woman relinquishes her legal rights in return for her husband's assuming responsibility for her and her children. It is clear that Edgar feels a certain amount of guilt for not satisfactorily holding up his end of the bargain, as is evidenced by his attempt to falsely present his financial situation to Kurt. Edgar also tries to shift his own guilt onto Alice by presenting her as money-grubbing.

Kurt is described as both tractable and bashful. He has suffered through the dissolution of his marriage and the parting from his children. Evidently, while in America, Kurt was able to pull some of the threads of his life together and to become a financial success. In practically no time at all,

Edgar and Alice succeed in unraveling his newly found peace of mind. Alice's wiles manage to break through Kurt's civilized and composed veneer. In the end, Kurt shows himself to be no better than any other human animal: "You have roused the wild beast in me, which for years I've been trying to kill by self-denial and penance. . . . Come to me! I will suffocate you — with a kiss." Alice believes she has liberated herself from one vampire only to find herself in the clutches of another jealous monster of her own creation. Even though Kurt initially seems to be in control of his feelings, we ultimately see that he cannot escape the drives and instincts of his species — the sins of the flesh.

As in *Miss Julie*, the environment of *The Dance of Death* (I) can be considered as contributing to the behavior of the characters. Alice and Edgar are not only psychically but also physically separated from the rest of the world. The feeling of confinement evoked by their surroundings strengthens Alice and Edgar's discontent with their marriage and fosters an oppressive boredom. The atmosphere of the prison is dark, and Alice suggests that her two children who died perished from lack of light.

Edgar, Alice, and Kurt are ruled by drives and passions they themselves do not fully understand. As Edgar muses in the final act: "So extraordinary that I can't believe it was I who behaved in such a despicable way." Edgar might find solace in Paul's words: "It is no longer I that do it, but sin which dwells within me." The Captain has allowed himself to be governed by the sins of his flesh, so he himself is not really responsible for his actions.

The tribulations of the spirit are somewhat more difficult to depict on stage. The necessity of this task, however, caused Strindberg to experiment with techniques that have been called expressionistic. But, as we have encountered modified naturalism in *The Dance of Death* (I), so we also find expressionism with limitations. Strindberg has chosen an essentially realistic mode for the play, and no matter how much he may exaggerate actions and scenic elements, he does not leave the realm of the possible and pass irretrievably into the supernatural. Strindberg supplies a rational explanation for everything, although he points toward alternative explanations.

To conceive of an expressionistic reading of the same play requires quite a shift in our perspective. Instead of a cause of behavior, the environment becomes a physical manifestation of inner psychic processes. Instead of scientific objectivity, the audience is exposed to the highly subjective inner turmoil of the characters. That is not to say that an expressionistic reading precludes the naturalistic reading; both levels are simultaneously present in the play.

From the naturalistic point of view, the atmosphere of the former prison was a cause of behavior; however, from an expressionistic perspective, the prison's presence is a symptom of a psychological state. Kurt remarks about the criminality that hangs in the air and about the sensation of having dead bodies beneath the floorboards. Later we hear from Alice how Edgar has "uprooted" all her friends and relatives. Alice accuses Edgar of locking her up in a tower, but actually the two are psychologically shackled to each other and share their confinement. For the most part, the chains binding Alice and Edgar have been forged by sexual attraction. Their spirits are confined to the "prison of the flesh."

The significance of the telegraph on the set is perhaps best explained in reference to some lines from a later Strindberg play, *The Ghost Sonata:* "Silence cannot hide anything — which is more than you can say for words. I read the other day that the differences in languages originated among the primitive savages who sought to keep their secrets from the other tribes. Languages are therefore codes."[8] Alice and Edgar's only communication with the outside world is quite literally in code. Edgar uses the code because he is afraid that the operators will overhear his secrets. He has also used the code to keep secrets from Alice. Alice proves her betrayal of the Captain by learning this code. She is also able to decipher the code of Edgar's spoken words: "I'm so good at translating his lies and can always get at the truth with my dictionary." Alice and Edgar are unable to communicate honestly with each other because they speak a language of lies.

Thus, in the first act we find Alice and Edgar firmly imprisoned in the flesh. Edgar has lost his belief in his own spirit, and believes that humanity is merely fertilizer for the garden. He believes that life is not worth much if he is not able to smoke and drink, that is, indulge the flesh. In the words of Paul, he has turned God's truth to lies. He now speaks only in lies.

Edgar's spirit is reactivated by his brush with death. After his revelatory attack and before he settles down for the night the following exchange occurs between Edgar and Kurt:

THE CAPTAIN: If you knew what agonies I am suffering.

KURT: Physical?

THE CAPTAIN: No, not physical.

KURT: Then they must be spiritual. There's no third alternative.

Then the Captain exclaims that he does not want to die because he is worried about the pain. His concerns are still centered around the body, when he should be worried about his soul. By the end of the night, however, he discovers the immortality of the soul. This is not yet a conversion, but merely the reaction of a proud and egocentric man in the face of impending oblivion.

In the second act, although Edgar has discovered his own spirit, he still tries to find some means for prolonging the life of the body. He stops drinking, consults a doctor, professes his intention of marrying a young wife, and practices vampirism on both Alice and Kurt. Edgar's fight with Alice and Kurt assumes the appearance of a military campaign; the set becomes nothing less than a battleground. In act 2, the Captain effects a change in the setting by changing his costume. At the end of this act, the Captain stands in dress uniform, reveals to Kurt and Alice how he has supposedly defeated them, and orders them to abandon the fortress. When confronted with his wife's infidelity, Edgar attacks her with his sword. Throughout the play, each of the characters is involved in a battle with the others. Each chooses a weapon and a strategy. The Captain takes Kurt's children as hostages and threatens to cut off all supplies to his wife. Alice uses sex as her weapon and takes Kurt prisoner to use him against her husband. Kurt seeks to remain a neutral power, but is eventually overwhelmed by Alice's propaganda. In *The Dance of Death* (I), the Strindbergian "battle of the brains" is presented with the verisimilitude of military maneuvers.

As previously noted, Strindberg, in his letter to Axel Herrlin, observed, "The longing for innocence and beauty makes itself felt the strongest after sinning!" In act 2, the Captain has fled from his brush with death into his most outrageous deeds to date. Edgar's extreme behavior acts as a catharsis and paves the road to conversion.

The masterful pantomime at the beginning of the final act portrays this conversion. As in the previous act, the Captain begins by playing a lone hand. He is engaged in solitaire but cannot get the game to come out right, and so he throws his strategy out the window. He ritualistically jettisons his whisky, cigarettes, and eyeglasses — all physical crutches. Instead of outward vision, Edgar is more in need of "in-sight." He then dispatches a number of his self-deceptions and illusions: his wife's laurels, the piano that played the military marches, his wife's picture, and their love letters. Now, having laid aside these concerns of the flesh, Edgar is prepared for a true conversion.

Via both naturalistic and expressionistic techniques, Strindberg was able to portray the struggle between the flesh and the spirit. But something is missing: these struggles must be given a divine context. Romans 1:20 tells us: "For the invisible things of him from the creation of the world are clearly seen, being understood by the things that are made, even his eternal power and Godhead." Strindberg had realized this several years earlier, as his diary bears clear witness through its numerous notations of natural phenomena that supposedly have divine significance. Thus, the remaining dramaturgical task was: how to show the intervention of the hand of God without departing from the fundamentally realistic mode of the play. Strindberg's hints at the presence of a divine will are many.

The theme of Eden and the Fall is pervasive throughout *The Dance of Death* (I). Strindberg's set description for the opening curtain reads: *"On either side of the big doorway are windows, in one of which are [pots of] flowers and in the other [a cage of] birds. . . . The glass doors are open, and an artillery man on sentry duty is seen down by the shore battery. . . . Now and then his sword glitters in the red light of the setting sun."* This arrangement has a familiar ring to it — which can be accounted for by comparing Genesis 3:24: "So he drove out the man; and he placed at the east of the garden of Eden cherubims, and a flaming sword which turned every way, to keep the way of the tree of life." Alice and Edgar have been cast out of paradise and find themselves subjected to the punishments of the outside world and the sins of the flesh. The verb *att falla* (to fall) is a leitmotif throughout the play. A character "falls into apathy," "falls to the floor," "falls in tears," and "falls on their knees." When Kurt is discussing humanity's fall from grace with Alice, she — who is herself a fallen woman — asks which fall he is talking about. The question is appropriate because, ever since the original Fall, humankind has not stopped falling. The continual repetition of the Fall is inescapable during life; it is part of humanity's punishment.

This leads back to Paul's letter to the Romans. Humanity is punished by sin. The primary sin in *Dance of Death* (I) is lust. Alice, Edgar, and Kurt are in a Swedenborgian hell-on-earth and are being punished by their own passions. Strindberg directly names the island on which they live Little Hell. The stormwinds blowing throughout the play indicate yet another literary hell: in the second circle of Dante's *Inferno,* carnal sinners are tossed about by an incessant storm. Strindberg eventually furnishes us with the following dialogue:

THE CAPTAIN: You're not so childish as to believe in hell, are you?

KURT: Don't you believe in it — you who are right in it?

THE CAPTAIN: Only metaphorically.

KURT: You've described your hell so realistically that metaphors, however poetic, are out of the picture.

Although the characters may be in hell, God has not abandoned them. At certain points, the hand of God seems to intervene in the fates of the characters. Although Strindberg does not give God any lines, he finds other ways for God to express Himself. The cards the characters play with serve as a divine oracle. In the first scene, when Edgar and Alice are playing, spades turn up as trump. Edgar is dismayed because in mystic circles spades are associated with winter, the ace of spades being a card that forebodes death. Doors slam and windows rattle as expressions of divine disapproval of the character's words and actions. The door slams when Edgar has demonstrated his atheism, and the window rattles when he shreds the portrait of his wife. Perhaps the closest that God comes to actually speaking is in the final scene of the play. Alice is driven to her knees in fervent prayer beseeching God to grant a way out of their crisis, and she promptly receives a direct reply by telegraph. This is as close to a *deus ex machina* as Strindberg can come and still maintain his realistic mode.

A central pointer toward the divine context is the dance-of-death motif indicated in the title. Edgar is engaged in a medieval dance of death and Strindberg sees to it that Edgar's dance is accompanied by music. First it is the music drifting over from the Doctor's party. Then it is Alice's rendition of "Entry of the Boyars," during which Edgar collapses. During the Captain's revealing conversion pantomime, the music used between the acts is supposed to continue. This is perhaps the most surrealistic effect in the play.

Edgar's dances with death spur him from atheism to an excessive bout of sinning, to repentance and resignation. On one level, the play ends where it begins with the discussion of the upcoming silver anniversary. But as both Sprinchorn and Lindström indicate, the Captain has, like Job, made a spiritual spiral upward. He has temporarily freed himself from his fixation with the flesh and waits for life to begin with the approach of physical death. He realizes that all are in need of pity and that all one can do in this life is clean house and submit to God's trials. Purity of spirit can be attained only when the individual sheds the corporal baggage that condemns humankind to a state of sinfulness.

Thus, the first act of the play is spent primarily sketching Edgar's existence for us. He is an atheist and a practiced sinner. However, this is altered when he suffers his revelatory attack. Edgar claims that he has been on the other side and what he has seen haunts him throughout the play. As Lindström points out, his conversation with Kurt after this attack is in essence *dialogus mortis cum homine*. Edgar's attempts to assimilate his vision first cause him to invent the immortality of the soul and then, in the second act, to flee from death. Of course, these attempts are doomed to failure.

The pantomime scene at the beginning of the final act is the point of Edgar's conversion and rebirth. When Alice enters the room and sees that Edgar has lit all the candles, she exclaims, "It looks like Christmas Eve in here!" Edgar's conversion has the same significance for himself in terms of redemption as the birth of Christ had for humanity. Sprinchorn interprets this scene as Edgar's vastation; however, it seems more likely that his vastation took place during his attack while he was actually on the other side. Edgar flees from the brutal truth of his vision into illusions and lies, only to come up against the truth again; whereupon conversion and resignation ensue.

Within this paper I have tried to indicate how the dramaturgy of *The Dance of Death* (I) arose almost naturally from the needs of Strindberg to express on the stage his own speculations about body, spirit, and their divine context. Scholarship has identified this drama as both naturalistic and expressionistic, and, as I have shown, both these judgments are true to a degree. However, Strindberg did not begin with the intention of writing a naturalistic or an expressionistic play. Rather, these techniques were the means through which Strindberg attempted to project his own view of the world.

This worldview has been described at length by Göran Stockenström.[9] It is a mystical vision of the universe with close ties to concrete reality, as can be seen in comments such as the following from *Inferno*: "Spirits have become positivists, in harmony with the times, and are therefore no longer content to manifest themselves only in visions."[10] Or, as Strindberg wrote to Anders Eliasson: "The natural explanations I accept as exoteric popular explanations but behind them there are the esoteric ones." In *The Dance of Death* (I), Strindberg reproduced nature as he perceived it. The supernatural dimension that lurks in the background is an essential component of his perception of nature. This dimension was all the more important to him because it grew out of a privileged view of the world. Not all possess enough penetration to interpret the divine will behind the naturalistic facade. In most of the post-Inferno plays, including the historical plays, Strindberg has exercised this privileged vision to interpret the divine meaning in the chaos of concrete reality.

In *The Dance of Death* (I), the concrete reality to be interpreted is a series of biological drives. Strindberg thought that he had discovered the divine purpose of these drives in Paul's letter to the Romans. Biological drives lead the individual to sin, and sin is a punishment in itself. Without sin there would be no repentance. These drives tyrannize the spirit so that the will to do good is often thwarted by diabolical urges. From Strindberg's point of view, the most attractive feature of this theory is that it absolves guilt, in Paul's words (cf. Romans 7:20): "It is no more I that do it, but sin that dwelleth in me."

With the exception of isolated flashes of insight, the characters of *The Dance of Death* (I) are unable to perceive and articulate the divine context of which they are a part. In the final act, the Captain asks Kurt, "Then what is the meaning of this mess?" Kurt answers, "In my better moments I have thought that the meaning was just that we should not understand, and yet submit." The knowledge of this meaning is the property of God and the playwright. At best, the characters can describe their own symptoms, which is essentially the function of naturalism. The playwright, however, possesses the insight to diagnose the disease.

When these restrictions are placed on the dialogue, when the characters themselves cannot explain the significance of the play's events, when there is no Delphic oracle to elucidate divine intentions, then this task devolves upon scenic means of expression. Decor, properties, lighting, music, sound effects, mime, gesture, movement, and so on must be made to speak. The necessity of enhancing the expressiveness of scenic elements caused Strindberg to develop techniques that changed the shape of modern theater. In *A Dream Play*, this tendency can be seen in full flower. The dialogue is secondary to the eloquence of the scenic elements. In *The Dance of Death* (I), Strindberg has primarily sought to resolve a religious question, but in the process he has begun resolving dramaturgical questions in a way that will ultimately have a profound effect on later movements in the theater.

PART IV

The Dream Plays: Dramatic Discourse and Stagings

14

Expressionistic Features in
To Damascus (I)

Timo Tiusanen

Calling *To Damascus* (I) "expressionistic" is, of course, nothing new. Rather, it reflects a consensus among many Strindberg scholars. Gösta M. Bergman calls *To Damascus* (I) "a monodrama" and says that German expressionist plays developed into monodramas following Strindberg's footsteps.[1] Or, to take a more recent phrasing by Kela Kvam, "With the Damascus trilogy Strindberg had foreshadowed the monologue play and the *Stationendrama* of expressionism."[2]

The Swedish-American scholar C. E. W. L. Dahlström published a study of *Strindberg's Dramatic Expressionism* in 1930. It is a many-sided discussion of the field of problems mentioned in its title — a study that may be somewhat dated but is not yet antiquated. Dahlström finds six distinctive features in expressionism and calls them control factors. I shall quote him in abridged form, giving you the first two phrases within each factor.

1. Radiations of the ego, solipsism
2. The unconscious, *Einfühlung*
3. *Seele, ur*-ishness
4. Music, objectification of inner experience
5. Religion, the search for God
6. The worth of man, social-political framework[3]

Dahlström translates the German expression *Ausstrahlungen des Ichs* into "radiations of the ego"; I have left a few other phrases in their German form. By "radiations of the ego," Dahlström means that the expressionist playwrights often went to the extreme of peopling their hero-centered stage with characters that were only thinly veiled aspects of the hero. The Beggar or the Confessor in *To Damascus* (I) have, of course, widely been taken as forces within the mind of the Stranger, and this interpretation concurs with the first of Dahlström's "control factors."

With Dalhström and his categories in mind, I shall now turn to another critic's effort to define expressionism in the context of Strindberg's plays. In the preface to his translations of Strindberg's eight expressionist plays, Arvid Paulson writes: "The term [expressionism] embraces fantasy and symbolism in general, and is especially applicable to works distinguished by upheavals of emotion affecting our inner view of the world, distortions of experience and thought, more or less abstract characters . . . and states of mind comparable to dreams or deliriums in which appearance, time, and space lose cohesion or continuity."[4] Whereas Dahlström admits that his factors may be partially overlapping, Paulson succeeds in gathering several distinctive features into a coherent sentence intended to be a definition of expressionism in drama.

I appreciate both these efforts to grasp the essence of expressionism. Yet I am not entirely happy with either one, nor have I been able to find a definition of expressionism in drama that would be totally satisfactory. Thus, I present a system based on the following distinctive features of expressionism in drama and will test *To Damascus* (I) against this list:

1. Distorted reality
2. Broken chronology
3. Expressive settings and lights
4. Monodrama: emphasis on monologues
5. Chorus and mass scenes
6. Pantomime and dance
7. Elements of nightmare
8. Social protests: against machine age and city life
9. Idea surpassing characterization
10. Sharp contrasts
11. Dynamic qualities

To Damascus (I) moves somewhere in the half-lit zone between reality and total fantasy — so much so that the play has been interpreted as a vision or dream of the Stranger. The distortion is most marked in the Asylum scene, yet Ollén is certainly correct in calling it a pioneering feature in the play that the representatives of the unconscious step into reality quietly and self-evidently.[5] There is no clear-cut borderline between realistic and expressionistic scenes, as there is in *Spring's Awakening* by Frank Wedekind, another play foreboding and heralding the later advent of expressionism.

"Broken chronology" — the second feature — is a more disputable point. The play proceeds in the present tense on the stage; it has no dual movement forward and backward in time as has *The Emperor Jones* by O'Neill, nor does it resort to flashbacks or to "flashes forward." Yet one might conjecture a disruption in the experience of the Stranger right at the core of the play, in the Asylum scene, where the protagonist wakes up with his memory temporarily out of action. Let us put a question mark beside this criterion.

No matter what stage style is chosen for a production of *To Damascus* (I), it is hardly imaginable that the play could be given a fully realistic treatment in the scenography. Some stylized or expressionistic settings and lights seem obligatory. The play is certainly a monodrama; it has chorus and mass scenes that must be realized on the stage with the help of at least pantomime, if not dance. The action in the early scene with the funeral guests in brown, and of the Asylum scene, is easy to envisage as stylized toward uniformity and mechanical manner of moving, as were many of the mass scenes in expressionism. There are, beyond a reasonable doubt, elements of nightmare in the play; there are sharp contrasts and dynamic qualities among its stylistic characteristics. Thus features three through six seem to be present in *To Damascus* (I).

"Social protest," on the other hand, is not a strong component in this play. If there is a protest involved, it is a very personal one — Strindberg's protest against his own sense of guilt and the intolerable dullness and mediocrity of life. In fact, just as *Spring's Awakening* originates one main branch of expressionism, which will be called socio-expressionism, so *To Damascus* (I) is a starting point for another branch, frequently called psycho-expressionism. Both subdivisions face and describe chaos in life: in the case of socio-expressionism, that chaos is caused by a turbulence in society; in psycho-expressionism, by a disorder within the protagonist's state of mind. Sometimes these two types of chaos coincide or overlap.

The last feature on my list — "dynamic qualities" — may not apply to *To Damascus* (I). The basic idea of the play is the long and unwilling pilgrimage of the Stranger to repentance — a theme growing out of Strindberg's Inferno crisis. The character somehow manages to balance between being merely a configuration of this theme and capturing our sympathy as a human being.

How many points does *To Damascus* (I) score in my test? There are eight affirmative answers, two question marks, and one negative outcome. Is *To Damascus* (I) an expressionistic play?

Before answering that question, I should like to state that my list of distinctive features stems from my studies in American and German expressionism, which I undertook long before I had read *To Damascus* (I) or found Dahlström's study. Dahlström puts a great deal of emphasis on the contents of expressionistic plays, whereas the main emphasis in my list is on formal elements. The aim of the entire mental exercise is to create a system that would be more coherent than most impressionistic definitions of expressionism yet fluid enough to permit a certain amount of variation. It remains to be stated, however, that a high number of expressionistic features in any given play is not, in itself, a sign of high artistic value. In fact, I am inclined to be suspicious of such purity. I favor instead a kind of stylistic eclecticism or mixture.

My last point is an effort to see *To Damascus* (I) from the perspective furnished not only by expressionism but by several conflicting and advancing movements in modern drama and theater. In one scene of the play, the Stranger, convalescing after the effects of a spiritual hangover, feels "the exquisite pangs of conscience" and he revels in his "body's pain while [his] soul floats like a cloud around [his] head." Passages like these are a constant problem for any scholar of Strindberg. How does one evaluate his embarrassing self-confessions? Or the ambivalence in the passage? To what extent is the passage formulated by a conscious artist whose relation to his own ego was as clinically analytic as that of Anton Chekhov to one of his less sympathetic patients? Was Strindberg a conscious or, as Sven Delblanc puts it, "an unconscious modernist"?[6] To what extent do we witness unfortunate lapses in taste, self-confessions that are almost too honest and awkward to be true and thus without any affectation at all in their rawness of emotion? To what extent did Strindberg merely polish and finish his literary themes, bit by bit and incident by incident, until he reached a sovereign mastery of matter and manner in the world of his creation?

I do not know. Perhaps it is true that the posthumous reaction to Strindberg, among expressionists and others, sees in the breaches and breaking points of his style, in its constant dives into the pitfalls of egocentricity, one of the most important pieces of evidence for his continuing modernity. He keeps us on tenterhooks. We never know when his characters switch from a concrete stage situation into a highly emotional and generalized outburst. From the point of view of orthodox dramatic strategies, this is one of his main vices — a vice that becomes a virtue, perhaps, when considered from the point of view of *avant-garde* developments in drama. In his very private sense of being justly and unjustly hurt by his neighbors, friends, enemies, and life itself, he surpasses most German expressionists, even if the latter were frontline soldiers from the chaos and ruination of World War I. August Strindberg has put so much of our despair and feeling of alienation, our nightmares and fears, our black humor and graceless state of sin into his words and stage situations that his despair sounds to us strangely familiar and almost consolatory, as if he were one among us, muttering on the stage.

15

Titanism and Satanism in
To *Damascus* (I)

Barry Jacobs

To Damascus (I) (1898), as the biblical allusion in the
title implies, is a play about religious conversion. After a series of increasingly ghastly experiences, a thoroughgoing materialist and nihilist, who is
identified only as the Stranger, is forced to acknowledge that some invisible
powers govern our lives and that death may not be the end of everything.
Shattered, but still somewhat skeptical at the end of the play, he agrees to
accompany the Lady into the church "to hear new songs." Is this really a
conversion? One is tempted to answer by echoing the Stranger's last
speech in the play: "Perhaps!" Although his titanic suffering has obviously
changed him, his "conversion" raises some difficult questions about how
we are to interpret the last scenes of this play. To suggest interpretations for
some of the problematical issues I see here, I will concentrate on the titanic
and satanic aspects of the Stranger's character and on their role in reshaping
his attitude toward guilt and the meaning of suffering.

In the first draft of *Inferno*, Strindberg wrote, "God became both a
scientific discovery and a need,"[1] and he described his own discoveries
about religious experience in three autobiographical works: *Inferno, Legends,*
and *Jacob Wrestles*. His famous "Inferno crisis, " which was a series of five
psychotic attacks (or psychological experiments, according to some),[2] followed a pattern that has been charted by Gunnar Brandell, who has shown

Titanism and Satanism in To Damascus *(I)*

in detail how the fears that plagued Strindberg during the first three crises — poverty (beggars) and alcoholism — were eclipsed by religious concerns when "a cult of Jehovah" emerged after the third crisis.[3] The last crisis (in November 1896) had a conscious moral and religious dimension: in *Inferno* and *Legends* Strindberg describes his spiritual growth, which he largely attributes to the wisdom and comfort he found in the works of Swedenborg: "By enlightening me as to the true nature of the horrors I had suffered during the previous year, Swedenborg had freed me from the electrical machines, the practitioners of black magic, the workers of spells, the envious alchemists, and from the madness I feared would overtake me. He had pointed out my only road to salvation: to seek out the demons in their lairs, inside myself, and then kill them by . . . repentance."[4]

Although it is extremely difficult to assess the synthetic religion that he created — his Confessionless Christianity, as he sometimes called it — it is much easier to see how his conversion affected his position as a literary figure: Strindberg, the great literary naturalist, the apostle of Darwinism, the ally and disciple of Nietzsche, now had "scientific proof" of God's existence. Moreover, he was aware that he was not alone; indeed he was in the vanguard of a new religious awakening.[5] All the recent converts — literary figures like Arne Garborg, Gustaf Fröding, and J.-K. Huysmans —had been sinners and blasphemers, but none so culpable as Strindberg. What could be more natural, therefore, than that he should compare himself to Saul, the Pharisee who persecuted Christians, and whose sudden overwhelming experience on the Damascus Road made him not only a Christian but the Apostle to the Gentiles? But although he insisted on interpreting his conversion in theological terms, Strindberg's profoundest insight was really psychological and concerned his guilt feelings. During the last of the Inferno crises, for example, he began to see that he was his own greatest enemy and that his sufferings came from within. The gradual realization that his persecutors were largely the creations of his own guilt feelings projected onto the outer world not only led to his "cure" but also provided him with the plot pattern of several plays. It first occurs in *To Damascus* (I), and it recurs in such works as *Advent* (1898), *Midsummer* (1900), and *Easter* (1900). At the beginning of these plays, his protagonists are obsessed with the notion that they are suffering innocently: characters like the Stranger and Elis (in *Easter*) initially find it impossible to reconcile their monumental sufferings with their relatively insignificant guilt (innocence). In the first scene of *To Damascus* (I), for instance, the Lady remarks upon the profound sympathy that the Stranger awakens in her:

THE LADY: Yes I have never seen another person, no one in my whole life, whose mere appearance brings me to the verge of tears

> . . . tell me, what do you have on your conscience? Have you
> committed some shameful deed that was never discovered or
> punished?
>
> THE STRANGER: That's a good question! I do not have any more
> crimes on my conscience than others who are going free — yes,
> one: I didn't want to be life's fool.
>
> (*SS* 29:10)

Here — like one of Job's comforters — she suggests that suffering is God's
punishment for sin, while the Stranger's reply leads us to the heart of his
problem: his rejection (or denial) of his own guilt.

Strindberg himself tended to regard suffering as punishment, and he
could usually resign himself to his own great sufferings only when he could
find a guilty deed or an evil thought to cancel each instance of physical pain
or mental anguish. Occasionally he could get his books to balance, but it
was a very delicate balance indeed. Before Swedenborg taught him to turn
inward to find the sources of his anguish, he pursued various exculpatory
ideas that might enable him to locate external sources for his guilt — and he
never entirely abandoned those ideas. One such idea — eloquently expressed in "Graveyard Reveries" — is the notion that life is a penal colony to
which we have been sentenced for crimes we have committed in an earlier
existence. Moreover, his analysis of his own dreams did not lead him into
his unconscious mind, but — in a most unFreudian manner — encouraged
him instead to believe in the phenomenon of the *Doppelgänger*:

> For the past several years I have made notations on all my dreams,
> and I am convinced that man leads a double life, that imaginings,
> fancies, dreams have a kind of reality. So that all of us are spiritual
> somnambulists and in our dreams do deeds that, according to their
> varying nature, persecute [förfölja] us in the waking state with a
> feeling of satisfaction or bad conscience, fear of the consequences
> . . . . I think that the so-called "persecution mania" often has a
> good foundation in remorse for evil actions committed "in sleep,"
> hazy recollections of which haunt us. And the fantasies of the poet,
> so despised by narrow, limited souls, are realities.
>
> (*SS* 28:280)

Finally — and this means of rejecting guilt is most relevant to *To Damascus*
(I) — Strindberg frequently flirted with belief in the transmigration of
souls. In a letter to Ola Hansson on January 3, 1888, when he was reading
Poe for the first time, he playfully suggested that the soul of Poe (who died
the year Strindberg was born) might have "smouldered down through
masses of media" to him. During the Inferno period, the possibility of this

sort of metempsychosis seemed to him a more serious matter. No one could deserve to suffer as much as he was suffering. From whom might he have inherited his guilt: Napoleon? Robert le Diable? Entries in the *Occult Diary* indicate that he frequently dreamed of Napoleon, and at various times even identified himself with him. In the 1890s he half-playfully signed several letters to his daughter Kerstin "August Bp." (Bonaparte) and "the Corsican."[6] True, Napoleon had much to answer for, but he was hardly demonic; therefore Strindberg became even more fascinated by the legendary medieval figure Robert le Diable, who, like Merlin and Gilles de Rais (called Bluebeard), incarnated the struggle between God and Satan.[7]

Strindberg first called the play that became *To Damascus* (I) "Robert le Diable." A reference to him in *Jacob Wrestles* (*SS* 28:337) indicates that Strindberg was familiar with some version of the rambling medieval romance devoted to this demonic figure who underwent ten years of humiliation to expiate his many violent crimes — he pretended to be a half-witted deaf-mute and contended with dogs for his food. Strindberg probably read the modern French version of this romance, which went through countless printings in the popular *Bibliotèque bleue* series in the last century, but his real inspiration seems more likely to have come from Meyerbeer's then still popular opera *Robert le Diable*. A notation in the *Occult Diary* indicates that Strindberg read Scribe's libretto for this opera (which he mistakenly attributed to E. Sue) around the same time that he was first reading Eliphas Lévi's *Les Clefs des grands mystères.*[8] Scribe was heavily under the influence of Weber's *Der Freischütz*; therefore he transformed this chaotic medieval French romance into a prime example of romantic satanism. Throughout the opera — and one should not overlook certain operatic tendencies in all Strindberg's so-called dream plays — the forces of evil (represented by Bertram) and the forces of good (represented by Alice) struggle within the protagonist, Robert, Duke of Normandy, who is constantly thwarted in his efforts to marry his beloved, Princess Isabelle. He is unaware that his constant companion and confidant, Bertram (who looks like the Devil) is really his demonic father who has been commissioned by the forces of evil to win his soul. Although Bertram's corrupting influence promises ultimately to succeed, it is not working fast enough; he is therefore informed that unless his task is accomplished by midnight a few days after the action begins, Robert will be liberated by a higher power. In the first act Robert's foster sister Alice, who is as good as Bertram is evil, arrives with their mother's testament. Expiring, the mother dispatched Alice to protect Robert from the evil power that constantly threatens him, and now (in Heaven) she continues to pray for his salvation. In Bertram Alice recognizes the Devil from the Saint Michael painting in her village church — a detail that may have suggested the use of the St. Michael painting in scene 9 of *To*

Damascus (I). After his encounter with Alice in Act I, Robert becomes aware for the first time that two contending tendencies are pulling him in opposite directions: one toward good, the other toward evil. In Act V, which takes place outside the Cathedral of Palermo, the prayers of chanting monks and the lyrical pleadings of Alice keep Robert from yielding to Bertram. While he wavers, the clock strikes midnight and he is saved. The earth opens to swallow Bertram and the scene changes to the inside of the cathedral where Robert meets Isabelle at the altar and his soul is redeemed through holy marriage.

Scribe's version of the story ends in a church and certainly for Strindberg at this period one of the most important aspects of this opera must have been its obsession with religion.[9] Like Scribe, Strindberg was well aware of the dramatic nature of religious ritual and his sense of its scenic potential is nowhere more apparent than in the Asylum scene, where the singing of part of *Dies irae* is followed by the horrifying reading of the curse from Deuteronomy with antiphonal responses by the ghostly inmates of "The Good Help" Asylum. Perhaps another link between *Robert le Diable* and *To Damascus* (I) is the satanic strain that flashes forth from the Stranger from time to time. In Scribe's text, where Robert is always conscious of his dual nature, Bertram looks like what he is — the Devil. In *To Damascus* (I), however, the Stranger, who occasionally resembles the Devil, only gradually becomes aware of his dual nature. In scene 1 when the Lady suggests that religion may alleviate his sufferings, he replies, "You mean that ringing bells and holy water would comfort me. . . . I have tried, but that only made things worse. It was the same as what happens when the Devil sees the sign of the cross" (*SS* 29:14). This figure of speech becomes real in scene 2, when the Doctor notices that the play of sunlight and shadow on his portrait of the Stranger have momentarily made him resemble the Devil. Later, in the first Kitchen scene (scene 7), the Old Man reports to the Mother that the superstitious peasants are already spreading tales about how horses shy when the Stranger approaches and how dogs attack him, while the boatman is claiming that the ferryboat floated higher in the water when the Stranger boarded it (*SS* 29:76).[10]

At an early age — long before he knew Meyerbeer's opera — Strindberg had derived a concept of the demonic from Schiller and Byron. He was 19 in 1868 when he first read Schiller's *Die Räuber* and, shortly thereafter, Byron's *Manfred*. Both works made a profound impact on him and informed his early demonic characters, Gert Bokpräntare (in *Master Olof* [1872]), Lucifer (in *The Epilogue to Master Olof* [ca. 1877]) and Falander (in *The Red Room* [1879]).[11] During the 1880s these satanic figures all but disappear from Strindberg's works, but after the Inferno crisis, they reemerge in more highly developed, subtler form. This refinement doubtless owes something

Titanism and Satanism in To Damascus *(I)*

to the French occultists and to J.-K. Huysmans. A few months before he wrote *To Damascus* (I), Strindberg made the following entry in his *Occult Diary*: "It is noteworthy how Huysmans' development follows the same course as mine. From magic and satanism to Catholicism." A year or so after publishing *Là-Bas* (1891), his novel about latter-day satanism, Huysmans had retreated to a monastery for a few weeks. Although his experience there failed to live up to his mystical hopes, during the years that followed he finally did "dwindle into" a Roman Catholic. In 1895 he published *En Route*, the novel about his conversion. At the time of writing *Là-Bas*, however, he was not so much a satanist himself as he was a literary naturalist bent upon writing a novel about satanism; most of his material came from his informants, Berthe Courrière and the infamous Abbé Boullan.[12] Strindberg was certainly not interested in the more lurid aspects of satanism: exorcisms, black masses, the image of Christ tatooed on the soles of the feet so that the satanist could ever tread upon the Savior — the sort of thing that attracted Huysmans; nor, one might add, would Strindberg ever have settled for the sort of aesthetic Catholicism that became a refuge for Huysmans. To him satanism had a much narrower meaning, which we can discover from a curious entry in the *Occult Diary* concerning modes of tuning a violin: "A E A E or C# A E A (Wagner). Country fiddlers sometimes tune their fiddles C# A E A, but they are loath to do so because it is 'demonic.' Cf. Cabala on the subject of bringing together what nature has separated: Perverse! . . . — Wagner is satanic. Satanism = to believe God evil (Cabala)" (*OD* 64). A few months after he completed *To Damascus* (I), Strindberg repeated this simple definition of satanism in a letter to his friend Emil Kléen (on July 22, 1898). He writes that he has been studying Sar Péladan's *Vice suprême* and finds it most remarkable: "Same satanism = belief in evil." It is really this notion of satanism — his belief in evil — (and not fleeting suggestions that he is the Devil) that makes the Stranger resemble Robert le Diable, that makes his last book so dangerous, and poisons his whole life. To the extent that they believe that they are innocent sufferers — that God allows evil to exist — many of Strindberg's post-Inferno protagonists are "satanic." And their only hope of salvation lies in confrontation with their own guilt.

Here one must distinguish between Strindberg's satanic and his titanic heroes. During the period when his outlook most closely approached Nietzschean nihilism (the late 1880s), he created Magister Törner (in *Tschandala*), a titanic figure who uses his enormous intelligence to triumph over his wily and ruthless foe. But as the case of Nietzsche himself seemed to prove, being a genius may well pose a threat to one's sanity.[13] That is why Strindberg's next important titanic hero, Inspector Borg in *By the Open Sea* (1889), is unable, despite his great intellectual gifts, to save himself from madness. Totally unlike the Blond Beast envisioned by Nietzsche, Borg is a delicate,

Barry Jacobs

hypersensitive man who in the early part of the book is capable of achieving a kind of reverse Nirvana by filling the universe with his own personality — in *To Damascus* (I) the Stranger experiences the same sort of apotheosis in scene 4, "By the Sea" (*SS* 29:54). During his meditations on nature, Borg derives great pleasure from allowing his mind to run up and down the evolutionary scale until he finds himself standing at the top; then — by analogy — he achieves self-mastery by exploring the past stages of his own individual development as far back as he can trace them. Without losing his integrity he can easily adapt himself to the society of others merely by descending the evolutionary ladder the requisite number of rungs and then by using memory as a guide to the thoughts and feelings of people at that particular stage of development. However, his unhappy love affair with Maria (the prototype of the Strindbergian vampire) and his inability to reshape her personality prove to be his undoing. He eventually loses his ability for self-mastery to such an extent that his personality begins to disintegrate. Unable to find any fixed point outside himself, he goes mad and commits suicide. His titanic aspirations as well as his tragic fate stem from his atheism.

The next great titan Strindberg created is that aspect of the Stranger that reveals itself most fully when he assumes the role of Jacob wrestling with the angel. The struggle takes place offstage (and in the consciousness of the Stranger) between scenes 8 and 9, that is, between the time he leaves the Rose Chamber and awakens from a coma of three months' duration in "The Good Help" Asylum. The Abbess tells all that is known about his case:

> You were found in the mountains above the ravine with a cross that you had broken down from a Calvary and with which you were threatening someone you imagined that you saw up in the clouds. You were feverish and you fell over a cliff. That's where you were found — unhurt, but delirious. And so you were brought here to the hospital and put in bed. Since that time you have been delirious, and despite the fact that you have complained of pain in one hip, we have been unable to find any injury. (*SS* 29:89)

In *Jacob Wrestles*, the fragmentary work Strindberg abandoned just before he began to write *To Damascus* (I), he describes how Christ daily used to "persecute" him all along the rue Bonaparte, accosting him from the windows of countless shops dealing in religious goods and how he used to take refuge in the church of Saint-Sulpice where he would fortify himself by contemplating Delacroix's picture of Jacob wrestling with the angel. Jacob, the wrestler who remains on his feet despite his wounded thigh, now becomes the paradigm for the Strindberg whose newly won religion was beginning to fill him with confusing emotions and confront him with contradictory dogmas. Strindberg had found "religion," but no peace. He was disappointed and angry — angry about the reverses, the betrayals, the frustrations, and the poverty that still seemed to plague him. In the fictional part of the work, he several times encounters a mysterious, Christlike figure to whom he pours out his heart. In these long tirades he experiences deep shame for all his past errors, lists all his doubts about which path to follow to find blessedness, and expresses all his bitterness about the lack of justice in the world; but every time that these negative feelings humiliate him — every time they bring him to the threshold of repentance — his old anger flares up and his rebellious spirit urges him once again to challenge the "powers" to single combat. The mysterious stranger, however, is hardly a worthy opponent for Strindberg; he not only withholds his blessing but speaks little and refuses to justify himself — not surprisingly, because many of Strindberg's most damaging arguments are *pensées de l'escalier.* It is easy to see why Strindberg found comfort in Delacroix's titanic patriarch.

Although the side of Strindberg that contends with the enigmatic Christ figure in *Jacob Wrestles* returns as the titanic side of the Stranger in *To Damascus* (I), this aspect of his character is slow to emerge in the play. At curtain rise the impoverished Stranger has reached an impasse: he has left his wife and children, abandoned his literary career, and feels threatened by alcoholism, madness, and death. While waiting at a streetcorner for the post office to open so that he can collect a letter containing money due him, his sharp yearning has "summoned" his newest acquaintance, the Lady. Although he feels that she must have some important role to play in his life, he finds it difficult to define the precise nature of her mission. Early in the first scene, he expresses the odd wish to be her old, blind father whom she would lead into marketplaces to sing (*SS* 29:16) — reminiscent of the Harper and Mignon in *Wilhelm Meisters Lehrjahre,* but by the end of the scene he reverses these roles and declares his intention to liberate her from her husband, whom she calls the Werewolf. In his career as a writer, he has always regarded himself as a liberator, but now he is beginning to become aware of forces that point beyond liberation to death and rebirth.

Before the action begins we are presented with two auditory images: Mendelssohn's funeral march establishes the fact that a death has occurred; and two bells ring a total of seven times (four strokes indicating the quarter hours; three strokes to toll the hour). The first image is specific — and sobering; the second — as yet vague — is prophetic. In the course of the first scene we become aware that the Stranger — despite his claim that he derives a great sense of power from the knowledge that he can always commit suicide if things become too grim — both fears death and hopes for rebirth. The most powerful image of rebirth (or rejuvenation) in the first scene is Medea's cauldron. At the end of her second interview with the

Stranger, the Lady asks him to accompany her into the church — not to hear a sermon, but just to be soothed by the beautiful music:

> THE STRANGER: No, not into the church. It is very painful for me there and it makes me aware that I do not belong, that I am a lost soul with as little hope of returning to the church as I have of becoming a child again.
>
> THE LADY: You already know all of that, do you?
>
> THE STRANGER: Yes, that much I know, and I have the sense that my dismembered body is simmering in Medea's cauldron. I shall either go to the soap factory or arise, rejuvenated, from my own juices. It all depends on Medea's skill.
>
> (*SS* 29:23)

This image of the painful process of destruction in the hope of transformation — later picked up and translated into the haunting sound of the ever-grinding mill — is ambiguous: the Stranger's suffering might lead either to rebirth or to total destruction. In both versions of the myth to which Strindberg here refers, success depends not on Medea's skill but on her will.[14]

In some curious way, the images of rebirth and renewal also finally coalesce with the repeated use of the number seven in the play. "Seven," as Thomas Mann observed," is a good handy figure in its way, picturesque, with a savor of the mythical."[15] In *To Damascus* (I) it seems to have the same high value it held for Mann. In addition to its general symbolic value — it is viewed as symbolic of perfect order, of a complete period or cycle; moreover, it is the number forming the basic series of musical notes, of colors, and of the planetary spheres. It is also the symbol of pain.[16] Seven is fraught with Christian significance: the seven deadly sins and their corresponding virtues; the seven sacraments; the seven words from the cross; and the Seven Sleepers of Ephesus — those seven young Christians said to have taken refuge in a cave during the Decian persecution in the third century who awakened two hundred years later, thus proving the doctrine of the resurrection of the dead.

A reference to the Feast of the Seven Sleepers of Ephesus (July 27) is, in fact, the means by which Strindberg launches the numerical symbolism that recurs at so many important points in the play.[17] At the opening of scene 2, ("At the Doctor's"), the Doctor and the Sister discuss the Stranger's impending visit. The Doctor wonders if his wife's guest is the same person who, as his schoolfellow, played a prank that caused him untold suffering. They also talk about the Stranger's latest book, which shows signs of madness. Both characters express such hatred and fear of him that within relatively few speeches Strindberg manages to charge the atmosphere with a superabundance of emotion — so much so that we expect lightning to strike when the "demonic" Stranger first encounters his embittered victim. Instead, when they do meet, both men appear to hide their deep emotional distress behind inconsequential chit-chat:

THE DOCTOR: Welcome to my home.

THE STRANGER: Thank you, doctor.

THE DOCTOR: You've brought nice weather with you, which we can certainly use, since it's been raining for the past six weeks.

THE STRANGER: Not seven? Isn't it supposed to rain for seven weeks if it rains on Seven Sleepers' Day? . . . but what am I thinking of . . . we haven't had Seven Sleepers' Day yet! How stupid of me!

(*SS* 29:36-37)

By caricaturing his own superstition, the Stranger once more rejects the ordered universe in which he has ceased to believe, but — ironically — he also invokes an image (the Seven Sleepers) that may briefly suggest resurrection or rebirth, just as the severed limbs in the icebox may momentarily recall both the hopeful aspects of Medea's cauldron and the horrifying carnage concealed in Bluebeard's castle. Although these ambiguities will ultimately prove connotative of fruitfulness, in this scene most of the imagery implies destruction or death. Upon entering, the Stranger seems to recognize the Doctor, falters, and then recovers; his composure is short-lived, however, for the scene is full of menacing objects (the surgical knives and the bees), incongruous elements (the strange turtle), and ghoulishly horrifying things (the contents of the icebox) that fill him with unbearable anxiety. Particularly disquieting for him are the two titanic figures: the Doctor's oddly shaped woodpile and the madman Caesar. The woodpile, which has twice been struck by lightning, suggests that in his own way the Doctor too is defying higher powers, while Caesar plays God by interfering with the normal life-cycle of plants. The titanic imagery that prevails in this scene surfaces again in scene 4, in which the Stranger feels his self swell out until it fills the universe; and it culminates in his role as Jacob, when he brandishes a cross at his imagined adversary in the clouds.

The specifically Christian significance of the numerical symbolism does not begin to emerge until after the titanic side of the Stranger's nature has been partially subdued. During his three-month-long coma, he has been something of a *sjusovare* himself — some complex, untranslatable pun may be embedded in this situation: *sjusovare* means dormouse, one of the Seven Sleepers of Ephesus, and sluggard. At the time of his awakening, he is a changed man. Although he is still confused, he now respectfully acknowledges the existence of some higher power. Of course, he still resists this power and feels that he is suffering unjustly, but he can no longer confidently take refuge in the idea that all ends in death. In short, now that he believes in some sort of god — albeit an unjust one — he has become "satanic." To be "satanic" is to be like Robert le Diable: to be in dire need of salvation and in imminent danger of damnation. In scene 11 (the second of the two Kitchen scenes), the full significance of the number seven becomes clear.

After a night of infernal tribulations, the haunted Stranger enters the dark kitchen, where rags and dishtowels agitated by the wind combine with other elements — auditory images (the sound of the wind, distant thunder of a waterfall, mysterious thumping sounds), and visual symbols (a crucifix, a stuffed bird of prey) — to create a perfect scenic realization of his mental state. Moonlight momentarily transforms the floor into a writhing snakepit. His overwhelming burden of guilt has just caused him to relive his entire life — to reexperience the vastation (*ödeläggelse*) that was verbally presented in the Asylum scene. Now — still unwilling to accept full responsibility for his guilt but beginning to see that he is far from innocent — the Stranger's Jacob side again comes into play as he challenges his invisible adversary once more. What happened offstage before is now enacted before our eyes: he feels that someone is tearing his heart right out of his breast; despite the Mother's repeated exhortations that he kneel to the Crucified Christ, he steadfastly refuses. When the crisis passes, he says he has been struggling not with death but with annihilation:

THE MOTHER: Annihilation of the divine — what we call spiritual death.

THE STRANGER *(seriously, without irony)*: So that's what you mean . . . then I am beginning to understand.

THE MOTHER: My son, you have left Jerusalem and you are on the road to Damascus. Go there! Take the same road you traveled to get here, and plant a cross at each station, but stop at the seventh. You do not have fourteen, as He had.

(SS 29:109-10)

This speech partially explains the title of the play by identifying the Stranger first with Saul and then — curiously enough — with Christ. It also points both to the palindromic structure of the play and to the Stranger's spiritual rebirth or his redemption.

The ambiguity of Medea's cauldron (and all the other symbols of transformation) also characterizes another complex of symbols that ultimately becomes associated with repentance, mercy, and redemption. The nuclei of this cluster are the color rose (the Rose Chamber) and the white Christmas rose, that is, the highly poisonous *Helleborus niger,* which also becomes one of the obsessive symbols for madness in the play. When she makes her second appearance in scene 1 (set sometime during the summer, apparently), the Lady is wearing a Christmas rose *(julros),* which normally flowers in midwinter. Although the first element in its popular name connects it with the birth of Christ and therefore (however faintly) with redemption, the Stranger immediately reads it as a negative symbol:

> THE STRANGER: . . . And I also know that the Christmas rose you are wearing on your bosom is a mandragora. According to the symbolism it means malice and calumny, but in the past it has been used as a medicine to cure madness. Will you give it to me?
>
> THE LADY *(hesitates):* As medicine, you mean?
>
> THE STRANGER: Naturally!
>
> (*SS* 29:20)

In scene 2 this association between the Christmas rose and madness is strengthened and linked to the titanic imagery in the play, when it is revealed that the madman Caesar puts the helleborus plants in the cellar during the winter and forces them to bloom in the summer instead — this must be the source of the Lady's (otherwise inexplicable) Christmas rose in scene 1. Although no stage directions mention the flower again, it mysteriously turns up in scene 15 (the second scene in the hotel room), when winter is beginning to give way to spring:

> THE LADY: . . . Have you noticed that it's spring again?
>
> THE STRANGER: I have noticed it because that Christmas rose is beginning to wither.
>
> THE LADY: But don't you feel that it is spring in the air!
>
> THE STRANGER: Oh, yes. I think that chilled feeling in my breast is beginning to diminish.
>
> (*SS* 29:124)

Presumably, the change of seasons and the withering of this ominous flower are connected with the Stranger's penitence and mean that the danger of madness is now past.

Much more elusive than the symbolism of the Christmas rose is the use of the color rose (the Rose Chamber), which has both sinister and reassuring aspects. In *Inferno* Strindberg describes how the color rose pursued him on his way to Austria in August 1896. At first he thought it betokened reconciliation with his estranged wife, Frida Uhl. When he discovered that the room he was to stay in during his visit with his Austrian in-laws was entirely rose-colored, he was enchanted, but later, when his erotic hopes were dashed, the color seemed to him a mockery.[18] No such neat reversal in symbolic development takes place in *To Damascus* (I). Strindberg's personal associations with this color — reinforced, perhaps, by the fact that a legendary eighteenth-century torture chamber in Stockholm was called the Rose Chamber[19] — seem to underlie the negative aspects of this Eden in which a second Fall occurs, when Ingeborg-Eve reads in the forbidden book and discovers the difference between good and evil. A sinister connotation still clings to the color at the end of scene 15 when she runs out of yarn and abandons her piece of needless crochet work. It is dirty and the Stranger suggests that it be washed — or dyed rose. "No, never!" she replies (*SS* 29:125). Perhaps she rejects the color because of the guilt feelings associated with the room where she broke her promise to him. Late in the play, however, the color acquires equally strong associations with mercy: as the Stranger prepares to leave "The Good Help" Asylum, the Abbess tells him that mercy is to be found in a rose-colored room (*SS* 29:96). On his second visit to the Rose Chamber, however, he finds that the room is partly dismantled (the curtains and flowers have been removed and the furniture is hidden beneath dust covers), and his encounter there with the merciless Mother suggests that the Abbess meant not the actual Rose Chamber but something more abstract. In scene 13, the Beggar tells him to follow the wheel tracks down to the sea and leave behind the expiatory chapels and memorial crosses because "they hinder thought's flight to the Rose Chamber" (*SS* 29:115); here it clearly seems to mean the Eden that the Rose Chamber was before Ingeborg-Eve's fall — in other words, a paradise that may yet be regained in some mysterious way.[20]

All the Stranger's "doubles" — the Beggar, the Doctor, and Caesar — play a role in the destruction of his old self (Medea's cauldron) in preparation for his rebirth (the Rose Chamber). The Lady, for example, seems to activate the faded — almost forgotten — guilt connected with the boyhood prank that earned him the nickname Caesar and caused the Doctor to lose faith in human goodness. Whereas the Doctor's other appellation, the Werewolf, suggests that he has a satanic side that never manifests itself on stage, the Doctor and Caesar are both titanic. Like the Mother and the Old Man, who are particularly aware of their punitive missions, all these doubles are also disciplinary spirits. The Swedenborgian notion of the disciplinary spirit, a person who is sent to punish or to torment the lost sinner back onto the paths of righteousness, was particularly vital for Strindberg around the time he wrote this play — entries in the *Occult Diary* show that he viewed both Dreyfus and Lucchéni (the assassin of the Empress Elizabeth of Austria) as disciplinary spirits. Among all the disciplinary spirits and doubles that dog the Stranger, however, none is so terrifyingly aware of his secret self as is the Beggar.

Of course, the Beggar incarnates Strindberg's (the Stranger's) fear of poverty and his arrogant desire to "walk in the gutter and experience *Machtgefühl*."[21] When he first enters in scene 1, picking through the trash in the gutter, he does seem to function primarily as a disciplinary spirit, a grim warning of what the Stranger will become if he continues to drink and to let his literary gifts go to waste. He arouses the Stranger's curiosity but certainly not his pity. Since he has not asked for a handout, however, he resents being called a beggar and asks the Stranger to guess his identity:

THE BEGGAR: Can you . . . guess who I am?

THE STRANGER: No, I neither can nor will — in a word, I'm not in the least bit interested in you.

THE BEGGAR: How does one ever know such things beforehand? Interest generally comes later, when it is too late. *Virtus post nummos.*

THE STRANGER: What? A beggar acquainted with the Latin language?

THE BEGGAR: You see! You're getting interested. *Omne tulit punctum qui miscuit utile dulci.*

(*SS* 29:17)

Although the first Latin quotation here (from Horace's *Epistles* [I,i,54]) may appear to be a good motto for a mendicant ("Virtue after money," i.e., "only the rich can afford to be virtuous"), it does not seem to have much connection with the Stranger's indifference. Törnqvist takes the Beggar's dependence on Latin maxims as an indication of his intellectual poverty; he therefore sees the Beggar, who considers himself "a free man," as the victom of an irony, but the Beggar is the real ironist here.[22] In this epistle Horace tells Maecenas that the first step toward virtue is to shun vice and folly and leave the pursuit of material goods to seek wisdom: it is quite possible that the Beggar bears a similar message to the Stranger, who is waiting for a registered letter containing money *(nummi)* at the post office, but refuses to fetch it because of his negative attitude toward the world:

THE STRANGER: But that beggar! He certainly is a disgusting person. Is it true that he resembles me?

THE LADY: Yes, if you keep on drinking, you will be like him. But now go in to the post office and get your letter. Then come along with me.

THE STRANGER: No. I'm not going to the post office. The letter probably contains nothing but court orders or judical acts.

(*SS* 29:29)

As long as the Stranger thinks ill of everything and perceives himself as an innocent sufferer — in other words, as long as he remains satanic — the Latin motto applies to him. But the motto must be reversed: "After virtue, money," it should read. In the final scene in the play, when the Stranger meets the Lady back at the street corner where the play began, he suddenly remembers the letter he scorned to fetch at the outset of the action:

THE STRANGER: . . . the post office. P, O, S, T. Listen, didn't I leave a registered letter unclaimed?

THE LADY: That's right. You did that because it contained only bad news or insults . . .

THE STRANGER: or court orders . . . *(Striking his forehead.)*

(*SS* 29:134)

The money has, of course, been there all along, and now that his attitude has changed, he is worthy to receive it. The operative word here is *post*: "P, O, S, T." By spelling it out he shows that he perceives a deep connection between the Latin maxim, the post office, and his new willingness to think positively.[23]

Having aroused the Stranger's interest by demonstrating a familiarity with Horace, the Beggar goes on to answer the initial questions. What he is really looking for is Polycrates's ring, but because the search may take quite some time, he is willing to settle in the meantime for a few cigar butts. Polycrates was the victim of an ironic situation. Alarmed by his unheard-of success and afraid that Nemesis would punish him, he cast a precious ring into the sea, but when it was returned to him by a fisherman, he knew that he faced imminent disaster. The Beggar ironically inverts the story to state a paradox: if the intended goal was failure, then failure is success. At first simply disgusted by the Beggar's unhygienic habits, the Stranger soon begins to be genuinely alarmed by the similarity of their situations. Earlier in the scene he had described the scar on his forehead (given him by his brother) as a sign of his total alienation from his fellow man; when the Beggar, tipping his hat, reveals a similar "Mark of Cain" — "I got it from a close relative," he explains (*SS* 29:18) — the Stranger is terrified. Unasked, he gives the Beggar money — too much money — to look for Polycrates's ring in some other part of town. The beggar insists upon returning most of the money so that he can regard this not as an alms or a bribe but merely as a display of friendship:

THE STRANGER: Display of friendship! Am I your friend?

THE BEGGAR: At least I'm your friend, and when you're all alone in the world, you can't be very fussy about people.

(SS 29:19)

Near the end of the first scene, when the Beggar shows up at the café and tries to order a bottle of wine, the identification between him and the Stranger is completed. The Innkeeper not only refuses service to the Beggar but tries to throw him out of the café, reading his description from a wanted sign: when the Stranger tries to intervene on the Beggar's behalf, the Innkeeper attacks him:

INNKEEPER: . . . Listen, let me look at this wanted sign and see if maybe the description fits you: 38 years old, brown hair, moustache, blue eyes; no steady employment; sources of income unknown; married, but deserted wife and children; known to harbor subversive social views, and gives the impression of not being in full possession of his faculties . . . Hey, it fits!

THE STRANGER: *(rises, pale and overwhelmed)*: What's going on here?

INNKEEPER: By God, I think it fits perfectly!

THE BEGGAR: Maybe he's the culprit and not me.

INNKEEPER: That's how it looks. Now I think you two gents just better lock arms and toddle off together.

THE BEGGAR: C'mon, let's us get out of here.

THE STRANGER: Us! This is beginning to look like some sort of plot!

(SS 29:27-28)

His putative resemblance to the Beggar has placed the Stranger in an infernal situation from which the Lady, drawn away from St. Elizabeth's Chapel by the force of his deep longing for her, rescues him.

The two negative encounters with the Beggar in scene 1 prove to be prophetic, for by the time they reach her childhood home in the mountains, the Stranger and the Lady have become indigent vagrants. Although they are both deeply ashamed when they discover that a place has been prepared for them at the "beggar's table" *(bettlarbordet)*, this institution points to the positive side of the beggar figure. "Never deny hospitality to a beggar," the Mother reminds the Old Man at the beginning of scene 7; "it might be an angel!" (*SS* 29:67). This admonition shows that she shares the popular folk belief that angels — or even Christ Himself — sometimes assume the most abject forms of human misery to inspire acts of true charity — in the tradition of Saint Julian the Hospitator.

The Beggar also appears as one of the ghostly inmates of "The Good Help" Asylum, where he joins all the Stranger's other "victims" in cursing him. In the first scene, he had claimed that he was a "free man with academic training" who had neglected to pay his taxes because he did not want to hold public office (*SS* 29:27). In the Asylum scene, the Confessor describes him as "a beggar who is unwilling to own up to his begging because he has studied Latin and been 'liberated' *(befriad)*." His insistence on "liberation" links him in yet another way to the Stranger, who had always regarded himself as a liberator. His earlier works, apparently full of Nietzschean nihilism, were intended to label and expose life-lies, to free people from outmoded political, social, and religious ideas; the Confessor even suggests that the madman Caesar has lost his reason as a result of reading the Stranger's "liberating" books. In other words, the Stranger here discovers that he was mistaken in his Promethean aspirations: instead of bringing light for Olympus, he may have been the emissary of the Prince of Darkness. Strindberg renders this realization with a gesture: "when he (the Stranger) raises his head, he sees the image of Saint Michael and lowers his eyes" (*SS* 29:93). This massive confrontation with his own guilt is a decisive factor in his "conversion": now he is on the road to salvation; now he must "seek out the demons in their lairs and kill them by repentance," as Strindberg had said in *Inferno* of his own case. After hearing the Confessor pronounce the terrifying curse, the Stranger says he is still suffering from fever and insists that he must leave the Asylum to find a real doctor. The Confessor, echoing an earlier speech of the Stranger's, says, "He who cures the 'beautiful pangs of conscience.'" He is referring, of course, to Christ, and next the Abbess tells the Stranger that if he ever needs mercy, he knows where that is to be found: in a rose-colored chamber. While the foregoing scenes repeat themselves in reverse order, the Stranger both repents and seeks mercy, as he approaches his unconventional "conversion."

On the Damascus Road, Saul recognized Jesus as the Christ, the long-awaited Messiah, and became His apostle, Paul; but neither Strindberg nor his complex character, the Stranger, was ever ready for a conversion of this nature. Since he was a youth Strindberg had consistently rejected the idea of the Redemption and found the notion of a suffering god repellent. Indeed — like Nietzsche — he felt nothing but contempt for Christians, who needed to make Christ their scapegoat and to cast all their crimes and sins onto Him. His sharpest criticism of Christine in the preface to *Miss Julie,* for example, is that she is "stuffed full of morality and religion that she uses as fronts and scapegoats, which a strong person does not need, since he can bear his guilt himself — or else reason it away."[24] Although the Inferno crisis led him back to a belief in God — or the "powers" — he continued to reject Jesus as a Savior. Therefore even if he could begin to understand the wrath of Jehovah during the mid-1890s, he was constantly bewildered by the Christ who pursued and "persecuted" him. In *Jacob Wrestles* he writes, "For more than a year I have been persecuted by the Savior, whom I do not understand and whose help I want, if possible, to render superfluous by bearing my cross myself, owing to a residue of manly pride in me which finds something repulsive in the cowardice inherent in the idea of projecting one's faults onto the shoulders of an innocent one" (*SS* 28:338). The only Christ he could understand or accept after his religious crisis was the Christ Child; in other words, although he came to accept the Incarnation — even in its highly developed Roman Catholic form — he always rejected the Redemption in favor of some notion that man's only salvation lay in acceptance of the role of scapegoat himself — so as not to project his sins onto an innocent, suffering Jesus.

After leaving the Asylum to follow the Abbess's injunction to seek mercy in the Rose Chamber, the Stranger encounters two former disciplinary spirits, the Mother and the Beggar, who now act as spiritual guides. Religious faith, however, has done nothing to soften the Mother, who seems (along with the Confessor and the Old Man) to represent dogmatic Roman Catholicism. She is more self-righteous than serene, and surely no one could be tempted to emulate her. The only characters in the play who really understand mercy and the need for suffering are the Abbess and the Beggar, whose religious views are probably very close to Strindberg's own — at the time he wrote the play. In scene 13 ("Along the Road") the Beggar, who — next to the protagonist — is the most enigmatic character in the play, identifies the Stranger with Saul. The expiatory chapel, the calvaries, and the memorial crosses that dominate the stage set for "Along the Road" (scenes 5 and 13) underscore the dreary penitential aspect of Christianity, that is, the aspect of religious experience represented by the Mother.

When the Stranger enters in scene 13, he encounters a transformed Beggar sitting by a chapel, holding a caged bird and a birdcatcher's lime twig. In other words, the shabby Beggar of scene 1 has now become a sort of Papageno. In *Legends,* a work that was completed shortly before he began work on *To Damascus* (I), Strindberg reveals the source of this transformation: "By chance (?) *The Magic Flute,* Schikaneder's libretto, has fallen into my hands. The ordeals and the temptations of the young couple make me think that I have let myself be taken in by seductive voices and that when I have been unable to endure the hardships and sufferings, I have bowed beneath them and submitted" (*SS* 28:301). Of course, it is altogether in keeping with Strindberg's subjectivism that whatever he happened to read could supply grist for the mill, but the elements he borrowed from Schikaneder to redefine the Beggar represent one of his most successful (and most genial) literary allusions.

Barry Jacobs

A prime example of Enlightenment mysticism, *The Magic Flute* is just the sort of text that would make a strong impression on Strindberg during the period of his life when he counted himself a disciple of Swedenborg. Its protagonist, Tamino, and his comic double, Papageno (literally "the parrot man," who talks too much) must undertake a perilous journey and undergo purificatory ordeals. To be initiated into the mysteries that will ensure their happiness, they must, above all, overcome their fear of death. While Tamino and his beloved Pamina do succeed in quelling their mortal fears, Papageno, who describes himself as a *Naturmensch,* lacks the strength of will and the intellect to follow their example. Although he does finally earn a mate, Papagena, he never qualifies for ultimate enlightenment. The talkative Beggar in *To Damascus* (I) becomes the Stranger's comic double in scene 13. When the Stranger enters he finds the Beggar sitting by an expiatory shrine with his lime twig and a caged starling. In scene 1 the Stranger had wished he were the Lady's old, blind father whom she led into marketplaces to sing; now the Beggar has a caged bird who supports them both by its whistling and singing. Because he has changed professions, he now rejects the title the Beggar *(Tiggaren)* in the definite form.[25] Although he no longer has to beg, he reveals that the lime twig, the prop that links him most closely with Papageno, is a feint — merely intended to suggest that he is actively involved in catching birds. His whole philosophy, he now ironically claims, is based upon appearances. In scene 1 the Stranger had remarked upon the difficulty of judging by appearances (*SS* 29:17); now the Beggar reveals the danger inherent in basing a worldview on such flimsy foundations:

> Speaking of flapping wings reminds me: a bird once told me about Polycrates and his ring, and how he got all the good things in the world, but he didn't know what to do with them. So he prophesied in the east and in the west about the great cosmic void [världsintet] which he had helped to create out of the empty everything [*tomma alltet*]. Now, I wouldn't insist it was you, except I'm so dead certain that I'd take my oath upon it.
>
> (*SS* 29:115-16)

Here the mysterious Beggar is recalling an exchange he was not privy to — early in scene 1:

THE LADY: Have you ever had visions?

THE STRANGER: Never. But I have often thought I noticed that two different forces control my destiny: one of them gives me everything I desire, but the other stands next to him and smears filth on the gift so that when I receive it, it is so worthless that I don't want to touch it. It is really true that I have received everything I wished for in life — but it has always proved to be worthless.

(*SS* 29:11-12)

This was the speech the Beggar was parodying later in the first scene when he ironically identified himself with Polycrates. Now we see the caged bird as the Stranger himself: it represents his earlier career as a crusader for the cause of nihilism, when he was a man who totally misunderstood reality, who only thought he was free and freeing others, while in reality he was trapped within the confines of his own limited philosophy of life. There is still another dimension to the bird symbol, however. Because of its ability to fly, the bird is a natural symbol of freedom and transcendence — the spirit. This aspect of the symbol comes out when the Beggar says to the Stranger:

Now listen to me: if you follow those wheel tracks in the mire, you'll arrive at the sea and there the road ends. Sit down there and rest and then you'll get a diffent view of things. There are so many accidents here, so many religious objects, and so many unpleasant memories that hinder thought's flight toward the Rose Chamber. But just follow the tracks. Follow the tracks. If it gets a bit muddy sometimes, just lift your wings and flap them.

(*SS* 29:115)

Because it potentially represents thought's flight toward the Rose Chamber, which has already been connected with mercy — and is now used to suggest a lost paradise — the bird must also symbolize humankind's power to transcend the mire along the road of life; therefore it is probably the counterpart of the only other animal that appears on stage in this play: the mysterious (and very earthbound) turtle in scene 2.

Instead of attempting the sort of transcendence symbolized by the bird, the Stranger has always tried to replace God with his own titanic ego. Early in scene 1 he shocked the Lady by defining his religion as the belief that when things became unbearable, he could always play God by deciding to commit suicide. Minutes later, he tries to make her his own by giving her a new identity:

THE STRANGER: Let me think what your name shall be. I've got it! You'll be called Eve. (*With a gesture toward the wings.*) Fanfare! (*One hears the funeral march.*) There's that funeral march again!

(*SS* 29:13)

Instead of the anticipated fanfare to glorify this transformation, we hear the ironic voice of death, a voice he largely ignores at that moment. Later in scene 1, when the Beggar offered him his friendship, the almost penniless Stranger attempted to put him in his place by uttering the (untranslatable) insult *hut!* ("what impudence!" seems much too mild to capture its force); in scene 13 the Beggar retaliates. Although his recent experiences have changed him greatly, the Stranger still finds it tempting to return to his old belief that there is no God — and consequently no afterlife. The Beggar, who finds the Stranger's continued titanic posturing richly comic, deflates him by playing Christ to his Saul:

> THE BEGGAR: Sir! You think the worst of everything and everybody and so the worst always happens to you. Try just this once to think the best — try it.
>
> THE STRANGER: I want to try it. But if I'm deceived, then I have the right to . . .
>
> THE BEGGAR: You never have the right to do that!
>
> THE STRANGER *(as if to himself)*: Who is reading my secret thoughts? Who is turning my soul inside out? Who is persecuting me? Why persecutest thou me?
>
> THE BEGGAR: Why persecutest thou me, Saul?
>
> THE STRANGER *(with a terrified gesture, exits. Chords from the funeral march are heard as earlier in the play.)*
>
> (*SS* 29:116)

Here the stations of the cross merge with the epiphany on the Damascus Road. Of course, the Beggar is not Christ — any more than he is Polycrates with whom he identified himself in scene 1; but at this moment he does manage to awaken and "liberate" religious sentiments that lie deep within the Stranger's consciousness. This awakening is signaled by the funeral march, which now returns in an ambiguous dramatic context where it might suggest both the Stranger's fear of death and the demise of his old worldview. The way is now open for his final conversion, which occurs in scene 14 ("By the Sea").

Scene 14 balances and, in effect, responds to the first scene by the sea, scene 4, in which the Stranger — like Inspector Borg in *By The Open Sea* — experiences a titanic apotheosis, followed by a vision. In the earlier scene the clouds are dispersed and his mood becomes expansive:

> This is what it means to live. Yes, now I am alive, now — very now! and I feel my self swelling, extending itself, becoming rarefied, becoming infinite: I am everywhere: in the sea, which is my blood; in the flowers; and my head reaches up to heaven. I look out over

the universe, which is myself, because I am He. I would like to take the whole mass in hand and knead it into something more complete, more permanent, more beautiful.

(*SS* 29:54)

This sort of blasphemy leads the Lady to compare him to the madman Caesar. A quarrel ensues and she tells him he is hypersensitive. To reinforce his claim to total self-sufficiency, he produces an unopened letter, which he thinks contains the money that is owing to him, but instead he finds only a royalty statement showing that no uncollected funds remain in his account. This injustice leads him to curse heaven and to challenge whatever principalities and powers there may be. At the end of the scene, he experiences a genuine vision: in the Lady's knitting he sees her mother and grandfather and their servants saying a rosary in the kitchen of their home.

This extraordinary scene is balanced by scene 14, in which the Stranger and the Lady, who have been separated since the end of scene 8, are reunited. The striking new visual element in this scene is the wrecked ship; its three masts transform the landscape into a Golgatha, where the Stranger at last discovers the true meaning of the cross. Time and again in the play he has been tempted to regard the Lady as a disciplinary spirit sent either to destroy him or to effect his salvation. Now he rejects that idea:

THE STRANGER: I do not want us to tear each other to pieces; instead I want to rip myself apart as a sin offering to the gods [*försoningsoffer*]. I shall say: the guilt is mine; I was the one who taught you to loosen your fetters; I was the one who enticed you; so you must put the blame for everything on me — both the deed itself and its consequences . . .

THE LADY: You can't bear it.

THE STRANGER: Yes, I can. There are moments when I feel that I bear within me all the sin and sorrow and filth and shame in the world. There are times when I believe that the wicked deed itself — the very crime one commits — is a punishment that has been imposed upon us! You know, I was recently sick with a fever and among other things — so much was happening to me — I dreamed I saw a crucifix without Our Lord on it. And when I asked the Dominican . . . what that might mean . . . He answered: "You do not want Him to suffer for you — so suffer all by yourself!" And that is why people have become so sensitive to their own sufferings.

(*SS* 29:119)

This speech — and not the Stranger's final consent to enter the church with the Lady (*SS* 29:119) — shows the essence of the religious experience that *To*

Damascus (I) was written to convey: the expansiveness of the earlier scene is here reversed; instead of rejecting the sorrow and filth of the world, he now encompasses them. Throughout the play, while he vacillated between titanic and satanic poses, the Stranger has been caught in an impossible — and endless — dilemma. The titan denies all guilt or attempts to cancel it by moving beyond good and evil, for — like Nietzsche's superman — he wants to replace God. The satanist, however, only denies his own guilt by insisting that God is punishing him unjustly, that God allows evil to exist. The Stranger began to find a way out of this dilemma in the fever dreams that haunted him during the three months that pass between the first scene in the Rose Chamber (scene 8) and the scene in the Asylum (scene 9). In the latter scene the Confessor tells him that during his delirium "there was hardly a crime or a vice" that he has not confessed to (*SS* 29:92). But not until the Beggar "liberates" him from his titanism and his satanism does the Stranger become fully aware of his own culpability. Once he has acknowledged the enormous burden of guilt that he has hitherto attempted to project onto others, he is able to escape from his dilemma, because now he can find a positive, redeeming value in his sufferings and thus embrace the role of the scapegoat. This psychological insight takes us very far in understanding the nature of Strindberg's post-Inferno protagonists and shows the real extent to which the Stranger has been "converted."

16

To Damascus (I): A Dream Play?

Göran Söderström

      Several scholars have written about the first performance of *To Damascus* (I), foremost being Ingrid Hollinger and Richard Bark. I will limit my discussion to the scenographic solutions of this production and how they correspond to Strindberg's intentions and, on the basis of this, I will try to answer the question: was *To Damascus* (I) intended to be a dream play or not?

      In August 1896 in Ystad in southern Sweden (At the Doctor's House in *To Damascus* (I)) when Strindberg was planning the novel *Inferno,* he spoke of it as a drama of penitence, in which the defiant man has suffered but gains peace of mind through working for his family — in this case, the mother and child. Strindberg was on his way back to his young daughter in Austria, where he presumed he would also join his wife, Frida. He intended to write his great novel of conversion there.

      In reality he was never to meet his wife again. But in the small villages of Saxen and Clam near Dornach, where he had spent his happiest time with his wife and daughter in the summer of 1894, he settled in with his wife's relatives, in particular his mother-in-law and her twin sister, Melanie. They were both eager Swedenborgians, and in their library he read the works of Emanuel Swedenborg in the original version for the first time since his youth. He was fascinated by Clam's strange geographical surroundings, which he thought corresponded exactly to Swedenborg's description of hell; he interpreted the various landscapes around him in an occult way. In a letter from Clam in October 1896, he wrote that he was convinced that people are already in Inferno because of sins committed in a previous existence. After a mental crisis in November, he was persuaded by his wife's family to return to Sweden.

At the beginning of the year 1897, he intended, however, to return to Paris via Clam; he wanted to write *Inferno* in Clam, in the company of his daughter. The official announcement of his divorce stopped the journey. In mid-March he began to write the novel in Lund but left off writing after only a few pages. The narrative of the novel breaks off just before the first meeting with Frida in Berlin in 1893. In Paris at the beginning of May 1894 the narrative picks up again, which in real life was the time and place of his last goodbye to Frida. He did not want to do harm to the mother of his child.

Inferno was written in French for French readers, especially those involved in the occult movement. To discuss the publication in person he returned to Paris in August 1897. Waiting for its completion, he wrote the second and third part of *Inferno* — *Legends*, and *Jacob Wrestles*. The manuscripts are illuminated on the order of medieval ones. However, around the beginning of the year 1898, he grew tired of this work. On January 19, 1898, after a break of almost six years, he began a new drama, *To Damascus* (I). Again he returned to the story of his marriage to Frida Uhl, but now in a very stylized and transformed way.

In the French edition of *Inferno* he had added *Efterspelet till Mäster Olof* (Epilogue to *Master Olof*), his mystery-play pastiche from 1877 in a revised version titled *Coram Populo, De Creatione et Sententia Vera Mundi, Mystère*. It is obvious that he now wanted to write a play very close to a medieval mystery play, wherein the various scenes are called "stations," as in the passion play. The word station is repeatedly used in Strindberg's drama by the Mother and the Stranger, indicating a direct connection between this work and the passion play.

Strindberg explicitly states that the three parts of *Inferno* (with the exception of the episode with the Unknown in *Jacob Wrestles*) are true stories. The narrative in *To Damascus* (I) is, on the contrary, completely fictional, although constructed from fragments of the author's life. The characters differ, with few exceptions, almost entirely from what I, for lack of a better term, call the models. The Old Man, for example, is a good-tempered, wise man like the grandfather in fairytales; in reality Frida's grandfather was a rather mean, rich, and lofty old lawyer, as Strindberg describes him in the later play *Advent*.

As in the medieval morality plays, there is one character in *To Damascus* (I), the Stranger (the Unknown), and all other roles become more or less symbolic personifications of the conflicting forces, the various self-reproaches in the inner moral struggle of the main character. As in the mystery plays, the scenery contains certain realistic objects that function as symbols, elevated above everyday reality by being presented as dumb coactors at the center of the action.

Still, there are perhaps more ties to Strindberg's two earlier fairytale dramas, *Lucky Per's Travels* and *The Keys of Heaven*, as Gunnar Brandell has pointed out. The hero travels from one point through the world and back again to the starting point, learning from disillusionments and troubles to be humble and tolerant. There are, however, important differences: in *To Damascus* (I), there are none of the surprising scene changes that play such an important role in the two fairytale dramas. The scenery changes only when the hero moves from one station to another, except for changes of the daylight in some scenes. The scenery for each station is very important for the play, but only as a permanent symbol. It is characteristic that Strindberg proposes, in 1909, that the Intimate Theater play *To Damascus* (I) with a single set, in which all the scenery for the different stations is represented by symbolic elements.

Strindberg had found the landscape surrounding Clam exactly like hell, as Swedenborg describes it. There are nine different sets in *To Damascus* (I) (and several of them reappear in *To Damascus* [II]), but only seven are called stations. Strindberg does not count the first and last scene or the scenes designated to be on the road. The real-life drama of Strindberg's marriage took place for the most part in big cities like Berlin and Paris, but *To Damascus* (I) is set entirely in the country (with the exception, perhaps, of the scenes At the Hotel Room). As I will show later, six of the nine sets are taken from the surroundings of Clam. The three remaining sets are the first and last stations. Scene 1, at the Doctor's House, is the house in Ystad in southern Sweden where Strindberg first got the idea to write *Inferno* — before his return to his wife's relatives in Dornach and Clam in 1896. The third and fifth stations (Strindberg again counts from the Asylum scene) are on the seaside, which certainly goes back to Strindberg's wedding on the island of Helgoland in April 1893, but the scenery for the play is borrowed from the archipelago of Stockholm and replicates two of Strindberg's own paintings. Last, there is the scene at the Hotel Room, which is hard to identify.

It is very probable that Strindberg got the idea of the reverse repetition of scenes, following the Asylum scene, from his return visit to Dornach and Clam two years after separating from his wife. It was autumn when he saw all the familiar places again, and, according to the play's stage directions, the scenery changes to autumn or winter after the turning point of the narrative.

In addressing the question of whether *To Damascus* (I) is a dream play, it is important to note that the different scenes follow one another in a very logical way, not as in *A Dream Play*, with its dreamlike transformations of scenery. The settings in the former play are reflections of real landscapes or interiors and get their occult quality from being perceived as "correspondences," in the Swedenborgian sense of the term.

It is obvious that Strindberg paid a great deal of attention to how the drama was going to be performed, especially the changing scenes. When Strindberg got the news in July 1900 that Emil Grandinson was to direct the world premiere of *To Damascus* (I) at the Royal Dramatic Theater in Stockholm, he immediately wrote to him and suggested that he should refer to the famous passion play of Oberammergau. It is apparent that Strindberg wanted to underline his drama's resemblance to the medieval mystery play.

It is, however, understandable that Grandinson could not immediately understand how the example of the great outdoor theater at Oberammergau, with its antique temple gable, could be used for the stage of the old Dramatic Theater. At the same time, the numerous and rapid changes of scenery created a difficult technical problem. Strindberg did not want a break for scene changes before the Asylum scene, as is evident from his letters to Grandinson. A radical solution, which Strindberg sketched out for Grandinson, was to entirely abandon all the scene changes and perform the play on a fixed, elevated, passion-play stage constructed according to medieval models. Grandinson evidently rejected this solution — the austerity of it was indeed entirely foreign to the Dramatic Theater's standard scenographic practice — but Strindberg returned to it again in 1909 as an alternative way to produce *To Damascus* (I) on the Intimate Theater's small stage. "That would say it all," he wrote, "and no other decor would be necessary."

It is not possible to determine whether it was before or after this suggestion that projected backdrops were tried. In an interview one year earlier, Strindberg had said that he wanted to try projecting glass scioptic slides onto a white screen as backdrops for his new plays. He writes about the experiments of 1900 in *Open Letters to the Intimate Theater*: "Sven Scholander did indeed project a backdrop sufficiently large and clear, but inasmuch as it had to be dark in front of the backdrop for it to be properly seen, the actors were less visible." Sven Scholander was a sculptor by profession, but it was of course in the capacity of photographer that he carried out these experiments; it is therefore difficult to conjecture about the quality of the projected pictures.

By the time he began discussing the *To Damascus* (I) production with Grandinson, Strindberg had procured a model theater to test various solutions to scenographic problems. He mentions this for the first time in a letter to Carl Larsson on August 5, 1900. The management of the Royal Dramatic

To Damascus *(I): A Dream Play?*

Figure 6. *Grabow's "By the Gorge."*

Theater had apparently given up after the unsuccessful experiments and had "gone to Grabow," the dominant scene studio of the day. Carl Grabow was very competent but worked entirely in a traditional style — to Strindberg he had come to personify antiquated and conventional theater decor.

Grabow's first sketch, "By the Gorge (fig. 6)," indicates that Strindberg from the outset had no direct communication with the artist. The sketch is cleverly executed, but had little in common with the real gorge at Clam, perhaps the most important of the Infernolike locales that had inspired Strindberg in Austria (fig. 7). The mill, the cart-house with the buckhorn, and the smithy, on opposite sides of the road in the play, are, in real life, on the upper part of the gorge. Here one can also find the rock shaped like a human profile. The real-life bridge is at the foot of the gorge, as in Strindberg's stage directions (fig. 8).

Grabow's first sketch is for an uncut landscape as backdrop. The later sketches, where we can find Strindberg's direct influence, are framed with red draperies (fig. 9) — but probably not because he intended the backdrop to be trimmed down. The trimming was accomplished by a framed, painted arch, which was in all probability Strindberg's own solution. The sketch for the arch has been preserved separately from Grabow's other sketches (fig. 20). It was first found in 1972 in Strindberg's library, and the circumstances surrounding this find make it very probable that he experimented with it in his own model theater and requested that it be returned after it had been

Figure 7. *The gorge at Clam today.*

copied in full scale. The arch is mounted in front of the backdrops in Strindberg's own photographs from the production.

By using the standing arch, Strindberg succeeded in giving the set (fig. 11) some of the character of the Oberammergau stage. During the idealistic and romantic renaissance of the 1890s, festivals in Roman-style theaters in the open air under half-dilapidated roofed stages had become fashionable. Strindberg describes this development in *Open Letters to the Intimate Theater* and pays homage to it as the impetus behind the simplification embodied in modern scenography. It is, of course, a question not only of the simplification of scenery but also of what Strindberg calls an "ennobling," an elevation above the commonplace to a higher, timeless plane. With the heavens looming over the "ruins" of the arch and a constellation of stars embellish-

Figure 8. The present-day bridge at the foot of the gorge.

ing the night scenes, *To Damascus* (I) takes on the character of classical open-air theater. It is a rather ingenious solution to the problems of idealization and distancing.

How much in the sketches and the final stage version comes from Strindberg's suggestions and how much from Grabow and Grandinson's? The sketch (fig. 12) and the set (fig. 13) for the scene at the Doctor's House is considerably like that of the actual house at Ystad (fig. 14) that was Strindberg's model and that also appears in *Inferno*. The scene On the Streetcorner by Grabow (fig. 15) is in the final version very much like the marketplace in front of the church in Clam, where Strindberg saw a funeral in 1896. The funeral processions in Clam still begin in front of the church (fig. 16), as in the first scene of *To Damascus* (I). Only Strindberg himself can have given

Figures 9 and 10. *Grabow's sketch for "The Asylum Scene" framed by red draperies (above). Classical arch inspired by the antique temple gable from the Oberammergau passion plays (below).*

Figure 11. The standing arch for the scene "In the Ravine" by Grabow.

Grabow the needed information, as we know that he did in the case of other artists who illustrated his literary or dramatic works.

The Asylum scene is of particular interest to the problem of whether *To Damascus* (I) is a dream play or not. In the first production the Stranger is a spectator, someone dreamlike looking in upon a scene behind the scene (fig. 17), which functions as a play-within-the-play and creates opportunities to effect a dream atmosphere (as Richard Bark has noted). This solution has no equivalent in the stage directions. Was this effect, then, Strindberg's intention or only Grandinson's?

We have recently been granted a new opportunity to study Strindberg's own intentions for the stage sets of *To Damascus* (I). His second daughter, Greta, who was an actress, toured in 1909 with a theater company in the Strindberg Tour. In September and October of that year, Strindberg tried to persuade the company to perform *To Damascus* (I). Several times he asked his daughter by mail to send the scene painter, a man named Hallengren, to him for sketches of the sets. The play was never produced by the company, but the sketches — in oil — were found in 1983.

Figures 12 and 13. *"At the Doctor's House": Grabow's sketch (above), the corresponding set (below).*

Figure 14. Strindberg's dwelling in Ystad, summer 1896.

Figure 15. "On the Streetcorner," sketch by Grabow

Figure 16. Contemporary funeral procession in Clam.

Figure 17. *"The Asylum Scene."*

They all show scenes painted on backdrops, as in the Grandinson production. The proscenium arch has been changed to a cave, and there seems to be only an empty stage between the proscenium and the back-drops (figs. 18 and 19). Strindberg probably took the idea of the cave from his own painting from around 1901, wherein the cave represents the one found in Plato's dialogue *Phaedo*: our terrestrial world is compared in this work to shadows on the walls of a cave, in contrast to the eternal universe outside. This symbolic cave underlines the Swedenborgian character of the drama.

I think that we can assume that the poor scene painter Hallengren had no solutions for the sets himself. Let us then see how, in 1909, Strindberg wanted the Asylum scene to be played. The scenery exactly follows the description in the stage directions, and there is no inner stage. It is most likely, then, that the dreamlike setting in the first production was Grandinson's own invention.

The other scenes also closely adhere to the stage directions. The gorge is much more like the real one at Clam than is the Grabow sketch. Especially interesting are the scenes where the stage directions are less definite. The scene on the seaside seems to be inspired by an old painting, *Kymmendö* from 1873; the second scene of that name resembles *Golgatha*, which Strindberg painted in Dornach in 1894. The scene At the Hotel Room, which Grandinson, as Ingrid Hollinger has shown, depicted as a shabby and depressing room, is in the Strindberg sketches a tidy, ordinary room, probably a portrait of a real room as Strindberg remembered it. The Kitchen scene, both in the stage directions and in the sketches, is similar to the kitchen-drawing room in the little house near the Danube; in the stage directions for scene 1 in *To Damascus* (I), Strindberg gives a very exact description of this house as seen from the outside. The house and the room still exist (fig. 21), but have been entirely rebuilt. The Rose Room sketch (fig. 22) and actual set (fig. 23) seem to be directly derived from the real house in Clam. In the stage directions On the Road resembles the real one between Clam and Saxen-Dornach (fig. 24).

In conclusion, according to Martin Lamm, dream atmosphere in a play is created when something dreamlike is introduced. Richard Bark says that dream atmosphere involves transformation, an abolition of time and space. In Strindberg's own stage directions and in the sketches made under his direct supervision, nothing infers a dream atmosphere. The scenes are realistic, although filled by correspondences, in the Strindberg-Swedenborgian sense. The drama is thus not a dream play but a mystery play in the form of a fairytale drama.

Figures 18 and 19. *Oil sketches by Hallengren: "By the Sea" (above), "The Asylum" below*

Figure 20. *"By the Sea," in the Grandinson production.*

Figure 21. *Plaque on the house in Clam, with the Rose Room, commemorating Strindberg's visit.*

Figures 22 and 23. *"In the Rose Room": sketch by Grabow (above), the corresponding set (below).*

Figure 24. The countryside Hand road between Clam and Saxen-Dornach.

Charles XII as Dream Play

Göran Stockenström

The starting point for Strindberg's dramatization of the history of Charles XII was a scene in the last act. It contains the king's final accounting for his life, moments before his death. The idea originated from the short story *The Wake at Tistedalen* (1890), in which the king's death was used for the purpose of historical retrospection. The dramaturgical principle appears from the earlier versions and in 1901 is still a powerful influence on the final form of the text. In the first version of 1899, this scene was called "the King's bad dreams" (Kungens onda drömmar) or "Visions of terror" (Skräcksynerna).[1] In it, all the victims of Charles XII's tyrannical rule, the prisoners of war, those executed for crimes against the state, the dead soldiers, et cetera, were to parade before the king in a dream on the battlefield at Fredrikshald. Bulman cited the famous scene in Shakespeare's *Richard III*, in which the king is visited by the ghosts of the slain on the night before the decisive battle on Bosworth field, as one of the models for these spectacular visionary scenes in historical drama.[2] Retrospective scenes usually served to demonstrate the political crimes of the protagonist. For Strindberg the specters of the past are internalized as materializations of guilt and explained with reference to the functioning of pangs of conscience.

Returning to the play in the fall of 1900, Strindberg makes a new attempt to unify the public—and private realms. This time he structures the whole action of the play as dream-images passing through the consciousness of the king. The opening and closing scene used the same scenic image of the silent king looking at the flames of a fire. This essentially literary or cinematic framework that defines the "now" of the action is a familiar dramatic device in Strindberg's dream plays.[3] The conflict between the historical world and the protagonist's inner world is eliminated. The painful question of innocent suffering also resolves itself when history is presented in dream images. With the assumption that life is a dream, the question of individual guilt and suffering loses its meaning. This was a familiar conciliatory idea for Strindberg and structurally present in his "former dream play *To Damascus.*" The scene is now called "Visions of ghosts" (Spöksynerna) and a whole period of Swedish history is reduced to a dream, in which the historical personages and events appear as ghosts in a nightmare.[4] The king's bad dreams are viewed in terms of the metaphysical order as punishments in the hands of the Eternal One and his "powers," identical to the poet's own sufferings during the Inferno crisis. This process is interpreted as one of moral purification and visualized scenically by the flames of the cleansing fire.

By transferring the historical and political world totally into the realm of the private, *Charles XII* loses any pretention of being a historical drama. In 1900 it emerges instead as a dream play, with close connections to *To Damascus* (I). Whether life is a dream or dreams themselves reality remains a central theme for a poet who no longer conceived of it (life) as merely a poetic figure. The repetition of history as fleeting images from a dream within the central consciousness of the protagonist relates to a familiar concept described in the drafts of the play: "Swedenborg: Visions, vastation: the past is reenacted but now" (Swedenborg: Syner, ödeläggelsen: det förflutna försigår omigen men nu).[5] The term vastation (ödeläggelsen) is a concept from Swedenborg's theosophy, referring to the last reckoning with existence in the spiritual world. It is described by Strindberg in *A Blue Book* (1907): "It is the balancing of books at the solstice. The whole past is summed up, and the debit-side shows a plus which makes one despair. Scenes of earlier life pass by like a panorama, seen in a new light; long-forgotten incidents reappear even in their smallest details. The opening of the sealed Book of Life, spoken of in the Revelation, is a veritable reality. It is the day of judgment. . . . Swedenborg calls this natural process 'the vastation' of the wicked.'"[6] Strindberg often associated this sequence of events with a well-known psychological phenomenon, the so-called life-review, that is, the panoramic overview of the past observed in moments prior to death. With reference to the king at Fredrikshald, Strindberg writes: "All of life passes by" (Hela lifvet drar förbi).[7] In Swedenborg this process is more closely associated with the biblical "doomsday book" and its theme of unmasking and weighing of good and evil from a metaphysical perspective. Strindberg, on the other hand, perceived vastation to be identical to the scourges visited upon him during the Inferno crisis and interpreted the process as one of moral purification, to which scapegoats like himself and Charles XII were exposed through divine intervention. In an interview from October 1900, Strindberg stressed "that he had now from Swedenborg found good insights to solve the dilemma of Charles XII's character."[8]

Had Strindberg pursued the "modernistic" idea to conceive of his play as a dream, he would have created a new version of *To Damascus* (I) in historical trappings. To transfer the action to a wholly psychological realm was possible in *To Damascus* (I) but hardly so in a historical drama that purported to imitate a historical reality shared by dramatist and audience. Strindberg put the history of Charles XII aside, devoted himself instead to that of Gustavus Adolphus, and returned to *Charles XII* in the beginning of the following year, still unable to complete it. The play as we know it was finally completed during May-June 1901.[9] Strindberg has now found a medium between the demands of the historical drama and his dramatic focus on the suffering and transcendence of his protagonist. The balancing of the private and public worlds in a dramatic action is achieved by keeping the king offstage when political accusations against his despotic rule are voiced by individuals and groups from all social strata within the Caroline society. The merciless and expedite execution of the "innocent" skipper of Snapp-Opp is particulary disturbing to the audience because it raises the question of Charles XII's moral responsibility, not only in the case we witness with great empathy on the stage but also in that of all the other accusations from the king's victims. To absolve Charles XII from any moral responsibility, Strindberg introduces a new character, the Sailor, in Act III to rebut the alleged innocence of the skipper. In contrast to the latter's assertion that only weather and wind had stopped him from being at the site of the "rendezvous," we now learn of his complicity with the Danes. Needless to say, Strindberg has no support at all in the historical sources for this reclamation of the king's honor.

It is, of course, impossible to keep Charles XII totally outside the political actions in a historical drama. In his attempts to fulfill his mission to save the kingdom, Charles XII becomes involved with the morally disreputable Görtz, baron and advisor to Duke Karl Fredrik of Holstein. Contrary to everyone's expectations, Görtz is made a minister to Charles XII in the latter's desperate attempt to save the finances of the country. The king must raise money for an army to conduct his last military campaign against Norway to compensate for the enormous losses on the European scene. The dramatic meeting between the two is prepared in Charles XII's audience with Horn and Gyllenborg. The silent king requests Horn's opinion on "the widely discussed Baron Görtz." Horn responds after a great deal of hesitation. Charles XII remains silent, but his reactions are recorded in Strindberg's stage directions:

HORN (*sits down unwillingly and seems distressed by the low, uncomfortable chair*): Your Majesty's request is certainly a command . . .

(KING *looks down at the table before him; picks up a pen and begins to draw geometric figures.*)

HORN: . . . but . . .

FEIF: His Majesty requests what you might call a brief characterization of the person mentioned.

HORN: For a task like that would be needed a closer personal acquaintance with the man, and I have to admit that Baron Görtz is not among my closer . . .

(KING *looks up and fixes his eyes on* HORN *who becomes deeply alarmed.*)

HORN: Well then, according to everything I've heard, Baron Görtz . . . (*Tries to discover with his eyes what the* KING's *opinion of* GÖRTZ *is, and to compare it with the expression on* FEIF's *face.*) . . . that man is . . . an exceptionally unusual personality, and his desire to be unusual can only be measured . . . in its strength . . . by his desire for power.

(KING *draws — without looking up.*)

HORN: They say that he thinks he's the center of the world, that he looks in the papers every morning to see if the destinies of Europe have undergone any change while he has been sleeping, and the learned Swedenborg . . .

(KING *pricks up his ears.*)

HORN: . . . assures us that if Görtz died today he'd set the kingdom of the dead against the heavenly powers.

(KING *quits moving his pen, but does not look up.*)

HORN: This overwhelming desire for honor he conceals . . . tries to conceal beneath a simple exterior and a condescending manner towards his inferiors.

(GYLLENBORG *shows his uneasiness.* KING *becomes red in the face.*)

HORN: Inferiors, whom he actually despises, just as he despises all humanity.

(KING *inclines his head toward his chest.*)

HORN: These outstanding characteristics of Baron Görtz, coupled with his most exemplary insensibility to the suffering of others, would seem incompatible with a religious spirit, but Baron Görtz is not without religion. One could say that he fears for God, without fearing God.

(FEIF, *until now inscrutable, fixes his eyes with horror on* HORN. KING *puts his fingers to his throat as if he were choking.*)

HORN (*goes on without noticing anything, completely unaware of the unconscious hints*): The learned and pious Swedenborg believes Baron Görtz uses religion as a sort of magic, through which he secures support and power for himself, even in his purely criminal activities . . . for example, in extorting funds, in getting revenge on enemies . . . because he also has the peculiarity of never being able to forgive anyone.

(KING *fixes* HORN's *glance as if he wanted to read his innermost thoughts and to see if he has any mental reservations. His mouth is open, and his upper lip quivers.*)

HORN: In a word, a great weakness . . . disguised so that it seems like a tremendous strength; a convulsive stubbornness that cannot break down his own wilfulness . . .

(KING — *there is a noise from his spurs.* HORN, *as if awakening from a dream and realizing the infernal aspect of the situation, becomes silent with horror. All look at each other with mutual embarrassment, without anyone's quite being able to break the silence. Someone knocks three time on the right door.*[10]

(120-121)

The king's vehement mime during Horn's demasking of Görtz serves to key the audience that this "scene within the scene" is, in fact, directed by powers beyond the control of Horn and the king. The dreamlike quality of this double entendre is explicitly pointed out in Strindberg's stage directions. It is the Eternal One who has spoken through Horn. What he has related as a medium is, in fact, a description of Charles XII from Swedenborg's *Diarium Spirituale* (1843-46). It is a paraphrase of Charles XII's vastation in the spiritual world.[11] The king has staged a scene to reveal the true identity of Görtz but in turn has himself become demasked. In Swedenborg's doctrines of the spiritual world, vastation is the process by which man's character from earth is stripped away step by step to reveal his true self.[12] This gradual unveiling layer by layer restores the lost correspondence between appearance and internal condition that makes it possible to differentiate between the dead in heaven and those in hell. For Swedenborg

Charles XII belonged unequivocally to the latter category. In Strindberg's play Charles XII is subjected to a succession of these defilements of shame through a wide variety of techniques. These dramatic confrontations become the stepping stones in the spiritual journey that Strindberg depicts. His own process of change is projected onto Charles XII, whose inner development in the course of the play opens to a religious awakening. By using his own religious evolution as the paradigm for the king, Strindberg's resolution of "the dilemma of Charles XII's character" is necessarily a different one than the philosopher Swedenborg's interpretation of the historical Charles XII. The discrepancy between Charles XII's authentic self and Horn's depiction creates an ambiguity that the dramatist explores with great skill. When Charles XII regains his composure, he evades the accusations by questioning Gyllenborg and Horn on Secretary Feif's character. Two totally divergent characterizations serve to sustain the ambiguity for the audience. In this manner Görtz is presented as a double to the king, exemplifying the inherent possibilities for evil that inevitably followed the anointed monarch in the public realm. The technique is familiar from *To Damascus* (I), in which the Beggar serves as a double to the Stranger.

The facts of history are subsumed into a larger metaphysical pattern in *Charles XII*. Even the politically momentous meeting between the two historical figures is framed by a symbolic vignette with metaphysical overtones. The one-eyed Görtz is presented by the dramatist so that *"his face seems dead—in profile"* (123). This symbolic theme is later clarified by Swedenborg, whose function in the play is to point to the divine truth. In this respect his role in relation to the king is similar to that of Görtz. The latter represents the forces of evil, which can ultimately lead to humankind's damnation; the former represents the forces of good, which can ultimately lead to humankind's salvation. By juxtaposing the king between these two doubles, Strindberg creates a theatrical metaphor that incorporates the inherent possibilities of human beings in the world from a religious perspective. This is why Strindberg's stage direction concerning Görtz is an ominous one. What the audience is to witness is not simply a famous episode from Swedish history, when the political fate of the nation was at stake, but a reenactment of the fall of man to test Charles XII's true moral fibre. That some of the king's advisers were one-eyed is a historical truth that is incidental to Strindberg's true purpose:[13]

SWEDENBORG: And New Year's! . . . Poor Görtz!

FEIF: He sits there with his one eye as if he were sighting with a gun. . . . It certainly is strange that the King has surrounded himself with one-eyed people these last few years!

SWEDENBORG: Oh no!

FEIF: Yes, indeed! Frölich, Müllern, Grothusen, and Görtz see only with one eye!

SWEDENBORG: It would be amusing if there weren't a hidden meaning in it!

FEIF: Bah! Pure chance!

SWEDENBORG: No, Feif . . . but that you'll never understand . . .

FEIF: Dreams, Swedenborg, I don't understand!

(160)

In Swedenborg's theology, seeing corresponds to the heavenly light and the capacity of seeing becomes synonymous with understanding the metaphysical realities. Inability to see, one-eyedness, and blindness were signs of a corresponding immersion in the material world.[14] The external reality in Strindberg's *Occult Diary* (1896-1908) could just as well as the historical reality in his sources offer this knowledge of the Invisible that is used as one of the many leitmotivs of the play.[15]

The economic disasters and the war are the central theme in the scene between Charles XII and Görtz, but Strindberg does not use the discourse primarily to discuss the political circumstances. The audience has already witnessed Charles XII's emotional turmoil when he perceived his own reflection mirrored in Horn's analysis of Görtz's character. This ambiguity concerning Charles XII's true nature is further penetrated in the momentous meeting between the two. Charles XII does not engage in any discussion of possible solutions to Sweden's economic and political dilemma. Strindberg focuses instead on Charles XII's moral reactions to Görtz's unabashed cynicism:

GÖRTZ: A person with luck a little here and a little there . . .

KING: *How* can one . . . how can one . . .

GÖRTZ: Your Majesty knows what people and the world are . . .

KING (*looks up; sternly*): What do I know? (*Pause.*)

(125-26)

The dramatic meeting culminates in the arrest of Görtz, who is taken away to be questioned and tortured. Not even the reason for this action is politically motivated. "Write one thing and mean another?" is Charles XII's shocked reaction to a world that he is later forced to acknowledge as "a web of lies."[16] In the end Charles XII succumbs to Görtz's temptations for political considerations. The inner drama is depicted in his successive orders to alleviate the conditions of Görtz's imprisonment. Charles XII's moral dilemma forces him to speak in his own defense:

KING: Difficulties, the land . . . and the people . . . of difficulties!

FIEF: The country is impoverished . . . and the people!

KING: And that is my fault! Did I cause the plague? Did I cause the crop failures? Did I cause the fires? . . . Have I declared the wars? . . . No, I have only defended myself, my country, my royal inheritance! (*Pause.*) Where did that Görtz go?

FIEF: He has been put into prison, I suspect!

KING *rings.* ADJUTANT *enters.*

KING: Baron Görtz is to be under detention only in his own rooms! And is to be treated respectfully!

(128-29)

Görtz is finally freed and his proposal accepted by Charles XII. After the catastrophic failures of his economic schemes Charles XII accepts his responsibility without evasion or attempting to blame Görtz. In the face of public opinion, he stands by him to the end, an action that testifies to the king's spiritual growth in the course of the play. The political ambiguities inherent in the relationship between Charles XII and Görtz are left unexploited by the dramatist. The complexities of the historical world are continuously skirted by invoking a "higher" level of reality with Charles XII's inner development.

All the symbolic leitmotivs in Strindberg's text relate in one way or another to the dramatist's presentation of the king's spiritual journey. Because history is created by the shared consciousness of audience and dramatist, Strindberg had to establish historical probability while he found scenic means to express the vastation theme. To solve this problem the dramatist takes recourse to a number of leitmotivs that are repeated in the action of the play and fused into scenic images at key points of the king's inner development. The use of the set, the stage properties, music and sound or lack thereof accompany and reinforce the central theme.

No other protagonist is so carefully depicted and choreographed in stage directions as Charles XII. The king is described as frozen, tired, and weak with a sickly, ashen-gray face. He rubs his eyes, brushes with his hands in front of his eyes, clutches his temples. Most of the time he remains silent or speaks in a low, barely audible voice. We learn from the other characters that he is sick, that he suffers from sleeplessness and anxiety, that he is expected to die soon. Charles XII also believes that he is sick, but we learn that his affliction is not physical in nature. He complains bitterly about his loneliness and alienation. Yet, on several occasions, he emphatically states: "I am not alone, Feif; I am never alone . . . I am never alone, I've said."[17] Charles XII is haunted by his memories whether he is sleeping on his bed or looking into the fire. A guilt-ridden past manifests itself not only in dreams and visions but, as Strindberg put it, "in whole stage-productions of complete realism"[18] directed by the "powers." All the victims of his despotic rule, dead and alive, revisit him. The king does not know any longer if he has slept and dreamt or if the dreams themselves are reality. The rubbing of eyes and brushing with his hands before his eyes are signs of this state of half-reality repeated in Strindberg's stage directions: "KING *brushes his hand over his eyes as if he were collecting his memories and his thoughts.* . . . KING *(brushes his hand across his eyes as if he wanted to free himself from a net)"* (123, 125).

The feeling that life is a dream is created through the "strange" perceptions of the protagonist. *Charles XII* is similar to *To Damascus* (I) in this respect. In *A Dream Play* the aesthetic object was to consciously manipulate the stage action to create within the audience the feeling that life is a dream. Strindberg had also experimented with the latter approach in *Charles XII*. By positioning the king on a bed during one fourth of his time on stage, either dreaming or silently staring into the fire, the audience is constantly reminded of that borderline between what is real and what is dream. Strindberg stresses this surreal quality throughout the play by a number of staging signs. In those scenes that belong to a recognizable historical reality, the dramatist resorts to setting, music, and sound-effects that are interwoven with the textual discourse.

The set for the opening scene relies heavily on Fryxell, but the creation of a ghostlike village with burnt sites and a crumbling cottage is the dramatist's invention.[19] By the symbolic figure of the Man, Sweden's past with its enormous suffering invades the present. Wind, rain, cold, and darkness reinforce the image of a border-region between land and sea where the space of the living touches the space of the dead. The first significant action of the play is the lighting of a fire, the purpose of which is to foreshadow the king's death. On Charles XII's arrival the element of fire is connected with his inner world as he faces its flames, calm and immovable, ignoring the clamoring pleas of a suffering people. The theme is pursued in the second act, in which a large fireplace with a lit fire is facing the king's simple bed. With Horn and Gyllenborg gazing into the fire, the dramatist introduces a new character, the Professor, whose sole function in the play is to make the audience repeatedly aware of the symbolic meaning of the fire. It is true that the historic Charles XII lived in Professor Hegardt's house in Lund, but his kind of local color would serve no historical purpose in relation to his audience.[20] The discrepancy between the king's impressive chair decorated with royal emblems and an ermine mantle and his simple army cot and a uniform jacket on a clothes tree illustrates scenically the conflict between the public and private worlds of the anointed monarch.

The cold, suggested by the creaking beams, sets the stage for the sad notes from Luxembourg's saraband composed by "Sebastian Bach the king of the Land of Sorrows and Pain." This "song of sorrow" floats over the stage after Horn's description of the absent king: "A dead man, whose spirit is walking the earth."[21] To Gyllenborg it sounds like the autumn wind or crying children. The death of sixty thousand children in the last pestilence, which came from Russia after Poltava, is another reminder of the inevitability of innocent suffering. The convergence of the fire and saraband as staging signs serve to define the theme of vastation. The saraband is connected in the discourse with suffering and death and is played by the dwarf Luxembourg, who is the first to utter the biblical warning not to trust rulers who are mortal men: "Put not your trust in princes."[22] Luxembourg's role in *Charles XII*'s history is of the same order as the king's bed, but within the fictive structure he is developed into a well-known figure in the world of historical drama. As himself and as part of vox populi, his music makes the transition to that "higher reality" that is represented on the stage by the fire. The element of fire is present on the stage for more than half the action. In the literary discourse only the theme of death can compete with it, both being referred to on more than twenty occasions. Its central symbolic role as the highest of the elements that liberates us from the material condition is well-known from *A Dream Play*. The panoramic overview of life, the balancing of books, the liberation from the material condition, the insolvable dilemma of innocent suffering are the themes brought together as Agnes enters the flames to return to her father in heaven at the end of the play.

The more Strindberg focused on the inner development of Charles XII, the more he needed symbolic devices to unveil the metaphysical pattern. This in turn encroached on the political and historical drama he had set out to write. A scene from the second act serves to illustrate this dilemma:

> (KING *closes his eyes again. The saraband is played on a violin outside on the street.* KING *opens his eyes but does not move.*)

> (PROFESSOR *enters from the back on tiptoe without noticing the* KING. *Goes up to the stove and stirs the fire with the poker and tests the damper. Then he goes out on tiptoe through the back.* KING *has turned his head to see who it was, says nothing, but only observes what the* PROFESSOR *does. Then he draws up his arms and puts his hands under his neck.*)

> (MAN, *the veteran from Siberia in the first act, comes in from the right, poorly dressed, with a cap on his head and a bludgeon in his hand. Goes slowly up to the* KING's *cot, stops at the foot of the bed, folds his arms over his chest, and stares insolently at the* KING. *The* MAN *has apparently been drinking and has lost his self-control.* KING *lies motionless and looks at the* MAN.)

> MAN: Villain!

> (KING *as before.*)

> MAN: Villain! I said! . . .

Figure 25. *The Man, Hunger, number fifty-eight in Taube's dragoons, confronts the king in a dream sequence. August Palme as Charles XII and Frans Enwall as the soldier's ghost in the first performance of the play at the Royal Dramatic Theater, February 13, 1902.*

(KING *motionless.*)

MAN: Can't you talk? *(Pause.)* So you're the King of Sweden who lies in bed for seven years while the country is being ruined . . . you're a king, who leaves his capital and his government, who doesn't dare to return to his home and his people up in Stockholm, because he is ashamed of his fiasco! Had sworn, of course, that he would return with an arch of triumph at North Bridge and have a conquered kingdom on every finger! . . . You're ashamed! . . .

(KING *motionless.*)

MAN: Do you know where I've come from? . . . From the mines of Siberia, from the deserts of Russia! I met your friends there . . . Piper, Rehnsköld, Lewenhaupt, the ones you left in the lurch when you were down in Turkey playing the fool. But I came by way of Denmark, where I saw your best man, your most faithful servant,

Stenbock, working in irons, because you refused to pay his ransom!

(KING *has moved slightly.*)

MAN: Villain! Do you know who I am? . . .

(KING *motionless, but stares at the* MAN.)

MAN: Do you remember Krasnokutsch? . . . Do you remember Taube's dragoons? Do you remember the cavalryman, who saved your life and got demoted to the infantry because in his eagerness to serve he prevented the King from saving himself as they put it?

(KING *raises himself on his elbow and stares at the* MAN.)

MAN: Yes, I was Hunger, number fifty-eight, in Taube's dragoons, and that I saved your life I now regret, because if you had gone under, there would have been no Poltava, and we would have enjoyed peace . . . six years of peace by now!

(KING *lies down again.*)

MAN: It has been marvelous to speak out for once! And now we can be just as good friends all the same . . .

(KING *rings.*)

MAN: Yes-s! No one will come, because there's no one out there! Oh yes, there is a lady, a little Polish queen without a throne . . .

(KING *rings.*)

MAN: And a king who used to be powerful protected her and her lord. And the king who used to be powerful was a dashing man who didn't squeeze his shillings. . . . There, the deuce, now someone is coming! . . . Then I'm going! . . . You're welcome! Don't mention it! (*Goes.*)

(KING *has raised himself and tried to call, but has not managed to get out a word. Rings again.* HULTMAN *comes in from the back.*)

KING (*rubs his eyes*): I believe I've slept! . . . Was anyone here?

HULTMAN: I didn't see anyone.

KING: Hultman! Give me the cavalry list for 1709, Taube's dragoons!

(HULTMAN *goes to a shelf and searches.*)

KING: A blue folio with a yellow back!

(HULTMAN *comes up with the desired folio.*)

KING: Open it to number fifty-eight under Taube!

HULTMAN (*looks in the list*): Number fifty-eight? . . . It says that has been vacant since 1707!

KING: Was it? . . . Look for Dragoon *Hunger!*

HULTMAN *(looks again):* Hunger? . . . An unusual name! . . . It isn't here!

KING *(rubs his eyes):* Then I have been dreaming! . . . That was horrible!

(130-32)

From the dramaturgical point of view, this scene provides the necessary historical retrospection of Charles XII's political actions during his reign. The accusations against the king are delivered by the Man in rags from the first act. As a prisoner of war, his story of suffering provides the continuity between the past and the present. In this way the Man comes to represent the suffering of the Swedish people. He reiterates the classic examples from the historical tradition critical of the king.[23] They address Charles XII's prolonged stay in Bender, the fracas of his military campaigns, the loss of the empire, the suffering of the Swedish people. Directly related to his own fate is Charles XII's refusal to ransom prisoners of war, among them, his friends and loyal generals Piper, Rehnsköld, Lewenhaupt, and Stenbock. The charge that Charles XII should have failed to provide for the deposed Polish king Stanislaus's wife, Katarina Leczinska, and her children is historically inaccurate. The psychological motivations offered by the Man are related to Charles XII's high-reaching personal ambitions, his merciless indifference and coldness of heart. Not even such highly critical historians as Voltaire and Fryxell operate with similar unqualified depictions in black and white. Regardless of all the historical facts brought to bear on the silent king, the purpose of the scene is not to penetrate the historical or political realities.

If we instead examine the scene in terms of Charles XII's inner development, its function becomes eminently clear. The historical motivation for this scene is weak to say the least. A drunk veteran from Charles XII's Russian campaign enters the monarch's chamber to confront a prostrated silent king with a bludgeon in hand. In the first version from 1899, this character appeared as a recognizable historical figure modeled on two of the most famous Caroline prisoners of war, Rehnsköld and Stobéus.[24] In that context the dramatic figure had a historically defined motif for revenge in a conspiracy plot against a despotic ruler. In 1901 he returns as an avenging angel to read the voluminous contents of the king's Book of Sins. One after another he conjures up the guilt-laden images that haunt Charles XII. His true function in relation to the protagonist is identical to that between the Confessor and the Stranger in the Asylum scene of *To Damascus* (I). The evolution of this character from the drafts of 1899 to the play of 1901 reflects Strindberg's shift of emphasis from a public historical world to the private inner world of his protagonist.

We recognize the convergence of a number of leitmotivs that serve to place the scene in this metaphysical context. Charles XII lies upon a bed, staring into the cleansing fire, his life passing in review. Even the Professor is brought back on stage to silently stir the flames, directing our attention to this recurring symbolic device in the action of the play. The sorrowful notes of Bach's saraband are replayed. It is easy to recall Strindberg's identical use of Beethoven's D-moll sonata, the so-called *Gespenstersonate*, at the fall of Maurice and Henriette at *Auberge des Adrêts* in the second act of *There are Crimes and Crimes* (1899). This scene also depicts a fall. Charles XII has just decided to follow Görtz's advice to save the kingdom. When this metaphysical reckoning takes place, Charles XII remains silent, moves around, raises himself on his elbow, tries to scream but chokes in a similar way to the previous time he was chastised in the demasking of Görtz/Charles XII. Afterward the king believes he was sleeping and had a nightmare. When Hultman checks the identify of Number 58 Hunger of Taube's Dragoons, in the first act presented as Number 73 of the Southern Scanian Regiment, the soldier in question is found to have been dead since 1707. The latter is confirmed in the third act, when the Man acknowledges that he is from the kingdom of the dead and recognizes his deceased wife Caroline, now betrothed to the Sailor from the Snapp-Opp. The king's cramps and choking on the stage have demonstrated that the chastising by the "powers" has had its effect. The simple word horrible contains in this context a sign of Charles XII's first glimpse into a world of spiritual realities. The structural model for this reckoning with the past was in Swedenborg's vastation, transposed from the spiritual world to Charles XII's life and history. The ideas and structures of Swedenborg were seen to be identical to Strindberg's own Inferno experiences and interpreted as a stage in a process of moral purification. In *To Damascus* (I) Strindberg could use his stagecraft to represent the inner realities of crime and guilt. This was not possible in *Charles XII* because of the very nature of the historical materials, but Strindberg still comes very close.

What Strindberg could not achieve in this dream-scene is remedied by the third act in which Charles XII is absent from the stage. In this ceremonial act the victims of the king process across the stage to the accompaniment of Luxembourg's saraband. It is the widows of the captured lords, the widows of the executed traitors to the state, the oppositional ex-Royalists, the President of the National Council, and the speakers of the four estates. The absent king is symbolized by the silent house that refuses to open its doors to a suffering people. The action is mediated to the audience by the symbolic figure Malcontent. The climax of these historical-political actions is the ceremonial announcement of Louis XIV's death, signified by the lowering of the flag and accompanied by muted drums and church bells. From a world-historical perspective the anachronistic death of Louis XIV marked the end of an era of absolutism and the imminent death of Charles XII. At the same time it heralded the dawn of the age of freedom represented by the two pretenders Horn and Gyllenborg. The power struggles around the king and the ensuing chaos after his death indicate that history repeats itself — that only the figures on its stage change. A peripety in the traditional sense it is not, no matter how strongly Strindberg argued to the contrary. The ruins of burned houses at the back and a smithy at the left are the only elements of the set with symbolic associations. The dramatist had long intended to have a burning fire in his smithy, but the audience's anticipation of local color must have been prohibitive to any such excesses.

The motif of love belongs to the prevalent conventions of historical drama. Strindberg centered the whole fourth act of *Charles XII* around it, with Emerentia Polhem's attempt to woo the king, Charles XII's meeting with his sister, Ulrika Eleonora, and Katarina Leczinska's confrontation with the king. In a subplot Emanuel Swedenborg appears as the fiancé to Emerentia Polhem. Strindberg used the parallel between the love pangs of Charles XII and Swedenborg to explore the conflict between a material world and a higher reality. The superb scene with Ulrika Elenora is the only one historically motivated through the struggle for succession. In Shakespeare love entanglements are often used to expose the larger conflicts between private and public worlds in which the values attached to each are challenged and questioned. For the most part love stories in historical drama imply a reduction of the historical world, the purpose being to entertain the audience.

The fourth act is set in a garden in Lund, which required a degree of plausibility. Apart from the king's bed and a statue of Venus, Strinberg's set operates within the accepted historical conventions. The statue of Venus in the center serves to remind the audience that sexuality is the ultimate source of human suffering. Swedenborg exclaims: "This is love! Earthly love! . . . Heaven above!"[25] Strindberg's use of the love motif may be a reduction of the historical world, but its purpose remains the same as elsewhere— to rewrite history from a spiritual perspective. The interweaving of the different love stories sets up a parallel between Charles XII and Swedenborg. At a point when the desperate monarch vacillates and doubts his divine mission, Swedenborg's ill-fated love reminds the king that their pain and suffering are the signs of the chosen: "Emanuel [Swedenborg's Christian name], pull yourself together and be a man! You, a Nazirite, born for great deeds and great dreams, what do you have to do with either women or wine? Are you going to put your head in a lap and let her clip the hair of your strength?" [26] Like the Nazirite Samson, Charles XII and Swedenborg have been selected by God to fulfill a mission. When his fellow brother fails to free himself from the fetters of earthly love, Charles XII reiterates: "Emanuel, that means God be with us!" [27] When the two scapegoats depart on their divinely ordained missions, Strindberg paraphrases Mark Antony's last command to his faithful servant Eros: "My sword! My cape! And my hat!" With the acceptance of suffering and death, Charles XII can meet with his destiny at Fredrikshald:

SWEDENBORG: Now I'll accompany Your Majesty!

KING *(points at the statue of Venus):* And not that goddess!

(157)

That Strindberg's aim ultimately is a spiritual reinterpretation of human history is revealed by a number of different staging signs in the text. Emerentia's attempt to seduce the king is framed by the following stage direction: "KING *(who has had his face buried in his hands looks up, and, when he becomes aware of* EMERENTIA, *he does not seem to know if she is a dream or a revelation. . . .)* " [28] The stage of history has been set by the "powers," and Charles XII no longer knows what is reality and what is dream. During Charles XII's meeting with Ulrika Eleonora, Strindberg repeats a familiar scenic image with the king falling asleep to the sorrowful tones of Luxembourg to evoke the transcendent perspective. Charles XII's greeting to Katarina Leczinska is equally ambiguous: "I dreamt about you." [29] It is not clear whether Charles XII is referring to his "dream" during the scene with the Man in act 2 or if he's suggesting a different dream. The important point is that the state of half-reality, of dreaming, haunts him like pangs of conscience.

To make the audience aware that Charles XII's sickness is spiritual in nature, Strindberg uses the characters around the king to provide the physical symptoms of his vastation. Sleeplessness, anxiety, sick, worried, and on the brink of death are some of the characterizations in the text. We see him impatiently pacing the stage, irritable and at time frightened. He clutches his forehead as if he suffers from headaches, and he drifts in and out of sleep. At the same time there is an awareness that his sickness is not physical in nature. To the suffering monarch the external reality takes on a bizarre, ghostlike quality, and he complains bitterly: "They don't say anything! *(Pause)* The whole city says nothing; the whole country says nothing! A silence as of death is beginning to close about us! *(Pause)* And besides I am sick! The streets are empty; no one comes to call! No one protests! . . . No

one says anything! *(Pause.)* Say something!" (144-45). The repeated reminders in combination with pauses and silence are effective scenic means to
establish a sense of the surreal within the audience. What the audience
perceives in the fourth act are the consequences of vastation. For the king it
is an intense struggle to accpet death, overcome his will to control, and
follow his divine mission. To accept responsibility for his actions and come
to terms with his guilt seems almost insufferable. The thought of death is
constantly on his mind.

Charles XII identifies with the suffering Christ in his lamentations in
the Garden of Gethsemane and on the cross: "My God, my God. Let this cup
be taken from me!"[30] In his identification with the suffering Christ, the king
is brought another step toward accepting his own pain and suffering as part
of God's divine plan. Charles XII's struggle to accept God's will is communicated in a monologue from his bed. It is the first time that the central character communicates directly with his audience. He attacks the false image of
himself and his mission that has been created during his absence from the
kingdom. The historical-political world is brushed aside in one line: "There
isn't one act I cannot defend but I do not deign!"[31] When the dramatist
reduces the public sphere to the private, the king's reflections on human
love sometimes verge on the pathetic. The distance to the historical world is
bridged. In accepting the inevitability of his death, Charles XII identifies
with the legendary Swedish hero Ragnar Lodbrok, who died in a snakepit
after being captured by the English king Ella in the ninth century: "The
moments of my life are ended, smiling I shall meet my death!"[32] Listening
once more to Luxembourg's sad song from the "Kingdom of Death and
Sorrow," Charles XII finally seeks acceptance and peace beyond all heroic
posturing: "Now I shall go to sleep! Sleep, the best there is! The next best. *(He
falls asleep. The saraband is played in the distance.)*"[33]

By not defending his acts in the public realm, Charles XII is again
evading the dilemma of innocent suffering. Luxembourg's warning to the
victims of Charles XII's rule the first time that he played the saraband comes
to full force: "Put not your trust in princes, nor in the son of man, in whom
there is no help. / His breath goeth forth, he returneth to his earth; in that
very day his thoughts perish. / Happy is he that hath the God of Jacob for his
help; whose hope is in the Lord his God: / Which made heaven, and earth,
the sea, and all that therein is: which keepeth truth for ever: / Which
executeth judgement for the oppressed: which giveth food to the hungry.
The Lord looseth the prisoners."[34] Charles XII may identify with Christ's
divine scapegoat mission, but he has failed to accept the very words that he
himself quoted: "Nevertheless, not what I will, but what thou wilt."[35]
Strindberg has an answer for Charles XII's suffering, but no explanation for

that of the Swedish people. The problem of innocent suffering remained unresolved for him. In *A Dream Play,* which emerged from his own sufferings during his September 1901 crisis, Strindberg again grappled with this universal question that demanded a solution in one form or other.

On Görtz return Charles XII has accepted his destiny and is now willing to be accountable for at least some of his political actions. The death of the king is unavoidable, but Charles XII's admittance of guilt is cautiously qualified by the dramatist in view of the divine scapegoat role they shared. In the same manner as in *A Dream Play,* it is the world order with its web of deceit that emerges as the real culprit. The demise of the kingdom and the apocalyptic end of an era is made parallel to that of the king and visualized through scenography. Charles XII's garden in Lund is removed from the realm of history and becomes expressive of the fate of the king and the country. At the iron gate on the right, the dead Siberian soldier and his deceased wife appear with Malcontent, the narrator of Sweden's woes. This "silent and horrible" chorus recreates symbolically the history of Sweden and its ruler. The death of the king and the apocalypse of an era is expressed by a group of shabby-looking men and boys, whose appearance on stage is keyed to the word freedom. No one on the stage seems to notice these ghostly figures. Görtz is the only character who senses their presence, although he is unable to "see," because they are his fellow creatures and correspond to his inner vision of man and the world. "Something is happening that makes me uneasy but then I do not understand . . . and there is a smell from poor people's clothes."[36] After Charles XII's departure the lost garden of Eden is invaded and eventually taken over: " *(Now the iron-grill gate is opened, and shabby figures steal in, silent, ghostlike, curious, and fingering everything; the figures by the wall silently join them)* " (158).

The last stage in Charles XII's inward development takes place at Fredrikshald. During his final vastation the king looks into the flames of the cleansing fire and accepts his destiny with stoicism as he rids himself of the material world.

> FEIF: [. . .] What is the king waiting for?
>
> SWEDENBORG: Who knows! . . . See how he's lying staring into the fire! A great rich life is passing in review . . .
>
> FEIF: Has passed by . . . a great man!
>
> SWEDENBORG: Great, not great! Can we give the measure of a man with a few small words? . . . Are you tired, Feif?
>
> FEIF: We all are!
>
> SWEDENBORG: Yes, perhaps!

FEIF: It's the first Sunday in Advent today! Soon it will be Christmas!

SWEDENBORG: And New Year's!

(159-60)

The king's life revue had already been made abundantly clear to the audience from the vastation scenes of the second act and the ceremonial third act. Charles XII has reconciled himself to his private destiny but no answer is offered for his actions in the public realm.

The historical drama's demand that private experiences achieve what meaning they have only within a public perspective forced Strindberg to abandon the idea of using the king's consciousness in this scene as the sole framework for the historical action in the play. The necessity to keep the private and public realms apart had its roots in the still unresolved question of innocent suffering. Our suffering must be given an explanation, and in his final monologue Charles XII attacks a cruel and unjust world order:

> KING: [. . .](*He rolls the letters into a ball.*) The whole of life is like this ball, a web of lies, mistakes, misunderstandings! To hell with it! . . . Forgive me for swearing! *(Throws the ball into the closest fire. Pause)* I cannot fight with lies and the father of lies. . . . My own sister. . . . Certainly I haven't been any angel, but so devilishly black I wasn't, either! Let the people amuse themselves! The Sabbath ended at six o'clock! *(The saraband is played.)* Who is playing my saraband?
>
> (163)

Luxembourg's reappearance illustrates a final time the discrepancy between the popular image of the king as a ruthless tyrant and his true self. In the ensuing conversation with his spiritual guide, the dreamer and philosopher Swedenborg, Charles XII accepts death as a liberation from the web of lies and deceit:

> KING (*to* SWEDENBORG): Life is like that; what can death be like?
>
> SWEDENBORG: Nature is consistent!
>
> KING (*looks about himself*): Are they shooting from the fortress, or what is it that's singing about my ears?
>
> SWEDENBORG: The night wind, I suspect . . .
>
> KING: The glass in the lantern just broke. . . . They must be shooting . . .
>
> SWEDENBORG: We ought to be able to hear it!
>
> KING (*gets up in anguish*): I do not know . . . but I would like a glass of wine!
>
> (163-64)

Göran Stockenström

The identification with the tragic scapegoat role of Christ is a recurring analogy from the fourth act. The symbolic use of the setting creates at this point the necessary distance between the nobility of the king and the corrupt historical world he has rejected. The intrusion of the political world occurs again in the form of a dispatch that according to the dramatist's historical sources confirms the inevitability of Charles XII's imminent death.[37] The king's stoic acceptance is revealed in his last words to Swedenborg: "Good night, Emanuel! Now I shall start the assault!"[38] The use of Swedenborg's Christian name had already been clarified to the audience: "Emanuel, that means God be with us!" These words were spoken by the king when Swedenborg was caught in the slings and arrows of human passion to remind him about the course of divine love that was ordained for them both. The destiny of the king is finally interpreted by his friend Swedenborg, the dreamer who best knows how to solve life's riddles:

FEIF: Do you see him?

SWEDENBORG: Yes! He's on his knees as if he were praying!

FEIF: Praying? What is he looking for up there?

SWEDENBORG: What he's looking for! . . . That strange man!

FEIF: Have you ever understood his destiny?

SWEDENBORG: No, and we'll probably never understand it! I have never understood *one* human destiny, not even my own insignificant one.

FEIF: Are you aware that we are talking as if he were dead?

SWEDENBORG: He is dead!

(*A flare lights up the stage and expires with a report. Everyone on stage is silent as if in death, and all look up towards the fortress. [. . .]*)

SWEDENBORG: God be merciful to his soul. . . . But where did the bullet come from?

FEIF *(points to the fortress):* From up there!

SWEDENBORG *(points to heaven):* From up there!

(165)

No shot is heard when Charles XII dies. (The only bullet fired in the play is in the first act.) Instead the stage is lit up by a ball of fire. The fire set at the beginning of the action has finally reached its goal. The same is true for the bullet which, as Swedenborg interprets it for the audience, was not a physical but a metaphysical reality.

After Charles XII's death everything lapses into chaos and darkness, but the emergence of a big lantern next to the dead king manifests both

242

individual resurrection and the coming of a new age after renewed terrors. The end of the play has the characteristic uplifting effect when the audience shares in Charles XII's death. It is the ending that Strindberg's audience had long anticipated. Strindberg makes a visual point through the painful symmetry of the opening and closing images of Charles XII in the play. On his first appearance the audience sees the silent king before the fire, calm and immovable, with his back to the kneeling representatives of the Swedish people. In the final image it is Charles XII who is kneeling in a pose of humility, awaiting the portal of fire through which he is to pass. It is similar to Richard II on his throne with Bolingbroke before him as a supplicant in the first scene and the roles reversed with Bolingbroke on the same throne and Richard's coffin before him in the last. Strindberg was very fond of these symmetrical parallels, but between the first and the last image of the king in *Charles XII* something of significance has happened. Suffering has been turned into transcendence.

As historical drama Strindberg's *Charles XII* is deficient when compared with his "master Shakespeare" that he advocated as his model from *Master Olof*. Shakespeare's historical world with its secular focus on a discernibly real world, its cultivation of multiple points of view, its balance of public and private perspectives, and its artistic mastery is a unique creation. It has been praised and analyzed by Strindberg in his *Open Letters to the Intimate Theater*. The nature of its achievement has been accounted for by Shakespearean scholars. Strindberg's contemporary critics could more easily perceive the flaws of *Charles XII* as historical drama than later critics using other models of interpretation. Through its dual character of historical drama and dream play, it opens divergent possibilities of interpretation and evaluation. Strindberg's dramaturgical dilemma is that he uses the historical drama for a purpose for which it was never intended. The vastation motif, the dream-structure, and the leitmotiv technique all served to portray a landscape of the soul, and the public world of politics is reflected only within the consciousness of the king or separated from him. The historical world restricted the imaginative freedom we find in plays such as *To Damascus* (I), *A Dream Play*, and *The Ghost Sonata*. An authority on historical drama, Herbert Lindenberger, concludes: "The whole historical framework of *Charles XII* serves primarily to illuminate the neuroses of an unpleasant and broken man who unluckily (for future Swedish history) happens to be the king."

With Strindberg the nineteenth-century historical drama, as a genre with its own system of character relationships, poetic language, and dramatic progression in time, is brought to its end. The revision of history from a spiritual perspective is not necessarily different from his revision of history from socioeconomic viewpoints in the first *Master Olof* (1873);

Strindberg could still perceive of it in terms of "realism." It was only that the facts of history had taken on a different meaning when he found similarities between them and his own experiences during and after his Inferno crisis. What had to be revised in 1873 was different from what had to be revised in 1901. On both occasions it reflected his own consciousness at an intersection of history. The continuity in the stories from history that he tells and retells is unbroken, but the perspective keeps shifting and expanding as layer upon layer are incorporated into his dramatic discourse. The traditional period designations are too narrow for Strindberg; they cannot encompass the seemingly divergent elements of continuity and change coexisting in his work.

In twentieth-century drama the human being is often represented as severed from an earlier religious, metaphysical, and transcendent context, dismayed by the fact that all his or her actions seem to inspire only an insoluble anguish. When Strindberg, after *Inferno* (1897), portrays history's seemingly meaningless course and senseless cruelty to a suffering people, the depiction is not one of absurdity but of compassion offered him by his religious convictions. In the chaos surrounding Charles XII's death, a large lantern emerges center stage to signify this transcendent perspective. It made it possible for him both to understand the sufferings of the Swedish people and still to resurrect the king, however difficult and painful this process was for him, judging from his long and laborious work on *Charles XII*.

18

Theories and Practice
in Staging A Dream Play

Ingvar Holm

In a research group some years ago at the Institute for Research in the Dramatic Arts in Lund, the students decided to study how Strindberg's plays actually stood in relation to what people in France, Germany, Norway, and elsewhere once called naturalistic theater. That question related mainly to plays such as *The Father, Miss Julie, The Creditors, Pariah*, et cetera. Another question concerned how Strindberg's work related to what Germany, in paticular, would later begin to call expressionistic theater. In the latter case our curiosity concerned plays such as *To Damascus, A Dream Play, The Great Highway*, and also, with reservations, the remaining late dramas *The Dance of Death, The Ghost Sonata, The Pelican*, and others.

We had several reasons for posing these questions. A classification of Strindberg's plays as either naturalistic or expressionistic appears, as we know, in our standard reference books. But at the same time, we know that there is often some slanting of the evidence when we talk about artistic schools. The criteria of styles have a tendency to gain polemic import. Therefore, we asked ourselves how these styles really appeared, and we carried out a close reading of drama texts to find the answer.

There are other reasons to use the two schools as a point of departure for a study of the staging history of Strindberg. As we know, the term naturalistic was originally applied to a style of drama wherein a psychological reality connected with the everyday life of the kitchen and living room was allowed to guide the formation of theatrical roles and plots. But during the 1890s this purpose directly led to a new analysis of acting. Soon after Antoine and Otto Brahms — and before them as regards developing a theory of acting — we find, following the artistic criteria of naturalism, none other than the old leader of the amateur stage in Moscow, Constantin Stanislavsky. Here we have one of the prime movers behind the interest in naturalistic theater.

Expressionism began in around 1920 in Germany and made use of a new technical approach, not only employing devices such as the revolving stage, cyclorama, lifts, and other stage gadgetry already known in the baroque theater but also using a new form of lighting — high-powered spotlights, footlights, et cetera, the likes of which had never been seen before.

In this way, we noted, the two styles could be surveyed by making an inventory of the two different semantic systems that were developed to formulate a message. Both systems arose during Strindberg's time or soon after his death. Theater people, schooled in the two styles, were prepared to handle his texts. To what extent they had an adequate language to produce Strindberg's plays was a question that was addressed by our research.

There is one more reason to study the two styles and relate Strindberg to them. It is bound up with Sweden's position in theater history, seen in international perspective. Sweden was a thinly populated land of forests; as late as 1850 there were still no more than four inhabitants per square mile. Urbanization came late and by the middle of the 1800s not more than 10 percent of the country's population lived in the cities; hence there was little room for the theater, the most urbane of the muses. This view of Sweden may perhaps seem a little too picturesque, but it is in fact realistic. Going over the lists of repertory, stage records, and other material for the established theaters and traveling companies in Sweden, we notice that such stages as could be found in the comedy and melodrama theater on the Continent, were in Sweden nearly nonexistent or in extremely poor shape. As a matter of fact, the eighteenth-century court theater in Sweden had been more up-to-date in its time than what was offered a century later. Scandinavia had fallen behind during the great heyday of the theater in nineteenth-century Europe. At the close of *Peer Gynt*, Ibsen's main character says: "To my final word I've still to arrive / One doesn't die in the middle of act five."

He was not exaggerating. According to the established dramaturgical practice of the time, one died at the close of act 5 and not in the middle, and that was all there was to it. By a deceptively simple innovation, Ibsen was thus able to escape the confines of Scandinavian theatrical practice. He had observed the melodrama theaters of Rome and Munich. When Strindberg wrote his famous note "Ett verksamt drama" (An effective drama) in *Samlade Otryckta Skrifter* (Stockholm: Bonniers, 1919), vol. 2, 172: "An effective drama should operate with insinuations, contain a secret which the spectator gets to know either at the beginning or at the end . . . an outburst of emotion, anger, indignation, a sudden but well-prepared reversal, a disclosure, a punishment, a humiliation (nemesis), a carefully prepared ending with or without reconciliation, a qui pro quo, a parallelism, a reversal (retirement), a setback, a sunrise, well executed," he had hardly been able to study the effect of such a drama in Stockholm. He was basing his observations on what he had seen in Berlin and Paris.

Thus Swedish theater began late, in around 1880. It appeared on virginal ground: conventions had little strength. New schools were new indeed! All this contributed to the development of strange manifestations on the path toward Strindberg's theater. But before I proceed to the stagings of Strindberg's plays, especially *A Dream Play*, I will further examine the two theatrical styles.

My students who worked with this problem proceeded rather pedantically (and no harm in that) from two periods: naturalism from 1872 to 1892 and expressionism from 1910 to 1925. The students collected the titles of thirty dramas of each style, which manifesto writers of the respective periods regarded as typical for each of these "isms." The manifestos were, in the case of naturalism, 352 in number and essentially French and German, and, in the case of expressionism, eighty-five in number and mostly German. The manifestos were often declarations of principles written by authors who had declared themselves to be adherents of a particular style, but other types of polemic pamphlets and accounts from the chosen periods were also part of the manifesto material.

The manifestos were perused to note which dramas were mentioned as characteristic of the school in question. In this way we obtained a list of naturalism's "international top thirty" and a corresponding list for expressionistic drama.

Gerhart Hauptmann's *Vor Sonnenaufgang* (Before Sunrise) topped naturalism's list. *Miss Julie* was number fourteen and *The Father* number twenty-one. The most frequently mentioned plays considered to be naturalistic were evenly distributed over the years from 1880 to 1890.

Heading the list of the thirty expressionistic dramas were two Toller plays, followed by two by Kaiser, after which came dramas by Goltz, Unruh, Johst, Werfel, and Hasenclever. The expressionistic plays came in two waves, the first from 1914 to 1915 and the second from 1919 to 1922.

I wish to point out some characteristics in the plays that we studied as a background to Strindberg's works. The first is seemingly slight but in reality of the greatest significance: The total quantity of *stage directions* is larger in naturalism than in expressionism—16 percent and 14 percent, respectively, of the total text mass. No great difference, but a difference nevertheless. This occurs in spite of the fact that the technical stage apparatus, which the expressionist playwright at least theoretically had a chance to use and refer to, was much more extensive and expressive than that which the naturalistic playwright had had at his disposal thirty years earlier.

This indicates as well a general trend at that time to let the director have more decision-making power than before. The difference in the number of stage directions in typically expressionist plays does demonstrate the playwright's abdication of control over purely theatrical devices and media, all to the director's advantage. This accords with the theatrical theory of expressionism, which claims that the writer is alienated from the play.

One could expect an analagous relationship in the case of Strindberg and expressionism. When Strindberg wrote his dream plays and Chamber Plays, no expressionist or even what we would consider modern stage convention had begun to be developed. And this fact is witnessed by the first productions of his plays. He could no more resort to an already refined theatrical style than could the first naturalists; yet, if we study some of his dramas, which were often referred to in the manifestos of the expressionists — such as *To Damascus* (I), *A Dream Play*, or the Chamber Plays *Storm Weather*, *The Burned House*, *The Ghost Sonata*, and *The Pelican* — it becomes apparent that he was significantly more generous with stage directions than "typical" expressionistic or naturalistic playwrights. *A Dream Play* and *The Ghost Sonata*, in particular, have a greater number of stage directions, in proportion to play length, than any expressionist or naturalistic drama. And of all Strindberg's plays that were studied, only *Storm Weather* has a proportionately smaller number of directions than the average number for either expressionism or naturalism. In addition, his stage directions are much more lengthy and detailed than is the case with either style. (In *A Dream Play* and *The Ghost Sonata*, they are more than twice as long.)

Strindberg had a new theater in mind when he wrote his dream plays and Chamber Plays, but, at the same time, he could act without being inhibited by the new attitudes on the part of the directors that a few decades later would come to restrict so much of the playwright's freedom of movement. On the contrary, in his letters and prefaces, he is able to encourage the theater personnel to release and develop the vision in his dramas. The number of instructions in *A Dream Play* for the use of stage space and props are 50 percent higher than in the average expressionist drama. Even for lighting, the prized plaything of the new theater, he gives twenty-two directions, as compared with twenty-five in the expressionist drama with the highest number of lighting directions.

But more things are to be considered in this dissimilarity between Strindberg and the expressionistic playwrights. One consistently finds in this theater style that the playwright refrains from entering directly into what was regarded more as the business of the director. In expressionism, the text was the playwright's domain, and the stage and set design the director's. Strindberg, however, although he was quite aware of the new things going on in Paris, of Maeterlinck's texts, and, after 1905, of Gordon Craig's theories, created his new drama, as we have already noted, in virgin territory. Thus he could approach the theater more boldly. He could suggest in his preface to *A Dream Play* a connection between the stage and the "disjointed but seemingly logical form of the dream," where "anything can happen, everything is possible and probable," and he could recommend that a certain scene be like "a mixture of memories, experiences, free-floating ideas, absurdities, and improvisations." He continues in his stage directions to explain how "characters are split, doubled, duplicated, evaporated, condensed, scattered, and converged." In a moment's blackout the basswoods wilt and the Officer ages. In the next scene the tree is transformed into a hat rack in the Lawyer's office, only to reappear as a candelabra during the scene when the doctoral degree is conferred. The billboard outside the opera house becomes covered with the proceedings from a trial and soon afterward with psalm texts; the rose window of the courtroom is seen in the next moment in the cathedral, and the Lawyer's bed canopy is transformed into the tent of the Quarantine Officer. The palace grows and burns while people are led with unseeing eyes through the happy land, placed on a school bench under threat of a birching, or situated among the instruments of torture, until the burning castle blossoms into a gigantic chrysanthemum. All this comes from the stage directions and recommendations of Strindberg for *A Dream Play*, which was written in 1901.

None of the features and none of the transformations described in this theatrical landscape would be strange to a director in the expressionistic theater twenty years later, but among expressionistic playwrights, with all their intense psychological effects and violent situations, there is almost a total lack of the kind of explicit and constructive stage directions that Strindberg gave. Strindberg, not yet having met any of the "demon" directors of the coming decades, could imperturbably write out what later on could be regarded as ideal expressionistic theater. In the introduction to *A Dream Play*, he makes the proud declaration: "But above all there is a consciousness, the consciousness of the dreamer: for him there are no secrets, no inconsistencies, no scruples, no law."

The dreamer that Strindberg speaks of here was identical to the poet. Nevertheless, the role of dreamer as described by Strindberg in his introductions and stage directions was sooner appropriated by the directors than by the coming generation of playwrights. This became apparent to us when we, as a group, systematized the written stage directions of the expressionist plays, as well as the corresponding stage conventions.

I will now show how the naturalistic and expressionistic directors made use of Strindberg's influence and how the Strindberg heritage was carried on. At first Strindberg's works were played too realistically, with atmospheric effects that were too weak. In such a production, when a scene, gesture, or line was given specifically to break the illusion — the total effect seen in the sober conventional framework — it tended to become baroque or even ludicrous. The director in such cases had not succeeded in communicating or grasping the vibrant intensity in the apparently everyday world. Mishaps in this direction were a result of the epoch's recently acquired and one-sided schooling in naturalistic theater. The staging of *To Damascus* (I) at the Royal Dramatic Theater in Stockholm in 1900 — from many points of view sensationally modern — furnishes examples of this sort of shortcoming, if the documentation is to be believed.

Even worse was the creation of an artificial Strindberg mold. It was well known that he was a troublemaker, blasphemer, and misogynist, and that his dialogue fairly sizzled with emotional violence. And so there arose a particular "Strindberg style": as soon as an actor got a role in a Strindberg play, he pulled down the corners of his mouth, dropped his voice into the bass range, wrinkled his brow like a washboard, rolled his eyes, gnashed his teeth, and in general carried on like a murderer from an old opera. The actresses remade themselves into venomous vampires, beautiful beasts of prey with long claws and forked tongues. Misadventures in this direction were linked to a failure to understand the basic concepts of expressionistic theater.

It is well known that Max Reinhardt, deeply rooted in expressionistic theater and cognizant of the staging history of the Strindberg plays, did in fact employ some elements of the previously described frightening picture in his guest performance in Stockholm (1921) of *The Pelican* and other plays.

But, more clearly than anyone else, the same Max Reinhardt saw that the richer the content of an iconographic sign, the more clear-cut would be its effect. If one of the actors in a production appears pinioned in a characteristic attitude with arms spread-eagle and head hanging limply and downcast, it can mean that an everyday tragedy has given rise to a scene of Golgotha. Many playwrights and directors have also interpreted the symbols in this way. When first Max Reinhardt and later Olof Molander placed the Lawyer in *A Dream Play* in that position, it was in accordance with the writer's intention: the crown of thorns is mentioned in Strindberg's stage directions. But it must be assumed that the spectators also understand such signs. In this case, since one of the most common signs of Christian iconography has been employed, a Western audience would certainly understand the message.

Equivalent examples are to be found in Max Reinhardt's lighting directions. A few weeks after the opening night of *A Dream Play* in Berlin, 1925, he placed intense spotlights on Indra's Daughter at crucial moments and thus got an almost predictable reaction from the audience to the Daughter: they saw her as having been "sent from the gods." This change in interpretation was decisive for the whole meaning projected by the performance. Among other things it allowed Indra's Daughter — Helene Thimig — to stress the pain, dirt, and oppression suffered by the characters in all the aspects of life that give significance to the line "Human beings are to be pitied." The role had previously been played ritualistically and solemnly. Throughout all the scenes Indra's Daughter had acted as if she were standing in front of God — at His high altar. After Reinhardt, in accordance with expressionist practice, had used light to place emphasis on Indra's Daughter, actresses could perform passionately without ever losing the nimbus of the divinely gifted.

Godard has said that there is a moral standpoint in a camera angle. This is one of the most important statements that has been made concerning the performing arts — in Godard's case it was film in particular. There is also a moral standpoint in a gesture, a tone of voice, a choice of role, a light accent, or a color used in a set. To speak of drama without considering this is an absurdity.

When Olof Molander created his stage designs for *A Dream Play* in 1947 and again later, he proceeded from his knowledge of the author's milieu and biographical situation. Allusions to Strindberg himself were boldly underlined in one or more of the key roles (the Poet, the Officer, and the Lawyer). Molander also worked with various conceptions of the dream as a psychological phenomenon, conceptions that he had gleaned from his research of several sources of information. In the essay "Drömstilen hos Strindberg och Kafka" (Dream structure in Strindberg and Kafka) in *Bonniers Litterära Magasin*, written in 1946, the Swedish critic Ebbe Linde discusses Strindberg's and Kafka's use of dreams. He claims that most people dream colorlessly, "as if the dream were on film, thereby giving rise to the expression 'the shadowy world of dreams.' Or more rightly said: colors occur only occasionally, isolated and random, such as the blue hair ribbon in a hand-colored photograph." Kafka's dream atmosphere appears in just that way,

251

says Linde, whereas Strindberg's atmosphere is blazing with color. There are the yellow sunflowers, the blue monk's hood, and the green fish net, among many other examples.

Molander, while working on a production of *A Dream Play* for the Malmö City Theater, wrote about the aforementioned Linde essay to the designer Martin Ahlbom in a letter of August 20, 1946. It struck him, he wrote, "that perhaps one should either make all projections like black-and-white photographic negatives or make some of them like positives with only certain sections colored. In this way the set could be painted in black, gray, and white with occasional touches in glowing colors in order to stress something in the dream." This quotation paraphrases Linde's 1946 article, the thesis of which Molander himself accepted and put into practice in staging *A Dream Play*.

Among other things, the director and the designer of this production discussed the closet, which is found in several scenes. When Molander went through the designer's sketches for the stage sets, he criticized Ahlbom's suggestion of making the closet large, distorted, and unreal. The closet is one of the reminders of the Officer's guilty conscience. Molander writes:

> [The closet] certainly draws the Officer's attention but it is because it "reappears" from his childhood . . . and perpetually recurs in the most bizarre situations. One can let it appear yet more often than the author has indicated. And because the closet can be present much more often than we had earlier allowed it to be, it gives me the thought that perhaps we could arrange the stage design with fewer details — but let them "reappear" perpetually. (Olof Molander, Letter to Martin Ahlbom, August 20, 1946)

This written arrangement was carried through in the production. Strindberg's own directorial suggestions were magnified and stressed and the closet returned repeatedly. Among other things, it could be identified as the door with the four-leaf-clover window in the theater corridor. More important was the recurrence of all the details observed on stage. All the objects gradually became familiar — they were recognized as something that had been seen before, something known and, for that very reason, peculiar-looking in their new surroundings. Reality was thus expressed with the marked clarity of a myth. If the main purpose in Strindberg's *A Dream Play* is to a reveal the properties of dreams, it is hard to imagine a more perceptive stage set than that of Olof Molander.

The director's interpretation called for the appearance in the final scene of a stage image that would show the cross on Strindberg's grave in Stockholm. Through such an ending, the play was thus even more closely associated with the author's personality.

Only half a year after the Malmö production, Molander produced *A Dream Play* at the City Theater in Gothenburg in 1947. The Gothenburg production was more stark and less lyrical than the Malmö one had been. The Coalheavers' scene with its social theme, which had been left out in Malmö, was included this time. More significantly, in the final scene the set included a large, simple wooden cross built around a background of black ruins: a vignette of postwar Europe had made its entrance upon the stage. This production of *A Dream Play* had taken a step away from the poet's private situation during the early twentieth century and, at the same time, the line "Human beings are to be pitied" acquired a topical connotation.

In spite of this, however, Molander's view is still fundamentally built upon biographical observation. The dream is delivered through acting, masks, accents, and images. The dreamer and his situation are carried over to the spectator. The social environment in which Strindberg had lived, his private conflicts, and the facts of his biography had been revealed earlier by literary researchers and had made incessant appearances on stage. The stage designs by Molander indicate the extent of Strindberg's conquest of the Swedish audience. At the same time, this development also became a threat to Strindberg's works: the audience began to know too much about the man and a set of "classical" stage conventions grew up around his plays. Strindberg as a person began to be a bit too interesting.

Every country has at some time experienced something equivalent in regard to its native classics. The psychological picture of the Poet in *A Dream Play* contained so many bizarre features that it could lead to caricature. *A Dream Play* contains scenes that undeniably have recognizable equivalents in key events of the author's life: poor Strindberg liked red cabbage but could not taste it! And the whole affair with the crooked candles and the untidy curtains — Strindberg himself was to be pitied!

Molander's Gothenburg staging was a small step on the road to discovering *A Dream Play* as the work of an anonymous poet who could also appeal to a new era. After the bizarre elements and symbols had settled into place more comfortably within the work of art, then the work, as a continually new text, could convey a new application of Godard's words: Let the stage set be a moral decision. To some extent we can compare this statement with the expressionists' theory of staging.

In spring 1955 Oscar Fritz Schuh produced *A Dream Play* at the Theater am Kurfürstendamm in Berlin. It was an important step in the history of stage design and a work of art that was created with its audience's environment in mind. The production showed, as had so many earlier versions of *A Dream Play*, disappointments and sufferings, Foulstrand and the veil of tears, the implements of tortue, and "pitiful mankind," but this time not against a background of the irritated nerves and painful religious cramps of a dead poet. A physical likeness of Strindberg was not included among the roles; no one in the Berlin audience would have recognized him anyway. And any knowledge about Strindberg's life that might have explained the bizarre things in the play — the cupboard door, the corridor in the theater, disappointment over the nonconferral of the doctoral degree, the blacka-moor in Foulstrand, and so on — could not be expected of the Kurfürsten-damm audience in the ruins of Berlin.

A Dream Play was also dreamed in Central Europe in the postwar years, a different dream from those in Malmö, Gothenburg, and Stockholm. No one was especially interested in giving certain architectural features of the set a resemblance to residential areas in Stockholm. However, the Blind Man, the Invalid, and other pitiful characters were forced into a horror format. The dream was adjusted to a new reality. On opening night the iron grip seizing the audience began to loosen up, and the dialogue between the Poet and Indra's Daughter, Agnes, gave the formula behind the Berlin production, quoting from Strindberg's text:

DAUGHTER: I feel that once before, somewhere else, we said these words.

POET: Then soon you will know what reality is.

DAUGHTER: Or dreaming.

POET: Or poetry.

> (From *Six Plays of Strindbergs* trans. Elizabeth Sprigge
> [New York's Doubleday Anchor, 1955])

A Dream Play had been set against the backdrop of the new Europe. The colors in the performance were gray — no flowering Garden of Eden or towering castle here. Instead there was a recurring and endless spectacle appearing on the round horizon. In this stylized scenery the projected shadows allowed for the suggestion of dream images in surrealistic sequen-ces. The scene changes occurred according to Strindberg's recommenda-tions: in front of an open curtain but in a light that cast grotesque shadows on the screens, accompanied by a flickering shadow-play of bars and lattice, which glided along the stage.

The grating was actually an element that was taken from an unassum-ing remark in Strindberg's stage directions, and yet it came to dominate the scenery of the whole production: the imagistic associations alluded to jails and escape. In the final scene liberation came into view as a cipher, as difficult to interpret as in Strindberg's text, but different from it. During the last monologue a light fell as if from a church window upon Indra's Daugh-ter. But she left the stage through a door toward a red dawn far behind the backdrop. There was a touch of humanity about her walk to the execution at sunrise. She left a prison, but she never entered Strindberg's flowering castle.

There is much to discuss in the personalized interpretation of Strindberg as seen in the Berlin production, and much to object to. But it was consistent, created by a director who read and listened not only to Strindberg but also to the Europe that would be able to follow, recognize, and be astonished and affected by *A Dream Play*. Something was lost in Oscar Fritz Schuh's interpretation, something of the poetry, the softness, the devout searching. But this interpretation compensated for that loss in its single-mindedness, anxiety, and impassioned immediacy.

The Berlin stage set made *A Dream Play* refer to a particular political and cultural situation. The set was the instrument that directed the audience's attention away from the generalities in the play, away from the author's private realm toward a certain real situation: after a devastating war, during an even more uncertain peace, in a city threatened with encirclement, isolation, blockades, and barriers. The relatively clear text of the Berlin production limited the use of the drama. Many possible associations were cut off, but others became clear and effective.

Among 200 stagings of *A Dream Play*, I have chosen to talk about these two in particular, because they succeed quite well in carrying on the staging traditions derived from the two schools of theater — expressionism and naturalism — which historically framed Strindberg's own creative work. Olof Molander's interpretation, following the path marked by Strindberg himself, produced stagings that have used the best of the naturalistic theater, such as it was interpreted by Antoine, Otto Brahms, and Stanislavsky. Oscar Fritz Schuh showed how a powerful expressionistic staging that keeps the audience and its history in mind can look when it is at its best. Between these two opposites — one author-centered and the other focused on the spectator and on the expression of the historical present — the theatrical history of *A Dream Play* is enacted. This history has evolved as a result of the extraordinary situation out of which the style of the play first arose — the historical conditions that gave rise to *A Dream Play*. Thus the work continues to be a provocation to actors and directors today.

19

Staging A Dream Play

Egil Törnqvist

The recent interest in theater semiotics has increasingly drawn attention to the communicative problem inherent in the difference between the drama text and the performance "text" (Elam, 214; Fischer-Lichte, 3:34-36). The fundamental question to be posed is this: in what way are the verbal (linguistic) signs of the drama text transposed into visual and/or acoustic signs in the performance text? A number of subsidiary questions can be derived from this basic one: To what extent and in what way are the signs of the two texts just referred to polyinterpretable, explicit/implicit? To what extent and in what way is the recipient (reader, spectator) able to decode the signals encoded by the playwright alone (drama text) or by him or her in conjunction with a production team (performance)? Do the signals refer to recognizable outer circumstances, do they allegorize an existential situation, or do they mirror a subjective, inner reality?

I will discuss questions of this kind with regard to various productions of Strindberg's *A Dream Play*, written in 1901, published a year later.[1] Besides the *obligatory* transpositions, determined by the change of medium, a number of *voluntary* ones will be dealt with: exclusion, amplification, rearrangement of elements appearing in (the stage directions of) the drama text. The scenes will be treated in the order in which they appear in the play.

Staging A Dream Play

Because *A Dream Play* loosely imitates a dream to evoke a feeling that life is a dream, it is important that this aspect is conveyed in production. A constant problem in this respect are the shifts from one scene to another. When the play was first produced, several critics regarded it as a closet drama. Thus one of them, Daniel Fallström, pointed out that the ghostlike, immaterial life of the dream does not suit the theater. Dramatic art means action and human beings of flesh and blood, not stalking dreamlike images (Bark, 84).

The critic might in fact have quoted Strindberg himself, who once remarked: "I don't want to see *The Tempest* performed, I want to read it and make my own scenery of mere air and lighting" (*SS* 50:201).[2] Not surprisingly, he was also extremely displeased with the first production of *A Dream Play*: "The whole performance was a 'phenomenon of materialization' instead of its intended opposite (dematerialization)." The "endless entre-acts" were a major reason for this (*SS* 50:289). In the drama text Strindberg indicates the fluid, dreamy nature of the play in his stage directions. Thus, at the end of scene 1, the backdrop "*slowly opens to the sides*"; at the end of scene 2, a screen is drawn aside; at the end of scene 3 "*the backdrop is drawn up*"; at the end of scene 4 "*the scene changes into the* LAWYER'S *office without lowering the curtain*"; at the end of scene 5 "*the stage becomes dark,*" a number of properties are changed, "*the backdrop is raised,*" and a new one becomes visible, and so on.

The scene shifts have always proved a problem to directors and have undoubtedly contributed to the view that *A Dream Play* is more cinematic than theatrical. Technical development within the theater has hardly made this any easier: scene shifts can be brought about more quickly with painted backdrops than with three-dimensional properties. On the other hand, as Strindberg himself remarked, what is painted "cannot represent unfixed, floating illusions" (*SS* 50:289). One way of solving the problem of scene changes is of course to use a permanent setting and a minimum of properties. This is what Strindberg himself suggested when planning a simplified production at the Intimate Theater. However, this necessarily means that the dream aspect is not visually accentuated by the scenery. Characteristically, it took an outstanding film director to overcome the problem regarding scene shifts. Settling for an extremely simple permanent setting with a minimum of properties, Bergman could bring about very swift and smooth scene changes.

Another dream aspect concerns the use of color and sound. While we are accustomed to regarding dreams as being devoid of these qualities, Strindberg calls for both in his stage directions (cf. his plea for color effects in *SS* 50:289). And yet in the theater an attempt has occasionally been made to use color and sound as dream characteristics. Thus Reinhardt, in his 1921

Stockholm production, which was otherwise marked by a rich and varied use of sound effects, had the characters move silently across the stage on felt-soled shoes to provide a dream effect (Kvam, 110). Again, Reinhardt was the first to attempt the idea of a black-and-white dream on the stage (Kvam, 124). This was later repeated by Molander in 1935 (Bark, 120) and, more consistently, by Bergman in 1970.

Despite the fact that the Prologue, witnessing the Daughter's descent from Heaven to Earth, does not belong to Strindberg's original conception — it was written some five years after the play (*SS* 36:364) — it has usually been included in the stage productions: apparently directors have found it essential to stress the metaphysical dimension from the very beginning. As Quigley (118) puts it: "It is in order to remind us that the play's action is occurring in an 'earthbound' . . . domain that the play begins just outside that domain." Inclusion of the Prologue also means that the play is given a logical and satisfactory circle composition or frame: when it opens we witness the Daughter leaving her celestial domicile to begin her earthly pilgrimage; the play closes with her return to her heavenly origins.

However, from another point of view, the Prologue creates problems because, unlike the rest of the scenes, it does not take the form of a dream — provided we suspend our disbelief in visualized divinities, as we willingly do in the theater. While the rest of the scenes contain a number of elements indicating that life is, or resembles, a *dream*, the Prologue is strikingly "normal," suggesting rather that we are partaking of another and truer *reality*.[3]

Inclusion of the Prologue would indicate that the Daughter is the dreamer in the (rest of the) play, which dramatizes life on earth. From her divine point of view she can hardly regard earthly existence as anything but a fragment — incomplete and therefore unreal.

Exclusion of the Prologue would rather indicate that the spectator is the dreamer. Once the Prologue is omitted, the drama is limited to an existence well known to us all, and the Daughter functions merely as a mediator between stage and auditorium, as a mentor to the audience.

At the play's world premiere in Stockholm in 1907, the director, Victor Castegren, had not made a clear choice between these two possibilities. On the one hand, the Prologue was included, on the other, a permanent entourage around the stage suggested that the spectator is the dreamer of the play. The front stage "was transformed into ground filled with red poppies, the symbol of sleep: above the stage behind this, a frame decorated with poppy-creepers was stretched out as an area for the dream images to appear and disappear."[4]

The same vagueness characterized the first German production of the play in 1916 directed by Rudolf Bernauer. Here again the Prologue was included, and the entire drama was acted out behind a gauze, turning the spectator into the dreamer of the play. By not using a decor of this kind, Max Reinhardt and Olof Molander indicated that in their productions the Daughter could be seen as the dreamer.[5] In a letter Molander significantly points out that it is the Daughter "who dreams, i.e. experiences the dream of human life."[6] However, in his last production of the play, at the Norrköping-Linköping City Theater in 1963, Molander did not stress this aspect but chose to exclude the Prologue.

Exclude or include? A third alternative was chosen by Ingmar Bergman in his 1970 Stockholm production.[7] The Prologue was partly included, but it did not open the play. Instead it was placed at the beginning of scene 4, "The Theater," in Bergman's "interpretation." In other words, the Prologue was turned into an interlude. Moreover, in this version Indra and his daughter were not alone. When they appeared at the back of the stage, they were observed by the Poet and by Agnes — Bergman's earthly equivalent to the divine Daughter — who were sitting at the front of the stage at the Poet's table (fig. 26). In this way Bergman was able to indicate — as he did throughout his production — that the Poet (rather than the Daughter) was the dreamer of the play and that whatever appeared on the stage was a product of his imagination.

Strindberg's stage directions for the Prologue read: "*Cloud formations resembling castles and citadels in ruins on crumbling slate hills form the backdrop. The constellations Leo, Virgo, and Libra can be seen, and among them is the planet Jupiter shining brightly.*"[8]

The airy castles indicated in this description obviously serve as a contrast to the castle stable where the Daughter is soon to be "imprisoned"; it is worth noting that the idea of a celestial castle is reintroduced at the end of the play when the Daughter is ready to take her leave from life on earth.

In the vertical Heaven-Earth dichotomy the intermediate clouds seem to be a visual expression of the fact that the Daughter has now reached "the dusty atmosphere of Earth." Viewed in this way, it seems quite logical that the ruined castles and citadels represent the ruined hopes of humankind, perhaps even the demolition of Christian faith in a paradisiac hereafter.

But why does Strindberg mention the three constellations and the planet Jupiter? Obviously because he is dealing with symbols of man, woman, justice — Libra being Latin for scales — and God, central points in the thematic pattern of the play (Delblanc, 76).

The question is now: how much of this can be transformed into theatrical signs? In Carl Grabow's sketch for the 1907 Prologue (*Dröms-pelet*, 1970-71, 16; fig. 27) the contrast between light (emanating from Jupiter) and dark is accentuated. It is as though the dark clouds below warn of the Daughter's fate on earth. To the spectator, unfamiliar with the drama text, it

Figure 26. The Poet and Agnes in the foreground, Indra and the Daughter in the background (Ingmar Bergman, 1970).

would be difficult to assess whether it is a cloud- or a rock-scape; in the distance a couple of cloud-citadels can be divined. The scenographer has visualized Strindberg's simile very expressively. It is interesting to note that what is a clear distinction to the reader — we are concerned with clouds resembling rocks, not the other way around — becomes a puzzle-picture for the spectator, where primarily the figure and movement of the Daughter (absent from Grabow's sketch) cause the cloud aspect to prevail. Strewn across the sky are many stars, all the same size, but there are no constellations.

In Strindberg's text the Prologue takes the form of a dialogue between the invisible god Indra and his visible Daughter, who first appears "*standing on the uppermost cloud,*" whereas at the end, when the cloud descends, she falls to her knees. In the given context, made clear by the dialogue, her kneeling is an appeal, and her final words — "I'm sinking!" — have an ethical quality.

We do not know how the descent of the Daughter was re-created in the 1907 production. If she turned her back to the audience throughout the Prologue, as she does on Gunnar Widholm's drawing relating to this pro-

Figure 27. "The Prologue," Grabow's sketch for the 1907 Castegren production.

duction (*Drömspelet*, 1970-71, 24), then the spectators significantly did not see her face until she was incarnated as a human being.

In Bernauer's 1916 Berlin production, the fairy tale aspect was emphasized in the Prologue. The Daughter, in a golden dress and surrounded by an aureole, descended to Earth, framed by a black, starlit sky.[9]

The Daughter's outstretched arms, found on Widholm's drawing, appear again on Alfred Roller's sketch for the 1921 Reinhardt production (Kvam, 121; fig. 28) but this time the Daughter turns her face toward the audience. Grabow's heavy thunder clouds have become even heavier, but the suggestive vagueness is lost: what we see are simply clouds, nothing else. Behind them the black sky is burning with stars of varying magnitude. The celestial light does not emanate from a god-planet (Jupiter) or from some hidden celestial source (as with Grabow) but from the Daughter herself, whose divine nature is hereby visualized. We seem to have come closer to dark, sinful Earth and farther away from the heavenly light in this black-on-black version.

Whereas Roller one-sidedly stressed the cloudscape, Isaac Grünewald, responsible for the projections in the 1935 Molander production, emphasized the rock aspect (Bark, 121; fig. 29). Painted on a second curtain was what must have looked like a snow-covered mountainous landscape to the audience, whose glance would be led via a meandering black "road" toward a couple of high rocks resembling castles. The landscape makes a

Figures 28 and 29. *"The Prologue": sketch by Alfred Roller for the 1921 Reinhardt production (above), Isaac Grünewald's depiction projected in the 1935 Molander production (below).*

desolate, fateful impression, and the kinship with the dreamy landscapes of the surrealists is evident.

A surprising device in this version of the Prologue was the visual absence of the Daughter. Only her voice could be heard. The dialogue between father and daughter was accompanied by various sound effects indicated in the drama text: shouts of joy, shots, bells, and voices singing praise. It is possible that Molander chose to abstain from visualizing the Daughter because he was aware that her descent in the Prologue can appear to be a rather trite theatrical marvel — a technical spectacle — rather than a significant event in the parabolic play context. In any case, this alternative signifies a dematerialization of the Daughter completely in line with the theme of the play: as a celestial creature she is merely air, merely voice, related to the winds she describes at the end of the play.

As I have already indicated, Ingmar Bergman's handling of Strindberg's *Prolog im Himmel* in his 1970 production was very different from those of his predecessors. He used the Prologue as an interlude and reduced its length by half. At the back of the stage, on a small platform, the Scald (rather than Indra) and Indra's Daughter appeared, while the Poet and Agnes remained in the foreground as mediators between the audience and the characters elevated at the back of the stage (Bark, 156). Bergman had clearly settled for a highly ironical version, full of *double-entendres.* Instead of a heavenly reality, the audience was confronted with the world of theatrical illusion, indicated by the fact that the Scald and Indra's Daughter entered a stage where they gave a theatrical performance for which they were applauded. Strindberg's independent divinities were transformed into products of the human brain, theatrical inventions, poetic fantasies.

The first scene of the play proper is set outside a castle. The stage directions read: *"The backdrop presents a mass of gigantic white, pink, scarlet, sulphur yellow, and white hollyhocks in bloom; over their tops can be seen the gilded roof of a castle with a flower bud resembling a crown uppermost. Along the bottom of the castle walls, heaps of straw covering cleaned-out stable litter. The side wings which remain throughout the play are stylized wall paintings, at the same time rooms, architecture, and landscapes."*

The audience is invited to an earthly paradise, where the castle (life) is seen as something organic. Note how Strindberg explicitly stresses the aspect of growth in his stage directions: it is not a crown resembling a flower bud; it is a flower bud resembling a crown.

It is clearly not easy for a scenographer to communicate visually both the crown and the flower aspect. In Dworsky's sketch for Reinhardt's 1921 Berlin production (Kvam, 135) a crown on top of a round, vaulted roof is a rather contrived attempt to combine the two aspects, whereas in Grünewald's very different solution for the 1935 production (Bark, 122), the spectator may find it difficult to recognize the crown. By shaping the wing of the castle as a leaf — an idea derived from the Glazier's line "and if you'll look, you'll see a wing has shot out on the sunny side" — Grünewald visually confirms that it is indeed a growing castle, unless the spectator prefers to see the flower bud on its column as a phallic symbol, a view in line with Sprinchorn's interpretation (174-75) of this scenic element.[10]

For scene 2, set in the Officer's room in the castle, Strindberg prescribes: "*The setting is now a plain, bare room with a table and some chairs.*" Skawonius, responsible for the three-dimensional settings of Molander's 1935 production (Bark, 124), adds a barred window, clearly inspired by the Daughter's line "You're a prisoner in your rooms."

For scene 3, which takes place in the Mother's room, Strindberg calls for "*a brown wardrobe-cupboard,*" which has a traumatic significance for the Officer. In Skawonius's version (Bark, 124), this cupboard was identical to the door "*with an air hole in the shape of a four-leaf clover*" appearing in the subsequent scenes. As a result the spectator would be inclined to regard the Officer's later concern with the clover-leaf door as psychologically rather than metaphysically determined.

Scene 4, set in the theater corridor, forms the nucleus of the drama. The stage directions for this scene read:

> *The backdrop is drawn up; a new one can now be seen, representing an old shabby fire wall. In the middle of the wall is a gate opening on a path which ends in a bright green plot in which is a gigantic blue monkshood (aconite). . . . To the right is a bulletin board. . . . Still farther to the right is a door with an air hole in the shape of a four-leaf clover. To the left of the gate is a slim linden with a coal-black trunk and a few pale green leaves; next to it a cellar opening.*

There are distinct contrasts in this scenery. In front there is an ugly, dark interior, in the distance an attractive, bright exterior. Vertically, there is also a noteworthy contrast between the green leaves of the linden and blue of the monkshood above and the black of the trunk and the cellar opening below. The Officer's remark that doors containing an air hole in the form of a four-leaf clover are to be found in entrances suggests that the corridor is a kind of entrance or waiting room. And indeed it is. Waiting here are all those who have not, in Bennich-Björkman's words (65), "received any chief parts on the stage representing the world." In line with this interpretation Bennich-Björkman sees the opening of the door as an expression of the revolt of those who suffer social discrimination; thus it is natural that the police should arrive to prevent the opening of the door. In this interpretation the attractive area, namely the stage, is found to the right offstage.

This indeed seems to be the case as far as the characters of the play are concerned. Yet to the audience the attractive part is to be found elsewhere: at the back of the stage, behind the shabby fire wall, in the sunny and airy exterior. It is as though Strindberg has combined the attractive exterior of scene 1 with the claustrophobic interior of scene 2 to suggest that being outside the castle-theater is much more desirable than being inside it. As a result of this, a highly ironical situation is created: unlike the characters who are concerned merely with worldly success, the spectator is aware of other, nobler values.

Actually the scenery carries very obvious metaphysical connotations. Thus the black cellar hole suggests hell, the fire wall purgatory, the gate the entrance to heaven, and the bright spot in the distance with its green (for hope) and blue (for heaven) connotes paradise. In this sense scene 4 anticipates scene 9, where Foulstrand (purgatory or hell) is seen in front, and Fairhaven (paradise) at the back. The Doorkeeper, aware of the fundamental difference between those who are engaged (the sheep) and those who are not (the goats), may similarly be seen as a kind of St. Peter guarding the gate of Heaven.

A realistic scenery, as found in Grabow's sketch for the 1907 production (*Drömspelet*, 1970/71, 16; fig. 30), fails to bring out these "allegorical" connotations. Instead of Strindberg's highly stylized linden, which conveys the idea, put forward in scene 1, that flowers grow out of the dirt into the light, Grabow settles for a completely recognizable, unexpressive tree. However, he does provide the door with the ambiguous air hole, thereby retaining Strindberg's idea that the hole has both the form of a four-leaf clover and of a cross.

This ambiguity is obscured in Roller's solution (*Drömspelet*, 1970-71, 36), in which the cross aspect is not very evident. Although Roller's scenery is certainly stylized, it differs somewhat from what is suggested in the stage directions. Thus his fire wall is massive, imprisoning rather than *"old"* and *"shabby,"* and his linden is extremely compact and rich in foliage, rather than *"slim"* with *"a few pale green leaves"*. A special problem is created by the bulletin board. Strindberg's word is *affischtavla*, and it seems evident that he included this property primarily to indicate that we are in a theater. The billboard, in other words, is used for posters advertising the repertoire. This idea is retained by Grabow, but Roller rather senselessly turns it into a notice board, possibly misled by an erroneous translation.

The compact — rather than slender — linden is again seen in Dworsky's sketch (Kvam, 136; fig. 31), which visualizes an enormous announcement board. (The air hole has a very definite clover-leaf form, which does not suggest a cross.) Dworsky's solution does not indicate that we are in a theater corridor; the many windows in the wall rather suggest that we are again outside the growing castle.

Figure 30. *"The Theater Corridor," sketch by Grabow for the 1907 Castegren production.*

In this respect Skawonius's solution (Bark, 124; fig. 32), is very different. Here the nature of the locality is made completely clear through a sign saying *Till scenen* (To the Stage) and through one of the bulletin boards mentioning the words *Theater* and *Opera*. Unlike their predecessors, Molander and Skawonius chose a recognizable local environment. Inspired by Martin Lamm's investigations into the biographical background of the plays, Molander chose to locate *A Dream Play* not only in Sweden but in Stockholm. To the 1935 audience at Dramaten it must have been evident that the growing castle resembled the horse guards' barracks at the outskirts of the Capital — the most beautiful building in Stockholm, according to Strindberg — and that the theater corridor looked out on Kungsträdgården, Molin's fountain, and the spire of Jacob's church, that is, that the staged theater corridor in fact corresponded to one in the old Stockholm opera house. Once these connections had been established, other elements of the play could assume a recognizable nature. Thus the Billposter with his dip net *"with a green handle"* might be associated with the (green) fishing boats by Nybron next to the Opera. In short, by locating the play in and around Stockholm, Molander and Skawonius stressed the autobiographical nature of the play as well as indicated the realistic basis of Strindberg's collage of visual fragments. This does not mean that their settings were altogether realistic. Although this was true of each detail, the combination of

Figures 31 and 32. *"The Theater Corridor": Dworsky's sketch for the 1921 Reinhardt production (above), Skawonius's set for the 1935 Molander production (below).*

them was surprising — unreal, dreamlike (cf. Bjurström, 123). The technique was, in fact, similar to and possibly inspired by that used by surrealist painters. This is also true of the special dream effect created by the theater corridor being made to seem part of both an exterior and an interior setting.

More interesting than scene 5, the Lawyer's office, is scene 6, which visualizes the church where the Lawyer is to receive his Doctor of Laws degree: "*The railing remains and now serves as the balustrade for the sanctuary in a church; the billboard becomes a bulletin board listing psalms; the linden-clothes hanger becomes a candelabra; the* LAWYER's *desk the* CHANCELLOR's *lectern; the door with the four-leaf opening now leads into the sacristy. . . . The backdrop is raised. The new one represents a single large organ with keyboard below and a mirror above. Music is heard.*"

In Svend Gade's sketch for the 1916 production (Kvam, 107), the properties called for by Strindberg are complemented by a crucifix in a central position below the huge organ pipes. A more definite Christian element was thus introduced. The other most striking characteristic was the oval-shaped extra proscenium surrounding the stage picture here as elsewhere in the play. In front of this "peep-hole," a dark-blue veil with stars was hung. When lit from the outside, the veil was no longer transparent and thus made scene shifts possible. According to one interpretation (Bark, 99-100), this arrangement accentuated the fact that the audience looked into a dream world. But since the oval shape might also be associated with the opening of a shell (Kvam, 105), in the play likened to Indra's ear, it may just as well be argued that the audience's looking into this world was equivalent to Indra's listening to it, and that the spectator, being an outsider, became a kind of "divine" instance.

The ambiguity about whether the setting is exterior or interior, earlier mentioned with regard to Molander's and Skawonius's theater corridor, also characterizes Dworsky's sketch for the Church scene (Kvam, 137). In it the locale can be seen as an interior, in which case it has a rather small organ, or as an exterior, in which case the view through the church door reveals merely a fragment of the organ. The air hole retains its misplaced, realistic clover-leaf form. This solution obscures Strindberg's suggestion that faith in worldly success (the four-leaf clover) must be replaced by faith in the meaning of suffering (the cross).

The most cinematic transformation takes place between scenes 6 and 7: "*Through a change in lighting the organ becomes Fingal's Cave. The sea dashes in swells under the basalt pillars and produces a harmonious sound of waves and wind.*"

The connection between the two scenes is strongly indicated in Dworsky's sketch (Kvam, 138), in which the pipes of the organ become stalactites in the cave. More abstract were Grünewald's projection for the 1935 production (Bark, 127) and Rolf Stegar's decor for a performance in

Helsinki in 1959 (Holm, 256); in these cases the audience was free to view the abstract visual elements as part of a cave, a shell, a gigantic ear, so that the symbolic significance of the grotto was emphasized.

The Lawyer's home, scene 8, shows: *"a very simple room next to the* LAWYER's *office. To the right a large double bed with a canopy; next to it a window. To the left a sheet-iron stove with cooking utensils on it.* KRISTIN *is pasting strips along the inner windows. At the back an open door to the office; poor people waiting to be heard can be seen out there."*

Judging by the reviews, this scene was quite effective in Max Reinhardt's pioneering Stockholm production. In it Roller excelled in harsh black-and-white contrasts (Kvam, 109). The expressionist stage picture showed, in Reinhardt's own words, "eine dunkle Gruppe von wartenden Menschen . . . dunkel (schwarz) gekleidet. Weisse, starre, schattenhafte Gesichter, dicht neben einander, verzerrt, böse, beängstigend, leidend, die Augen nach vorn ins Zimmer gerichtet" (a dark group of waiting people . . . dressed in dark [black]. White, stiff, shadowlike faces, close to one another, distorted, evil, anxious, suffering, with eyes staring in front of them into the room) (Kvam, 111). One critic rightly spoke of a mood à la Munch.

A similar black-and-white effect, the faces of the clients appearing as white spots against the surrounding darkness, was found in Skawonius's somewhat more realistic version of this scene (Bjurström, 122). It was characteristic of this setting that certain properties (easy chair, small table with candle on it) were identical to those appearing in scene 3; this correspondence underlined the fact that the Daughter was now in a situation similar to that of the Mother in the earlier scene.

Scene 9, Foulstrand, appears after a:

> *Change on stage: the bed with its canopy becomes a tent; the stove remains; the backdrop is raised; to the right in the foreground one sees burned-over mountains with red heather and black and white stumps after a forest fire; red pigpens and outhouses. Below, an open gymnasium in which people are exercised on machines resembling instruments of torture. To the left in the foreground, part of the quarantine building's shed with hearths, furnace walls, and plumbing pipes. The middle area is a sound. The back of the stage is a beautiful shore with trees in foliage, piers (decorated with flags) to which white boats are tied; some of them have their sails hoisted, some not. Small Italian villas, pavilions, kiosks, marble statues can be seen among the foliage.*

Foulstrand or, literally, Shamestrand is clearly a place where the sinful are punished. This important aspect is hardly brought out in Grabow's sketch (*Drömspelet*, 1970-71, 17); nor is the contrast between Foulstrand and Fairhaven accentuated. Whereas this scenographer set the scene in day light, Roller (*Drömspelet*, 1970-71, 36) preferred to set it in pitch-darkness.

269

The suggestion of nature — of Swedish archipelago — in Strindberg's stage directions, retained in Grabow's sketch, was completely absent in the German version. It showed a terrace overlooking a sound with city lights in the background. There was a constructivist touch in the monstrous machines of exercise, which advertised their infernal significance.

The antithesis between Foulstrand and Fairhaven was more clearly worked out in Molander's 1935 production (Bark, 129) where Fairhaven significantly figured as a bright projection above, contrasting with three-dimensional, dark Foulstrand, below. The vertical arrangement was reminiscent of the one found in medieval mystery plays with their sharp Heaven-Hell dichotomy. However, it may be doubted whether Grünewald's cluttered, naivistic version of Fairhaven effectively suggested paradise.

For scene 10, Fairhaven, Strindberg gives rather detailed stage directions:

> When the light comes on again, the shore of Foulstrand can be seen in the shadow at the back. The sound lies in the middle area and Fairhaven in the foreground, both fully lighted up. To the right, a corner of the clubhouse with its windows open; couples can be seen dancing inside. . . . To the left a yellow wooden house. . . . In the foreground a dock with white boats and flagpoles with flags waving. Out on the sound a warship rigged with cannon openings is anchored. But the whole landscape is in its winter dress with snow on leafless trees and on the ground.

The playwright further calls for a porch with a bench, a box, and a piano. In the 1935 production (Bark, 129), Foulstrand was projected as a sterile winter landscape above — the scenographer seems to have been inspired by the words about *"stumps black and white after a forest fire"* in scene 9 — while Fairhaven, now three-dimensional, was seen below.

The suggestions of Stockholm archipelago were lacking in the 1947 Malmö production for which Martin Ahlbom constructed a setting spread out horizontally to meet the demands of the huge stage (Bjurström, 153). In Ahlbom's sketch Foulstrand is merely indicated in the background by a dark, wavelike strip, and the clubhouse is reduced to a free-standing wall. Time and place — nineteenth-century Sweden — are indicated by a huge Oscarian bust, two emblematic Swedish union flags above the door (revealing that the action is prior to 1905 when the union between Sweden and Norway was dissolved), and a sailing ship in the distance. There is a suggestive combination of exteriors and interiors; thus the stairs left with railing and hanging lamp seem to be part of an interior setting, whereas the stairs at right with pruned trees next to them — corresponding to the pruned birches left and right — are clearly part of the exterior. Everything seems covered by ice and snow and wrapped in a wintry haze. The domi-

Figure 33. *"Fairhaven," Mörk's set for the 1970 Bergman production.*

nant impression is one of chastised nature, sterility, winter sleep. It is obvious that Ahlbom's extremely atmospheric multiple setting comes very close to the surrealist paintings of the Swedish Halmstad group, which were in vogue around this time. Utterly simple, by comparison, was Lennart Mörk's design for Bergman's 1970 production (Bark, 158; fig. 33). Here the transference from Foulstrand to Fairhaven was simply established by means of a change from a black to a totally white setting. The spatial antitheses within each scene were left out, as were, on the whole, the properties called for by Strindberg. Thus Fairhaven was simply indicated by a white backdrop, a large table at center covered by a white spread, a huge spotlight on the backdrop suggesting a bright sun, and a lot of people, all of them — except the Poet, the dreamer — dressed in white.

In Strindberg's text the Fairhaven scene embraces the short and nightmarish School scene, usually very effective on the stage but scenographically of little interest. Much more interesting from this point of view is scene 12, usually referred to as the Coalheavers' scene. This scene is some times omitted in stage productions, presumably because it does not seem wholly integrated in the play. On the one hand, it is the only scene set outside a recognizable Swedish environment, while on the other, it is the only one that explicitly focuses on a social rather than a metaphysical problem. Actually, it has a valid ideological place in the unfolding of the action (Törnqvist, 150-51). The stage directions read: *"A shore on the Mediter-*

Figures 34 and 35. *"The Coalheavers' Scene": sketch by Grabow for the 1907 Castegren production (above), sketch by Roller for the 1921 Reinhardt production (below).*

ranean. To the left in the foreground can be seen a white wall, over which branches of fruit-bearing orange trees are hanging. At the back, villas and a casino with a terrace. To the right, a large pile of coal with two wheel-barrows. At the back to the right, a strip of the blue sea."

Paradise (Fairhaven) and Hell (Foulstrand) are now placed side by side. White versus black, rich versus poor, the unpunished (rather than the innocent) versus the punished (rather than the guilty).

In Grabow's sketch (*Drömspelet*, 1970-71, 17; fig. 34), the black-and-white contrast is certainly brought out, but the wall is not completely white, possibly because the scenographer wanted to suggest a visual link between the wall in this scene and the fire wall in scene 4. The trees towering above the wall (not called for by Strindberg) seem to be included merely to indicate the locality.

In Roller's scenography for this scene (*Drömspelet*, 1970-71, 37; fig. 35), the black-and-white antithesis was almost completely neglected; the coal heap was hidden in a shed. There was a vertical contrast between the high, massive, white wall and the casino towering above it at left and the low, rickety, wooden shed at right, suggesting the uneven power distribution in a class society. The height of the wall combined with the fruit bearing branches hanging over it effectively suggested the pains of Tantalus suffered by the coalheavers. An interesting device was the arrangement of the foliage, which was extended from the terrace above and across the upper part of the proscenium opening, indicating perhaps that the luxurious terrace continued into the auditorium — that the audience was part of the capitalist group under attack.

In Bergman's production, the scene was drastically — and successfully — integrated in the Fairhaven scene, that is, transposed from Italy to Everywhere. As the blackened coalheavers entered, the movements of the white-dressed vacation celebrators at Fairhaven — tennis players, dancing couples — were frozen. In this imaginative manner Bergman could retain, in simple fashion, Strindberg's black-and-white pattern.

For scene 13, Fingal's Cave II, the following stage directions are given: *"Fingal's Cave. Long, green waves roll slowly into the cave; in the foreground a red sounding buoy rocks on the waves. The buoy sounds only at indicated places. The music of the winds. The music of the waves."*

From these directions it appears that the acoustic element tends to overrule the visual one in this scene. After all, the audience finds itself in Indra's ear, a circumstance of which they are hardly made aware in Grabow's realistic version of the cave (*Drömspelet*, 1970-1971, 18). In his sketch for the backdrop, Grabow paints a calm sea — one that would hardly be able to produce any *"music of the waves."* Very different is Svend Gade's approach (Kvam, 105; fig. 36). Here the Daughter and the Poet are found in what looks much more like a giant shell of an ear than a cave — although the breaking waves and the wrecked boat help to indicate the realistic aspect. At a distance Christ, surrounded by an aureole, can be seen walking across the water, appearing, as it were, inside God's ear.

In Molander's 1935 production a number of dark stripes, resembling both organ pipes and stalactites were projected onto the backdrop (Bark, 131), while Rolf Stegar for the 1959 Helsinki production devised huge, abstract set pieces and projected light onto them (Holm, 256; fig. 37). In this last case the spectators were free to interpret the visual abstractions as they wished, although the dialogue would certainly guide them in definite directions.

The differences among Grabow's realistic, Gade's symbolic, and Stegar's abstract solution are of principle interest. Whereas Grabow confirms one aspect of what is communicated verbally (the cave aspect), Gade confirms another (the shell aspect), and Stegar keeps everything open and invites the spectator to interpret.

In Bergman's reductive version no cave at all was to be seen (Bark, 159). The lines were divided between the Poet, sitting at his table, Indra's Daughter, and the Scald; Agnes, next to the Poet, representing humankind, remained silent.

Scene 14 is again in the theater corridor. And the final scene (15) is again outside the castle: "*The same scenery as in the first tableau in the first act. But the ground at the base of the castle is now covered with flowers (blue monkshood, Aconite). At the very peak on the tower of the castle roof is a chrysanthemum bud ready to burst. The castle windows are illuminated with candlelight.*"

Toward the end of the scene, the Daughter prepares herself for a rebirth through fire, a return to heaven: "*She takes off her shoes and puts them into the fire.*" From which we must conclude that there is a fire, although Strindberg does not mention it in his stage directions. This is followed by the *défilé*: a number of characters enter and sacrifice what is dear to them to the fire — a desire, a need, sometimes concretized in the form of an object, sometimes not.

The *défilé* has both an objective, parabolic aspect and a subjective, psychological aspect. On the one hand, it indicates that humankind has learned from the Daughter the transient nature of all earthly matters; on the other hand, it infers that the Daughter's end is near. The Poet says, "everything and everyone rushes by in a single procession."

The play ends in a spectacular way. The Daughter "*goes into the castle. Music is heard. The backdrop is lighted by the burning castle and shows a wall of human faces, asking, sorrowing, despairing. . . . When the castle burns, the flower bud on the roof bursts into a gigantic highly symmetrical chrysanthemum.*"

In Gade's art nouveau sketch (Kvam, 106; fig 38), the burning castle is

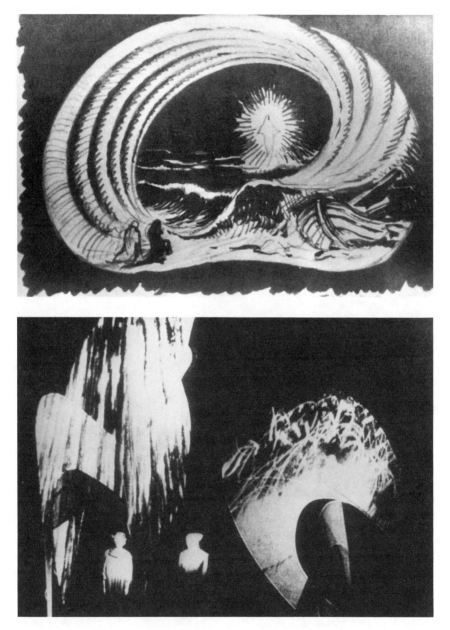

Figure 36 and 37. *"Fingal's Cave": sketch by Gade for the 1916 Bernauer production (above), Stegar's set for the 1959 Helsinki production (below).*

Figures 38 and 39. Final scene "Outside the Castle": sketch by Gade for the 1916 Bernauer production (above), projection in Molander's 1935 production (below).

also a growing castle, the flames corresponding to the leaves of the giant chrysanthemum bursting into bloom. In this way the central idea of the play that destruction is inevitably linked to rebirth, that losing one's life means gaining it, is visually expressed. For the sacrificial scene or *défilé* Gade provides an altar in classical style.

Roller's solution (*Drömspelet*, 1970-71, 37; sketch in Kvam, 122), was to use an overgrown castle rather than a growing one, surrounded by ghostly light against a background of darkness. Instead of an altar, there was a heap of logs in the foreground gathered for the sacrificial fire. Instead of entering the castle, the Daughter mounted the funeral pyre to the tune of a gay Swedish melody and then sank through the floor — "like Mephistopheles at the Opera" (Ollén, 1982, 455).

In Molander's 1935 production (Bark, 132; fig. 39), the castle was projected on the backdrop. In front of it, center, was a simple altar with two tall, white candles, conveying Christian rather than classical or primitive connotations. When the *défilé* was over and the Poet and the Daughter were left alone on stage, the music of "I call Thee Jesus" was heard. Toward the end of the Daughter's monologue, the horizon turned red: the castle was afire. On her last word, "farewell," the projection of the castle disappeared and the horizon turned blue. A cross was raised on the altar with the inscription *Ave crux spes unica*, a text wasted on those spectators who were not familiar with Latin, Catholic churchyards, and/or Strindberg's own grave. On the backdrop a collage consisting of anxious human faces of different sizes was projected (Bark, 133), while the Poet remained alone on stage as the spokesman for humankind.

The heap of logs returns in Ahlbom's sketch for the 1947 Malmö production (*August Strindberg 1912-1962*, 56), where the lighted windows of the castle can be seen in the distance. The dreamy haze that generally characterizes Ahlbom's sketches is found here too. The cross and the collage of faces used in the Stockholm production were also used in this production.

In the 1947 Gothenburg performance (Holm, 233) Molander and Ström again copied the horse guards' barracks in Stockholm when designing their growing castle, a compact, somber building with black (rather than illuminated) windows, surrounded by blackness, a scenographic solution not very different from Roller's conception. At the end (*August Strindberg 1912-1962*, 71; fig. 40), the Poet was again shown alone on stage below a huge black cross towering over the black ruins of houses, reminiscent of those found in European cities bombed during World War II. The accent was clearly on the suffering of (postwar) humanity rather than on the growth into another reality. The somberness of this stage picture combined with the aspect of growing characterized Max Bigneus's scenography for the 1957 Basel production (Holm, 238; fig. 41). Bigneus, apparently inspired by the

Figures 40. Final scene "Outside the Castle," set by Ström for the 1947 Molander production (above), set by Bigneus for the 1957 Basel production (below).

Figure 42. *Final scene "Outside the Castle," set by Mörk for the 1970 Bergman production.*

line about the flowers, which do not thrive in the dirt but rush up toward the light to bloom and die, designed a highly surrealistic stage picture, accentuating the dynamic aspect of a plant rather than the stable one of a castle. Actually the castle, with dark bricks below and bright buds above, was no more than a wall, a façade, full of gaping windows. Rather than resembling an attractive castle, it looked like an entangled, poisonous plant.

A similar conception was used in Bergman's 1977 production in Munich, where roots were "curling like snakes among decomposing mortar" (Kahle, quoted from Ollén, 1982, 462).

Again, Bergman and Mörk's 1970 version was very different (Bergström, 89; fig. 42). He used no castle, a purely symbolic fire — a large, nonfigurative, red design on a permanent screen — and instead of an alter the Poet's table, where the characters sacrificed their attributes, that is, took leave of their roles in token of the fact that they were merely products of the Poet's imagination.

At the end of this production, the Poet stepped forward and all the others gathered around him while he (rather than the Daughter, as in the drama text) spoke the final lines about the schizophrenic predicament of humanity: the desire to leave and to stay. Then the stage was left almost empty. "The spotlight on the Poet's table was extinguished. The final image was no Strindbergian picture of a flowering castle of redemption and deliverance, but simply a glimpse of Agnes, the woman who has taken upon herself all mankind's suffering in her heavy gray shawl, still seated alone on the empty stage, her hand pressed convulsively to her face in speechless anxiety" (Marker, 109-10) — clearly a realistic understatement of Strindberg's *"wall of human faces, asking, sorrowing, despairing."*

In his stage directions, Strindberg sometimes indicates certain sound effects, nearly all of them relating to music. Thus in the theater corridor the Officer sings his "Victoria," in the church *"music is heard"* in connection with the degree ceremony, and later the Daughter *"plays a Kyrie"* on the organ, *"but instead of organ music human voices are heard."* In Fingal's Cave I, there is *"a harmonious sound of waves and wind."* In the Fairhaven scene, the waltz indoors is competing with Bach's Toccata and Fugue no. 10, which Edith is playing on the piano outside. In Fingal's Cave II, the sound of the buoy can be heard and the Daughter is said to *"recite to soft music"* — it is an open question whether Strindberg refers to the *"music"* of winds and waves he has just mentioned or to "real" music. A little later the crew of the ship in distress sing a Christ Kyrie, obviously corresponding to the one played earlier on the church organ. In the theater corridor, Victoria sings from above. And when the Daughter enters the burning castle at the end, *"music is heard."* These are about all the references to sound effects in the play.

It is obvious that wherever Strindberg gives no instructions, a director would have to select the music. Thus, for the church scene, both Molander and Bergman selected Chopin's Funeral March. But in addition to the sound effects indicated by Strindberg, any production of *A Dream Play* would inevitably include many more, and some directors would go very far in this respect. An extreme case is Max Reinhardt, whose 1921 productions excelled in all kinds of sound effects, often arranged in very definite patterns. Thus, in the Prologue, the Heaven-Earth dichotomy was also illustrated acoustically from above when could be heard, in Reinhardt's own words, "seltsame, fremde, sphärische Klänge — seltsame Harmonien" (strange, alien, spherelike tones — strange harmonies), strongly contrasting with "ein chaotisches Gegeneinander — Glocken und Schreie — Orgel und Schüsse — Janichzen und Schlagen — Maschinenlärm und Pfiffe — Gewitter, Donner, Wind und Sturm" (a chaotic collision — bells and screams — organ and shots — piddling and drumming — machine noises and sirens — tempest, thunder, wind and storm) (from below Kvam, 108). When the Daughter descended, the harmonious sounds faded out and the cacophony increased.

A contrary sound progression occurred at the end of the play, where first "das klagende Stöhnen von zahllosen Stimmen, musikalisch gefasst" (the lamenting moaning from countless voices musically conceived) was heard. But "dann setzen hell die Rhytmen von Oben ein, steigern sich mächtig und erlösend bis zum Schluss. Das Chaos in der Tiefe versinkt, bleibt noch hörbar, verklingt bald in ferner Tiefe" (then arise the light rhythms from above, intensifying in power and redemption up to the end. The chaos of the abyss fades away, still remaining audible, soon disappears in the distant depths) (Reinhardt, in Kvam, 119). The example demonstrates how the Daughter's descent to and ascendance from Earth is suggested through purely aural means.

Unlike the scenery, the outward appearance of the characters is rarely commented on by Strindberg. This is true even of the central figure. Only from the fact that she is the daughter of an Indian god may we possibly infer that she looks oriental. This was the case with the first actress who played this part, Strindberg's ex-wife Harriet Bosse.[11]

On a photo from the 1907 production (Ollén, 1982, 437; fig. 43), she appears with clasped hands in a white dress, which suggests her divine, pure nature. There is an oriental touch in the Javanese cloak she wears over her shoulder and in the diadem across her forehead.

The long white dress with wide sleeves was seen again in the costume of Inez Lundmark, who played the Daughter in a 1916 Gothenburg production (*Drömspelet*, 1970-71, 26); the hair with its long serpentine curls looks somewhat Cretensian; in contrast to Bosse, Lundmark did not wear any jewellry. Jessie Wessel's Daughter in Reinhardt's 1921 Stockholm production was at times strikingly oriental (*Drömspelet*, 1970-71, 26), studded with pearls that sensually emphasized her navel and nipples.

A classical tragedienne was brought forward in the appearance of Tora Teje, who played the lead in Molander's 1935 production (*Drömspelet*, 1970-71, 27; fig. 44). The hairstyle resembled that of Lundmark. But with regard to costume, Molander decided upon black — introduced by Reinhardt in his Berlin production (Kvam, 138) — rather than white, even adding mourning crepe. Indeed, mourning became this unadorned Daughter — the director had just produced O'Neill's trilogy! — for humankind is sinful and to be pitied in this vale of tears.

The black or, at times, dark gray long dress has been retained for the Daughters in later Swedish productions of the play, with slight variations (*Drömspelet*, 1970-71, 27-29); sometimes the divine origin has been stressed (Kavli, 1947; Tretow, 1959), sometimes the human incarnation (Tidblad, 1947, fig. 44; Prytz, 1952; Wållgren, 1955). Occasionally the black dress has been trimmed with a white collar, a visualization, as it were, of the Daughter's innocent origin and the fall her descent to Earth signifies. By splitting the figure in two — the divine Daughter and the earthly Agnes — Bergman was

Figure 43. *Strindberg's third wife, Harriet Bosse, in the role of Indra's daughter in the 1907 Castegren production.*

Figure 44. Tora Teje (left) and Inga Tidblad (right) as Indra's daughter in the Molander productions of 1935 and 1947 (Malmö).

free to costume both according to their respective natures. Thus the Daughter (Kristina Adolphson) appeared in a long white robe with a mantle attached to it, whereas Agnes (Malin Ek) wore a simple pale blue or gray dress with a white collar, completely unadorned (*Drömspelet*, 1970-71, 30), a weak — and representative — member of mankind, deprived of the possibility to return to a consoling celestial origin.

Strindberg states about the Officer that he wears *"an extremely unusual contemporary uniform"* when we first meet him in scene 2, and later, in scene 4, *"he is dressed in frock coat and a top hat."* How he is dressed in the school scene (scene 11), dramatizing his feelings of immaturity, the playwright does not tell us. In Molander's 1963 production, he appeared in the school scene as a civilian, in what looked very much like a frock coat (Lindström, 207), whereas in Rouleau's 1970 Paris production, the *"contemporary uniform"* was retained (Måtte Schmidt, 11). Moreover, whereas the Officer was costumed in very much the same way as the surrounding boys in the Swedish version, his uniform set him off strikingly against the school costumes of the girls in the French one. The feeling of unripeness was expressed in both cases, but it is arguable which version was the more suggestive.

The discrepancy between the signs of the drama text and those of the performance text is especially obvious with regard to what we loosely term stage action. A playwright would normally comment only incidentally on such matters as positions, movements, gestures, facial expressions — that is, on the thousands of *momentary* stimuli communicated to the spectator in any play production. It is especially in this area that directors find a rich field for amplification. Two examples might suffice to illustrate this.

In the Church scene Strindberg calls for a gesture, the symbolism of which is difficult to ignore. While the Officer, who has done nothing to deserve it, receives his laurel wreath at the degree ceremony, the Lawyer is denied his; says the Daughter: "I'll give you a wreath . . . that will be more becoming for you! (*Places a crown of thorns on his head.*)." This striking gesture, turning the Lawyer into a Christ figure, has clearly inspired directors and scenographers to various embroideries. It is presumably the reason why Gade chose to include a crucifix in his setting. Reinhardt went so far as to place the Lawyer in the position of the Crucified in front of a large black cross (Tideström, 282; fig 45). Molander, in his 1947 Gothenburg production, had the Lawyer make the gesture of the Crucified as the Daughter placed the crown on his head (Ollén, 1961, 413; fig. 46). In Bergman's version of the degree ceremony, three extras incarnated an altar piece visualizing the Crucifixion. The crown of thorns was taken from the crucified Christ and placed upon the Lawyer's head (fig. 47). "One final ironic pirouette punctuated the scene. After the crown of thorns had been cast aside, the Poet strolled forward from the background, picked it up and tried it on for size before a mirror (the audience!), cocked it at a rakish angle, like a *chapeau claque*, and strolled away" (Marker, 109).

The example illustrates how all the directors have enlarged upon Strindberg's acting directions. Whereas most of the amplifications match the idea suggested by the drama text and are thus merely complementary, Bergman develops the crown-of-thorns motif along completely new lines in accordance with his adaptation of the play.

My second example demonstrates how amplifications that are very similar can be applied to completely different parts of a play. The School scene is often regarded as the most nightmarish scene in *A Dream Play*. Reinhardt stressed this when he had the Officer leave his bench and triumphantly step up on the table only to discover " dass er nur mit einem Hemd bekleidet ist. Alle weisen mit Fingern aufihn, er versucht gewaltsam sein Hemd herabzuziehen, seine Blösse zu decken und schreit schliesslich gepeinigt auf" (that he is dressed only in a shirt. All point their fingers to him, he tries by force to pull his shirt down to cover his nakedness, and finally screams with pain) (Reinhardt in Kvam, 115; trans. Göran Stockenström).

Figure 45. The Lawyer in the "Church scene," photo from the 1921 Reinhardt production.

Figure 46. *The Lawyer in the "Church scene," photo from the 1947 Molander Gothenburg production.*

Compare this to the following description of the Lawyer's behavior in Bergman's version of the church scene:

> Entering this bizarre scene, the Lawyer . . . found himself literally trapped in a nightmarishly logical Chaplinade from which he could not extricate himself. This "terribly ugly, unsuccessful, embittered character in an old tailcoat, shiny with use, that hangs around his shoulders" (Zern) stumbled onto the stage, bowed to the assembly — and then discovered that he was still wearing his galoshes. Desperately, he tried to unbuckle and remove them — only to be assaulted by the foul smell of his wretched old coat, heavy as all his clothes are with "the stink of other men's crimes." Quickly the sniffing spread; soon everyone present was holding his nose. In his mortification the Lawyer then tried to remove the offending coat — with the result that his trousers fell down, and he was reduced to

Figure 47. *"The Church scene" with the degree ceremony in the 1970 Bergman production.*

the ultimate indignity of hopping about, unable to pull them up again. (Marker, 108-9)

Although there is clearly a difference in tone between Reinhardt's altogether serious version and Bergman's postabsurdist slapstick variant, both directors have chosen to visualize essentially the same dream situation. It is an open question whether Bergman has been inspired mostly by his general knowledge of psychoanalysis or by an awareness of how earlier directors — in this case Reinhardt — had produced *A Dream Play*. It goes without saying that directors influence one another and that every play production belongs in a stage tradition. Reinhardt, for example, undoubtedly set himself off against Bernauer, just as Bergman, by his own words (Bark, 153), set himself off against Molander. With regard to details, directors are undoubtedly often inspired by earlier approaches, and their solutions frequently depend much more on those of their predecessors than the audience might realize.

As for the general tone of individual productions, the time and place of the performance are of course of importance. Thus Bernauer's consoling 1916 production, stressing the fairy tale element in the play, reflected the hopeful atmosphere in Germany at that time, just as Reinhardt's nightmarish productions five years later mirrored the chaotic postwar situation. A similar contrast is found between Molander's summer blond 1935 production and his dark 1947 alternative, in which the protest of mankind against the world order was accentuated.

"Time and space do not exist," Strindberg says in the explanatory note preceding the drama, referring to one of the most striking innovative aspects of his *Dream Play*. But in many productions time and place do exist in the sense that the audience is aware that the action takes place in a recognizable environment. Molander's attempts to turn *A Dream Play* into a Swedish play have usually been hailed by Swedish critics. The argument has been that because Lamm and other biographers have made it clear that Strindberg was inspired to many ingredients in the play by his Stockholm environment, there is every reason to reproduce this environment on the stage. Yet, in the stage directions, Strindberg has not been particularly anxious to present a Swedish, let alone Stockholm scenery — and for good reasons: after all, he is concerned with the plight not of the Swedes but of mankind. And because every tendency to paint a *couleur locale* would make the audience feel either at home or estranged, as the case may be, it inevitably narrows the scope of the play.[12]

As we have seen, Strindberg's ambiguous scenery — castle-flower, cave-shell-ear, vacation spot-(pseudo) paradise, etcetera — presents great difficulties for scenographers and directors. Either the realistic or the symbolic aspect dominates. Several scenographers have compensated for this lack of ambiguity by adding a visual one indicated by Strindberg himself when he suggests that the side wings be *"stylized wall paintings, at the same time rooms, architecture, and landscape"*; the uncertainty is whether we are dealing with an exterior or an interior setting.

As for decoding the signs of the performance text, generally the more abstract they are, the greater the variety of possible interpretations. The red nonfigurative design appearing in Bergman's 1970 production is a case in point (see figs. 26 and 47). It was variously interpreted among the critics as "the burning castle of the dream," "the human circulatory system," "flickering flames from the earth's interior," and "the inside of the eyelid as we see it when we doze off" (Marker, 102).

Whatever incidental solutions he chooses, every director of *A Dream Play* would be confronted with the question in which manner or style he or she wants to stage the drama. Given that Strindberg's stage directions are followed — as is usually only partly the case — does this mean that the signs of the script are transformed into illusionistic (realistic) or nonillusionistic (expressionist, surrealist) signs in the staged text? The variables are considerable here. In Pfister's words(45): "Bleibt die Bühne als Bühne bewusst (Illusionslosigkeit, bzw. Anti-Illusionismus) oder soll sie als etwas Anderes erscheinen, als sie ist (Illusionismus)? Das sich zwischen diesen beiden Extrempositionen . . . wieder eine ganze Skala von Möglichkeiten entfaltet, ist evident" (Does the stage remain a stage [nonillusionistic or anti-illusionistic]? or shall it appear as something else as it is [illusionistic]? It is evident that between these two extreme positions . . . a whole range of possibilities unfold."

However, since a dream by definition appears to be both real and unreal, the logical style of production for a play imitating a dream would, it seems, be one that combines illusionistic and nonillusionistic aspects. For this reason Molander's approaches to the play represent a fruitful synthesis of Castegren's all too illusionistic and Reinhardt's far too non-illusionistic versions.

For if *A Dream Play*, in its staged version, does not impress us as a *recognizable* (imitation of a) *dream*, the emotional impact of the message that life is (like) a dream is lost and the production has failed. In this difficult settling for a medium position — with regard to scenery, sound, character appearance, acting — lies the major problem with regard to the staging of *A Dream Play*.

References

Bark, Richard. *Strindbergs drömspelsteknik-i drama och teater.* Lund: Studentlitterature, 1981.

Bennich-Björkman, B. "Fyrväpplingen och korset. Om symbolmeningen i Strindbergs *Ett drömspel*," ed. G. and S. Bergsten, in *Lyrik i tid och otid. Lyrik-analytiska studier tillägnade Gunnar Tideström.* Lund: CWK Gleerup, 1971.

Bergman, G. M. *Den moderna teaterns genombrott 1890-1925.* Stockholm: Bonniers, 1966.

Bergström, B. *Teater ögonblickets konst fångad i bilder.* Stockholm: Bonniers 1976.

Björkman, R. *Scenisk konst* 9 (Stockholm, 1907).

Bjurström, P. *Teaterdekoration i Sverige.* Stockholm: Natur och Kulture, 1964.

Delblanc, Sven. *Stormhatten. Tre Strindbergsstudier.* Stockholm: Alba, 1979.

Elam, Keir. *The Semiotics of Theatre and Drama.* London and New York: Methuen, 1980.

Fischer-Lichte, E. *Semiotik des Theaters.* Tübingen: G. Narr, 1983.

Holm, Ingvar. *Drama på scen.* Stockholm: Bonniers, 1969.

Kvam, Kela. *Max Reinhardt og Strindbergs visionaere dramatik.* Copenhagen: Akademisk Forlag, 1974.

Lindström, G. M. *Dramatik.* Stockholm: Uniskol, 1966.

Marker, Frederick, and Lise-Lone Marker. *Ingmar Bergman: Four Decades in the Theater.* New York and London: Cambridge University Press, 1982.

Måtte Schmidt, T. "Drömspelet på Comédie-Française, ett reportage," *Meddelanden från Strindbergssällskapet* 47-48 (1971)

Ollén, Gunnar. *Strindbergs dramatik*. Stockholm: Sveriges Radios Förlag, 1961.

———. *Strindbergs dramatik*. Stockholm: Sveriges Radios Förlag, rev. ed. 1982.

Pfister, M. *Das Drama*. Munich: Finks, 1977.

Quigley, A. E. *The Modern Stage and other Worlds*. New York and London: Methuen, 1985.

Sprinchorn, Evert. *Strindberg as Dramatist*. New Haven and London: Yale University Press, 1982.

Strindberg, August. *Samlade skrifter (SS)*, 55 vols, ed. J. Landquist. Stockholm: Bonniers, 1912-21.

Strindberg, August. *Drömspelet. Dramaten Lilla Scenen* (playbill, 1970-71).

———. *A Dream Play and Four Chamber Plays*, trans. Walter Johnson. Seattle and London: University of Washington Press, 1973.

———. *A Dream Play. Adapted by Ingmar Bergman*. Introd. and trans. Michael Meyer. London: El Secker & Warburg, 1973.

———. *August Strindberg 1912-1962*. Brussels: 1962.

Tideström, G. *Dikt och bild*. Stockholm: CWK Gleerup, 1965.

Törnqvist, Egil. *Strindbergian Drama. Themes and Structure*. Stockholm: Almqvist and Wiksell; Atlantic Highlands, NJ: Humanities Press, 1982.

20

Directing A Dream Play:
A Journey through the Waking Dream

Susan Einhorn

— What is poetry?
— Not reality, but more than reality.
Not dreams, but waking dreams.

The Poet and Agnes, *A Dream Play*

The best plays, the ones that last, are communal dreams.

Marsha Norman, *'night, Mother*

Before January 1981 I had never read or seen *A Dream Play*. Yet in February 1981, I directed what turned out to be a successful production of the play, using an essentially bare stage and only eight actors. Lynn Michael, artistic director of The Open Space Theatre Experiment in New York City, was the producer and initiator of this project.

What I hope to do in this paper is relate how I responded intuitively to the images, myths, and symbols in the text and how I turned those responses into a theatrical exploration that was innovative, untraditional, and, ultimately, dramatically viable.

So that you can get a sense of the response the staging evoked, I am going to quote from several letters I received from audience members:

Susan Einhorn

The [version of *A*] *Dream Play* that I saw in my mind as I read it in
my room was a beautiful play full of ideas, hopes and mystical
insights into the nature of material/illusion/reality. . . . But the play
that you directed was even more beautiful and even more profound, and the images from your work continue to spin around in
my mind! It was a breathtaking production![1]

I was never really interested in this particular Strindberg play and
the other metaphysicals like it because I didn't think they worked
dramatically. I thought they could be staged as theatrical treatises
and no more. Not only did it work dramatically but your production handled this mysticism with such simplicity that I thought I
was getting the Hindu philosophy for the first time. I think it is one
of the most exciting productions of a classic play I have ever seen in
NYC. The clarity and simplicity in the direction of such dense
material was overwhelming. I am compelled to reread *To Damascus*
and *Ghost Sonata* as well as *A Dream Play.*[2]

What made me happy about your staging was not at all the fact
that it was an hommage à Strindberg but rather the disrespect —
the new translation which made him a writer of our time, the dras-
tic abbreviations and above all the joy that sparkled in so many
scenes (the Officer!) without losing the dark content. The most
awful thing of all is when *A Dream Play* is turned into liturgy where
the audience is squirming from boredom. *A Dream Play* should function like the clown who performs before God's mother, it can be
almost dancing and should go home to young people who have
never heard the name of Strindberg and who, if they have heard it,
quickly forget what they have learned in the overpowering presence of the stage. Then *A Dream Play* has been realized. That's what
happened at the Open Space. A sensation was among other things
the simplicity in your method of catching the dream character by
means of the mirrors in floor and backdrop and by the unaffected
play with the tulle curtains. . . . I suppose that the press has been
unfavorable to the Open Space Performance — as it is so often
when something unexpected turns up.

The latter quote was from a letter my dramaturg Elinor Fuchs received from
Ingvar Holm.[3] Fortunately, his prediction about the critical response was
wrong.

The final paragraph of Mel Gussow's review in the *New York Times*
gives a good summary of the design elements and their effects:[4]

Directing A Dream Play

Ursula Belden's sets are uncluttered — a few chairs and tables substitute for houses full of furnishings. There is one mysterious door
to nowhere. The floor is a large reflecting surface, the walls are plain
panels struck by the inventive lighting of Victor En Yu Tan. The
designers and the director communicate the polarities that are so
essential to the play, light and dark, pleasure and pain, beauty and
ugliness. An additional asset is Skip la Plante's score which moves
from waltz music to an ingenious simulation of the sound of the
wind and the waves as well as the tears of humans weeping. At The
Open Space . . . the company evokes a cohesive environment of
eternal lamentation and eventual reconciliation.

And from *The Soho News:*[5]

Strindberg mentions at least a dozen sets . . . and differentiates 50
characters. . . . The Open Space presents this play with one set
and eight actors . . . with not the slightest sense of stinting. It gives
us all of *A Dream Play*, in addition to a number of those shivers we
experience at moments in the theater when an artistic effect is
brought off perfectly.

The aspects of the play that my staging stressed are: (1) the Buddhist/
Vedic tone of the play, which is the core of all of its paradoxes, dualities, and
apparent contradictions; (2) the alchemy theme hidden in the play, which is
the root of so many of its textures and images and also defines the spiritual
journey; (3) the male/female principle, which is the through-line of the
"plot" of Agnes and the three men whose sufferings she comes to witness
and to understand; and (4) the humor in the play, for amid the wails and
moans of a complaining humanity are the seeds of the laughter of recognition of our common destiny.

The play is not about a single dream or a single dreamer, nor is it about
several simultaneous dreams. Its challenge does not lie in discovering who
the dreamer is or in using Freudian analysis to reduce the dream visions to
phallic objects. The play is humanity's dream, humanity represented literally by the trinity of the Officer, the Lawyer, and the Poet. The play shows us
that our whole lives are dreams and that we are all of us dreaming, even
when we are awake.

DAUGHTER: Why do flowers grow out of dirt?

GLAZIER: They don't like the dirt, so they shoot up as fast as they
can into the light — to blossom and to die.[6]

Is there a simpler, clearer explanation of the nature of human life and the desire to escape from suffering? This expresses the Buddhist view of human suffering as *karma*, or self-caused inevitability, the settling of debts in this life accrued from the sins of previous lives, and emphasizes the human desire to be liberated from this earthly body into the realm of pure consciousness. The entire journey of the play is humanity's search for light, for sun, for growth, and then for transcendence. This is what the bursting of the chrysanthemum signifies: a sign of the ascension of a consciousness into a higher sphere — in other words, Agnes's return to heaven.

In Chinese alchemical doctrine, the highest state of enlightenment is designated by the symbol of the golden flower, and the thousand petals of the lotus is the major icon of Vedic tradition.

The Buddhist theme defines the dramatic action of the play, which is the conflict of opposites, the clashing of dualities, the torture and painful struggle to distinguish between what is real and what is illusion, what is spirit and what is matter, what is good and what is evil, what to love and what to hate, what action goes toward the light and what action goes toward the darkness, what is true and what is false. As Strindberg wrote in his diary on November 18, 1901: "The sum total of it all is a ceaseless wavering between sensual orgies and the anguish of repentance. . . . On this same morning I saw the Castle, illuminated, as it were, by the rising sun. Indian religion, therefore, showed me the meaning of my *Dream Play* and the significance of Indra's Daughter, and the Secret of the Door: Nothingness. Read Buddhism all day."[7] And the Lady in *To Damascus* (III) says: "What do we know of reality, child? It is not reality which meets your eye but the image of reality. And the image is only the appearance, not the thing itself."[8]

In the church scene in *A Dream Play*, Agnes and the Lawyer discourse as follows:

AGNES: Do you know what I see in this mirror?
The world as it should be. For as it is, it's upside down.[9]

LAWYER: How did it come to be upside down?

AGNES: When the copy was made.

LAWYER: Ah! You have said it — the copy!
I always felt this must be a poor copy, and when I began to remember the original nothing satisfied me.

(215-6)

These concepts were the basis of the stage design by Ursula Belden. The entire floor was mirrored with a mylar substance, the backdrop was a huge cyclorama made of several rows of curving scrim panels, with a central periaktoi on wheels. There was one door, situated on the revolving periaktoi, with a cloverleaf design cut out of it. A ceiling piece of a mirrored mandala hung over the center of the space so that the actors were reflected twice, from below and from above. The only furniture was one table and two chairs. The set won the Villager Award for Outstanding Design that season.

The inherent paradoxes in *A Dream Play* are what gave us the courage to do the production in such a sparse, minimalist way. Props were reduced to an absolute minimum, colors were used very selectively: silver, beige, white, and black with red accents. The one remembered cloverleaf door became all doors.

"For him who keeps the sun in his heart, there is no evil." This is the translation of a Sanskrit chant we used in the church scene, which ties in with the strong alchemical themes in the play. The golden sun, the quest for gold, and the golden flower are the enemies of the evil spirits with which Strindberg was so obsessed in his Inferno years.

Strindberg's alchemical experiments were as much about the desire to rid himself of his despair, to purify himself through suffering, and thus to be reborn to a cleaner, purer self, as they were about changing base metals into gold. This mystical transformation from the earthy, impure being to a higher being is, I believe, the basis for the birth, death, and rebirth themes in the play. The Officer is born, the Lawyer dies, and the Poet is reborn.

The philosopher's stone, which was necessary to turn lead into gold, was often described not as tangible but as being made out of fire and water. The four elements, air, water, earth, and fire, run throughout the play, in the wind and the waves, the manure and the mud, and the burning sulphur and the fire of the ascension.

It is fascinating that black, red, and white are the colors traditionally used to depict the body, spirit, and soul — the mercury, salt, and sulphur that supposedly united to form the philosopher's stone. And this is how Strindberg describes Foulport[10] where cholera victims came to be purified in the heat of the sulphur ovens: "Charred hills covered with red heather and black and white stumps of trees left after a forest fire; red pigsties and out-houses" (223).

The Lawyer corresponds to the color black, or the body element, the Officer to the white of the soul, and the Poet to the red of the spirit. In Alchemy, *nigredo* is the term of the black stage when what was initially a substance is dead and putrefying. The Lawyer is "black" with the sins and sufferings of humanity and uses sulphur to fumigate his office. This reference is repeated in the blackamoor, the black-faced Quarantine Master who also disinfects with sulphur.

In the painting series called *Splendor Solis* by sixteenth-century painter Salomon Trismosin, which is in the British Museum, there are paintings of the *Bath of Rebirth* that depict a black, charred figure whose arms and head are beginning to turn red, emerging from a hot, cleansing bath into the arms of a goddess/madonna figure holding a red robe. This startling image connects both with the Lawyer who can never be cleansed of his self-imposed blackness and is therefore essentially dying and with the Poet who takes the place of the Lawyer by taking his mudbath, thus signifying the purification before his rebirth.

My final point about the alchemy in the play is perhaps the most interesting in reference to symbolism. An alchemical formula for making the philosopher's stone[11] is to make a circle (using a man and a woman), then a square, within a triangle, then a larger circle.

The basic elements of the mandala, a form that when looked at can induce a state of meditation, is a circle, representing the sky, inside a square, representing the earth. Indra's daughter descends from the sky (circle), enters the earthly plane (square), interacts with a triangle of men, and returns to the sky (circle) again.

Because our setting was bare, I was able to create these simple patterns and shapes in the blocking formations throughout the production. Thus the play's primitive symmetry was exposed and celebrated.

Strindberg initially conceived of writing *A Dream Play* with two characters — one male and one female — and I think this is still apparent in the finished product. All the possible male/female relationships are explored in the play:

Male	Female
Indra	Indra's Daughter
Glazier	Agnes/Daughter
Officer	Agnes/Mother
Lawyer	Agnes/Lover-Wife-Mother
Poet	Agnes/Sister

Agnes is the goddess who makes herself manifest in human form to unite with each aspect of humanity: she is maternal with the Officer, intellectual/sexual with the Lawyer, and spiritual/artistic with the Poet. She shatters each one's illusions by demonstrating the true nature of reality, teaching each one the lesson he is seeking, and giving each one the answer he deserves and is capable of understanding.

One of the most important aspects of my staging was the assignment of roles in the casting. The small cast brought out the patterns of the male/female union and the archetypes hidden in the recurring images in the play. Besides the quartet, two women and two men played all the other parts as follows: one actor played the Glazier, the Quarantine Master, and the Dean of Law. The other played the Father, the Prompter, He, the Naval Officer, the Schoolmaster, and the Dean of Theology. The Father's turning

Figure 48. Agnes (Susan Stephens) and the Officer (Charles Shaw Robinson) in the castle tower. From Susan Einhorn's production at the Open Space Theater, New York, 1981. Photograph by Carol Rosegg, © Martha Swope.

Figure 49. Agnes and the Poet (Bruce Somerville) in Fingals Cave. Photograph by Carol Rosegg, © Martha Swope.

Figure 50. *The Officer and the doctoral candidates. Photograph by Carol Rosegg,* © *Martha Swope.*

into the Schoolmaster was particularly effective in terms of the living archetypal pattern that emerged.

The first actress played the Mother, the Doorkeeper, the Singer, Kristin, Alice, and the Dean of Medicine. The transformation from Mother to Doorkeeper to Kristin was very illuminating in its implications. The second actress went from Lina, to Victoria, to Dancer, to She, to Ugly Edith, to the Dean of Philosophy, with the magical transition from Victoria, to She (someone else's Victoria), to Ugly Edith. The beauty/ugliness duality was thus breathtakingly exposed.

Another significant aspect of my concept of the play was what I called the theme of the silver thread that Agnes talks about in Fingal's Cave. The same two pieces of fabric were worn and used by all the women in the play to dramatize the mythical theme of weaving that is so prevalent in Strindberg's work. The first appearance of Agnes was as a breathing form under a blanket made from silver thread, which was meant to portray her soul looking for and finding a body for her journey to earth. This fabric reappeared in the Officer's home and then became, in succession, the star coverlet of the Doorkeeper, the fabric on which the doctoral wreaths were carried at the graduation ceremony, the canopy during the wedding ceremony, the tablecloth in the domestic scene, the prayer mat in Fingal's Cave,

Figure 51. *Agnes and the Lawyer (Martin Treat) at their wedding ceremony.*
Photograph by Carol Rosegg, © *Martha Swope.*

and the sacrificial altar on which the final burying took place. The white
shawl given to the Mother became the Gatekeeper's shawl of nettles,
Agnes's wedding veil, and her marital shawl. I hope the irony of this
continuum is clear. The simplicity of this device heightened the dreamlike
quality of the appearance and reappearance of this web of material.

I could not imagine approaching this play without a sense of humor,
although I understand that many others have, because even the most
painfully true and deadly serious moments in Strindberg's plays are inevitably funny. It is merely a question of how loudly you allow yourself to laugh
or enable the audience to laugh. The marriage scene in *A Dream Play* is as
funny in its savage, ironic, and witty view of domestic compromise and
misery as anything ever written on the subject.

In a play in which humankind is repeatedly said to be pitiable, and in
which tears and wailing are omnipresent, I introduced as much actual
laughter as possible. The first human sound we heard from Indra's Daughter, signifying her entrance into Agnes's body, was laughter, the giggling of a
little girl playing hide-and-seek with her father, the Glazier. Surely our
entrance into this life is as comical as it is portentous.

Laughter also echoed through the halls of the theater corridor, when the Officer conversed with the Billposter, and the first offstage sound, which introduced us to the Poet coming for his mudbath, was his own raucous laughter. Indeed Foulport was full of the black laughter of the Quarantine Master, the aging and comical blabbermouth. I staged this scene to resemble a Fellini circus. He and She appeared on the "boat" as masked doll-like copies of the Officer and his idealized Victoria.

In addition to the sounds of laughter there was an unusual and most original soundscore composed by Skip la Plante, who works with instruments that he makes. We followed the mystical theme throughout, using bells, chimes, and vibrating metal objects that induced a state of calmness and meditative attention in the listeners. The sound of the tears of the world was made with broken glass fragments; the Buddhist hymn mentioned earlier was an a cappella chant sung by the company as witnesses to Agnes's marriage proposal to the Lawyer. I staged this as a subtle seduction, reenacting the play of Māyā and Brahma. The sound of the wind and the waves in Fingal's Cave was achieved live by the invisible company blowing into glass bottles of various sizes and shapes in carefully composed rhythms.

For the final Fingal's Cave scene and the farewell outside the Growing Castle, the sound of a handmade harmonium underscored the action, adding extraordinary tension and momentum.

I cannot adquately describe the lighting effects, except to say the lights bounced off the mirrored floor and created beautiful patterns on the scrim panels. The changes in season, the trees and the flowers as well as the final bloom, were created through lighting projection. Many scenes were lit in candlelight glow, which was refracted throughout by the mirrors. The cobblestones of the theater corridor were made out of pools of light through which the waiting Officer walked as he aged, and these very same pools of light created the prison of the Schoolroom to which he was forced to return.

My production length was about 103 minutes (Ingmar Bergman's was 105) without intermission. We made substantial cuts and adaptations in the Elizabeth Sprigge text. Although we rehearsed the Coalheaver's Mediterranean scene, I cut it before opening. I regret this now. I staged it as a scene of impending physical violence, where all the men in the company surrounded Agnes in a large circle and taunted her, assaulting her with their grumblings about their working conditions. It was the only scene that ended in a blackout. I saw it as Agnes's nightmare.

The images of the triangle and the square were further highlighted by staging several moments when the action stopped and the Poet, the Lawyer, the Officer, and Agnes looked at one another. This began with the Daughter of Indra, in full regalia, being surrounded and aided by the three while she prepared for her earthly appearance. They removed her goddess's

Figure 52. Agnes, Edith (Bonnie Brewster), and the Officer listen to the tears of the world. Photograph by Carol Rosegg, © Martha Swope.

gown and crown and gave her shoes. Such a moment for the triangle in the square recurred before the Lawyer's office, again after the Blind Man's monologue in Fairport, and finally, before Agnes's fiery ascent. These moments were wondrously strange because they were so theatrical and had nothing to do with words. The powerful gazes among these four seemed to suggest ancient memory, present intimate knowledge, future intimacy, and strangeness, all at once.

Thus I complete the account of my journey through the waking

Figure 53. The Officer and the Schoolmaster (Paul Peeling). Photograph by
Carol Rosegg, © Martha Swope.

dream. Directing *A Dream Play* provided me, as a member of humankind,
with only those answers I deserved and was able to grasp at that time in my
life's dream. I look forward to directing it again because it is a theatrical
masterpiece and therefore will bear me new answers from the seeds of my
next set of questions.

The Tower of Babel:
Space and Movement in
The Ghost Sonata

Sarah Bryant-Bertail

Roland Barthes, in *Sur Racine,*[1] uses semiotic analysis of various sign systems in conjunction with anthropological and psychoanalytical approaches to arrive at what he calls Racinean space. He projects an architectural design within a landscape, outlines its borders, and rationalizes this space through interpretation of the plays. Whereas the projection of Racinean space is only part of Barthes's work in *Sur Racine,* it is Anne Ubersfeld's whole task in "The Space of Phèdre," one of several articles in a recent issue of *Poetics Today*[2] that is devoted to theater semiotics. The theatrical text that is the object of a semiotician's study must always encompass both the written text and its projected performance or spatial and temporal materiality. Barthes and Ubersfeld read the relation between Racinean movement and space from the movement and placement of various characters in relation to each other, from patterns of spatial imagery, and from patterns formed by objects visible on a projected stage or alluded to in the dialogue. Any systematization of how a play creates and moves through its own space and time is of course an interpretation. Interpretation, whether by an actor or a spectator or a reader, is the discovery or elucidation of certain principles by which a work produces meaning. The main task of any semiotic analysis is to observe the process of how the play sets up its own codes of meaning. Patrice Pavis, in *Languages of the Stage,*[3] argues on behalf of precisely the kind of work that Barthes has done in *Sur Racine*. Pavis urges that semiotics be used not to undermine but to refocus and strengthen through self-awareness the traditional disciplines of theater and drama criticism, to prod us all toward an examination of what the stakes of our disciplines are. However, any semiotic study, including this one, fundamentally departs from more traditional approaches on some points: by refusing to admit the existence of any intrinsic, permanent meaning in a work of art, and refusing, in consequence, to privilege any one point of entry into the text or to grant the preeminence of ideological, historical, or biographical sources over the work itself. This paper will use a semiotic approach to analyze and try to bring into a coherent aesthetic pattern the scenic space as it is delineated by the placement of objects, the movement of characters, and the metaphorical systems of the play. My goal is to observe and interpret the play as a dynamic system, an approach that assumes a work of art is more than a neutral locus wherein preexisting "sources" are reflected.

Umberto Eco's notion of the three-part sign will serve as an operating theory of how meaning is produced.[4] The play can be seen as a kind of meta-sign, a play of signification encompassing playscript and performance, actor, spectator, and reader. The sign consists of the signifier, which is analogous to form, the signified, which is analogous to content, and the referent, that is, what it refers to in real life. Semiotics is mainly concerned with the signifier and signified, inasmuch as its task is to observe *how* a work means rather than *what* it means, to study the formation of content, rather than form *and* content.

An indication of the shape of the play's space is offered explicitly in Strindberg's stage directions.[5] In the beginning of the play, we are outside on the city street looking at the façade of the house with its round room. Later we move inside this round enclosure for the Ghost Supper, then farther away from the center of the house to the Hyacinth Room. Finally, house and city street disappear and we are out on the water looking at an island in the distance, Böcklin's painting *The Isle of the Dead*. The movement of the scene has proceeded from outside the house to inside to a more extreme outside. Given the limitations of the physical stage, the "circular" walls of the round room must actually be presented as semicircular, with the spectators and auditorium closing the circle. Likewise, the circular seating pattern at the ghost supper must draw in the spectator as well.

If we follow the visible movements of the characters as indicated by the stage directions, a few basic patterns emerge: Hummel rolls along in his wheelchair or walks on crutches; his first large movement is around the corner of the house so that he can eavesdrop on the people gathered behind it. In the round room, he circles from the statue around the room and back. The impetus of Hummel's movement is to see others or to avoid being seen, to hear or to avoid being heard. In other words, he either stalks or hides from the others. At the supper, he sits down as the others form a circle about him, and gets up again for the last time only when they force him to go into the closet where he is grotesquely elevated by hanging himself. Looked at as a continuum, his movement has taken him in an uneven spiral from outside to the extreme interior of the house, and from a lower to a higher elevation. The house opens itself to him only to seal him into its deepest enclosure, one that remains masked and dark for the spectator. Thus the progressive views of the house make up the movement through space. The house can be seen to move the play along as if the latter were unwrapping itself and then vanishing.

To move beyond what is actually seen, it is useful to introduce two categories of space distinguished by the semiotician Michael Issacharoff, whose article "Space and Reference in Drama" also appears in *Poetics Today*.[6] Issacharoff divides the dramatic space into the mimetic and diegetic spaces, the mimetic being what is seen on stage and the diegetic what is indicated by dialogue or metaphoric allusions. These divisions reveal some interesting patterns of movement when applied to *The Ghost Sonata*, particularly when action shifts from the diegetic to the mimetic or vice versa. A striking instance of such a shift is the movement of the house from the diegetic to the mimetic space: the house that collapses in the diegetic space before the play begins is a ghost of the house that we see before us on stage. To use another example, we see Hummel circling about the exterior of the house in his wheelchair, then about the round room on his crutches; this takes place in the mimetic space, while in the diegetic space he tears down buildings, creeps into houses, takes them apart stone by stone, and binds people to himself. Although he could *appear* to be a pitiful old cripple in the mimetic space, he is made into a vampire or venomous spider in the diegetic one. For the thematic structure of *The Ghost Sonata*, the dialectical movement between the two spaces is of particualr importance.

Hummel's overall movement is associated with the unwrapping and disappearance of the house. The sequence of dramatic action moves in a circular pattern, with time appearing to reverse its direction. Evert Sprinchorn argues that Arkenholz actually has died before the play begins, at the point when he rescues the child from the collapsing house.[7] The moment that the child seems to disappear from his arms is the moment of Arkenholz's death; thus everything that follows is after the material fact. The pattern of collapse, death, and removal to another space has occurred before the play begins and is repeated at the end. In the original production at the Intimate Theater in Stockholm, Strindberg had copies of Böcklin's painting appear to the left and right of the proscenium, a spatial arrangement that suggests a repeated or circular progression. If we "read" this moment of production from left to right, as with a line of writing, we see that the play has taken place — literally filled the now empty space — between the two identical scenes representing beginning and end.

The spiraling movement of Hummel, from outside to center, does in fact imitate that of a spider weaving a web. The web is repeatedly signified through various means. Drawn as a map, with the characters' relationships to one another represented by intersecting lines, the community of the play resembles a complex tangle of lines all converging at the figure of Hummel. Critics have long made the point that the network is intentionally tangled, and have attached to Strindberg's image various referents: the network is said to mean nineteenth-century society, humanity's corrupted moral state, or Strindberg's confused life and mind. Finding the original or correct referent for this image—or signified, to use semiotic terminology—lies outside the reach of this study. Of more interest here is an exploration of how several signification systems collaborate to produce the web, and how this image in turn relates to other signifieds and to the whole play as a dynamic meta-sign.

There are many allusions to Hummel as a spider and vampire. When Hummel touches Arkenholz, the latter says, "Let go of my hand; you're taking my strength; you're freezing me" (201). Later Johansson warns Arkenholz that it is not as easy as he believes to leave, "once he [Hummel] has the net over your head" (205). And Hummel himself implicitly compares the narrative of his life to the travels of a spider: his life, he says, is "like a book of fairy tales, though the tales are different, they all hang together on a thread, and the theme recurs regularly" (198). He says that people are "bound together by crimes and secrets and guilt" (212). Finally, hanging on the end of the thread, he dies.

But even benign-looking objects in the mimetic space tend to move invisibly within the diegetic one, conspiring in spiderlike activities. Arkenholz complains that the fragrance of the hyacinths acts as a venom: "[It] confuses my senses, deafens me, blinds me, . . . bombards me with poisonous arrows" (220). Likewise, Hummel says that words conceal secrets whereas in silence one can hear thoughts and see the past. The status of language is in fact of direct thematic interest to Strindberg. In the ghost supper scene, he has Hummel say: "The difference between languages really arose among primitive peoples in order to conceal the secrets of the tribe from the rest, so languages are symbols and the one who finds the key understands all the languages of the world" (215-16). In other words, Strindberg ironically has the weaver of tangled webs introduce the idealistic seeker of truth. The "fall" of human society from a unified and pure state into a divided, tribal one is reflected in the diversification of language, but it is still thought possible to return to an unfragmented origin. The above passage explicitly suggests the possibility of returning to a pre-Babel state. Arkenholz, as a student of languages, is entrusted with the task of finding the key that will untangle truth from falsehood. In a play called "The Ghost Sonata," only Arkenholz sings, matching human language with the "universal language" of music. The notion of music as an uncorrupted, spiritually elevated language was of course widely held at the end of the nineteenth century.

But the association of human communication with concealment is carried out on less obvious levels. A catalog and semiotic analysis of objects in the mimetic and diegetic space reveals three predominent patterns: first, there are several "lines of communication" displayed on stage or mentioned in the dialogue. The bulletin board, for instance, acts as a shield toward which the adulterous couple go so as not to be overheard. Thus the board's normal function has been reversed. Other lines of communication include the newspaper, behind which Hummel hides, the playbill, the telephone, the telegraph, the handbell, and the church bells. The church bells are heard when the curtain is raised and serve to define the dramatic space as a city of which we see only a part. The bells set an emotionally ambivalent tone that could represent an alarm, a proclamation of joy, or simply a sign of the passage of time. The telephone, telegraph, and newspaper extend the dramatic space outward to include the world. Through the display of this indefinitely expanding network, Strindberg amplifies the spider web pattern, moving it beyond the stage and Swedish city to implicate the rest of the civilized, technologically connected world.

The second group of objects, which seem to be part of a single signification system that in turn relates to an overall one, consists of those with reflecting surfaces: the mirrors, the fountain, and the windowpanes that flash in the sunlight. These objects are surfaces that trap the images they reflect, give back deceptive reflections, and draw one space into another. The Old Woman in the window uses a gossip mirror to spy upon people below. Hummel says of her: "The gossip mirror is the only mirror she uses because in that she doesn't see herself, only the outside world, and from two different directions. But the world can see her; she hasn't thought of that" (203). There is also a mirror in the round room. On a proscenium stage, it would probably reflect part of the auditorium, again implicating the spectators in the scene and using them to complete the so-called circle of friends.

The third pattern that emerges is that of objects that cover or wrap: white sheets of mourning hung in the windows, curtains covering the statue, the mummy's cloth, a blanket hung on the balcony rail, window shades, winding sheets on a corpse, bedclothes over the window ledge, wallpaper covering the door, and, at the center of the house's interior, the

Japanese screen that covers death itself. As time goes on, these wrappings can be seen to move from their innocuous utilitarian function in a naturalistic setting to a new position as signifiers within a system that associates concealment with immorality, suffocation, and death. The stage properties surreptitiously come to life, transforming themselves into murder weapons.[8] By association through patterns of imagery, the lines of communication also become contaminated with the signification of death. They are transformed into lines that strangle and entrap. No system of the play can remain isolated from the others. Of the Hyacinth Room, the Young Lady says: "This room is called the room of ordeals — it's beautiful to look at but consists of nothing but pure flaws." To which the Student replies, "Unbelievable; but one must look into that. It's beautiful but a little cold" (223).

The lines of communication are perverted in their function, concealing rather than relaying messages, just as the mirroring surfaces produce a reversed and distorted reflection. Spatially and temporally the action takes place and the scene shifts as if the play were "unwrapping" itself.

The various signification systems, traditionally called motifs or recurring imagery, are still theatrically incoherent until they can be seen to move toward a larger signified that relates them all to one another. This is not to suggest that there can be a clear indication of which referent is the correct one. One cannot prove, for instance, whether the signification system of wrapping and unwrapping refers to Strindberg's personal life, nineteenth-century Christian morality, Buddhism, or Madame Blavatsky's spiritualism. Semiotic theoreticians Charles Peirce and Umberto Eco have introduced the referent as the third element of Saussure's two-part sign to try to deal with the fact that meanings of a single work of art can change when they are mediated by the passage of time, the crossing of national borders, and other circumstances. The need for the concept of a referent is demonstrated in the history of theater production by, for example, the fact that sexual abstinence is no longer automatically connected with altruism, as it no doubt was for Strindberg's earliest spectators.

The metaphorical complex of the eyes exemplifies how a signifier seems to become more coherent when it draws closer to other sign systems. Strindberg's conscious — and unconscious — preoccupation in the play with communication, words, and hidden and overt signs, is striking. The play carries on a kind of commentary about its own process of communication. The characters directly converse about the failure of language and the impossibility of preventing multiplicity of meanings from developing. Even seeing is not believing. Arkenholz and Hummel observe bedclothes being hung over the balcony and try to guess what this simple act may be concealing: "That is complicated, I think!" / "Yes, . . . any way you look at it. Though it seems simple" (200). My own recognition of Strindberg's concern

for the process of signification is not a claim that the author was intentionally provocative. On the contrary, such a recognition is mediated by the
current concern about the overcoded nature of what Lyotard calls the
postmodern condition.[9] From this present-day standpoint, Strindberg's
work seems to mark the shift from an imagination that used organic — that
is, plant and animal — metaphors to one whose metaphors are drawn from
linguistic processes.

The eye, for instance, belongs to both the organic and the linguistic
metaphorical fields. It is the part of the body most frequently mentioned in
the play. The Student's eyes are bathed by the Milkmaid so that he will not
contract infection. Hummel uses his eyes to entrap Arkenholz: "I've had my
eyes on you a long time" (200). The cook draws out her victims' blood with
her eyes (205). The mummy stays in the closet because "her eyes can't
stand the light" (218). Eventually, the signification of evil is attached to
seeing without being seen. One-way sight is as evil as binding without
being bound; both are associated with the organic imagery of vampirism.

The play of signification of the eyes is in turn related to that of light
and darkness. When Arkenholz sings, "I saw the sun, so I seemed to have
seen the Hidden One" (227), the ultimate light is dialectically joined to the
ultimate darkness or concealment. Walter Johnson notes that in the original
Swedish, the "Hidden One" is *Den Fördolde,* a term that connotes "one who
is veiled or concealed."[10] Thus the "motif" of the eyes is a signifier of the
larger signified, which is the pattern of concealing and revealing. Referents
have been suggested by Johnson and others on what the eyes could *stand
for.* A psychoanalytic critic, for instance, might point out that Strindberg's
preoccupation with eyes is a sign of his paranoia. No doubt this is true.
However, the point here is not to argue whether such observations are valid
or invalid. As Pavis and Barthes have said, the reader ought to be free to
begin reading from this or any other point of entry. Nevertheless, to exit via
such a referent would seem to do unnecessary injustice to oneself as a
reader, because it would short-circuit the pleasure of the text, to borrow a
phrase from Barthes again.

On the other hand, not to exit at all from the seemingly infinite chains
of signifiers and signifieds would not be a pleasure either, for any reader.
Therefore, I would like to move toward the meta-sign, in the direction of an
interpretation — not a fixed referent that would trap and mummify the play.
Pavis advises that the semiotics of theater not try to elevate itself to the
status of a discipline but remain a flexible "point of view." In concurrence
with this advice, I want to point out one more system of signification and to
connect this in turn to some empirical observations.

Now that some of the interdependent patterns of movement, space,
and time have been suggested, these patterns can be followed as they move

toward a larger signifier and signified, which can be called the sign of Babel. As a narrative sequence and a physical space, Babel can be associated with *The Ghost Sonata*. The circularity of the playing space has been mentioned. The spiral movement upward and downward would also be the direction one would have to travel if one were living inside a tower. The narrative of Babel is also "reflected" in fragmentary form as well as in large action sequences of the play. The house collapses before the play begins, and again at the end, when the whole set suddenly disappears. There are a great many allusions to the destruction of buildings, streets, and squares, which can in turn signify the tower and the city called Babel. In act 1 Arkenholz describes the collapse of the burning house: "I was drawn to the ordinary street where the house later collapsed . . . [a] building I had never seen before. . . . Then I noticed a crack in the wall, and heard the floor splitting"(199). Hummel, at the other extreme, is a figure accused of causing such ruin. In spinning his net and stalking his victims, he destroys the systems and edifices of civilization. In the words of the character Johannsson, he first "looks at houses," then "breaks into them," "creeps in through windows," "tears them [houses] down," "takes them apart stone by stone until they fall," "opens streets," and "settles squares"(204-5).

There is another classification of objects in the mimetic and diegetic space that has not been mentioned, a group that can be called "useless objects" or "blatant symbols." But the fact that they are blatantly semiotic does not make them easier to analyze. On the contrary, they are completely coded, iconic signs unto themselves, as well as part of the play's signification pattern. That is, each one is its own signifier, signified, and referent in one. The coat of arms, signet ring, book of peerage, key, snowflake, shallot, flowers, and statue of Buddha fall into this classification. The coat of arms and signet ring, for instance, are symbols in a hierarchical social system, unquestionable signs of aristocratic status. And yet Hummel, by "throwing the book" — that is, the book of peerage — at the Colonel, proves that even these signs can be falsified and the whole system behind them — their referent — exposed as arbitrary. The military rank of the Colonel was eradicated by a change in the Swedish government, a power play over which he had no control. When the Colonel is stripped of his "good name," he loses his status as an entity because the standards of what is legitimate have been changed by the arbitrary play of political, historical, and social signification. He is finally not just an uncovered man, but a nonentity according to these institutionalized signification systems.

A great deal of critical attention has been focused on these objects already, much of it a tracing of the text back through the already fully articulated systems outside the play to which these symbols refer. However, in their relation to the rest of the text these objects too are caught up in the unresolvable dialectical oscillation between signifying good and signifying evil. Like the other objects, what at first seems to mean only good is later found to conceal malevolence.

The house in *The Ghost Sonata* glitters and appears clean and sound from the outside, but the language used in it gradually lends it the atmosphere of a rotting chamber of horrors. The character Bengtsson says: "When a house gets old, it gets moldy, and when people are together tormenting each other for a long time, they go crazy" (208). The decline of morals is further linked to physical decay by such passages as: "She has lost the desire to live. . . . She withered in this air which breathed crimes, deception, and all kinds of falseness" (216). The language of the house is also infested with repulsive animals, again in the diegetic space of metaphor: appearing as images are the spider, the scorpion, the mythical lamia, the rat, the deathwatch beetle, and the bloodsucker. Even the flowers are not free of such vermin; we recall Arkenholz's remark to the Young Lady that her flowers have poisoned him with the venom of their fragrance (220). He also explicitly transforms the house into a metonym for a civilization that is connoted by the term Babel: "this madhouse, this reformatory, this charnal house" (227). In other words, "Babel" has, over the passage of time, come to signify human institutions that try to *contain* and simultaneously *convey* our confusion and violence.

In the Genesis version of the Babel narrative, the descendents of Noah have been spreading outward from Mount Ararat for several generations, and settle on a plain where they build a city called Babel. The King James Version reads as follows:

> And the whole earth was of one language, and of one speech.
> 2 And it came to pass, as they journeyed from the east, that they found a plain in the land of Shinar; and they dwelt there.
> 3 And they said one to another, Go to, let us make brick, and burn them thoroughly. And they had brick for stone, and slime they had for mortar.
> 4 And they said, Go to, let us build us a city and a tower, whose top *may reach* unto heaven; and let us make us a name, lest we be scattered abroad upon the face of the whole earth.
> 5 And the LORD came down to see the city and the tower, which the children of men builded.
> 6 And the LORD said, Behold, the people *is* one, and they have all one language; and this they begin to do: and now nothing will be restrained from them, which they have imagined to do.
> 7 Go to, let us go down, and there confound their language, that they may not understand one another's speech.

8 So the LORD scattered them abroad from thence upon the face of all the earth: and they left off to build the city.
9 Therefore is the name of it called Babel; because the LORD did there confound the language of all the earth: and from thence did the LORD scatter them abroad upon the face of all the earth. (Genesis 11:1-9)

In God's eyes the people have built the city and tower for the wrong reason: to make themselves a name and to unify themselves. God attributes this offensive act of imagination to a too effective system of communication and institutes confusion as the law governing language.

However, in Strindberg's play, the characters continually try to rebuild it, and to alternately unite with and escape from one another. A chosen few, such as Arkenholz, still retain enough audacity and imagination to study languages, altruistically searching for a key that will lead them back to the unity supposedly present at the origin of civilization. Such a key can, it is hoped, act as a code breaker, breaking the power of the law of confusion. As in the story of Babel, the main structural edifice in *The Ghost Sonata* is also part of a city. Like Babel, too, the house and city are built from the material that happened to be available, and not according to God's specifications, as Noah's ark was built.

Walter Johnson, among others, cannot pinpoint a particular significance in the name Arkenholz, although he admits it is evocative. Arkenholz, he points out, sounds like the German terms for ark and wood.[11] The word Arkenholz also closely resembles *Arche Noahs,* which in German simply means Noah's ark. Both ark and *Arche* derive from the Latin *arcene,* meaning to enclose. With this in mind, "Arkenholz" could signify any enclosure made of wood, from a house to a chest to a boat. The Ark of the Covenant, for instance, is the chest that holds the stone tablets inscribed with the Ten Commandments. Even the Holy Law is contained in an enclosed, artificially created space. The name Arkenholz can of course also signify "wood of the ark." Whatever connotations may be possible, there is evidence in Strindberg's handwritten manuscript that this word was not chosen at random: the notation "Arken + Holz" appears in one of the drafts of the play.[12] In any case, Strindberg gives this overcoded name to a wandering picaresque hero, truth-seeking, self-sacrificing, poetic, musical, a student of languages whose values oppose those of Hummel, even though one character sometimes sounds like the other. Some directors have given Arkenholz and Hummel the same stage appearance, that is, the same costume and makeup; this could be called a staging *sign* of their relationship. Indeed they exemplify two sides of one dialectic of signification. Hummel's speeches often touch on the same topics as those of Arkenholz, but Hummel tends to move from the theological, philosophical level to the "low" level of domestic intrigue, whereas Arkenholz reverses this pattern, working "up" from gossip to theological and philosophical discourse.

Continuing this interpretive line, it is Arkenholz who seems to have just arrived from Ararat, whereas the others have lived in Babel for a long time. Between the biblical stories of the Flood and Babel, there is only a genealogy of Noah's descendants, with information on where they traveled. The characters in the story of Babel belong to the same family that God thought worth saving from the Flood. The two chapters are part of one circular or repetitious narrative in that each chapter ends with catastrophe as punishment. Looked at in a somewhat heretical light, it is God who is arbitrary and humanity who is consistent in being "imaginative" — that is, able to use images. God's law forbidding unity of language ensures the continuation of deception, war, and hatred. Because Strindberg was an artist, it would be understandable that he might have ambivalent feelings about the implications of Babel. God appeared to tolerate the work of human imagination until it began to encroach upon his heavenly space. Strindberg's ambivalence toward the deities God and Buddha is evident throughout the play. Arkenholz utters a prayer to close the play and, as if incidentally, to kill the very girl for whom he is praying. The prayer is addressed to the dying girl and only *refers* to a deity: "May the Lord of Heaven be merciful to you on your journey"(228).

The sudden disappearance of the house at the end of the play is a repetition of the collapse of the building from which Arkenholz rescued the child. With the corresponding mythical framework of the Flood and Babel in mind, the play's ending can be linked to these narratives. The fountain and windows of the set may recall the biblical passage: "the fountains of the great deep [were] broken up, and the windows of heaven were opened" (Genesis 7:11). There is a certain potential for disaster "written into" these objects. Also in act 1, Hummel looks up at his daughter in the window and says to Arkenholz: "I think it's getting cloudy. What if it should rain? Then I'd be in a nice mess"(202). Immediately afterward are the stage directions: *"It becomes cloudy and darkens: the old woman by the gossip mirror closes her window"*(203). Nevertheless, it does not seem to actually rain during the play, only to darken, with everyone going inside until the set disappears. The disappearance of the house can thus also be associated with the biblical deluge. Even the sun and clouds belong to the signification pattern of concealer and concealed. When Arkenholz claims "I saw the sun, so I seemed to have seen the Hidden One" (227), he is linking ultimate light and ultimate darkness into the same unresolvable dialectical opposition.

The white light and appearance of the landscape of Böcklin's *Isle of the Dead* can now be associated with the return of the sun and, to employ the words of the Bible again, "the fountains . . . of the deep and the windows of heaven were stopped" (Genesis 8:2). Since the Isle of the Dead is seen in the distance from out upon a calm body of water, the scene may even represent the first view of land from the window of the ark as the water recedes. The real arch of the proscenium, the encloser and framer of the play, ought also to be remembered here. In the original production Strindberg may have hung the painting on both sides to signify both the circling back to an origin *and* the repetitious pattern of renewal and destruction. Whether this scene moves the action into the past or future remains ambiguous and finally undecidable. Having the double image seems to undermine the whole notion of time as a "forward-moving" narrative.

Material from the Strindberg archives offers what might be called empirical evidence in support of the interpretation ventured here. Several short works, published and unpublished, bear the title Babel, revealing that the author worked consciously with the notion of Babel as a unifying metaphorical structure. Babel was in fact a fashionable topic for artists at that time.

Nevertheless, I am glad that this empirical discovery did not come before, and thus short-circuit, the semiotic analysis and interpretation, because to begin with Babel as a more or less ready-made structure would have reduced *The Ghost Sonata* to a kind of example. Such so-called proof does less damage to the theatrical text when used as an avenue of exit rather than a rigid framework of analysis. The question no doubt remains: of what use is a semiotic approach? My answer is that it offers a way to study the written text and projected performance as one dynamic meta-sign, a unique system of signification in operation, and that it attempts to see the play at work rather than to "work it over" by driving it back at all costs to its ideological, historical, or biographical "sources." The main methodology followed here has been to look for patterns that might explain why and how the play moves and how we, the reader and spectator, are pointed toward particular interpretations. My initial setting up of headings such as "objects in the mimetic space," "objects in the diegitic space," "movement of characters in mimetic space," "parts of the body," "animal references," and so on, was an operation that preceded the writing of this paper. It was an attempt to dodge for a time the almost hypnotic influence of the narrative plot and ready-made ideological and religious structures, as well as literary ones such as expressionism, Faustian conflict, et cetera. Since Strindberg himself was consciously trying to escape the theatrical norms of time and space, it seemed of interest to try to follow him in this experiment. Long catalogs were listed beneath each of the initial headings and gazed at until certain recurrent patterns began to emerge. By this point at the latest, all pretense of scientific objectivity ought to be abandoned. For the choice of particular headings and the recognition of patterns is mediated by all the experience, training, cultural institutionalization, political ideology, and literary and theatrical genre expectations that make up the changing horizon of the critical reader or spectator. Thus it is unrealistic to think of semiotics as a new discipline; it can function only in conjunction with traditional theater studies and all else that mediates between the play and its audience. With this necessary mediation in mind, I would like to quote Pavis's explanation of what a semiotic study attempts to accomplish: "Semiology sets out from stage signs to reconstruct, by comparing, adding up, and checking the redundancy of signifying systems, the double system of content and form. . . . Instead of explaining everything by means of a ready-made structure, semiology aims to determine which structuration of the performance the spectator can set up."[13]

A structure such as Babel certainly appears to be ready-made and would have been useful to the most entrenched intentionalist critic. By the same token, a semiotic method can be used to make one text conform to any number of ready-made structures. Nevertheless, such an approach at least allows us to have an inkling of the complex signification processes at play in a work like *The Ghost Sonata.*

Discourse and Scenography in *The Ghost Sonata*

Jon M. Berry

August Strindberg's *The Ghost Sonata* is the most produced of his Chamber Plays. Its complexity and depth allow a great many
directorial approaches and absorb countless interpretations. Perhaps this is
one reason for its popularity: expressionism, symbolism, and realism can all
be found in the work and can each, when used as a major production style,
produce valid, powerful results. From the realistic interpretation given the
play by Olof Molander, to the divergent expressionistic approaches taken
by Max Reinhardt and Ingmar Bergman, *The Ghost Sonata* has been proven
to be a remarkable play capable of communicating its complex ideas
through many voices.

Part of the play's success in this regard may be a result of the form of
the work itself — a form that combines realism and symbolism to create a
tension between the material and the immaterial concerns of the drama.
Such a tension enabled Strindberg to make a difficult theme not only
dynamic but also dramatic and allowed him to complete a theatrical experiment in which he had been engaged for years. As Evert Sprinchorn has
pointed out, Strindberg, through his scientific experiments beginning in
1891, searched for the great coherent principle in nature and so attempted to
"combine the realms of inorganic and organic matter in one grand synthesis
in which the universe would display a kind of order without having any

teleological end."[1] Further, Strindberg expanded his pursuits to include not only matter but also mind. In his own terms, his intention was to eliminate "the frontier separating matter from what was called mind."[2] In his later works, including *The Ghost Sonata*, one finds a further attempt to eliminate not only the frontiers separating matter from mind but those separating matter, mind, and spirit.

Consequently, Strindberg strove in his scenic experiments to expand even the concept of reality until it was seen to be a single and unified fabric consisting of a homogeneous blend of matter and mind, material and spirit, subjective and objective modes of perception. All phenomena would thus be seen to exist concurrently and coproductively. As with Freud, the map of reality is enlarged. But for Strindberg, it has become all-inclusive, leaving nothing outside its boundaries.

The Ghost Sonata represents a major step in Strindberg's theatrical experiments in staging this broadened reality. In it, realism plays a large role in the staging, but it is a realism that is inclusive rather than exclusive of spiritual and metaphysical concerns. The first scene establishes the context of the play visually as well as verbally. The audience is induced to view the drama from a broadened perspective — a perspective that Strindberg may have regarded as being a primary state of awareness before abstractions are enforced.

Indications for this perspective are immediate. Note, for example, Strindberg's changes within the layout of the set. From the opening moments of the play, one is not looking out upon a street or an exterior environment from inside a drawing room, as was customary, but is looking in upon the interior action from an exterior advantage. The view is from "the other side," both literally and figuratively, and quickly establishes an important context: one enters the house — the small interior world of humanity — from the far side of life; and one's interpretations of the subsequent action will be partially determined from this bias.

Thus, the standard or the norm by which one will view the scene will be that of the world of the Milkmaid — that outer realm that interpenetrates the inner. This does not mean, however, that this play is simply a dream play. It is a dream play and much more. For the world of the Milkmaid is complex and multidimensional. She exists in several realms that operate simultaneously. The Student can see her at the fountain although Hummel cannot. This is possible because she is of the spirit world, visible only to the Sunday child. Neither can Hummel see the dead Consul. Yet, moments later when Hummel boasts of having saved a drowning girl in Hamburg, the Milkmaid appears to him. She is now of the world of dreams — of the drama of mind — and it is Hummel's conscience that "sees" her.

Had Strindberg chosen to present the Milkmaid in verbal discourse alone, or had he not been careful to have her enter the scene, fully visible to the audience, *before* the Student, and to have her use the physical fountain because she feels the heat of the day, her role in the opening scene and the perspective that she represents may have been reduced to that of a psychological aberration — a sign of strain on the mind of the Student. Moreover, had the Milkmaid been visible only to the Student and not to Hummel (who we know is not a Sunday child), her citizenship in multiple worlds would not have been depicted. The audience sees her in several connections, and her reality is therefore a more complete one. Hers is that wide realm in which all partial "realities" (material, spiritual, and psychological) are merely modes of one whole reality.

The play takes on a semidreamlike quality, to be sure, for there are a number of private dreams staged; and, more importantly, one is not used to viewing the world in the way that Strindberg shows it. One is more inclined to believe in the "reality" of Hamlet's murdered father stalking the parapets than in that of a drowned milkmaid wandering the streets of Stockholm. The one reality is theatrical, but the other — Strindberg's — oversteps its theatrical bounds. Strindberg does not ask, as does Shakespeare, that one willingly *suspend* one's disbelief, he asks that one actually *change* one's beliefs to accord with his own. That is, Strindberg seems to require that his audience accept his personal vision (minus a modicum of artistic exaggeration, of course) as a true depiction of the way things are. How is one to make this change? The Milkmaid herself is not ready to accept the reality of this interpenetration of realms. She is not so much frightened at seeing the Student as at being seen and spoken to by him. He is special. He has an expanded vision almost like that of the audience, who will now view the whole of the real world at once rather than piecemeal. The action of the first scene not only establishes the relationships between characters and the exposition of antecedent action needed for the audience to better understand the play but also determines the way in which the play will be viewed. It eases the otherwise unwilling audience into the proper frame of reference.

When this context is established, the audience finds itself peering into a new house, probing into the lives of living people, descending into the material depths. Appropriately, the guide for this stage of the journey is Hummel, for he is alive, rooted firmly to the material mode, and complexly related to the other people in this living inferno. He leads the Student and the audience through an examination of the house and the people within it.

This house is one of many houses talked about in the play; but because of its similarity to the others, it comes to represent society at large. We know that one house has collapsed — the house of the elder Arkenholz is in shambles — and we realize that this one may someday end in the same way.

Societies come and go, as do families and nations, and this new house in a new style is no exception. For the moment, however, it seems to resist decay. It appears so perfect and so inviting. The student remarks with an unabashed ardor:

> I have already looked at it — very carefully. . . . I went by here yesterday, when the sun was glittering on the panes — and dreaming of all the beauty and luxury there must be in that house, I said to my friend, "Imagine having an apartment there, four flights up, and a beautiful wife, and two pretty kids, and twenty thousand crowns in dividends every year. (745)[3]

The Student has looked at the house. He says he has looked very carefully. But he has not looked into it. He has seen only the outside of the house and the few objects visible to him through an open window — objects of luxury and elegance that are also visible to the audience at the opening of the curtain: *"When the curtains are drawn and the windows opened in the round room, one can see a white marble statue of a young woman surrounded by palms and bathed in sunlight. On the windowsill farthest to the left are pots of hyacinths — blue, white, pink."* The house itself is finely decorated: *"Through the door can be seen the hall and the staircase with marble steps and balustrade of mahogany and brass. On the sidewalk on both sides of the entryway are tubs with small laurels"(739).* If appearances mean anything, this is a place to be desired. It is a scene of material perfection, both beautiful and opulent, into which everyone dreams of entering — the beggars at the back door, the Student, and Hummel.

To this vision are added the peeling bells and distant organ tones of a Sunday morning. Ships' bells in the harbor signify the beginning and end of different journeys. The atmosphere early on is reminiscent of that at the close of Goethe's *Faust.* For salvation is in the air, and the best that life has to offer stands bathed in sunlight on a glorious morning. If appearances mean anything, the Student has stumbled into an earthly paradise. But unlike Faust's kidnapping from the mouth of hell, any salvation that will be open to Strindberg's seeker after knowledge lies on the far side of hell. He must first descend into its depths, experience pain, love, confusion, and anguish; his eyes and his mind will be opened until he can no longer bear to see or to know. When his knowledge and his vision crush him, and his love crumbles away, he will have discovered both the reason and the need for faith. Like the outside of this modern new house, the Student will find the promise of this particular Sunday morning a mere façade behind which something rots.

As the ships' bells toll, the Student's journey into the house of Man begins. He has gone through one passage and approaches another. As he grows to physical and spiritual maturity, he leaves the vanished child behind and presses on through *The Valkyrie* into the round room and the room of ordeals. Hummel has come full circle to the end of his own journey. Life and death meet in the person of the Milkmaid; and the theme is reiterated in the scene. Even in this radiant place where every detail breathes success, *"Hanging on the railing of the balcony on the second story are a blue silk bedspread and two white bed pillows. The windows to the left are covered with white sheets signifying a death in the house"* (739). As spruce twigs are scattered on the ground, one journey through this life is accomplished, and another begins.

Overtly symbolic of this rhythm of comings and goings, life and decay, is the statue of the Colonel's wife. "Was she so wonderful?" inquires the Student. Then, in a non sequitur that belies his own love of beauty for beauty's sake, he adds, "Did he love her so much?" Hummel replies: "Suppose I were to tell you that she left him, that he beat her, that she came back again and married him again, and that she is sitting in there right now like a mummy, worshiping her own statue. You would think I was crazy" (746). In the idealistic Student's eyes, something is crazy. For how could ugliness reside in beauty? How could the truly beautiful decay? He does not understand, as yet, the rhythms of life.

In the first scene of *The Ghost Sonata,* matter and mind, life and death are depicted as a confluence of realms interdependent on each other. The action in one sphere defines the action in another; and causes and effects are so interwoven that no amount of analysis could ever unravel them into their separate strands. This complexity of causation and relationship has grown from its initial articulation in the preface to *Miss Julie* to include every conceivable kind of determinism. After Hummel tries to give the Student an idea of the interconnections among the persons in the house, he adds, "Complicated, don't you think?" To which the Student can only respond, "It's damned complicated!" Indeed it is, to borrow Hummel's words, inside and outside. The complicated outside of *The Ghost Sonata* —the context — is established.

Unlike the first scene, the second presents space and the objects within it in the convention of the bourgeois drama. The atmosphere of this interior scene will be darker and more terrible than that of the exterior scene; but, perhaps with the exception of the death screen, the scenery will not be. The darker mood will be established through action, characterization, and language rather than through the visual symbolism of Strindberg's scenography.

The scene is the round room, a conventional drawing room whose furnishings are indices of a particular time and place. The place is an upper-class set of apartments in Strindberg's own Stockholm. The milieu, as many have pointed out, is highly specific; and if the universal can be found in the particular, the universal might be found here. For Strindberg has brought along the baggage and the trappings of naturalism. He does not, however, treat the properties and the setting as mere decoration. The objects in the round room will not function simply as indices of time and place, class and taste, nor will they be, for the most part, overtly symbolic. The objects will play the role of objects in the material world. As characters in the drama, they will represent that material world in the same way that human characters represent humanity. Furthermore, these objects will function as that material stuff through which the human characters must battle.

In terms of the set, the round room is pierced with several doors that lead into other rooms with other doors. There is always a way into or out of a room in this labyrinthine drama of passage and passages. Life is lived in a series of interconnected spaces. In this connection, the role of the Mummy's closet takes on a special function. There is a door, a passage, which leads into a closed room. The purpose of this room is for storage; it was never intended to be a place to live. Much like the psychological niche into which the Mummy has retreated, the closet is a cul-de-sac. It is part of the round room and is not. The parrot-character is in this world and is not. Thus the Mummy lives on the fringe of life and passes now this way, now that, through the papered door — now taking refuge in oblivion, now returning of necessity to eat or to drink in the great round.

Resuming my discussion of the physical objects within the scenic space, the realistically individuated properties of the rich interior constitute a repetition of "things" to which the inhabitants of the house are inextricably wed. Ironically, these inhabitants are both masters and prisoners of their own possessions. In the context of the multiple dimensions established in the first scene, this statement is both sociological and ontological. Sociologically, these bourgeois characters are tied to the objects that support them in their station. The humans are thus defined by their property to such an extent that they would cease to be what they are if their material worth were at all diminished.

For example, in verbal discourse, the Colonel is stripped by Hummel of his stations as a noble and as a military man. These have been the credentials upon which the Colonel has been able to extend his credit, accumulate the hallmarks of his apparent wealth, and move up in the world. Without them, he would have been nothing; and to lose them destroys even his ability to rebuild. He has lost his possessions to Hummel and, by extortion, his ability to recover from the loss.

Yet Hummel does not stop at this. He continues. "Take off that wig of yours and have a look at yourself in the mirror. And while you're at it, take out those false teeth and shave off that moustache and let Bengtsson unlace your metal corset" (766). Much of what appears to be the Colonel is a fabrication, in a literal sense, laid upon the animal. His appearance is supported by objects that have become a part of his character. The Colonel and the other members of his household are indeed trapped in a deteriorating social structure, as Maria Bergom-Larsson has suggested;[4] but they are also trapped in the world of things, of physical objects and a physical being, from which they cannot escape. Societies change, a person's dreams may be altered, but the human condition as Strindberg so often depicts it, is rigid. For the round room is also *Kāma-Loka*, the realm of desires, the world of flesh and material need. In this more ontological context of the scene, the human characters are bound to the physical matrix of the great round of life; and they cannot be freed from that bondage without physical death. Strindberg plunges his characters into the agony of an existence they can in no way alter. As Harry Carlson puts it: "The pain in this world of lies and illusions is not simply a result of social injustice, it is existential. Social evils must be remedied, but the great round of life creates and devours in a rhythm that is not governed by human concepts of order and justice."[5] Ethics, it would seem, are a manufactured sociological expedient that have no permanent place in the natural world.

There is, however, a great difference between total capitulation to the material mode of reality and the recognition of that mode as *Māyā* — a veil over a deeper and more complete reality. Hummel has capitulated. He has given himself over not only to satisfying survival concerns but to taking into himself every good thing that crosses his path. Perhaps no character in the play is so deeply rooted in the physical as is Hummel. One of his first acts in the round room after banishing the servants is to roam about that room fingering objects. In one respect, he is taking inventory after having purchased all the Colonel's debts. His action thus sets up the next scene in which he strips the Colonel. In another respect, however, he is making love to the house, touching it, petting it — stimulated by the sight of the statue of the woman who had come to represent for him all of this wealth. He took *her* when he could not take *it*. Now he has returned to take *it*. Hummel becomes, for the audience, the incarnation of lust and greed that he threatened to become in Johansson's introduction of his character to the Student in the first scene:

> — All day long he rides around in his chariot like the great god
> Thor. . . . He keeps his eye on houses, tears them down, opens up
> streets, builds up city squares. But he also breaks into houses,
> sneaks in through the windows, ravages human lives, kills his
> enemies, and forgives nothing and nobody. . . . Can you imagine
> that that little cripple was once a Don Juan? (754)

If the world were simply material, Hummel and his ilk would not be in the wrong. Survival of the fittest would be the only ethic.

There is, however, something more to life, and the Mummy points this out when she turns on Hummel in the climax of the supper sequence: "We are poor miserable creatures, we know that. We have erred, we have transgressed, we, like all the rest. We are not what we seem to be. At bottom we are better than ourselves, since we abhor and detest our misdeeds" (770). Hummel has been, like everyone else, in the "wrong." But the Mummy does not come to this conclusion simply because she is on the losing end of a material battle. Rather, she has discovered the value of human cohesion after having come to recognize the realm of desires for what it is. That realm is *Māyā;* and *Māyā* in *The Ghost Sonata* is the clutter of the physical mode — the illusion created by both pretense and the "reality" of physical objects. It is the shroud that hides the individual soul from its true, nonmaterial nature.

The round room up to this point has stood as a symbol for the great round of life — the cycle in which all living things feed on one another. We see now, however, that the round room has a secondary symbolic meaning tied to late T'ang Buddhist philosophy — that of the Round Enlightenment and its consequent defilements of the real. On the path to Round (perfect) Enlightenment, all *Māyā* must be removed to escape the realm of *Kāma-Loka;* and the participants in the ghost supper are doing much more than waiting upon all-conquering death to liberate them. They are engaged in sloughing off their bondage to the material mode and to the illusions that they have constructed through a lifetime of ignorance and misunderstanding.

In the Mummy's phrase "at bottom we are better than ourselves," the human existence is split. The Mummy is voicing a concern of the soul, the eternal portion of the human. The recognition of the physical aspect as *Māyā* is made from this more spiritual perspective; and once *Kāma-Loka* is revealed for what it is in truth, the individual soul, in Strindberg's syncretistic blending of Buddhism and Christianity, can move to make reparations with its fellow souls. Reconciliation is sought with both human beings and God. Although complete reconciliation waits upon death, preparations must be made.

When Hummel points to the clock, which he uses to signify finite human nature — when he points to linear time, which winds down and brings all things to a close, the Mummy ripostes by offering a different perspective: "But I can stop time in its course. I can wipe out the past, and undo what is done. Not with bribes, not with threats — but through suffering and repentance" (770). She cannot stop material time, this woman who wears its ensign more than any other character in the play; but she speaks from a vantage point of timelessness, from a knowledge that the physical life is just one ordeal to be passed through. She stops time in the sense that she knows that it too is *Māyā*. This life will end for her, and therein lies hope. The first stage in the movement toward perfect enlightenment is accomplished in the banishing of lust and greed made manifest in the destruction of Hummel. This act is the initial step in the deconstruction of all *Māyā*.

Although the human characters in this scene are more than physical and possess eternal souls, the realm of *Kāma-Loka* is no illusion. As one has seen in the first scene, the existence of one mode of reality does not negate the existence of all others. The realistic properties in the round room play the role of a very tangible *Māyā*. For it is the people and their language (their verbal discourse) and not their material environment that is half in and half out of *this* world. It is verbal discourse that makes the environment appear to be illusory: for it is through that discourse that the soul voices its aphysical nature. To pit the world of objects against the world of the soul, the scenographic discourse is borne out realistically in the tradition of the illusionistic theater. In this way, the major conflict in the scene is recognized as being not between Hummel and all others, nor between the characters and a fictive life, but between the human soul and the necessity of living in a material body in a material world. The harsh character of this material world advances through the realistic staging.

Scene 3 is played in the hyacinth room, and one discovers quickly that the ordeals borne in this place are extensions of those so graphically depicted in the last scene. The theme is repeated, although the point of attack is much earlier — closer to the moment when innocence comes face to face with decay. Yet, even though the theme is reiterated, the third scene is not merely a repetition of the second. The second scene has served, in combination with the first, to prepare the audience for the difficult concepts and discourse of the final movement of the sonata. Leitmotivs have surfaced and resurfaced to foreshadow what will become the dominant strain of the third scene.

The scenographic depiction of the realm of desires is also reiterated when the language of the two human characters parades before the mind's eye a series of psychological scenes in which the material mode seems to act in direct opposition to the human will. That will is the will of innocence to create the best of all possible worlds, and Strindberg shows that such a world cannot exist in the corrosive presence of realistic detail. Although there is little to unmask in either the Student or the Young Lady, an unmasking does in fact take place. It is the unmasking of the scene, which not only serves to reveal the true nature of the hyacinth room but also operates as the dramatic event by which the Student and the Young Lady are led to the transcendence of a world of *Māyā*.

The scene is initially "transported" by the presence of objects symbolic of transcendence. Strindberg's stage directions treat these objects simply:

> *A room decorated in a bizarre style, predominantly oriental. A profusion of hyacinths in all colors fills the room. On the porcelain tile stove sits a large Buddha with a bulb of a shallot* (allium ascalonicum) *in its lap. The stem of the shallot rises from the bulb and bursts into a spherical cluster of white, starlike flowers. . . . The Student and The Young Lady (Adèle) are near a table, she seated at her harp, he standing beside her.* (773)

A room in a bizarre oriental style breathes a mysticism that is reinforced by the Buddha with his shallot. The hyacinths splash the stage with color. A harp echoes the final tones of an unheard song. The scene is at once transported in time, place, and mood from the grimness of the preceding scene.

Yet that grisly scene lingers: "*In the rear to the right, a door leads to the round room. The Colonel and The Mummy can be seen in there sitting motionless and silent. A part of the death screen is also visible*" (773). This is a haunting reminder that one has not left the earth, that one has not been transported to Shangri-La, and that, as yet, love has not been able to conquer all. Paradise, or at least a small touch of heaven-on-earth, is juxtaposed to the hell-on-earth of the previous scene. To the rear at the left, like an umbilical life-support for the human beings in this other-worldly plenum, is the door to the kitchen. Strindberg has left no doubt about the context in which this third scene will be played.

As the action begins, the Student tries to leave things as they appear to be. He and the Young Lady, like Dante and Beatrice before them, stand atop purgatory in an earthly paradise looking into heaven. To heighten the reality of their situation into this dreamworld, the Student constructs some symbolism. "Is this the flower of your soul?" he asks. The flower in question is the hyacinth; and by linking it to the Young Lady's soul, he develops a resonance between it and the transcendent nature of her spirit. The mood darkens momentarily as the Student recognizes another resonance. The flower was created, according to legend, in the commingling of blood and earth — in the death of Hyacinthus, whose brains were dashed out by a discus hurled by his lover Apollo and blown awry by the jealous Zephyr. This unspoken legend foreshadows the Young Lady's death in the final moments of the play, but the Student has another reason for avoiding it. He is still determined to put the best face on their situation. He hastily drops the subject and proceeds to create another myth — a symbolic meaning for the flower and a symbol of hope for himself and his companion.

> First you have to interpret it. The bulb is the earth. . . . Here the stalk shoots up, straight as the axis of the world, and here at its

> upper end are gathered together the six-pointed star flowers. . . .
> It's an image of the whole cosmos. That's why Buddha sits there
> with the bulb of the earth in his lap, watching it constantly to see it
> shoot up and burst forth and be transformed into a heaven. (774)

The Student has settled on the dominant metaphor of the Buddhist "empti-ness" philosophy — *K'ung-hua,* "the flower in the air as the symbol of an empty mirage of a flower *(hua)* grounded on empty space *(k'ung)*."[6] The Student, however, transposes empty Nirvana to a heaven — something more approachable by the Christian Young Lady and her Christian audi-ence. This world, symbolized by the flower, may someday become a heaven. The young couple is excited about this prospect as if in the creation of such a myth they could make the idea it represents become a reality.

As they re-create the world in the light of their own hopes, the young couple surround themselves with a tentative Eden. They are insulated form an oppressive reality by symbols, flowers, music. They console each other with the notion that earth can indeed be made into a heaven. After this act of creation, the Student proclaims, "We have given birth to something together. We are wedded."

As with the original tenants of Eden, knowledge will be this couple's undoing. The Young Lady's reply, "No, not yet," picks at the thread that begins the unraveling of this make-believe universe. To be truly wedded (as well as to be truly enlightened), time, testing, and patience are required. The testing has begun. From this point on, the scene of beauty will be stripped away in a protracted analysis of the environment. A tension is created between symbolism and reality — that is, between the object as it is used symbolically and the same object in its material function. In this way, the objects in the scene end by working as all objects do: to subdue, to con-strain, to poison the ideal with the real. Clearly, the fabrication of a symbolic transcendence *within* a material existence cannot hold for long. For the imposition of symbolic nature upon an object interrupts only briefly its material function, and the materials used to signify spirituality soon decay into those functions.

In this room of ordeals, as the Young Lady calls it, examples of this fact abound. The Young Lady takes the Student on a verbal tour of the room and of her trials and tribulations within it. She speaks of the furniture, the stove, the windows, the laundry, and so on, through a chorus of things and chores that keep her battling to "keep the dirt of life at a distance." An example of the imperfections within the room is the writing desk, which, even though it is verbally presented in only a matter of seconds, encapsulates the nature of all the household objects and symbolizes the plight of the Young Lady herself. "Do you see that writing table?" she asks the Student. He replies,

"What an extraordinarily handsome piece!" The Young Lady continues: "But it wobbles. Every day I lay a piece of cork under that foot, but the housemaid takes it away when she sweeps, and I have to cut a new piece. The penholder is covered with ink every morning, and so is the inkstand, and I have to clean them up after her, as regularly as the sun goes up" (777). Her tale of woe is not merely an indication of the untidiness of a maid who ought to be dismissed; it is a parable about the problem of living. Although the writing table is a beautiful piece of furniture, it is also an artifact with a utilitarian function. Its defect, its one short leg, does nothing as yet to impair its beauty but does impair its function. The table wobbles. Therefore, its functional aspect must be ministered to regularly. But its use as a writing table impairs its beauty, for because it is used, its top gets messy and must be constantly cleaned.

Like everything else in the room, the writing table has a functional aspect (a material aspect) that works against its symbolic or aesthetic aspect. Moreover, the functional aspect of each object is imperfect. It is difficult to write on the table. It is nearly impossible to keep a fire going in the stove. It is impossible to marry and have children with the Young Lady.

The symbol enlarges metaphorically: the Young Lady is beauty or the keeper or repository of it. She also has a functional self. Beauty, here equated with purity and innocence, coexists with utility in a combative relationship within the same person. On the ontological level, the functions of the human woman in her daily life compel constant ministering to keep beauty alive. Sociologically, the household and the Young Lady's way of life can be maintained only at great cost. She has been buoyed up upon a sea of people who have labored to support her in her pristine state. But as the sociological structure breaks down, and as the Hummel family of vampires eats away at the foundations, the Young Lady gets ever closer to the filth that is the basis of all material life. In the first scene, the Student claims he had marveled at an apartment that was four flights up. One no longer wonders why that apartment is now on the ground floor.

The worldly paradise tentatively established by the young couple crumbles back into purgatory and the inferno. The Student rages at a world of appearances that kills the individual (the idealistic individual) with its insidious realities. He ends by stripping away even those insulatory secrets that the Young Lady had asked him to let her keep:

It was a Sunday morning, and I stood looking into these rooms. I saw a colonel who wasn't a colonel. I had a magnanimous benefactor who turned out to be a bandit and had to hang himself. I saw a mummy who wasn't one, and a maiden who — speaking of which, where can one find virginity? Where is beauty to be found? In nature, and in my mind when it's all dressed up in its Sunday clothes. Where do honor and faith exist? In fairy tales and plays for children. Where can you find anything that fulfills its promise? Only in one's imagination! (781)

Indeed, the illusions of reality are a construct of the Round Enlightenment mind. But as the *Māyā* gives way to understanding and emptiness, *Kāma-Loka* falls away. Likewise, as the Young Lady comes under the blows of the Student's revelations — as she is confronted with the truth against which she no longer has any defense, her hold on life is loosened. Her sickness "at the very core of life" kills her psychologically because she cannot bear the oppression of living while knowing that her life is borne upon pretense. It physically kills her because, without the hope that the pretense had given her, she is no longer strong enough to keep tying that knot that binds her body and her soul together. She is freed spiritually as her mind and body pass into oblivion. To borrow words used by Yeats in another connection, "the ceremony of innocence is drowned" — drowned first in the wash of a decaying civilization and a decaying body and then drowned in the knowledge of its own impermanence. The Young Lady's soul escapes her body and leaves the room of ordeals behind.

In the final sequence of *The Ghost Sonata*, the material mode of reality is passed through. But the clarity of the vision of the life beyond is obscured. How is this vision of the purely immaterial to be expressed in a physical theater without using clichéd images of the afterlife? And if the Buddhist motif is still used, how would one depict "emptiness"? Strindberg knows not to portray too much. His initial intent was to deny the eye any concrete image on which to focus. The lessons of the third scene would teach this much. Therefore, the senses are transported to another level. All visual signs blur, when the walls of the house fall away, into pure light — a radiantly white incandescence. Likewise, speech and all other auditory signs pass into music. The movement of the senses is thus from an object plane to an ephemeral plane. This would have been the more powerful ending to the play.

Strindberg could not, however, use the magnesium light that he wanted, so he called for his set to dissipate into a two-dimensional vision —a painted backdrop of Böcklin's *Isle of the Dead* seen as a continued mode of reality. One sees the Young Lady moving across a Stygian stretch of water into another portion of her life in which the earthly *Kāma-Loka* is finished.

Once it is clear that the material mode is to be traversed — that is, lived through rather than capitulated to (as in the case of Hummel) or avoided (as in the case of the Mummy in her closet) or poetically dressed in its Sunday best — then the *Māyā* falls away and nonrealistic staging takes over. To get to this point, however, the realistic depiction of the material scene provides a theatrical vehicle for the character of the human soul whose vehicle is the language of the dialogue. Since conflict can exist only between characters that are truly opposed, Strindberg has, in *The Ghost Sonata*, brought both characters face to face. He has pitted humanity's spiritual nature against its physical nature.

Textual Clues to Performance Strategies in *The Pelican*

Paul Walsh

Despite its popularity in Scandinavia, *The Pelican* has been performed only rarely in the United States, and it has not attracted the kind of close critical attention given Strindberg's better known works. At first glance, the dramaturgical innovations in *The Pelican* strike one as slight compared, for example, with those in *The Ghost Sonata*, and the tone and tenor of the language, the catalog of mundane concerns, and the tangled skein of domestic relationships seem to reduce the play to a pathological melodrama about an unfortunately peculiar family. This was the reaction of the Stockholm critics to the premiere performance of *The Pelican* at the Intimate Theater. August Brunius, for example, wrote that although "the opening note of the play was interesting and, had it been carried out with energy, would have had a beautiful result," the play lacked "real conflicts, dramatic drive and power. The author foregrounds trivialities, an unending squabble over food and fuel." Sven Söderman found the play a depressing witness "to its author's inner brokenness" and "exclusively pathological" even in its strong scenes. Vera von Kraemer considered the question of food "the essential tragedy of the piece which functioned as incessantly pure parody."[1]

The critics of Strindberg's day were more intent on preserving distinct levels of representational style than are critics today. Consequently, they were baffled by the deliberate mixing of stylistic levels employed in the drama and chose to view its hyperbolic and symbolic domestic situations in relation to daily life — the referent usually postulated in realistic drama — rather than to the stylized and often exaggerated psychological states postulated as the referent in poetic tragedy. Thus, when judged by the standards of the conventional domestic *drame*, which had served as the basic organizing principle of the play, it was considered a pathological and grotesque testament to the author's obsession with trivialities. This initial assessment blinded critics to the dramaturgical innovations in the play — the deliberate mixing of stylistic levels, the conscious intensification of verbal and visual metaphors capable of intimating deeper significance, and the dual perspective achieved by the intentionally ambiguous parallel development of two carefully linked dramatic structures.

In the dramas of his naturalistic period, Strindberg had experimented with a dramaturgy based on surface action and psychological subtext. In the Chamber Plays he extended this experiment, focusing attention on the moments when surface and subtext change positions, while at the same time extending the subtext of the drama to include metaphysical resonances. In so doing, he shifted the weight of the drama away from the surface action to a second parallel action that intimates the presence of a metaphysical order operating beyond the physical action of the drama, although communicating and communicated through the same entanglements of domestic, mundane concerns.

The surface action of *The Pelican* moves forward with calculated precision, adhering as Ingvar Holm has demonstrated to Freytag's model of a "rising and falling action," which reaches its high point when Fredrick finds the posthumous letter from his father. The scenes that follow show the Mother humiliated as the children take their revenge, leading to a moment of recognition and the final catastrophe.[2] Parallel to this, however, is also a latent action in which the Mother is first tested and then punished by a power outside the realm of human control, which employs naturally explicable phenomena as agents. The compounding of two stories — the one a story of crime and retribution carried out by characters physically embodied by actors on the stage, and the other a story of guilt and punishment carried out not by physically embodied characters but by absent "powers" whose presence is made manifest in the stage properties and *mise en scène* — leads to inevitable and intentional ambiguities for actors and audience alike. The first story turns on the uncovering of a consciously concealed crime leading to externally motivated retribution; the second, on the internal recognition of unconscious guilt leading to a moment of reconciliation. That moment follows the catastrophe when Fredrick and Gerda are transported from the realistic scene onto a higher plane of spiritual enlightenment dramatized in the reverie of light and the talk of "summer holidays" beginning.[3]

The psychologically ambiguous motivations of the Mother are central to this parallel development and allow for the dramatic elaboration of the post-Inferno perspective in which "there are crimes and crimes." Without the surface action, and the suspense it affords, the more subtle structure would lose its dramatic intensity and theatrical viability, devolving into the florid poetic fantasies associated with the French symbolists of the 1890s and evident in the fragment *Toten-Insel*, which Strindberg set aside to write *The Pelican*.[4] It was to avoid such undramatic, overly significant flights of poetic fancy that Strindberg developed his theory of "new naturalism," elaborating in the Chamber Plays a new form to communicate his new perspectives on life.

Today we are better prepared to appreciate the deliberate mixing of representational levels in a play like *The Pelican* and the parallel development such mixing facilitates. On close examination, we see that the seemingly obsessional concern with mundane trivialities simultaneously serves as pivotal marker both to objectify the metaphysical dimension of this new perspective on life in concrete and familiar terms that can be realized on stage and to dematerialize these familiar and concrete objects into metaphoric vehicles for the metaphysical intimations associated with them in the text. Modern scholars generally agree that *The Pelican* shares central themes and motifs with the other Chamber Plays, among them the perception of the world as a "web of illusions and lies," the motif of sleepwalking in which psychological motivations are compounded by a reverie of escape into an idealized past, and a latent concern for the Swedenborgian settling of accounts.[5] As yet, however, the particular strategies for integrating these concerns and motifs into the drama and communicating them on the stage have not been examined, nor have the dramaturgical consequences of these strategies been appreciated.

Like the other Chamber Plays, *The Pelican* demands the audience divide its attention between plot and character on the one hand and the thematic development and tonal motifs on the other. To aid this shift in attention and to intensify the ambiguity generated by the parallel development of conflicting stories, both turning on the central character of the Mother, Strindberg has employed a number of textual markers to actors and audience alike, which can be read as deliberate clues to performance strategies.

Strindberg's own attention to stagecraft and the art of acting in the *Open Letters to the Intimate Theater* suggests that close critical attention to the markers and clues written into the text can prove valuable. Although it is perhaps premature to speak of a deliberate vocabulary of textual clues based predominantly on the evidence of a single text, the particular textual clues I examine here proved valuable to the actors I worked with in a production of *The Pelican* at the University of Toronto in October 1982. Furthermore, they point with self-verifying consistency toward the explicit elucidation and elaboration of the dual movement in the drama outlined above and the dual perspective generated by it in the audience.

In his *Open Letters to the Intimate Theater*, Strindberg writes about the actor penetrating and "mastering the role."[6] He speculates that the actor becomes entranced, enters the role, and in fact becomes it, filling it from within with his own personality.[7] In the "Third Letter" he writes: "*Being* the character portrayed [*rollen*] intensively is to act well, but not so intensively that he forgets the 'punctuation'; then his acting becomes flat as a musical composition without nuances."[8] In the "First Letter" Strindberg cautioned the actors of the Intimate Theater not to slur over consonants and to pay particular attention to the internal rhythms of a speech, whether *legato* or *staccato*. Above all, the actors must remember they are "talking to an audience of many people whether . . . [they] want to or not."[9] The *legato* that Strindberg asks his actors to observe "means that all the words in the phrase steal after each other in rhythmic movement in keeping with one's breathing"; *staccato*, he says, "has its justified effect, as we know, when one is excited or angry and is gasping for breath."[10] It is my contention that the phrasing, rhythms, and stylistic alterations in *The Pelican* not only mark emotional nuances but also serve to underscore thematic transitions and juxtapositions that facilitate the shift of attention from plot and character to tonal and thematic development and back, while at the same time facilitating the elaboration of the parallel structure.

To illustrate the particular use Strindberg makes of textual markers in *The Pelican* and the integrating function they serve, I would like to examine closely a few selected segments in the drama, beginning with the opening of the third scene, which strikes me as particularly complex. In this brief exchange between mother and daughter, several themes from the first scene are compounded and reiterated in light of the expanded context supplied in the second scene. The segment is composed of nine elliptical sentences constituting three exchanges. In the first, the Mother asks if Gerda recognizes the music that is being played:

MOTHER: Do you recognize it?

GERDA: The waltz? Yes![11]

In the second exchange the Mother expands upon Gerda's curt answer, compounding her memory of the wedding and her hidden desires for Axel, which were exposed in the last part of scene 1 and in scene 2. The tone here suggests that of a dream as the Mother passes with unself-conscious ease from direct address to private reverie: "Your wedding waltz, which I danced right through to morning!" Gerda's response is again terse — "I? — where is Axel?" — but the elliptical progression of thought, marked in the text by the dash that separates the first and second sentence, is readily supplied by the audience from the information gleaned from the preceding scene. Knowing that Gerda has become aware of her mother's hidden desire for Axel, the audience follows Gerda's progression from the ambiguous personal pronoun to the accusatory, possibly cynical, and certainly direct question. The Mother's response — "How should I know?" — is psychologically ambiguous. It is either a direct evasion or a self-conscious denial that Gerda has penetrated the secret desire concealed in her momentary reverie. In Swedish the interrogative is contracted *"Va[d] rör det mig?"* (How should I know?), facilitating a *staccato* delivery that marks the heightened emotion of agitation or bewilderment. The ambiguity is partially resolved in Gerda's final response — "So! Quarrelled already?" — and the exchange of glances that fill the pause that follows it. Again this line is marked in Swedish by a contraction and ellision: *"Seså! Han I grälat redan?."*

Recalling Strindberg's insistence that such contractions be avoided on stage, we can assume that here they are employed to mark a moment of particular intensity and significance. The final unanswered question reverberating in the pause is in fact a direct echo of the Mother's question to Axel in scene 1 where the audience learned from Axel that the wedding was "particularly successful," and that the Mother first cried and then "danced every dance" so that Gerda was "almost jealous" (229):

> MOTHER: What? Aren't you happy?
>
> SON-IN-LAW: Happy? Sure, what's that?
>
> MOTHER: So? Have you quarrelled already?

In Swedish, the moment is again introduced by a contracted interrogative *(Va?)* and intensified by Axel's dejected slang response. Axel then goes on to say that he and Gerda have done nothing but fight since the engagement began, calling into question his peculiarly truncated statement that the wedding was "particularly successful. Particularly" (229).

On further reflection, it is not only the line "Have you quarrelled already?" but the whole scene between Axel and the Mother that is echoed in the pause following the elliptical opening exchange of scene 3: the reverie called up in the Mother by mention of the wedding waltz; the question, "Where is Gerda?" (228), echoed in Gerda's question, "Where is Axel?"; Axel's dejected denunciation of the possibility of happiness so carefully amplified and extended, revealed in the dialogue between Fredrick and Gerda in scene 2 (244-47); and the Mother's dawning realization of her own entrapment. On a deeper level, the sense of déjà vu recorded in the exchange of glances during the pause reinforces the dramatic reversal of roles in the closing of scene 2 when Gerda invited Fredrick and Axel into her kitchen for steak and sandwiches (257-58). Linking this reversal with the revelations of scene 1 compounds the pause with a sense of the settling of accounts as past moments and perceptions return to haunt the present.

On stage, I would suggest, this last sense is further intimated by the book Gerda is holding, which can be treated as a multivalent sign conjuring up the metaphysical themes associated with the inventory and the settling of accounts. In this way, the pause and the exchange of glances serve as a transitional marker into the subsequent dialogue about the cookbook, at which point the actors' and audience's associations with the book change. We know that Strindberg used such transformational strategies in *A Dream Play* and *The Ghost Sonata*, in which both stage properties and characters split, double, and multiply. Whereas there is no direct textual evidence or specific stage direction to suggest that the book be treated one moment as inventory ledger and the next as cookbook, or that Gerda one moment can embody the presence of the testing powers and the next the ethos of the revenging daughter, such an interpretation underscores the implicit connection between the real inventory discussed in the opening scene, the inventory of crimes and recriminations dramatized in the surface action of the play, and the inventory of a soul's progress intimated in the latent structure. By writing into the drama text specific clues that mark segments where the surface and latent actions change positions, Strindberg allows the audience to follow the parallel development and encourages the dual perspective in which a thing is both itself and something else. At the same time, he draws the audience into an experience of the duality of human motivation and the multivalent nature of physical phenomena.

What is most surprising is that the subsequent dialogue about the cookbook proceeds as if the earlier exchange had not taken place. It is of course up to the actors to treat this earlier segment in such a way as to call its reality into question, marking the transition from one stylistic level to another, but Strindberg has given the actors sufficient clues for this and, in the transitional pause, has given the audience time to absorb the moment, catch its echoes, and carry the necessary associations into the subsequent dialogue.

In the Toronto production I chose to heighten the sense of dislocation in this segment and bring the metaphysical action deliberately to the surface by allowing the realistic tenor of the action to recede momentarily. This was marked in the *mise en scène* by increasing the intensity of the lighting. As the Mother danced the hypnotic wedding waltz, the actor playing the part of Gerda entered with book and pen, indicating gesturally the action of taking inventory of the contents of the room. When the Mother tried to extend her moment of internal reverie, she was confronted by a series of testing questions and accusations emanating not so much from the character Gerda as from the situation of inventory-taking. The truncated and abbreviated exchanges were deliberately phrased to echo the earlier moments in the drama to which they refer. At the end of the segment, the "powers" relinquished control of both Gerda and the Mother, with a demonic laugh emanating from the actor playing Gerda, after which the lighting changed back to what had been established as normal and the actor resumed her previous role. The pause served as a transitional marker between stylistically distinct levels of representation and as a pivotal point on which the actor playing the Mother could turn from internal reverie to characteristics associated with the Mother in the surface action, while the actor playing Gerda could turn from the embodiment of the testing powers to the character identified by the audience as Gerda.

The recapitulatory exchange at the beginning of scene 3 plays almost like a false start, ending with a showdown of unanswered questions. A similar exchange begins the play when Margret enters the sitting room already occupied by the Mother. Three times the Mother asks Margret to "Close the door please" (215). There is no indication in the text that Margret does. Instead she asks, "Is Madam alone?" to which the Mother responds by drawing attention to the "dreadful weather," and the Mother repeats her command. Only after the third repetition do the characters make contact and let the dialogue get under way.

As with the opening of scene 3, and throughout the play, the dialogue here can be psychologically explained and motivated, but the unsettling effect on the audience of the triple repetition and the disjointed *staccato* of unanswered questions cannot be denied. The ambiguity of dual perspectives is both deliberate and essential here as well. If the beginning of scene 3 serves as recapitulation, the opening of scene 1 serves as premonition, establishing the mood of enclosure, isolation, and nervous agitation that permeates the play. The abrupt shift from the repeated command to "Who is that playing?" — marked in the text by a dash — and Margret's apparently unconnected reference to the weather establish an unconscious link between the music, which only later we learn Fredrick plays to keep warm (216, 218), and the wind that invades the room twice, endowing both music and wind with an inexplicable sense of mystery while subtly and succinctly establishing the parameters of the room by the sounds that both surround and permeate it. The brief exchange serves further to indicate, and alert the audience to, the disjointed form of exposition employed in the play, which proceeds by intimation and the gathering of associations.

When a few lines later Margret asks why the Mother remains in the apartment where her husband died, she answers that the landlord will not let them move, nor can they so much as stir (216).[12] Here again a pause is used to indicate a transition in thought as the Mother's attention is drawn to the sofa: "Why did you take the cover off the red sofa?" On the surface the pause marks a change of focus; on a deeper level, however, it serves to underscore the preceding line, linking it with the subsequent one. The disjunction draws attention to the psychological thought process whereby the Mother associates her entrapment with the death of her husband. On the surface level of crime and retribution, the sofa, which later the Mother says "looks like a bloody butcher's block" (238), becomes a concrete symbolic reminder of her own part in her husband's death *and* of the possibility that she will be found out. On the metaphysical level, the sofa is not only a reminder but a scourge. The terrifying prospects of imprisonment that motivate the mother's hysterical denial of responsibility for the death of her husband later in the scene (239) are presaged here with the added ironic intimation that the Mother's fear of unjust imprisonment — that is, imprisonment outside the letter of the law — itself constitutes a prison for an act outside the letter of the law. While the Mother may be able to cover up her past actions, she cannot escape from their consequences. On the metaphysical level, both past actions and consequences are objectified in the room itself and its furnishings as items to be counted in the inventory. Again, the author's close attention to indicating within the rhythms and pauses of the text both surface motivations and latent metaphysical intimations, and the careful clues to actors and audience, establish implicit connections and associations without overweighing the realistic tenor of the scene. The room that the Mother had thought to take possession of at the death of her husband has in fact taken possession of her and holds her captive.

The mystical implications of this are subtly suggested in Margret's response, the naturalness of which is intruded upon by the pause that follows it: "I had to send it to be cleaned. (*Pause.*) Madam knows that, well, he drew his last breath on that sofa; but take it away then." (210). Margret, the chattering maid, functions on the metaphysical level as an agent of the testing "powers" that strive throughout the play to wake the Mother to consciousness. Here, as at the beginning of scene 3, the pause serves as a pivotal point on which the actor can turn from the embodiment of the testing "powers" to the realistically portrayed maid. It is Margret who has uncovered the sofa, the first in a long series of uncoverings; it is she, moreover, who has sent the cover to be cleaned. Her tasks as maid are at once realistic and endowed with metaphysical resonances.

The skill with which this opening scene is crafted ensures that, if the actors are conscious of the multiple levels of development, effect, and association here, these can be directly conjured up in the mind of the audience through only the most subtle accents on the part of the actors. The ambiguity of multiple messages is essential. The pauses and phrasing intimate the deeper significance and mark moments of stylistic transition, freeing the actors to respond naturally to the realistic flow of the scene. The pauses thus serve a dual function as pivotal points for the actors, marking the interchange of surface and latent actions, and as clues to the audience, indicating the psychological and metaphysical significance of the dialogue.

If we turn briefly to the other pauses in the opening dialogue, we see this strategy repeated. The pause that precedes Margret's suggestion that she light a fire echoes the unspoken accusation contained in her interjectory "Yes, yes . . .," which had likewise prefaced her previous speech about the underdeveloped Gerda (217-18). Again the pause intensifies the transition, connecting the children's weakness and the money that cannot be accounted for with the unlit fire. The cold stove becomes another objectified accusation. At the same time, Margret's repeated interjection turns on and magnifies the psychological ambiguity of Margret's motivation, suggesting both that she has heard this all before and that she chooses to set aside the Mother's excuse for a more appropriate time and place.

On the metaphysical level, the repeated interjections mark the actual process of the inventory being taken while imputing into the scene a sense of testing as the unseen "powers," through the agency of Margret, offer the Mother the opportunity to recognize and acknowledge her guilt and its consequences. This last sense is further amplified in the next pause, following the Mother's admonition, "Watch yourself, Margret." (218). In the intervening lines Margret has stated her accusations more directly; the Mother responds first with nonchalance, then with a sense of dismissal, and last with agitation. At this point the progression is disrupted by a significantly ambiguous pause in which the Mother tries to locate a sound she has apparently heard from outside the room: "Is there someone out there?" Margret denies anyone is there, compounding the audience's momentary confusion and marking the haunting presence of the unidentified "power" hovering around the parameters of the room, presaged in the opening scene. This haunting presence, which gradually materializes out of the Mother's fear of punishment and her unacknowledged guilt, will remain ambiguously identified with both the dead husband and the benevolent "powers," aiding the simultaneous development of the surface action of crime and retribution and the parallel structure of testing and punishment, while subtly integrating the two.

The first pause after Fredrick's entrance, like those in the scene with the maid, is naturalistically motivated, as the stage direction indicates: Fredrick "pretends to read" (221). However, it follows the Son's verification of the chill in the room, calling up Margret's attempts to light a fire, which had been similarly marked. Again the pause serves as a transitional pivot from the chill to the inventory and on the metaphysical level from "the death-like cold," which, Brian Rothwell writes, is "literally the past,"[13] to the settling of accounts. The precision with which the scene not only conjures up the chill in the room but links it with the metaphysical structure of the play, making both reverberate in the pause, identifies the cold not only as the past but as the haunting presence of the past in the present. Also prevalent is the chilling terror that, because palpably present in the furnishings and atmosphere of the room, the past will be found out. Here as elsewhere, the pause serves both to mark a transition and to draw connections on a level beneath the surface of the action.

The tone of profound exhaustion and the escape into a private reverie of dreams and memories, identified in the text with metaphors of sleepwalking, is marked by a similar series of textual clues, and connected implicitly with the profound sadness over the impossibility of happiness. This minor tonal motif, introduced in the initial exchange between the Mother and Axel, is amplified in the second scene between Gerda and Fredrick. "Are *you* happy?" (244), Fredrick asks, pausing after his declaration that he will never get married. "*Jaha!*" (Oh yes!) Gerda answers; "When one finally has what one has always wanted one is happy." A few lines later, after Fredrick has prompted Gerda to examine the facts of her situation — that Axel has gone off to a restaurant on their first evening home and that the honeymoon was cut short because Axel missed their Mother — he asks if Gerda "had a nice trip." "*Jaha!*" (245) she answers again, this time with less conviction, prompting Fredrick's compassionate "Poor Gerda." Later we learn that Axel struck her on their wedding night (254), a fact which Gerda tries both to cover up and to forget. On the psychological level, the revelation of that slap (Fredrick has apparently learned about it from the Mother, "who can use the telephone better than anyone" [245]), is intimated in the pauses that precede Fredrick's questions. On the metaphysical level, this discovery of Gerda's innermost secret intimates the eventual uncovering of all secrets, whether acknowledged or not. The complexity of this segment and its entangled exposition serve to implicate all the members of the household in the web of lies and illusions that is the world of the play. At the same time, Fredrick's simple statement of compassion — "Poor Gerda" — remains as a strikingly real moment of connection between brother and sister. This formula is repeated with growing intensity and frequency toward the end of the play; the phrase "poor mamma" appears four times in the closing reverie of the play after the Mother's death.

The mood of profound sadness and the compassion it generates is heightened and tied to the motif of sleepwalking when Gerda acknowledges that "the greatest pain" is to discover the emptiness of one's fondest happiness (*"den högsta lyckans intighet"*) (247). Here too the statement is preceded by Fredrick's repetition of the phrase of compassion and interrupted by a signifying pause, and further marked by the substantive *lyckan* (happiness). This devastating admission follows Gerda's attempt to escape into a reverie of past memories: "Let me sleep!" The transition is marked in the text by a decelerating tempo and a three-part movement from direct address, through transitional impersonal pronoun, to a first-person present-tense recreation of a past moment: "Do you remember as a child . . . people called one evil if one spoke the truth. . . . You are so evil, they always said to me . . . " (246). Here as elsewhere in the drama, the escape into reverie is exposed by the presence of the other. Like the accusations physicalized in the furnishings of the room and in the intrusion of the outside power as wind and warning knocks, the moment of reverie brings the past palpably into the room as the actor physicalizes the moment recreated by the character from her memory.

In the foregoing analysis I have shown how Strindberg employs particular textual clues to mark important transitional segments in the drama where subtext surfaces and surface action recedes, or where past actions and motivations become palpably present on the stage, momentarily compounding the fictional present tense of the drama with the fictional past-made-present. I have shown how the interchange of surface and subtextual actions results in an alteration of stylistic levels of representation that integrates the tonal and thematic concerns of the drama into the surface action while intimating their deeper metaphysical resonances.

The most significant dramaturgical consequence of this experiment resides in the freedom it gives the dramatist to develop two contrary although parallel actions in the drama. The latent structure of testing and reconciliating can be seen to encircle the surface action of discovery and retribution; at the points where the surface action decelerates, the metaphysical process intensifies. Aware of the dramaturgical power of the suspense generated in the surface action, Strindberg carefully paces the intrusions into the room by the unseen "powers," whether represented scenographically (lights, sound, wind) or through the agency of one of the characters, so as not to interfere with the "rising and falling" pattern of the surface action. The deliberate ambiguity of contrary movements, like the deliberate mixing of stylistic levels and referents, enhances the peculiar sense of dislocation in the drama while allowing the latent metaphysical parallel action to change places with the surface action at carefully marked moments, enhancing the duality and otherworldliness of the dramatic experience.

I trust these few illustrations sufficiently suggest the parallel structure I have identified and confirm the internal integrity of the play and the function of the intentional mixing of representational styles. Further I hope these illustrations demonstrate the function of such textual clues as contractions, repetitions and pauses that serve as directives to both actors and audience, underscoring and amplifying the dynamic vision and shifting the perspective that informs the drama. Once these textual clues have been identified and explored, it remains for the actors and director to make them physically present on the stage. But without a doubt, the particular decisions and strategies that director and actors choose should not seek to resolve intentional ambiguities or ignore deliberate markers necessary for the shifting perspective demanded by the drama.

Notes

Notes

Preface

1. Eugene O'Neill, "Strindberg and Our Theatre," from a playbill for *The Spook (Ghost) Sonata,* in *New York Times,* Jan. 6, 1924, cited from Oscar Cargill, *O'Neill and His Plays* (New York: New York University Press, 1966), 108-9.

2. Letter from O'Neill to Macgowan, Apr./July 1924, cited from R. Bryer Jackson, *The Theatre We Worked For* (New Haven and London: Yale University Press, 1982), 50.

3. Letter from O'Neill to Macgowan, Feb. 8, 1951, in Bryer Jackson (1982), 267.

4. "Spook Sonata, Milestone in Dramatic Season in New York," in *The Pennsylvania Register,* Jan. 9, 1924.

5. Agnes Boulton, "An Experimental Theatre," in *Theatre Arts Monthly* (Mar. 19, 1924), 187-88.

6. Alexander Woolcott, "The Play," in *New York Times,* Jan 8, 1924.

7. Karl Decker, "The Spook Sonata, An Odd Squawk," in *New York Telegraph,* Jan. 7, 1924.

8. Eric Bentley, *The Playwright as Thinker* (New York: Reynal and Hitchcock, 1946), 192.

9. John Gassner, *The Theatre in Our Times* (New York: Crown Publishers, 1954), 170.

10. Martin Esslin, *The Theatre of the Absurd,* rev. ed. (New York: Doubleday Anchor, 1969), 304-6.

11. See Ralph H. Haugen, "American Drama Critics' Reactions to Productions of August Strindberg" (Minneapolis: University of Minnesota, Ph.D. thesis, 1959).

12. From an unpublished article by Göran Stockenström, "Strindberg in America 1987: A Perspective on the Present," in *Strindbergiana* 1987-88, (Stockholm: Strindbergssällskaped, forthcoming).

13. Haugen, "American Drama Critics' Reactions," 9-10.

Chapter 2. Strindberg and the Superman

1. Bernhard Diebold, *Anarchie im Drama* (Frankfurt am Main: Suhrkamp, 1921), 197-99.

2. Una Ellis-Fermor, "Strindberg," in *The Oxford Companion to the Theatre,* ed. Phyllis Hartnoll, 2d ed. (Oxford: Oxford University Press, 1957), 776.

3. F. W. Lucas, *The Drama of Ibsen and Strindberg* (New York: Macmillan, 1962), 458, 472.

4. Ibid., 45.

5. Friedrich Nietzsche, *On the Genealogy of Morals,* trans. Walter Kaufmann and R. J. Hollingdale (New York: Viking Press, 1969), 3d essay, sec. 27, 161.

6. Harald Beyer, *Nietzsche og Norden,* 2 vols. (Bergen: John Griegs boktr., 1958-59), 2:49-65.

7. August Strindberg, "Mitt förhållande till Nietzsche," in *Samlade skrifter*, ed. John Landquist, 55 vols. (Stockholm: Bonniers, 1912-21), 54:323-24.

8. Evert Sprinchorn, "Ibsen and the Immoralists," *Comparative Literature Studies* 9, no. 1 (Spring 1972): 58-79.

9. It is also quite possible that the ideas expounded in the story, ideas about the extirpation of the weak by the strong and about the moral rights of the superior individuals, came from Max Nordau's *Paradoxes psychologiques* (Chicago: L. Schick, 1885). For evidence of Nordau's presence in Strindberg's writings, see Hans Lindström, *Hjärnornas kamp* (Uppsala: Almqvist and Wiksell, 1952), especially 261-67 and 287-88; and Harold H. Borland, *Nietzsche's Influence on Swedish Literature, with Special Reference to Strindberg, Ola Hansson, Heidenstam and Fröding* in Göteborgs Kungl. Vetenskaps- och Vitterhets-Samhälles Handlingar, sjätte följden, ser. A., band 6, no. 3 (Göteborg: Wettergren and Kerbers, 1956), 31-40.

10. Strindberg, *Samlade skrifter*, 12:375.

11. Strindberg to Ola Hansson, Apr. 3, 1889, in *August Strindbergs brev*, ed. Torsten Eklund, 15 vols. (Stockholm: Bonniers, 1948), 7:302.

12. Strindberg, *I havsbandet*, ed. Hans Lindström, *August Strindbergs Samlade Verk, National-upplagan*, ed. Lars Dahlbäck et al. (Stockholm: Almqvist and Wiksell, 1981-85), 31:181.

13. Nietzsche, *Thus Spoke Zarathustra*, in *The Portable Nietzsche*, ed. Walter Kaufmann (New York: Viking Press, 1954), 238 (part 2, "On Scholars") and 233 (part 2, "On the Land of Education").

14. Nietzsche, *The Gay Science*, bk. 5, *The Portable Nietzsche*, 448.

15. Nietzsche, *Beyond Good and Evil*, trans. Walter Kaufmann, (New York: Viking Press, 1966), sec. 243, 177.

16. Strindberg, *I havsbandet*, 182-83.

17. Nietzsche, *The Will to Power*, trans. Walter Kaufmann and R. J. Hollingdale (New York: Viking Press, 1968), 363.

18. Letter from Strindberg to Ola Hansson, Jan. 28, 1889, *Brev* 7:236. This quotation from Strindberg does not mean that in depicting Borg's mental decline in the last pages of the novel he was putting his own experiences on paper. The detailed description of Borg's delirium is based in good part on what Strindberg had read, especially the accounts of insanity in Henry Maudsley's then standard work on the subject, *The Pathology of Mind* (London, 1879). See Strindberg's essay "Själamord," *Samlade skrifter* 22:189-91; and Torsten Eklund, *Tjänstekvinnans son* (Stockholm: Bonniers, 1948), 445.

19. Letter from Strindberg to Algot Ruhe, Apr. 20, 1898, *Brev* 12:296.

20. That the germinal idea for *By the Open Sea* came from Nietzsche's insanity has been suggested by Borland, *Nietzsche's Influence* (23), and by Walter A. Berendsohn, *August Strindbergs skärgårds- och Stockholmsskildringar* (Stockholm, 1962), 136, 146.

21. Letter from Strindberg to Littmansson, Nov. 1, 1900, *Brev* 13:327; and Strindberg to Frida Uhl, Aug. 15, 1896, in *Meddelanden till Strindbergssällskapet*, nos. 63-64 (May 1980): 25.

22. Eric O. Johannesson has interpreted the novel in Jungian terms as the "story of a divided self, a self in conflict due to an over-emphasis on the rational faculties and a corresponding repression of feelings and senses" (*The Novels of August Strindberg* [Berkeley: University of California Press, 1968], 170).

23. Letter from Strindberg to Georg Brandes, Apr. 22, 1890, *Brev* 8:36.

24. In 1898 Strindberg saw that the up-to-date equivalent of the superman would be a product of occult studies, a Swedenborgian androgynous angel, insusceptible to physical love. ("Swedenborg i Paris," *Samlade skrifter* 27:611-12.)

25. Nietzsche, *The Antichrist*, in *The Portable Nietzsche*, 630-31.

26. In this paper I have concerned myself mainly with those aspects of Nietzscheanism that Georg Brandes emphasized and labeled "aristocratic radicalism." Other aspects of

Nietzsche's philosophy — his skepticism regarding Darwinism and science in general, and his critique of causality — would have won the approbation of the post-Inferno Strindberg.

Chapter 3. Strindberg and the Dream of the Golden Age

1. Hayden White, *Metahistory* (Baltimore: The Johns Hopkins Press, 1973), 30-31.

2. August Strindberg, *Metamorphoses*, trans. Horace Gregory (New York: New American Library, 1960), 34-35.

3. All references to Strindberg's works in this chapter are to *Samlade skrifter* [Collected works], 1-55 (Stockholm: Albert Bonniers Förlag, 1912-21). The volume number appears in italics, the page numbers in roman. All translations, except where otherwise indicated, are my own.

4. See "Inledning till Lycko-Pers resa," *August Strindbergs dramer*, vol. 2 (Stockholm: Bonniers, 1962).

5. Strindberg, *Brev* 11:295.

6. See *Samhällets fiende* (Stockholm: Tidens förlag, 1961).

7. Strindberg, *The First and Second Discourses*, trans. Roger D. Masters and Judith R. Masters (New York: St. Martin's Press, 1964), 141-42.

8. Cited by Harry Levin, *The Myth of the Golden Age in the Renaissance* (New York: Oxford University Press, 1969), 159.

9. White, *Metahistory*, 25.

10. Levin, *The Myth of the Golden Age in the Renaissance*, 159.

11. *The Adventures of Don Quixote* (Harmondsworth, Middlesex: Penguin Books, 1950), 149.

12. Hesiod, *The Works and Days*, trans. Richard Lattimore (Ann Arbor: University of Michigan Press, 1959), 37.

13. Strindberg, *Brev* 2:254.

14. *Encyclopedia Brittanica*, 11th ed. (1911), 2:858.

15. Sabine Baring-Gould, *Curious Myths of the Middle Ages* (New York: Oxford University Press, 1978), 137.

16. Gunnar Ollén, *Strindbergs 1900-talslyrik* (Stockholm: A. B. Seelig and Co., 1941), 289 n. 1.

17. Michael C. Putnam, *Virgil's Pastoral Art: Studies in the Eclogues* (Princeton, NJ: Princeton University Press, 1970), 138.

18. Strindberg, *Brev* 15:123.

19. Martin Lamm, *August Strindberg*, trans. Harry G. Carlson (New York: Blom, 1971), 334.

20. Harry G. Carlson, *Strindberg and the Poetry of Myth* (Berkeley: University of California Press, 1982), 93-123.

21. James George Frazer, *The New Golden Bough: A New Abridgement of the Classic Work* (New York: Criterion Books, 1959), 559-60.

22. Mircea Eliade, *Patterns in Comparative Religion* (New York: Meridian, 1963), 391-92.

Chapter 4. *Charles XII* as Historical Drama

1. August Strindberg, *Open Letters to the Intimate Theater*, ed. Walter Johnson (Seattle and London: University of Washington Press, 1966), 113.

2. Göran Stockenström, "Strindberg och historiens Karl XII," *Meddelanden från Strind-bergssällskapet* 47-48 (May 1971): 17-18 (especially n. 10).

3. Strindberg, *Open Letters to the Intimate Theater*, 249.

4. Strindberg, *Ockulta dagboken*, facsimile ed. (Stockholm: Gidlunds, 1977), 104.

5. Stockenström, "Kring tillkomsten av *Karl XII*," *Meddelanden från Strindbergssällskapet* 45 (May 1970): 26-32.

6. Ibid., 42 (especially n. 77).

7. See Walter Johnson, *Strindberg and the Historical Drama* (Seattle: University of Washing-

ton Press, 1963), 155-74, and Gunnar Ollén, *Strindbergs dramatik* (Stockholm: Sveriges Radios Förlag, 1982) 405-14.

8. Stockenström, "Strindberg och historiens Karl XII," 47-48 (1971): 15-18.

9. Strindberg, *Open Letters to the Intimate Theater*, 301.

10. Stockenström, "Strindberg och historiens Karl XII," 47-48 (1971): 29-36.

11. Strindberg, *Samlade skrifter* 53 (Stockholm: Bonniers, 1916), 50.

12. Strindberg, *The Chamber Plays*, trans. Evert Sprinchorn (New York: Dutton, 1962), 73-74. (Rev. ed., Minneapolis: University of Minnesota Press, 1981.)

13. Stockenström, "Strindberg och historiens Karl XII," 47-48 (1971): 20-27.

14. Ibid., 20-22, and "Kring tillkomsten av Karl XII," 45 (1970): 21-22.

15. Stockenström, "Strindberg och historiens Karl XII," 47-48 (1971): 21.

16. Ibid., 21 (especially nn. 1-2).

17. Strindberg, *Queen Christina.Charles XII.Gustav III*, trans. Walter Johnson (Seattle: University of Washington Press, 1955), 161. All citations to this edition are abbreviated as *Charles XII*; all revisions of quotations from this text are annotated in the corresponding notes. All translations are my own.

18. See Stockenström, *Ismael i öknen: Strindberg som mystiker* in Acta Universitatis Upsaliensis; Historia litterarum 5, (Uppsala: Almqvist & Wiksell, 1972), 403-22, 428, 443-49.

19. Strindberg, *A Dream Play*, in *Six Plays by Strindberg*, trans. Elizabeth Sprigge (New York: Doubleday Anchor, 1955), 260.

20. Strindberg, *Inferno*, trans. Mary Sandbach (London: Hutchinson, 1962), 171.

21. Strindberg, *Open Letters to the Intimate Theater*, 123.

22. See Harry V. E. Palmblad, *Strindberg's Conception of History* (New York: Columbia University Press, 1927), 68-90, and Herbert Lindenberger, *Historical Drama: The Relation of Literature and Reality* (Chicago and London: University of Chicago Press, 1975), 87-88.

23. Lindenberger, *Historical Drama*, 12-14.

24. Strindberg, *Open Letters to the Intimate Theater*, 118.

25. Stockenström, "Kring tillkomsten av Karl XII," 45 (1970): 41-42.

26. Ibid., 43.

27. Lindenberger, *Historical Drama*, 88.

28. Strindberg, *Open Letters to the Intimate Theater*, 261.

29. Stockenström, "Strindberg och historiens Karl XII," 47-48 (1971): 23-27 and "Kring tillkomsten av Karl XII," 45 (1970): 28-29 (especially n. 34).

30. Strindberg, *Open Letters to the Intimate Theater*, 262.

31. Strindberg, *Charles XII*, 109-10.

32. Lindenberger, *Historical Drama*, 99.

33. Strindberg, *Open Letters to the Intimate Theater*, 266.

34. Stockenström, "Strindberg och historiens Karl XII," 47-48 (1971): 18-20.

35. Ibid., 19-20 (especially nn. 18-19).

36. Peter Szondi, *Theorie des modernen Dramas* (Frankfurt: Suhrkamp, 1956), 20. (English trans: *Theory of the Modern Drama*, trans. Michael Hays [Minneapolis: University of Minnesota Press, 1987], 13).

37. Strindberg, *Open Letters to the Intimate Theater*, 262-63.

38. Quoted from Ms. "C XII:1-4," in "Drafts to CHARLES XII," *SgNM: II:6* (Stockholm: Royal Library), repr. 1903, 2nd German ed. of *Königin Kristina*.

39. Strindberg, *Open Letters to the Intimate Theater*, 260.

40. Ibid., 261.

41. Stockenström, *De historiska källorna till Strindbergs drama Karl XII*, thesis for Fil. Lic. (University of Uppsala: Litteraturhistoria med poetik, 1969), 189-95.

42. Ibid., 195-97.

43. Strindberg, *Charles XII*, 152.

44. Stockenström, *De historiska källorna till Strindbergs drama Karl XII*, 183-288.

45. Lindenberger, *Historical Drama*, 45-53; see also Szondi, *Theorie des modernen Dramas*, 37-42.

46. "Drafts to *Charles XII*," *SgNM II:6* (Stockholm: Royal Library), had act designations; later changed to "Tableaux I-V."

47. Strindberg, *Open Letters to the Intimate Theater*, 260-61.

48. Ibid., 260.

Chapter 5. Strindberg and the Tradition of Modernity

In some passages I make use of thoughts from my book *Rollenspiel und Welttheater. Untersuchungen an Dramen Calderóns, Schillers, Strindbergs, Becketts und Brechts* (München: Fink, 1980).

1. Eugène Ionesco, "Mes critiques et moi," in *Arts* 22-28 (Feb. 1956), in *Notes et contre-notes* (Paris: Gallimard, 1962), 65-68. My translation.

2. Maurice Gravier, *Strindberg et le théâtre moderne: I. L'Allemagne* (Paris: Lyion IAC, 1949); Anthony Swerling, *Strindberg's Impact in France 1920-1960* (Cambridge: Trinity Lane Press, 1971); Marilyn Johns Blackwell, ed., *Structures of Influence: A Comparative Approach to August Strindberg* (Chapel Hill: North Carolina University Press, 1981); Marianne Kesting, "Strindberg und die Folgen," *Vermessung des Labyrinths* (Frankfurt: S. Fischer, 1965), 126-38.

3. Samuel Beckett, with Georges Duthuit, *Bram van Velde* (1949) (London: Calder and Boyars, 1965), 109.

4. August Strindberg, *Tjänstekvinnans son, Samlade skrifter 19* (hereafter, *SS*), ed. John Landquist (Stockholm: Bonniers, 1912-21), 217-18.

5. Strindberg, *En blå bok II, SS* 47:681-82.

6. Strindberg, *Tjänstekvinnans son, SS* 19:42.

7. Strindberg, *Inferno, SS* 28:204.

8. Ibid., 113, 121.

9. *Vivisektioner*, ed. Tage Aurell and Torsten Eklund (Stockholm: Bonniers, 1958), 127-29.

10. Strindberg, *Fröken Julie, SS* 23:103-4. *Strindberg: The Plays*, vol. 1, trans. Michael Meyer (London: Random House, 1982), 94.

11. Helmut Müssener, *August Strindberg: Ein Traumspiel. Struktur- und Stilstudien* (Meisenheim, 1965), 24.

12. Meyer, *Strindberg: The Plays*, 1:95 (*SS* 23:104).

13. Ibid., 2:175 (*SS* 36:17).

14. Strindberg, *Tjänstekvinnans son, SS* 18:218.

15. Georg Büchner, *Dantons Tod*, in *Sämtliche Werke und Briefe*, ed. Werner Lohmann (Hamburg: Wegner, 1967), 41.

16. Leo N. Tolstoy, *Diary 1898*, in *Dramen*, trans. August Scholz (Reinbek: Roholt, 1966), 241.

17. Ionesco, "Victimes du devoir," in *Théâtre I* (Paris: Gallimard, 1954), 226: "Nous ne sommes pas nous-mêmes. . . . La personnalité n'existe pas. Il n'y a en nous que des forces contredictoires ou non contredictoires."

18. Bertolt Brecht, *Anmerkungen zur "Dreigroschenoper,"* in *Gesammelte Werke in 20 Bdd.* (Frankfurt: Suhrkamp, 1967), 17:999.

19. Strindberg, *Fadren, SS* 23:12. Cf., Meyer, *Strindberg: The Plays*, 1: 34: "It's bad luck on the girl, yes. But it's bad luck on the boy, too." Meyer fails to render the note of compassion in the Swedish — "Det är synd om . . ."

20. Meyer, *Strindberg: The Plays*, 1:29 (*SS* 23:12).

21. Ibid., 1:71 (*SS* 23:87).

22. Ibid., 1:4 (*SS* 23:12).

23. Ibid., 1:61, 60 (*SS* 23:69, 67, 66).

24. Paul Watzlawick, Janet H. Beavin, Donald D. Jackson, *Pragmatics of Human Communication: A Study of Interactional Patterns, Pathologies, and Paradoxes* (New York: Norton, 1967).

25. Jürg Willi, *Die Zweierbeziehung. Spannungsursachen — Störungsmuster —Klärungsprozesse — Lösungsmodelle* (Reinbek: Roholt, 1975).

26. Meyer, *Strindberg: The Plays*, 1:74 (*SS* 23:92).

27. Ibid., 1:75 (*SS* 23:93).

28. Ibid., 1:96 (*SS* 23:105).

29. Ibid., 1:61 (*SS* 23:68).

30. Letter from Strindberg to G. ap Geijerstam, Mar. 17, 1898, in Egil Törnqvist, *Strindbergian Drama: Themes and Structure*. (Stockholm: Almqvist and Wiksell, and Atlantic Highlands, NJ: Humanities Press, 1982), 95.

31. Strindberg, *Till Damaskus, SS* 29:12.

32. Ibid., 9.

33. Ibid., 9.

34. Martin Lamm, *August Strindberg*, trans. Harry G. Carlson (New York: Blom, 1971), 319.

35. Strindberg, *SS* 29:16, 13.

36. Ibid., 54.

37. Soren Kierkegaard, *Sygdommen til Doden*, in *Samlede Vaerker*, ed. A. B. Drademan, J. L. Heiberg, and H. O. Lange (Copenhagen: Gyldendal, 1901-6), 11:189.

38. Strindberg, *SS* 29:11.

39. Ibid., 135.

40. Ibid., 102.

41. Ibid., 133.

42. Letter from Strindberg to G. ap Geijerstam, Mar. 17, 1898, in Törnqvist, *Strindbergian Drama*, 95. My emphasis.

43. Gunnar Brandell, *Strindberg in Inferno*, trans. Barry Jacobs (Cambridge: Harvard University Press, 1974), 251.

44. Meyer, 2:235 (*SS* 36:299).

45. *SS* 36:249.

46. Meyer, 2:250-51 (*SS* 36:324).

47. Strindberg, epilogue to *Master Olof, SS* 2:313-19, prologue to *Inferno* in *Inferno* (Paris: Mercure de France, 1966), 16-26. There are significant differences between the two texts from 1878 and 1897 respectively, juxtaposed in translation by the author. Cf. Karnick, *Rollenspiel und Welttheater*, 273-97, where the two pieces are printed in full.

48. Aristotle, *The Poetics*, trans. W. Hamilton Fyfe (London: Heinemann, and Cambridge: Harvard University Press, 1953), 35.

49. *Aristotle's Poetics*, trans. S. H. Butcher (New York: Hill and Wang, 1961), 52.

50. Ibid., 64.

51. Georg Wilhelm Friedrich Hegel, *Ästhetik. Mit einer Einführung von Georg Lukács*, ed. Friedrich Bassenge (Frankfurt o.J.: Europäische Verlagsanstalt, 1966), 2:551. (Translation by Göran Stockenström).

52. Pedro Calderón de la Barca, *El gran teatro del mundo* in *Obras completas*, ed. A. Valbuena Briones (Madrid: Aguilar, 1952), 3:208. (Translation by Göran Stockenström).

53. Strindberg, *Till Damaskus, SS* 29:177.

54. Lamm, *August Strindberg*, 301.

55. Beckett, *Endgame*, in *Dramatische Dichtungen in drei Sprachen* (Frankfurt: Suhrkamp Verlag, 1963), 1:462.

56. Jakob Michael Reinhold Lenz, *Der Hofmeister*, in *Sturm und Drang: dramatische Schriften*,

ed. Erich Loewenthal and Lambert Schneider (Heidelberg: Verlag Lambert-Schneider, 1963), 1:207; Büchner, *Dantons Tod*, 1:41; Strindberg, *Mäster Olof*, ed. C. R. Smedmark (Stockholm: Bonniers, 1947-48), 160.

57. Reinhard Baumgart, "Kein Nutzen aus Beckett," in *Literatur für Zeitgenossen* (Frankfurt: Suhrkamp Verlag, 1970), 167.

58. Büchner, *Dantons Tod*, 1:41.

Chapter 6. Strindberg "Our Contemporary"

1. Evert Sprinchorn, *Strindberg as Dramatist* (New Haven: Yale University Press, 1982), 154.

2. Bonnie Marranca, *The Theatre of Images* (New York: Drama Book Specialists, 1977).

3. See selections from Hegel's *Aesthetik* in Bernard F. Dukore, *Dramatic Theory and Criticism* (New York: Holt, Rinehart and Winston, 1974), 543-45.

4. Quoted in Jacques Robichez, *Le Symbolisme au théâtre: Lugné-Pöe et les débuts de l'Oeuvre* (Paris: Editions de l'Arche, 1957), 49-50. My translation.

5. Strindberg comments on the Parisian mystery play rage in *Jacob Wrestles*: "Young men don the monk's cowl . . . dream of the monastery, write legends, perform miracle plays. . . . The Middle Ages!" in *Inferno, Alone and Other Writings*, ed. and trans. Evert Sprinchorn (Garden City, NY: Doubleday, 1968), 306.

6. I know of no written evidence that the Hartmann cycle inspired Strindberg's world-historical triology, but the circumstantial link is strong — yet another in the chain connecting Strindberg's later plays to the dramatic experimentation of the 1890s. The Hartmann plays may be found in English translation in Sadakichi Hartmann: *Buddha, Confucius, Christ: Three Prophetic Plays*, ed. Harry Lawton and George Knox (New York: Herder and Herder, 1971).

7. For Péladan's rules see Robert Pincus-Witten, *Occult Symbolism in France* (New York: Garland, 1976), 33-34.

8. The theory that psychological collapse led to Strindberg's late plays is most interestingly reversed in a paper by Evert Sprinchorn, "Strindberg and the Wit to Go Mad," reprinted as "The Guinea Pig" in Sprinchorn, *Strindberg as Dramatist*, 63-74.

9. Antonin Artaud, *The Spurt of Blood*, in *A Treasury of the Theatre*, ed. John Gassner and Bernard F. Dukore (New York: Simon and Schuster, 1970).

10. This play appears in English under the title, *The Baden Play for Learning*, in *Brecht*, ed. Erika Munk (New York: Bantam Books, 1972).

11. Richard Gilman, *The Making of Modern Drama* (New York: Farrar, Straus and Giroux, 1974), 105.

12. Christopher Norris, *Deconstruction: Theory and Practice* (London: Methuen, 1982), 26-28.

13. Jacques Derrida, "Freud and the Scene of Writing," *Writing and Difference*, trans. Alan Bass (Chicago: University of Chicago Press, 1978).

14. Norris, *Deconstruction: Theory and Practice*, 41.

15. All quotations from the play are taken from the Sprinchorn translation in *The Genius of the Scandinavian Theatre* (New York: New American Library, 1964).

16. Preface to *Miss Julie*, in *The Plays of Strindberg*, vol. 1, trans. Michael Meyer (New York: Random House, 1972), 103.

17. Roland Barthes, *Roland Barthes*, trans. Richard Howard (New York: Hill and Wang, 1977), 168.

18. *Rumstick Road* is the second play in Gray's autobiographical trilogy, *Three Places in Rhode Island*. It has been performed in three different runs in New York City; the original one was in the spring of 1977 at the Performing Garage. The text may be found in *Performing Arts Journal* 3:2.

19. See Carolee Schneeman, *More Than Meat Joy* (New Paltz, NY: Documentext, 1979).

20. Actress Ruth Maleczech used photographs of her father and son in *Hajj*, performed at the Public Theatre in New York in spring 1983.

21. For a definition of the term, see Jonathan Culler, *On Deconstruction: Theory and Criticism After Structuralism* (Ithaca, NY: Cornell University Press, 1982), 95.

22. Harold Bloom, *The Anxiety of Influence* (New York: Oxford University Press, 1973), 30.

23. Sigmund Freud, *Totem and Taboo*, trans. James Strachey (New York: Norton, 1961), 95.

Chapter 8. Strindberg's Dream-Play Technique

1. Letter from August Strindberg to Axel Lundegård, Nov. 12, 1887, in *August Strindbergs Brev* (Stockholm: Albert Bonniers Förlag, 1958), 6:298. Unless otherwise indicated, all translations are my own.

2. For more detailed information about these productions, see Richard Bark, *Strindbergs drömspelsteknik — i drama och teater* (Lund: Studentlitteratur, 1981).

Chapter 9. The Camera and the Aesthetics of Repetition

1. See, e.g., Wayne Booth, *The Rhetoric of Fiction* (Chicago: University of Chicago Press, 1961).

2. Interview with Ingmar Bergman in Frederick J. Marker and Lise-Lone Marker, *Ingmar Bergman: Four Decades in the Theater* (New York and London: Cambridge University Press, 1982), 222.

3. John Orr, *Tragic Drama and Modern Society* (Totowa, NJ: Barnes and Noble, 1981), 52. Strindberg's contemporary critics, particularly in Sweden, considered him to be a pathological madman whose writing bore witness to the fragmentary nature of his mind. Only after Max Reinhardt presented his productions of the Chamber Plays in Sweden did the predominantly negative view of them change there too. See Kela Kvam, *Max Reinhardt og Strindbergs visionaere dramatik* (Copenhagen: Akademisk Forlag, 1974); Göran Stockenström, *Ismael i öknen: Strindberg som mystiker* (Uppsala: Almqvist and Wiksell, 1972), 483; and Freddie Rokem, *Tradition och förnyelse* (Stockholm: Akademilitteratur, 1977), 27-34.

4. Susan Sontag, "Theatre and Film," in *Styles of Radical Will* (New York: Farrar, Straus and Giroux, 1976), 103-4. See also, e.g., Nils Beyer, *Teater och film* (Stockholm: Bonniers, 1944); and Allardyce Nicoll, *Film and Theatre* (New York: Thomas Y. Crowell, 1936).

5. Sontag, "Theatre and Film," 104.

6. Martin Lamm's important study on Strindberg, originally published in 1918-20, made the correlation between Strindberg's private life and his art, and many later critics have followed suit. (See n. 17).

7. See, e.g., Peter Wollen, *Signs and Meaning in the Cinema* (Bloomington: Indiana University Press, 1972); William Luhr and Peter Lehman, *Authorship and Narrative in the Cinema* (New York: Putnam, 1977); and Christian Metz, *The Imaginary Signifier* (Bloomington: Indiana University Press, 1982).

8. Rune Waldekranz, "Fröken Julie i filmiska gestaltningar," in *Perspektiv på Fröken Julie*, ed. Ulla-Britta Lagerroth and Göran Lindström (Stockholm: Rabén and Sjögren, 1972), 135-52.

9. August Strindberg, *Samlade skrifter* (Stockholm: Bonniers, 1914-21), 23:186. All translations of citations from this source are my own.

10. Ibid., 111-12.

11. Evert Sprinchorn, *Strindberg as Dramatist* (New Haven and London: Yale University Press, 1982), 28.

12. Roland Barthes, *Camera Lucida*, trans. Richard Howard (New York: Hill and Wang, 1981).

13. See, e.g., C. E. W. L. Dahlström, *Strindberg's Dramatic Expressionism* (Ann Arbor:

University of Michigan Press, 1930), for an interesting expressionistic interpretation of Strindberg's naturalistic plays.

14. See Peter Szondi, *Theorie des modernen Dramas* (Frankfurt am Main: Suhrkamp, 1956), 40-42, who calls this structure "station drama." (English trans: *Theory of the Modern Drama*, trans. Michael Hays [Minneapolis: University of Minnesota Press, 1987], 25-28.)

15. Strindberg, *Brev* (Stockholm: Bonniers, 1970), 12:279-80. Letter of Mar. 17, 1898. My translation.

16. Strindberg, *Samlade skrifter* 36:215.

17. Lamm, *Strindbergs dramer* (Stockholm: Bonniers, 1966), 217; Sprinchorn, *Strindberg as Dramatist*, 156-58.

18. Lamm, *Strindbergs dramer*, 331. My translation.

19. Strindberg, *Samlade skrifter* 36:309.

20. Richard Bark, *Strindbergs drömspelsteknik i drama och teater* (Lund: Studentlitteratur, 1981).

21. Harry Carlson, *Strindberg and the Poetry of Myth* (Berkeley: University of California Press, 1982), 165.

22. Strindberg, *Samlade skrifter* 36:282.

23. Søren Kierkegaard, *Repetition: An Essay in Experimental Psychology*, trans. W. Lowrie (New York: Harper and Row, 1941), 52-53. On Kierkegaard's importance for Strindberg see, e.g., E. Johanneson, *The Novels of August Strindberg* (Berkeley: University of California Press, 1968); and Gunnar Brandell, *Strindbergs Infernokris* (Stockholm: Bonniers, 1950).

24. Sprinchorn writes: "It is worth noting that Strindberg composed *The Ghost Sonata* and liberated drama from its long enslavement to character and motivation in the same year that Picasso painted *Les Demoiselles d'Avignon* and shattered the old concepts of the relationship of art to nature" (*Strindberg as Dramatist*, 276). Sprinchorn does not, however, elaborate the details of the pictorial similarities between the two artists. It is also important in this connection to stress Strindberg's own work as a painter. See Göran Söderström, *Strindberg och bildkonsten* (Stockholm: Forum, 1972).

25. Tom Stoppard, *Rosencrantz and Guildenstern Are Dead* (London: Faber and Faber, 1969), 20.

26. S. Rimon, "The Paradoxical Status of Repetition," *Poetics Today* 1, no. 4 (1980): 151-59, has, on the basis of Lacan's work, analyzed different categories of repetition that are applicable to modern literature. Metz, in his analysis of film (see n. 7), extends these to include the act of viewing itself as a constant repetitive return to the primal scene of the parents.

27. Strindberg, *Samlade skrifter* 34:7. See also Rokem, "Dödsdansens första tur," in *Tidskrift för litteraturvetenskap* 1 (1981), where I have indicated how Searle's speech-act theory (John R. Searle, *Speech Acts* [London, New York: Cambridge University Press, 1969]) can be applied to an analysis of the opening scene of *The Dance of Death* (I) in order to understand the dramatic tensions this kind of unresolved speech-act pattern generates. In the opening scenes of Ionesco's *Chairs*, it is clear that the old couple is involved in a "game" that has definitely been played a number of times before.

28. References are to Strindberg, *Samlade skrifter* 45.

29. Egil Törnqvist, *Strindbergian Drama: Themes and Structure* (Stockholm: Almqvist and Wiksell, and Atlantic Highlands, NJ: Humanities Press, 1982), 205. See also his more detailed analysis in *Bergman och Strindberg: Spöksonaten — drama och iscensättning Dramaten 1973* (Stockholm: Bonniers, 1973).

30. Strindberg, *Samlade skrifter* 45:211.

Chapter 10. Strindberg's Vision

1. The translations from August Strindberg's *The Father* are my own. (The translation of

Hebbel's epigram from *Europa* is by Göran Stockenström.)
2. Adalbert Stifter, *Sämtliche Werke* 5 (Hildesheim: Ulms, 1972), part 1, 4. Translation by David Luke in Stifter, *Limestone and Other Stories* (New York: Harcourt, Brace and World, 1968), 22.
3. Ibid., 6, and ibid., 22-23.
4. Ibid., 5-7. (Translated partially by Göran Stockenström.)
5. Maurice Maeterlinck, "Le tragique quotidien," *Le Trésor des Humbles* (Paris: Mercure de France, 1902), 187-88. Translation by Alfred Sutro in Maeterlinck, *The Treaure of the Humble* (New York: Dodd, Mead and Co., 1905), 105-6.
6. Knut Hamsun, "Fra det ubevidste Sjaeleliv," *Samtiden* 1 (Bergen, 1890), 325-27. My translation.
7. Strindberg, *Tjänstekvinnans son, Samlade skrifter*, ed. John Landquist, 55 vols. (Stockholm: Bonniers, 1912-21), 18:374-76. My translation.
8. Georg Brandes, *Kritiker og Portraiter*, 2d rev. ed. (Copenhagen: Gyldendal, 1885), 370. My translation.
9. Ibid., 364-65. My translation.
10. Ibid., 375. My translation.

Chapter 11. Strindberg and the French Drama of His Time

1. August Strindberg, in Torsten Eklund, *Före Röda rummet, Strindbergs ungdomsjournalistik* (Stockholm: Bonniers, 1948), 80-81.
2. Ibid. Both quotations are from Strindberg's review of the productions of Shakespeare's *Comedy of Errors* and Labiche's *Powder in the Eyes* at the Royal Dramatic Theater in Stockholm in *Dagens Nyheter*, Feb. 1, 1874.

Chapter 12. Love without Lovers

1. See Ingmar Bergman, *A Project for the Theatre*, ed. and intro. Frederick J. Marker and Lise-Lone Marker (New York: Frederick Ungar Publishing Co., 1983). "Love without Lovers" was first published in a shorter, condensed version in *A Project for the Theatre*, together with the authors' translation of Bergman's *Julie*. All excerpts from the play are from that edition.
2. Interview with the authors, first published in *Theater* 13 (Summer/Fall 1982): 51.
3. August Strindberg, preface to *Miss Julie*, trans. Evert Sprinchorn, in *Dramatic Theory and Criticism*, ed. Bernard F. Dukore (New York: Holt, Rinehart and Winston, 1974), 570.
4. Strindberg, *Open Letters to the Intimate Theater*, trans. Walter Johnson (Seattle: University of Washington Press, 1966), 132.
5. Quoted in Frederick J. Marker and Lise-Lone Marker, *Ingmar Bergman: Four Decades in the Theater* (New York and London: Cambridge University Press, 1982), 97.
6. These manuscript emendations are described in detail in *August Strindbergs dramer*, ed. Carl Reinhold Smedmark (Stockholm: Bonniers, 1964), 3:498-506.
7. Interview with Per Allan Olsson in *Dagens Nyheter*, May 14, 1981.
8. Katarina Egerman's line in *From the Life of the Marionettes* (New York: Pantheon, 1980), 76.
9. Interview in *Theater* 13:51.
10. *August Strindbergs dramer* 3:498.
11. Interview in *Theater* 13:52.
12. Ibid., 51.
13. Ibid., 49.
14. Sprinchorn translation, *Dramatic Theory and Criticism*, 570.
15. Interview in *Theater* 13:52.

Chapter 13. Naturalism or Expressionism

1. Karl-Ivar Hildeman, "Strindberg, *The Dance of Death*, and *Revenge*," *Scandinavian Studies* 35, no. 4 (1963): 267-94.

2. Hans Lindström, "Vad händer i *Dödsdansen?*" *Från Snoilsky till Sonnevi: Litteraturvetenskapliga studier tillägnade Gunnar Brandell* (Stockholm: Natur och Kultur, 1976), 62-75.

3. Evert Sprinchorn, "Hell and Purgatory in Strindberg," *Scandinavian Studies* 50, no. 4 (1978): 371-80.

4. August Strindberg, *Ockulta dagboken*, Kungliga Biblioteket (Sg NM:72), Sept. 9, 1900.

5. Strindberg, *Skrifter av August Strindberg* (Stockholm: Bonniers, 1916), *SS* 34:1-122. All further references to this work are translations from *Five Plays of Strindberg*, ed. Elizabeth Sprigge (New York: Doubleday Anchor, 1960), 125-87.

6. Letter to Axel Herrlin, Dec. 11, 1900, *Brev* (Stockholm: Bonniers, 1972), 13:349.

7. Strindberg, *Inferno and From an Occult Diary*, trans. Mary Sandbach (New York: Penguin Books, 1979), 126.

8. Strindberg, *Skrifter* 12:339.

9. Cf. Göran Stockenström, *Ismael i öknen: Strindberg som mystiker* (Uppsala: Almqvist and Wiksell, 1972).

10. Strindberg, *Inferno*, 145-46.

11. Letter to Anders Eliasson, Oct. 28, 1896, *Brev* 11 (Stockholm: Bonniers, 1969), 369.

Chapter 14. Expressionistic Features in *To Damascus* (I)

1. G. M. Bergman, *Den moderna teaterns genombrott* (Stockholm: Bonniers, 1966), 348-49.

2. Wilhelm Friese, ed., *Strindberg und die deutsch-sprachigen Länder* (Basel and Stuttgart: Helbing and Lichtenhahn, 1979), 266.

3. C. E. W. L. Dahlström, *Strindberg's Dramatic Expressionism* (Ann Arbor: University of Michigan Press, 1930), 80.

4. August Strindberg, *Eight Expressionist Plays*, trans. and intro. Arvid Paulson (Toronto, New York, London: Bantam Books, 1965), 1.

5. Gunnar Ollén, *Strindbergs dramatik* (Stockholm: Prisma, 1966), 116.

6. Sven Delblanc, *Stormhatten* (Stockholm: Alba, 1979), 63.

Chapter 15. Titanism and Satanism in *To Damascus* (I)

1. Cited by Gunnar Brandell in *Strindberg in Inferno*, trans. Barry Jacobs (Cambridge: Harvard University Press, 1974), 160.

2. Two recent studies of Strindberg promote this view: Olof Lagercrantz's *August Strindberg* (Stockholm: Wahlström and Widstrand, 1979), and Evert Sprinchorn's *Strindberg as Dramatist* (New Haven: Yale University Press, 1982). Lagercrantz regards the Inferno crisis as no more than a myth (321) and asserts that Strindberg "arranges delusions and is not their victim" (331). Sprinchorn follows Lagercrantz in emphasizing Strindberg's application of "occult" terminology to his psychological "experiments," and both take the "esoteric" and the "exoteric" Strindberg very seriously. Sprinchorn compares Strindberg with Freud: "The fact that Strindberg was a scientist and explorer of the mind using methods similar to those of Freud and following a parallel avenue of inquiry puts a work like *To Damascus* into a special category: art as science" (84).

3. See Brandell, 98-100. In the second chapter of *Strindberg in Inferno* ("The Inferno Psychoses," 66-97), he gives a full account of the five crises.

4. August Strindberg, *Samlade skrifter*, ed. John Landquist, 55 vols. (Stockholm: Bonniers, 1912-21), 28:190. References to this edition will hereafter be cited in the text as *SS*, followed by the volume and page number(s), separated by a colon. For the sake of stylistic consistency, I

have made my own translation of all citations from Strindberg's works, his letters, and his *Occult Diary* (cited in the text as *OD*).

5. In his *Occult Diary* Strindberg notes with grim satisfaction the tragedies that darken the lives of important figures who continue to cling to naturalism; for example, he followed the Dreyfus affair with special interest because he felt that Zola was totally wrong and was being punished. He was also fond of listing former atheists who had been converted as a result of horrifying experiences: J.-K. Huysmans, François Coppé, Mrs. Schram, Johannes Jorgensen, Arne Garborg, Gustaf Fröding, Emil Kléen, Paul Cavallin, Helena Nyblom, Ola Hansson, and so on. Part of this diary is available in English translation: see *Inferno: From An Occult Diary*, trans. Mary Sandbach (New York: Penguin Books, 1979). In Swedish there is a facsimile edition of this famous diary: see *Ockulta dagboken (1896-1908)*, 2d ed. (Stockholm: Gidlunds, 1977).

6. See especially the letters he wrote to her between Dec. 18, 1896, and Mar. 2, 1897 (*August Strindbergs brev*, vol. 10, ed. T. Eklund [Stockholm: Bonniers, 1968]). A number of entries in the *Occult Diary* attest to his obsession with Napoleon in 1897-98. Not only did he read a good deal about Napoleon, he frequently dreamed he was related to him. On Feb. 26, 1898, he "saw" Napoleon's famous monogram in the wrinkled surface of his bed curtain.

7. See Göran Stockenström's careful analysis of Robert le Diable and Merlin in his *Ismael i öknen: Strindberg som mystiker* (Uppsala: Almqvist and Wiksell, 1972), 287-89. Stockenström shows that both figures became important to Strindberg during the Inferno period because they are scapegoats in disguise. They also attracted him because they incarnate the radical dualism of spirit and matter, good and evil, God and the Devil. Durtal, the hero of Huysman's *Là-Bas*, is a writer who has abandoned the clichés of naturalism to write the life of the diabolical fifteenth-century figure Gilles de Rais surnamed Bluebeard (not to be confused with the villain of the widespread folktale who systematically marries and then murders three [or seven] sisters). Durtal is primarily fascinated by Gilles de Rais because he incarnates three incompatible personalities: the brave fighting man, the refined and artistic criminal, and the repentant sinner and mystic.

8. *To Damascus* (I) was written between Jan. 19 and Mar. 6, 1898. According to an entry in the *OD* (53), Strindberg first read Lévi on Jan. 29, 1898. This book later assumed such great importance for him that he wrote on the title page of the *OD* that it contained the explanation for the diary.

9. See Patrick J. Smith's excellent discussion of Scribe the librettist in *The Tenth Muse: A Historical Study of the Opera Libretto* (New York: Alfred A. Knopf, 1970), 210-32.

10. See Egil Törnqvist's suggestive study of this play in his *Strindbergian Drama* (Atlantic Highlands, NJ: Humanities Press, 1982), 71-95. Törnqvist carefully lists all instances of this identification between the Stranger and the Devil (or Lucifer), concluding with the pictorial representation of Michael slaying the Evil One in the Asylum scene, and observes: "In scene 1 the Stranger had expressed his joy at 'battling dragons'; now he has discovered that he is himself the dragon: when he looks at Michael he feels ashamed" (85). Perhaps it is better to say that the Stranger has begun to be aware that good and evil forces are struggling to gain control of him.

11. Of course, all such conceptions of "satanic" or fallen man ultimately derive from romantic misreadings of Milton's Satan. See "The Metamorphoses of Satan" in Mario Praz's *The Romantic Agony*, trans. Angus Davidson (New York: Meridian Books, 1956), 51-91.

12. For a lively account of popular satanism and the occultist movements that flourished in Paris at this time, see "Mystiques, occultistes et satanistes" in André Billy's *L'Epoque 1900* (Paris: Tallandier, 1951), 142-78. Brandell carefully assesses Strindberg's knowledge of and relation to the Paris occultists (108-110).

13. During his brief correspondence with Nietzsche (Nov.-Dec. 1888), Strindberg had at first been extremely gratified by Nietzsche's enthusiastic response to *The Father*, then increasingly alarmed by the megalomania — bordering on insanity — that manifested itself in his

letters. On Dec. 31, 1888, he wrote to Strindberg that he had summoned the princes to Rome and would have the young emperor shot. This letter was signed Nietzsche Caesar, whereas his next — and final — communique was signed Der Gekreuzigte. See Harold H. Borland's *Nietzsche's Influence on Swedish Literature with Special Reference to Strindberg, Ola Hansson, Heidenstam and Fröding* (Gothenburg: Wettergren and Kerbers, 1956), 21-24.

14. In one version of the story, Medea offered to destroy Jason's enemy, King Pelias, by means of a trick. She appeared to Pelias's daughters and offered to rejuvenate their aged father. To demonstrate her powers, she transformed an old ram into a bleating lamb by chopping it to pieces and boiling it in a cauldron with some magic herbs. Pelias's daughters were thus persuaded to cut their father's throat, dismember him, and toss him into the pot, but because Medea omitted the magic herbs, he remained irrevocably dead. In the second version, Jason asked Medea to add some years to the life of his aged father, Aeson. To accomplish this task, she had herself borne off in a winged chariot to a desert place, where she gathered magic herbs. Upon her return, she put Aeson into a deep sleep, drained his aged blood, and renewed him in her cauldron. Seeing her success, the daughters of Pelias begged her to do the same for their father; she agreed, but tricked them by omitting the herbs.

15. See *The Magic Mountain*, trans. H. T. Lowe-Porter (New York: Alfred A. Knopf, 1953), 706. Mann's fascination with the number seven is, of course, well known. In fairy tales, as Bruno Bettelheim observes, "the number seven often stands for every day of the week and is also a symbol of each day of our life." See his *The Uses of Enchantment: The Meaning and Importance of Fairy Tales* (New York: Vintage Books, 1977), 84.

16. See, for example, the entry "Numbers" in J. E. Cirlot's *A Dictionary of Symbols*, trans. J. Sage (New York: The Philosophical Library, 1962), 220-27.

17. Although the Feast of the Seven Sleepers is celebrated on July 27 in the Roman rite, it falls between Aug. 2 and 4 and again between Oct. 22 and 23 in the Byzantine calendar.

18. For a complete discussion of this development, see Brandell, *Strindberg in Inferno*, 91-92. Because Frida remained aloof, and their little daughter Kerstin was terrified of him, Strindberg's hopes for reconciliation soon collapsed; then the color rose began to "persecute" him so that he could not escape it — he even found one rose-colored sheet in a package of cigarette papers he bought! He finally realized that this was not the color of erotic hopes but of infernal flames.

19. Strindberg himself calls attention to this detail in *Inferno* (SS 28:171-72).

20. Perhaps the mysterious connection that Strindberg wishes to establish between mercy and the color rose is reinforced by the submerged reference to roses that Törnqvist discerns in the Lady's preference for Saint Elizabeth's Chapel in scene 1 (see Törnqvist, *Strindbergian Drama*, 90-91). The cult of Saint Elizabeth of Hungary (Thuringia), although unknown in Sweden, is widespread in middle Europe, and Strindberg may have had it in mind in insisting on this saint as the particular object of the Lady's devotion. Saint Elizabeth is usually represented holding roses in her cloak, an allusion to the legend that relates how, when her uncharitable husband demanded to see what was concealed in her cloak, the loaves of bread she was carrying to the poor were miraculously turned to roses. Charity, the chief expression of her sanctity, may also serve to connect her with the Beggar.

21. See Brandell, *Strindberg in Inferno*, 99 and 256. Strindberg's old friend, Jean Lundin, a former military officer who had become a derelict, doubtless served as the model for some aspects of the Beggar in *To Damascus* (I); for more on this connection see Brandell, *Strindberg in Inferno*, 73-74, and Lagercrantz, *August Strindberg*, 318-20.

22. See Törnqvist, *Strindbergian Drama*, 77. His discussion of the Beggar (76-79) is full of interesting insights and suggestive details.

23. This also accounts for the fact that when the Stranger is deeply disturbed (in scene 2) by the unwelcome strains of Mendelssohn's funeral march from the neighboring estate, he is

told that the pianist is the woman who runs the post office (*postfröken*).

24. *August Strindbergs dramer*, ed. C. R. Smedmark (Stockholm: Bonniers, 1964), 3:306. The statement I translate here was cancelled by Seligmann, whose edited version of *Miss Julie* was the only one available to Landquist when he produced his edition of Strindberg's complete works. Using the original manuscript, which has since been found, Smedmark has restored this cancelled observation about Christine's dependence on scapegoats.

25. At the risk of overinterpreting the text, I call attention to the Beggar's only Latin quotation in Scene 13, "*Ille ego qui quondam*," which is the first half-line of the so-called false opening of the *Aeneid*, the four lines (quoted by both Donatus and Servius) in which Virgil explains why he has ceased to write lyric and pastoral poetry and has now turned to epic themes. Strindberg may have had in mind the idea that the Stranger, should he resume his writing career, would have both a new style and a new message to proclaim. The fact that the Beggar is now — so to speak — gainfully employed may also suggest that the Stranger's money worries are soon to end.

Chapter 17. *Charles XII* as Dream Play

1. "Drafts to *Charles XII*," SgNM: II:6 (Stockholm: Royal Library); see also Göran Stockenström, "Kring tillkomsten av *Karl XII*, *Meddelanden från Strindbergssällskapet* 45 (1970): 26-34. Unless otherwise indicated, all translations are my own.

2. Joan Bulman, *Strindberg and Shakespeare* (London: Jonathan Cape, 1933) 210-11.

3. "'His Former Dreamplay *To Damascus*,'" in *Strindbergs Dramen im Lichte neuerer Methodendiskussionen* (Basel: Helbing & Lichtenhahn, 1981), 222-23.

4. "Drafts to *Charles XII*," SgNM: II:6; see also Stockenström, "Kring tillkomsten av *Karl XII*," 34-40.

5. "Drafts to *Charles XII*," *SgNM: II:6*.

6. Strindberg, *Zones of the Spirit: A Book of Thoughts* (New York and London: G. P. Putnam's Sons, 1913), 41.

7. "Drafts to *Charles XII*," *SgNM: II:6*; see also Stockenström, "'The Journey from the Isle of Life to the Isle of Death': The Idea of Reconciliation in the *Ghost Sonata*," *Scandinavian Studies* 50, no. 2 (Spring 1978): 139-41.

8. "Kring tillkomsten av *Karl XII*," 22, 36-43 (especially n. 15).

9. Ibid., 21-24.

10. Strindberg, *Queen Christina. Charles XII. Gustav III*, trans. Walter Johnson (Seattle: University of Washington Press, 1955), 123. All citations to this edition are abbreviated as *Charles XII*.

11. Emanuel Swedenborg, *Diarium Spirituale 1-7* (Tübingen: Jo. Fr. Im. Tafel, 1843-1846), secs. 4741, 4748; see also secs. 4750, 4884; cf. Stockenström, *De historiska källorna till Strindbergs drama Karl XII*, thesis for Fil. Lic. (University of Uppsala: Litteraturhistoria med poetik, 1969), 149-66, and "Kring tillkomsten av *Karl XII*," 43, and "Strindberg och historiens Karl XII," *Meddelanden fran Strindbergssällskapet* 47-48 (1971): 35-36.

12. "His Former Dreamplay *To Damascus*," 218-22.

13. Stockenström, *De historiska källorna till Strindbergs drama* Karl XII, 200-201.

14. Emanuel Swedenborg, *Arcana Coelestia 1-9* (Christianstad and Stockholm, 1864-89), secs. 4403-21, 4525-34; see also secs. 994, 2383, 2701 (translations from 1907 Rotch Edition of *Swedenborg's Works*, vols. 1-32 [Boston and New York: Houghton, Mifflin and Co.]); cf. Stockenström, *Ismael i öknen: Strindberg som mystiker* in Acta Universitatis Upsaliensis; Historia litterarum 5 (Uppsala: Almqvist & Wiksell, 1972), 33-109.

15. *Ockulta dagboken*, facsimile ed. (Stockholm: Gidlunds, 1977), 115-16; see also "Drafts to *Charles XII*," *SgNM: II: 6*.

16. *Charles XII*, 127.

17. Ibid., 123-24.
18. Stockenström, " 'His Former Dreamplay *To Damascus,*' " 217-18.
19. Stockenström, "Kring tillkomsten av *Karl XII,*" 37-38; see also Stockenström, *De historiska källorna till Strindbergs drama* Karl XII, 134-38.
20. Stockenström, *De historiska källorna till Strindbergs drama* Karl XII, 146-47.
21. *Charles XII,* 135-36.
22. *Charles XII,* 116 (changed to reflect King James Version of Psalms 146:3).
23. Stockenström, "Kring tillkomsten av *Karl XII,*" 28-30 (especially n. 34).
24. Ibid., 26-30, 36-38 (especially nn. 29, 34, 66).
25. Strindberg, *Charles XII,* 144.
26. Ibid., 155 (change: "a Nazarite").
27. Ibid., 155.
28. Ibid., 145-46.
29. Ibid., 153.
30. Biblical quotations are from the King James Version. "E'lo-i, E'lo-i, la'-ma sabachtha'ni," which means, "My God, my God, why hast thou forsaken me?" (Mark 15:34); and "Taketh this cup from me. Nevertheless, not what I will, but what thou wilt" (Mark 14:36).
31. Strindberg, *Charles XII,* 152 (change: "deign").
32. Ibid., 152.
33. Ibid., 152.
34. Psalms 146:3-7.
35. Mark 14:36.
36. Strindberg, *Charles XII,* 157.
37. Stockenström, *De historiska källorna till Strindbergs drama* Karl XII, 204.
38. Strindberg, *Charles XII,* 164.
39. Herbert Lindenberger, *Historical Drama* (Chicago and London: The University of Chicago Press, 1975), 122.

Chapter 19. Staging *A Dream Play*

1. For analyses of individual productions of *A Dream Play,* see Gunnar Ollén, *Strindbergs dramatik* (Stockholm: Prisma, 1961, 1982), 451-69; Kela Kvam, *Max Reinhardt og Strindbergs visionaere dramatik* (Copenhagen: Akademisk Forlag, 1974), 103-39 (Reinhardt, Molander); Richard Bark, *Strindbergs drömspelsteknik — i drama och teater* (Lund: Studentlitteratur, 1981), 83-86 (Castegren), 98-103 (Bernauer), 118-35 (Molander), 153-60 (Bergman); and Frederick J. Marker and Lise-Lone Marker, *Ingmar Bergman: Four Decades in the Theater* (New York and London: Cambridge University Press, 1982), 97-113 (Bergman). Translations from German by Göran Stockenström.
2. The abbreviation *SS* stands for August Strindberg's *Samlade skrifter* (Stockholm: Bonniers, 1912-21). References are to volume and page.
3. The idea that earthly existence is a dream, whereas pre- and post-existence represent the true reality, is paramount for Strindberg after the Inferno crisis.
4. Rudolf Björkman, *Scenisk konst* 9 (Stockholm, 1907). Quoted from Bark, *Strindbergs drömspelsteknik,* 84. Strindberg's own sketch for a simplified, never-realized production at the Intimate Theater in Stockholm interestingly combines the prologue with the rest of the play. The growing castle, symbolizing the Earth surrounded by clouds, was to form a permanent background for the various scenes, which were to be acted out at different localities on both sides.
5. The fact that the Poet is often provided with a Strindbergian mask is certainly not enough to turn him into the Dreamer of the play.
6. Letter from Olof Molander to Holger Ahlenius, Sept. 15, 1955, Royal Library, Stockholm.
7. His stage version has been published in English as August Strindberg, *A Dream Play.*

Adapted by Ingmar Bergman, trans. Michael Meyer (New York: Random House, 1973). However, the stage directions in the translation have very little to do with Bergman's production. Cf. Frederick J. Marker and Lise-Lone Marker, *Ingmar Bergman*, 252 n. 50.

8. Here and elsewhere I quote from Walter Johnson's translation, *A Dream Play and Four Chamber Plays* (Seattle and London: University of Washington Press, 1973).

9. As Bark points out in *Strindbergs drömspelsteknik* (100), director and scenographer — indeed Strindberg himself (cf. Bergman, *A Dream Play*, 303-4) — have been clearly inspired here by the cloud chariot, *la gloire*, of baroque theater.

10. A consistent psychoanalytic scenography in line with Sprinchorn's interpretation — theater corridor = vagina / cave = vulva, etc. — has, as far as I know, never been presented.

11. It is well known that Strindberg wrote the play with his third wife in mind while they were still married. "You are from Java," he used to tell her.

12. Admittedly, certain Swedish customs turn up in the text, and these may present difficulties when the play is performed abroad; obvious examples are the degree ceremony and Kristin's pasting strips along the inner windows (Ollén, *Strindbergs dramatik*, 465, 468).

Chapter 20. Directing *A Dream Play*

1. Eva Charney, Mar. 15, 1981.

2. Jed Cooper, Mar. 22, 1981.

3. Mar. 26, 1981.

4. Mar. 7, 1981, 15.

5. Wayne Lawson, Mar. 4, 1981, 55.

6. August Strindberg, *Six Plays of Strindberg*, trans. Elizabeth Sprigge (New York: Doubleday, 1955), 199. All further quotations from *A Dream Play* are from this translation; pages are cited parenthetically in the text.

7. Strindberg, *From An Occult Diary*, trans. Mary Sandback, ed. Torsten Eklund (London: Secker and Warburg, 1965).

8. Strindberg, *The Plays of Strindberg*, vol. 2, trans. Michael Meyer (New York: Random House, 1976), 222.

9. Sprigge translates this as "wrong way up." Elinor Fuchs changed it to "upside down" for our production.

10. Sprigge translates this as "Foulstrand." Fuchs changed it to "Foulport."

11. Richard Cavendish, ed., *Man, Myth and Magic: An Illustrated Encyclopedia of the Supernatural*, vol. 1 (Italy: PBC Publishing, 1970), 51-57.

Chapter 21. The Tower of Babel

1. Roland Barthes, *Sur Racine* (Paris: Seuil, 1963). (English trans: *On Racine*, trans. Richard Howard [New York: Hill and Wang, 1965]).

2. Anne Ubersfeld, "The Space of *Phèdre*," *Poetics Today* 2, no. 3 (1981): 201-10.

3. Patrice Pavis, "Discussion on the Semiology of Theatre," in *Languages of the Stage*, trans. Tjaart Potgieter (New York: Performing Arts Journal Publication, 1982).

4. Umberto Eco, *A Theory of Semiotics* (Bloomington and London: Indiana University Press, 1976).

5. August Strindberg, *The Ghost Sonata*, in *A Dream Play and Four Chamber Plays*, trans. Walter Johnson (Seattle and London: University of Washington Press, 1973), 183-231. All subsequent text citations are to this edition.

6. Michael Issacharoff, "Space and Reference in Drama," in *Poetics Today* 2, no. 3 (1981): 211-24.

7. Evert Sprinchorn, *Strindberg as Dramatist* (New Haven and London: Yale University Press, 1982).

8. See Walter Benjamin, *The Origin of German Tragic Drama*, trans. John Osborne (London: NLB, 1977), discussion of space, 98-102; discussion of stage properties, 132-42.

9. Jean-François Lyotard, *La Condition postmoderne* (Paris: Editions de minuit, 1979). (English trans.: *The Post Modern Condition*, trans. Geoff Bennington and Brian Massumi [Minneapolis: University of Minnesota Press, 1984]).

10. Johnson, notes on *The Ghost Sonata*, 230.

11. Ibid., 229.

12. Strindberg's notation in one of the drafts to *Spöksonaten* (SgNM: 3[12]), Alrik and Cleyonne Gustafson Strindberg Collection, University of Minnesota Library, Minneapolis.

13. Pavis, "Discussion on the Semiology of the Theatre," 27.

Chapter 22. Discourse and Scenography in *The Ghost Sonata*

1. Evert Sprinchorn, "The Zola of the Occult," *Strindberg and Modern Theatre* (Stockholm: Strindbergssällskapet, 1975), 102.

2. August Strindberg, *Samlade skrifter* 28:35, cited by Evert Sprinchorn, *Strindberg and Modern Theatre*, 106.

3. Quotations are taken from Evert Sprinchorn's translation of *The Ghost Sonata* in *August Strindberg: Selected Plays* (Minneapolis: University of Minnesota Press, 1986).

4. Maria Bergom-Larsson, "*Spöksonaten* — ett drama om borgarklassens kris," in *Dagens Nyheter*, Oct. 29, 1972.

5. Harry G. Carlson, *Strindberg and the Poetry of Myth* (Berkeley: University of California Press, 1982), 210.

6. Whalen W. Lai, "Illusionism (Māyavāda) in Late T'ang Buddhism: A Hypothesis on the Philosophical Roots of the Round Enlightenment Sūtra (Yüan-chüeh-ching)," *Philosophy East and West* 28, no. 1 (Jan. 1978): 43.

Chapter 23. Textual Clues to Performance Strategies in *The Pelican*

1. Quoted in Gunnar Ollén, *Strindbergs dramatik* (Stockholm: Radiotjänst, 1949), 33.

2. Ingvar Holm, *Drama på scen* (Stockholm: Bonniers, 1969), 180-81.

3. Brian Rothwell, "The Chamber Plays," in *Essays on Strindberg*, ed. Carl Reinhold Smedmark (Stockholm: Beckmans, 1966), 31, draws attention to the section "The Examination and Summer Holidays" in *En blå bok I* in which the fictional teacher describes how "the dissonances of life increase with the years" until one comes to live "more in memory than in the moment." This section of *En blå bok* elucidates both the psychological and the metaphysical processes explored in *The Pelican* and deserves fuller attention. Of particular importance here, however, is the metaphysical connection between testing and release, and the suggestion that this pattern of testing and release is a vital process of old age, when one has faith in an afterlife. This connection, indicated in the title of the section, is intensified in the closing line in which the "and" of the title is replaced by the stronger conjunction "with": "Examen med sommarlovet!" (Examination with summer holidays!). See *Samlade skrifter av August Strindberg*, 46, ed. John Landquist (Stockholm: Bonniers, 1912-21), 247-48.

4. See Ollén, *Strindbergs dramatik*, 226-28. Ollén considers the discarded fragment, printed in *Samlade otryckta skrifter av August Strindberg* (Stockholm: Bonniers, 1918), 1:293-310, as "an introduction" to *The Pelican*, which, he suggests, traces the events on Earth following the burial of the main character in *Toten-Insel*. Martin Lamm, *Strindbergs dramer* (Stockholm: Bonniers, 1926), 2:404, suggests that *The Pelican* represents an attempt by the author to rework in a new form the autobiographical material that had inspired *Toten-Insel*. Lamm does not, however, go on to examine how this new form allows the author to express the metaphysical convictions of *Toten-Insel* in a dramatic form that communicates both to the converted symbolist and to a wider public.

5. See, for example, Rothwell, "The Chamber Plays," 30-33; Evert Sprinchorn, *Strindberg as Dramatist* (New Haven: Yale University Press, 1982), 273; and Egil Törnqvist's illuminating study "The Structure of *Pelikanen*" in *Strindbergs Dramen in Lichte neuerer Methodendiskussionen* (Basel: Helbing and Lichtenhahn, 1981), 69-81.

6. August Strindberg, *Open Letters to the Intimate Theater*, trans. Walter Johnson (Seattle: University of Washington Press, 1966), 26-27.

7. Ibid., 23.

8. Ibid., 132.

9. Ibid., 25.

10. Ibid., 27.

11. Strindberg, *Samlade skrifter* 45:259. All parenthetical page references in the text refer to this volume.

12. See Törnqvist, "The Structure of *Pelikanen*," 77, for a reading of the psychological and metaphysical connotations of this exchange. Törnqvist points out the existential character of the situation, which, he says, suggests "man's imprisonment in life, his awareness of his shortcomings and his concomitant fear of death." To this I would add the metaphysical intuitions of the link between testing and release suggested by the previously cited passage from *En blå bok I.*

13. Rothwell, "The Chamber Plays," 32.

Index

Index

365

Index

Index

Index

Dreyfus, Alfred, 194, 356n5
Dumas, Alexander the Elder, 147
Dumas, Alexander the Younger, 143, 145
Dürer, Albrecht, 5
Dürrenmatt, Friedrich, 61
Dworsky, Franz (set designer), and *A Dream Play* (1921), 263, 265, 267, 268. *See also* Reinhardt

Eames, Clare (actress), *xi*
Easter (Påsk), 11, 91, 151, 183
Eastern religious figures. *See* Brahma, Buddha, Confucius, Māyā
Eco, Umberto, 304, 308
Edqvist, Sven-Gustaf, 29
Einhorn, Susan (director), xvii, 297
Eisenstein, Sergei, 119
Either/Or (Kierkegaard), 122
Ek, Malin (actress), 283
Eliade, Mircea, 37
Eliasson, Anders (physician and Strindberg correspondent), 173
Eliot, T. S., 26, 74: *The Waste Land*, 18
Elizabeth, Saint, 197
Ella, King of England, 239
Ellert, Gundi (actress), 160, *162*
Emperor and Galilean (Ibsen), 34
The Emperor Jones (O'Neill), 179
En Route (Huysmans), 187
En Yu Tan, Victor (lighting director), 293
Enwall, Frans (actor), 233
Ernani (Verdi), 100
Essen, Siri von, 54
Esslin, Martin, xii, xiii
The Eumenedes (Aeschylus), 99
"The Examination and Summer Holidays" ("Examen med sommarlovet!"), 361n3

Falkner, Fanny (actress), 150
Fallström, Daniel (theater critic), 257
The Father (Fadren), 99, 111, 124; adherence to theatrical conventions of, 50, 51, 53, 91, 92; centrality of scientific imagery in, 131, 132, 139-40; and naturalism, 146-47, 167, 245, 247; sex roles as predetermined in, 62-67; mentioned, xiii, xvi, 15, 112, 356n13
Faust (Goethe), 69, 319
Faust (legendary figure), 26, 314
Fichte, Johann Gottlieb, 29

Fletcher, Angus: *Allegory: The Theory of a Symbolic Mode*, 84
The Foundling (Edward Moore), 141
Fourier, Charles, 12
Frazer, James George, *The Golden Bough*, 35
Frederick the Great, 38
Fredrik of Hessen, 47, 53
Fredrik I (unfinished play), 49
Der Freischütz (Weber), 185
Freud, Sigmund: and humanism, 6, 16: and interpretation of *A Dream Play*, 117, 293; and the relationship of writing and consciousness, 80; and Strindberg, 147, 184, 317, 355n2
Freytag, Gustav, 331
Fröding, Gustaf, 183, 356n5
Fryxell, Anders (Swedish historian), 43, 44, 53, 231, 235
Fuchs, Elinor, xv, 292

Gade, Svend (set designer), and *A Dream Play* (1916): 104, 268; Christian symbolism used in, 273, 274, 277, 284; set sketches for, *275, 276. See also* Bernauer
Garborg, Arne, 183, 356n5
Gassner, John, xii
Geijerstam, Gustaf af, 116, 120, 121
On the Genealogy of Morals (Nietzsche), 18
Genet, Jean, 122
Ghosts (Ibsen), 92, 116
The Ghost Sonata: dream atmosphere of, 98, 103-5; and expressionism, 101, 245, 248; influence on modern theater, x, xii, 330; scenography and spatial metaphors of, 110, 124-28, 316-29, 335; spatial and metaphorical signsystems of, 169, 303-15; mentioned, *xi*, xvi, xvii, 31, 96, 140, 243, 292
Gilles de Rais (Bluebeard), 185, 191, 356n7
Gilman, Richard, 79
God: and *The Ghost Sonata*, 311, 312, 313, 323; and the historical drama, 46-47, 224, 227, 239; as represented in *To Damascus (I)*, 184-87, 191, 192, 201, 204; as represented in *The Dance of Death (I)*, 165, 166, 170-73; as represented in *A Dream Play*, 259, 274, 292; as represented in *The Father*, 65; as represented in *Historical Miniatures*, 34-37; Strindberg's conception of, 10-12, 17, 68-73, 198, 199; Strindberg's scientific

Index

Index

Index

of dream atmosphere in, 105, 251-52, 253, 258; the Daughter in, 259, 281; directorial style of , 255, 289, 316; production photos of, *262, 267, 276, 278, 286*; prologue in, 263; set designs for, 264, 266, 268, 270, 274; mentioned, 280, 287, 288. *See also* Grünewald, Skawonius, Ström

Mörk, Lennart (set designer), and *A Dream Play*(1970), 271, 279. *See also* Bergman

From Morn to Midnight (George Kaiser), 78

Morris, Mary (actress), *xi*

Munch, Edvard, 108, 269

"The Mysticism of World History" ("Världshistoriens Mystik"), 33, 46

Mythological figures: Aeneas, 81; Apollo, 325; Astarte, 35; Astraea, 28, 35; Eros, 238; Hercules, 21, 25, 26,; Hyacinthus, 325; Jupiter, 73; Medea, 189, 190, 191, 192, 194; Nemesis, 196; Polycrates, 196, 200, 201, 202; Prometheus, 73, 198; Venus, 237; Zephyr, 325 ; Zeus, 31, 34

Napoleon I, 38, 40, 185, 356n6

Nazimova, Alla (actress), xiii

Nero, 35, 38

Newton, Sir Isaac, 139

Nietzsche, Friedrich: Brandes's reception of, 18, 346-47n26; evidence of influence in Strindberg's writings, 19-22, 25, 187, 198, 204; as microcosm of late 19th-century Europe, 14-15, 17; and Strindberg, xv, 6, 23-25, 26, 183, 356n13; mentioned, 76. Works: *Beyond Good and Evil*, 18; *The Case of Wagner*, 18; *On the Genealogy of Morals*, 18; *Human All Too Human*, 18; *Thus Spake Zarathustra*, 18. *See also By the Open Sea* and *Tschandala*

The Nightingale of Wittenberg (*Näktergalen i Wittenberg*), 6, 88

Nora (Bergman production of *A Doll's House*), 152

Nordau, Max, *Paradoxes psychologiques*, 346n9

Notes from the Underground (Dostoevsky), 6

Novalis (pseud. of Baron Friedrich von Hardenberg), 136

Nyblom, Helen, 356n5

Occult Diary (*Ockulta dagbok*), 185, 187, 194, 229

Oedipus Rex (Sophocles), 51

Ollén, Gunnar, 117,178

O'Neill, Eugene, x, xii, xiii, 281; *The Emperor Jones*, 179

Open Letters to the Intimate Theater (*Oppna brev till Intima teatern*): on acting, 153, 332, 333; on a free theater, 91; on historical drama, 41, 44, 51, 89, 243; on sets and scenery, 208, 210

Open Sea, By the (*I havsbandet*): and the conflict between social Darwinism and humanism, 8, 9; and the conflict between scientific and poetic imagination, 90, 137; and the influence of Nietzsche, 16, 18, 20-26, 287; mentioned, 202

Orr, John, *Tragic Drama and Modern Society*, 108, 109

Overskou, Thomas, 142

Ovid, *Metamorphoses*, 27, 29

Le Pacha (*The Pasha*) (Scribe), 143

Palme, August (actor), 104, 233

The Pamphleteer (Smädeskrivaren) (Johan Jolin), 141

Panofsky, Erwin, 109-10

Pariah (*Paria*), 92, 245

Parker, Theodore, 29

Paul the Apostle. *See* Biblical figures

Paulson, Arvid (critic), 178

Pavis, Patrice, 304, 309, 315: *Language of the Stage*, 303

Peeling, Paul (actor), *302*

Peer Gynt (Ibsen), 76, 89, 94, 108, 246

Peirce, Charles, 308

Péladen, Joseph (self-titled Sar), 77: *Vice suprême*, 187

The Pelican (*Pelikanen*): and expressionism, 248, 250; stylistic levels of , 330, 331, 332; on textual markers to transition between levels of, 333-41; mentioned, xvi, xvii, 96, 245, 361n3

The People of Hemsö (*Hemsöborna*), 9

Peter the Great, 45

Phaedo (Plato), 218

Picasso, Pablo, 122: *Les Demoiselles d'Avignon*, 353n24

Pico della Mirandola, 5

Pillars of Society (Ibsen), 144

Pinter, Harold, xiii, 122

Pirandello, Luigi, 61

Index

Index

Index

Göran Stockenström has been a professor in Scandinavian studies at the University of Minnesota since 1976. He previously taught at the University of Uppsala in Sweden and the University of Oslo in Norway. Stockenström received his Fil. Dr. in comparative literature from the University of Uppsala in 1973. He has published extensively on August Strindberg and modern drama. With Dr. Karin Petherick of University College in London, he is currently preparing a critical edition in English of Strindberg's *Occult Diary, 1896-1908* (University of Minnesota Press, forthcoming).